# Work-Oriented Design of Computer Artifacts

D1559363

*Pelle Ehn*

# Work-Oriented Design
# of Computer Artifacts

Arbetslivscentrum
Stockholm 1988

© Pelle Ehn & Arbetslivscentrum

Graphic design:
Gary Newman & Nini Tjäder

Cover illustration:
Elisabeth Slote

Typeface:
New Century Schoolbook &
ITC Galliard (cover) from
Adobe Systems Inc.

Paper:
Munken Book & Tre Kronor (cover)

Printed by:
Gummessons, Falköping, Sweden 1988

Second edition 1989

ISBN 91-86158-45-7

To My Daughter Malin

# Contents

# Acknowledgements

The research for this book on design of computer artifacts for skill and democracy at work started some fifteen years ago. Hence, my gratitude is spread far and wide, and it seems difficult, if not impossible, to do justice to the intellectual, practical and emotional support from all 'co-authors' whose names will not appear on the cover of the book.

My colleagues and personal friends for many years in the DEMOS and UTOPIA projects – 'scholars' and 'ordinary workers' – definitely speak in these lines I have written. I can never adequately discharge my debts to them: without them there would not have been a book. It is that simple. To list and thank each of them individually would have been most appropriate, but given the risk of unintentionally forgetting some of them I have avoided this temptation. However, a few names must be mentioned. My many years of collaboration with Åke Sandberg during and after the DEMOS project have intellectually had an immeasurable impact on my research views on democracy at work. My years of collaboration with Morten Kyng before, during, and after the UTOPIA project have had a similar influence on my views on design of computer artifacts. The workers and trade unionists participating in these research projects have meant just as much to me personally and intellectually. Nils Bivall, Gunnar Kokaas, Bernt Eriksson, Malte Eriksson, and many others out there in the practical struggles for industrial democracy taught me most of what I know of the politics and morals of work-oriented design. The remainder of my debt to friends from DEMOS and UTOPIA I have tried to discharge by references in the pages that follow.

As to the actual writing of this book many people have read several chapters of earlier drafts and provided incisive and extremely valuable criticism. The list of people to whom I am especially grateful includes Liam Bannon, Gro Bjerknes, Niels-Ole Finneman, Joan Greenbaum, Jens Kaasbøll, Jerker Lundeqvist, Kim Halskov Madsen, Lars Mathiassen, Hans-Erik Nissen, Ole Skovsmose and Pål Sørgaard.

However, two colleagues have helped me far beyond what can be expected from colleagues and friends. Kristo Ivanov played the, sometimes unpleasant, role of the 'devil's advocate'. His criticism, with detailed comments and suggestions on virtually every page of the manuscript in preparation, made me spend an extra year in clarifying my position; any remaining unclarity is definitely not his fault. Susanne Bødker played the just as demanding role of 'the one who cares'. Not only did she read the whole manuscript more than once, providing most useful comments, and many late night discussions, she also helped in a thousand other ways, and encouraged me to go on when I despaired.

Kristen Nygaard was neither directly involved in our research that led to this book, nor in my actual writing of it. Nevertheless, without his visions of a new kind of cooperation between researchers and trade unions in the field of work-oriented design of computer artifacts, without his pioneering work, or his criticism and loyal support during many years of collaboration the book could not have been written.

More formally, I am indebted to the Swedish Center for Working Life in Stockholm – this unique research center for democratization of working life – where I had the pleasure of working when we carried out most of the research on which this book is based. I am also in debt to the Department of Computer Science at the University of Aarhus, where on a grant I spent the first year writing this book, and to the Department of Information and Media Science at the same university, where I was given the time needed to finish off the work.

This book is a 'desktop publishing' product, which does not at all mean that I as the author am without debts to others in preparing the manuscript for print. Gary Newman designed layout and typography, and Nini Tjäder helped 'implement' the typographic design. These new computer-based tools in desktop publishing have wonderful facilities for spelling control, something that has been most useful to me. However, there is more to language than spelling, as any one who has tried to express himself or herself in a foreign language knows. David Minugh had to work hard to make the text more readable in English.

It goes without saying that none of the persons mentioned is to be held responsible for the remaining obscurities, for controversial opinions I may have expressed, or for defects of any kind contained in the book.

Pelle Ehn
Århus, Denmark
March, 1988

# Prologue

*'Thus worthy work carries with it*
*the hope of pleasure in rest,*
*the hope of pleasure in our using what it makes,*
*and the hope of pleasure in our daily creative skill.*
*All other work but this is worthless; it is slaves' work –*
*mere toiling to live, that we may live to toil.*
*Therefore, since we have, as it were,*
*a pair of scales in which to weigh the work now done in*
*the world, let us use them.*
*Let us estimate the worthiness of the work we do,*
*after so many thousand years of toil,*
*so many promises of hope deferred,*
*such boundless exultation over the progress of civilization*
*and the gain of liberty.'*

William Morris in *Useful Work versus Useless Toil*

# From DEMOS and UTOPIA to Work-Oriented Design

## Work-Oriented Design of Computer Artifacts

Computers and coffee machines are perhaps the two most striking artifacts of a Scandinavian workplace today. To understand these artifacts we have to understand how people at work use them. For example the coffee machine is not just used to produce a stimulating drink; more importantly it offers an opportunity for people to meet, for communication in the workplace.[1] Similarly, computers are not just instrumental means of production: they also condition and mediate social relations at work.

Both computers and coffee machines are artifacts in the sense that they are human creations, created as means to an end. They are designed. However, in designing artifacts we do not merely design the artifacts themselves: deliberately or not, we also design conditions for their human use. Neck strain or isolation from fellow workers are just as important results of the design process as the instrumental functionality of an artifact. Conditions for human development such as learning of new qualifications and democratic participation and communication are designed, just as well as the technical aspects of an artifact. Sometimes a 'bad' or a 'good' use situation

---

[1] For the importance of the coffee machine see Weinberg, G.M.: *The Psychology of Computer Programming*, Van Nostrand Reinholt, New York 1971.

has been considered and anticipated in the design process, on other occasions the designers have simply not been able to anticipate the consequences.

This book is an inquiry into the human activity of designing computer artifacts that are useful to people in their daily activity at work. The background is my experience with design and use of computer artifacts in Scandinavian working life since the early 1970s, and my commitment to two design ideals:

The first is *industrial democracy*, the attempt to extend political democracy by also democratizing the workplace – the social life of production inside the factory gates and office walls.

The second is *quality of work and product*, the attempt to design skill-enhancing tools for skilled workers to produce highly useful quality products and services.

My reflections on these design ideals and their realization in the Scandinavian social and political setting are what I will refer to as *work-oriented design of computer artifacts*.

## A Scandinavian Challenge

The Scandinavian countries are often seen as states somewhere in between capitalism and socialism, or as a bit of both. Opinions differ, but there should be no doubt that in these countries the labor movement and especially the trade unions have played a major role in the struggle for democracy and quality of work.

Certainly trade unions, as most large organizations, exhibit contradictions in terms of their internal democracy, and with regard to oppression of weaker groups and minorities, etc. However, in a historic perspective, there is strong evidence that the only real social 'carrier' of the ideals of work-oriented design is the trade unions. Employers and their organizations may from time to time be interested in skilled workers and in participation, but their attempts to stop democracy at the factory gate, or to replace workers and their skill by machinery and detailed division of labor is far too well-known to be ignored. Hence, it is hard to see how an approach to work-oriented design of computer artifacts could have any real practical implications if not based on strong trade union support and involvement. Practice along the lines of such an approach has developed in Scandinavia during the last 15 years. This book reflects part of that practice and outlines some of its theoretical implications – a Scandinavian work-oriented challenge to design and use of computer artifacts.

This approach is a challenge to rethink traditional understanding of the process of design and its relation to the use of computers in working life. However, work-oriented design of computer artifacts is, as I see it, not only a strategy to include users and their trade union activities in the design process, but more fundamentally to include a cultural and anthropological understanding of human design and use of artifacts, to rethink the dominating objectivistic and rationalistic conception of design. At least in this sense, the work-oriented design of computer artifacts espoused in this book reaches beyond the borders of Scandinavia.

## Theory and Practice

My inquiry in this book is truly interdisciplinary in the sense that I claim importance for the social sciences and the humanities as well as the natural sciences in the design of computer artifacts. However, neither the perspective of natural sciences (which understands 'social effects' as consequences for other sciences to deal with) nor the perspective of the social sciences and the humanities (often taking a purely observing, interpretative, critical or analytic approach to technology) is accepted. There are disciplinary boundaries to overcome in work-oriented design of computer artifacts.

There is also the boundary between theory and practice to overcome. The limits for work-oriented design are not only theoretical. They do not solely depend on the dominating 'scientistic' perspective in computer science or on the 'academic' approach taken by most social scientists. As I see it, work-oriented design of computer artifacts has to be not only theory but also practice for social and technical change. The approach I advocate is not only inter-disciplinary but also action oriented. In research as well as in design, it includes the working people that ultimately will be exposed to its results.

This kind of politically significant, interdisciplinary and action oriented research dealing with resources and con-trol in the labor processes of design and use has con-tributed to what is abroad often seen as a specifically Scandinavian approach to the design of computer arti-facts.

However, the political reason for involving end users in the design process, and for emphasizing their qualifica-tions and participation as resources for democratic control and changes, is only one side of the coin. The other is the role of skill and participation in design as a creative and communicative process.

This complementary concern in work-oriented design of computer artifacts has grown out of my dissatisfaction with traditional theories and methods for systems design, not only with how systems design has been politically ap-plied to deskill workers, but more fundamentally with the theoretical reduction of skills to what can be formally de-scribed. Hence, one can say that the *critique of the political rationality* of the design process points to a *critique of the scientific rationality* of methods for systems description.

In this book I do not argue for a reinvention of the wheel: the instrumental power of systems thinking for purposive rational action is beyond doubt, and many of the computer applications that function well today could not have been designed without rationalistic design methods. Instead I suggest a reinterpretation of design methods to take us beyond the so strongly embedded Cartesian mind-body dualism and the limits of formalization, towards an understanding that hopefully can support more creative designer ways of thinking and doing design as cooperative work, involving the skills of both users and designers.

Hence, the work-oriented design approach I outline is an attempt to include subjectivity in a double sense. I claim the importance of rethinking the design process to include structures through which ordinary people at their workplace more democratically can promote their own interests. I also claim the importance of rethinking the use of descriptions in design, and of developing new design methods that enable users of new or changed computer artifacts to anticipate their future use situation, and to express all their practical competence in designing their future.

*The dialectics of tradition and transcendence – that is what design is all about.*

## How I Came to Write This Book

As mentioned above, my perspective in this book is not really truthful to the division of scientific labor between the the natural sciences, the social sciences, and the humanities. This can be illustrated in terms of the academic organizations I have belonged to. I started my research work in the social sciences at a department of information processing. I went on to an interdisciplinary and trade union oriented research center. The next stop was a computer science department of a natural science faculty. Now I work at a department of information and media science in the humanities faculty. Hence, I think it may help the reader if I tell my own story about how I acquired my perspective on work-oriented design of computer artifacts.

After a few years of practice as a computer programmer and systems designer I started as a Ph.D. student at the Department of Information Processing at the University of Stockholm. This was in the early seventies, a politically turbulent period in society in general, as well as at the universities. Influenced by this political 'climate', and by my limited practical experience my field of interest was systems design and democratization. The infological approach to systems design, developed by Börje Langefors and his colleagues,[2] offered an environment for this interest. This approach, which did not reduce systems design problems to producing correct specifications for a piece of code, but really addressed questions of practical use of information systems and computer technology in organizations, seemed most useful. I think I learned a great deal, and I am grateful to those who taught me. However, as a research assistant in the ISAC (Information Systems for Administrative Control) project I came to view this approach in practice as theoretically and politically too management oriented to be a base for my research interests. When I decided to reframe the questions of systems design and democratization in a sociological context I was encouraged to do so. (This was not exceptional. Such openness to alternative approaches was typical for the department Börje Langefors had created. Kristo Ivanov[3] was for example supported in developing a view based on the system approach by the pragmatist philosopher C. West Churchman, and Hans-Erik Nissen[4] developed inspired by phenomenology a new view on computer applications. Their work was an important ingredient in the environment at the department.)

Two years later I summarized my new understanding in *Bidrag till ett kritiskt socialt perspektiv på utvecklingen av datorbaserade informationssystem* (A Contribution to a Critical Social Perspective on the Development of Computer-based Information Systems),[5] whose truly academic title stressed its scientific claims. I proposed an

---

[2] See e.g. Langefors, B.: *Theoretical Analysis of Information Systems*, Studentlitteratur, Lund 1966, and Lundeberg, M.: *Some Propositions Concerning Analysis and Design of Information Systems*, TRITA–IBADB–4080, Royal Institute of Technology, Stockholm 1976 (dissertation).

[3] Ivanov, K.: *Quality Control of Information*, Royal Institute of Technology, NTIS no PB219297, Stockholm 1972 (dissertation).

[4] Nissen, H.E.: *On Interpreting Services Rendered by Specific Computer Applications*, Gotab, Stockholm 1976 (dissertation).

[5] Ehn P.: *Bidrag till ett kritiskt social perspektiv på datorbaserade informationssystem*, TRITA–IBADB–1020, Stockholm 1973.

interdisciplinary perspective for research into systems design and democratization. The research approach I advocated was action research together with trade unions, and here I was strongly influenced by Paulo Freire and his 'pedagogy of the oppressed'[6] as well as by Kristen Nygaard and the work he was doing together with the Norwegian Metal Workers' Union.[7] The report put me in contact with other researchers in Scandinavia thinking along similar lines. This in turn led to full time work on practical research projects in cooperation with trade unions for the next decade.

## DEMOS

The first project we[8] set up was DEMOS (Democratic Planning and Control in Working Life – on Computers, Industrial Democracy and Trade Unions)[9]. Among the original members of the group were the sociologist Åke Sandberg,[10] who had done work on the theory of demo-

[6] See e.g. Paulo Freire's *Pedagogy of the Oppressed*, Herder & Herder, New York 1971.

[7] See e.g. Nygaard, K. and Bergo, O.T.: *The Trade Unions – new users of research* in Personal Review 4, no 2, 1975.

[8] I prefer to refer to activities in the DEMOS project, and later on in the UTOPIA project, in the we-form, since these projects were deliberately designed as interdisciplinary, collective and cooperative efforts. However, in this book I will only elaborate on research activities in which I personally have been actively involved. Furthermore, the we-form should not be taken as an evasion of my occasional responsibility as project leader.

[9] The ideas behind the DEMOS project are described in Carlson, J., Ehn, P. Erlander, B., Perby, M-L., and Sandberg, Å.: 'Planning and Control from the Perspective of Labour: A Short Presentation of the Demos Project' in *Accounting Organizations and Society*, vol 3, no 3/4, 1978.

[10] In the beginning of the project Åke was finishing his PhD dissertation: Sandberg, Å.: *The Limits to Democratic Planning – knowledge, power and methods in the struggle for the future*, Liber, Stockholm 1976. After the DEMOS project he has among other projects been leading several more reflective and comparative trade union oriented research projects, including the Meth-

cratic planning, the mathematician Bo Göranzon,[11] who
had worked as an operations researcher and with a computer manufacturer, and the engineer Maja-Lisa
Perby,[12] who had some experience from study circles on
new technology together with trade unions. My main interest was systems design and design methods. This was
in 1975, the time when new laws on working life democracy were being enacted in Sweden. The use of computers
became an issue of codetermination and negotiation between employers and trade unions. Which resources were
needed for local trade union participation in planning and
use of new technology, and how could they be developed?
Together with a more theoretical understanding of the limits and possibilities of democratic planning in working
life, these were the questions we set out to work with.

ods Project on action research in working life, documented in
Sandberg, Å. (ed.): *Forskning för Förändring – om metoder och
förutsättningar för handlingsinriktad forskning i arbetslivet,*
Swedish Center for Working Life, Stockholm 1981, and the FRONT
project on trade union strategies on new technology and work,
documented in Sandberg, Å. (ed.): *Framtidsfrågor på arbetsplat-
sen,* Swedish Center for Working Life, Stockholm 1984. He is now
leading new trade union oriented projects on managerial strategies, new technology, work organization, qualifications, etc. See
e.g. Sandberg, Å. (ed.): *Ledning för alla – Om perspektivbryt-
ningar i företagsledning,* Swedish Center for Working Life,
Stockholm 1987.

[11] Bo left the DEMOS project at an early stage to set up the PAAS
project (a Swedish acronym for Perspective on Analysis, Tools
and Working Methods in Systems Development) documented in
Göranzon, B. et al.: *Datorn som verktyg,* Studentlitteratur, Lund
1983, and Göranzon, B. (ed): *Datautvecklingens filosofi,* Carlsson
& Jönsson, Malmö 1984. In the PAAS project and later on in the
program on Education–Work–Technology he has complemented
the trade union approach with a focus on skill, extending into a
dialogue with the arts.

[12] After the DEMOS project Maja-Lisa has continued to work with
the questions of skill and computers. See e.g. Perby, M-L.:
'Computerization and the Skill in Local Weather Forecasting' in
Bjerknes, G. et al.: *Computers and Democracy – A Scandinavian
Challenge,* Avebury, 1987.

In doing this we were facing a double problem: Workers and trade unions had neither very much experience in influencing design and use of new technology, nor experience from encouraging research to support their interests. As we saw it, there was a need for research which differed from the traditional commission-directed variety, where investigations are made by experts at the request of management. The results of such traditional work-oriented research are normally used as a basis for decisions by the management of an organization, and they are in practice exclusively used by management rather than by those who are ultimately affected. The workers often do not have the means available to judge the results produced by the experts. In our opinion, this type of research method thus worked against the workers' struggle for democracy at work.

The work-oriented action research method we applied in the DEMOS project meant that local unions themselves, through the use of 'investigation groups', made inquiries into the conditions in their 'own' enterprises. As researchers we took part in the investigation groups as 'resource persons' – our academic knowledge and our research time were at the groups' disposal. However, the starting point in the groups was the workers' own experience and competence.

Investigation groups were established at four different enterprises: a repair shop, a newspaper, a metal factory, and a department store. Being a 'resource person' at the repair shop and at the newspaper meant the work in these investigation groups formed my working life for several years.

In the repair shop the investigation group researched and developed alternatives concerning computer-based production planning. The group rejected a system based on detailed division of labor, and suggested a system that could support group work and developments of skills. We also developed and tried out a systems design model based on negotiations.[13]

At the newspaper the investigation group worked with the introduction of 'new technology', i.e. the transition from lead composing to computer based text processing and phototypesetting. The focus was on changes in content of work, and in the cooperation between different groups of workers. This meant intervention into managerial and technical plans for manning, education, investments, etc. The systems design 'negotiation model' was further developed here.[14] For me, personally, the involvement in the investigation group at the newspaper also meant the beginning of a decade-long involvement in the design of new technology in the newspaper industry and cooperation with graphic workers' unions all over Scandinavia.

As a 'dialectic' complement to the activities in the investigation groups we in the research group conducted more traditional academic studies of preconditions and restrictions on the development of skill and democratization in working life. Marxist labor process theories and the practical experience of the investigation groups together formed the basis for this theoretical activity. To us this theoretical side of the project was of great importance, since very little theory on organizational planning, systems design, and use of computers had a workers' perspective. After all, though the socio-technical approach had begun to have some influence on Scandinavian workplace design, the dominant perspective was still 'scientific management', the method for fragmentation of work and control of the worker that the engineer Fredrick Taylor developed at the beginning of this century.[15]

---

[13] Ehn, P. and Erlander, B.: *Vi vägrar låta detaljstyra oss*, Swedish Center for Working Life, Stockholm 1978.

[14] Ehn, P., Perby, M-L., Sandberg, Å.: *Brytningstid*, Swedish Center for Working Life, Stockholm 1984.

[15] Taylor, F.W.:*Principles of Scientific Management*, 1911.

In summary, our action research method aimed at building up knowledge in the investigation groups, a kind of knowledge which elucidates and widens the range of possible action. In a dialectical relation with these practical investigations traditional theoretical studies were carried out. This interplay between practical interventionistic investigations (as opposed to gathering of data) and parallel theoretical reflection (as opposed to detached theoretical reflections *a posteriori*), this is what we at times have referred to as *practice research*.

It was a central idea and integrated aspect of the project that we would share the experiences and results with workers at other places. This was carried out via education and the central trade unions. Hence, besides writing local reports together with the investigation groups, we spent much time and really worked hard on developing a textbook and other educational material on planning and use of computer artifacts from a work perspective to be used by workers.

The extensive use that trade union courses made of the textbook *Företagsstyrning and Löntagarmakt*[16] (Organizational Control and Labor Power) that I wrote together with Åke Sandberg was more than reward for our pains. I still see that book as a good example of the possibility of breaking the barrier between the academic world and ordinary working people, and – as the most important book I have contributed to – as my *practical* dissertation. Nor do i regard the fact that it also became used at many universities all over Scandinavia as in any way undermining this position.

Despite our heterogeneous disciplinary background when the DEMOS project started its organizational base was the Department of Information Processing at the University of Stockholm. However, when the work life reform in Sweden led to the establishment of the Swedish Center for Working Life as an interdisciplinary research

[16] Ehn, P. and Sandberg, Å.: *Företagsstyrning och löntagarmakt*, Prisma, Stockholm 1979.

institute to support democracy in working life, it was natural for us to move the project there. This important
environmental change for the project happened late in
1976.

At the end of the 1970s and of the DEMOS project plans
for a new project were growing. In the DEMOS project we
had done considerable work on participatory and democratic aspects in the design of computer artifacts. However, given the situation in Swedish working life we had
basically developed a *reactive* approach. It was a strategy
to make clear the harmful effect on work, that division of
labor and use of new technology had in a capitalistic economy, and to reduce it, rather than a strategy for exploring
organizational and technical alternatives. As good
Marxists we knew that this was not our business: we
knew that the design of the future workplace was the task
of the working class, and not a question of utopian ideas.
However, more and more people started to ask for good
worker oriented alternatives, and I must admit I very
much myself wanted to participate in a more *proactive*
*approach*, I wanted to participate in a project that really
explored and designed technical and organizational alternatives.

We first approached the office workers' unions, since
there were many signs that the office was the next place
in line for rationalization and massive use of computers.
However, at that time the office workers unions' found
the idea of researchers, systems designers and workers
designing the future office too utopian.[17]

----

[17] When in 1986 we subsequently suggested a utopian proactive
project on new technology and work organization in the office, the
trade union skepticism had turned into strong support of the idea.
The KNUT project is now a network connecting trade union
experiences with research at the Swedish Center for Working
Life, and external competence on ergonomics and systems design
with users.

## UTOPIA

Instead the UTOPIA project (in the Scandinavian languages UTOPIA is an acronym for Training, Technology, and Products from the Quality of Work Perspective) came to be carried out in cooperation with the graphic workers' unions. This was due to our earlier cooperation in the DEMOS project, and more importantly to the problematic situation in the printing industry. Strategically the graphic workers could not just say 'no' to new technology. To defend their craft they also had to come up with alternatives. The UTOPIA project offered such a possibility.

Our own motives for a complementary research emphasis and a shift from reactive work based on investigation groups as in the DEMOS project, to the proactive work in the UTOPIA research and development project can be found in the research program from 1980.[18]

Trade union practice and our own research in the 1970s into the ability to influence new technology and the organization of work at local levels highlighted a number of problems. One fundamental experience was that the 'degrees of freedom' available to design the content and organization of work with existing technology often were considerably less than those required to meet trade unions demands. Or, as we expressed it: Existing production technology more and more often constitutes an insurmountable barrier preventing the realization of trade union demands for the quality of work and a meaningful job.

Our focus was still at the workplace, but as we saw it, in order to support the local unions in their struggle for influence on technology, training and organization of work,

[18] See Ehn, P., Kyng, M. and Sundblad, Y.: *Training, Technology, and Product from the Quality of Work Perspective,* A Scandinavian research project on union based development of and training in computer technology and work organization, especially text and image processing in the graphics industry. (Research program of UTOPIA), Swedish Center for Working Life, Stockholm 1981.

an offensive, long-term strategy conducted by the central unions was needed. The trade unions at the central level had to assume responsibility for working towards collective solutions to the local demands in the areas of training, technology and organization of work, in addition to giving central support for actions taken at the local level.

To conduct a trade union technological research and development project was seen as one contribution to such a strategy. The UTOPIA project could hopefully contribute to changing the trade union's range of possible actions at the local level: Instead of defending the status quo, an offensive strategy was to be developed for another type of technology and improved products.

The practical overall objective of the UTOPIA project was to contribute to the development of powerful skill-enhancing tools for graphic workers. Thus, not only the development of technology, but also human qualifications and training were stressed. Quality of work and product was very important. The labor processes of page make-up and image processing in integrated computer-based newspaper production were the key issue.

The organization of such a research and development project had to differ from that of the DEMOS project.

The Swedish Center for Working Life was still a good base both because of its trade union orientation and because of its interdisciplinary environment, but it had to be complemented with computer science design skills if we really were to design alternative systems in accordance with our objectives. Yngve Sundblad and his colleagues at the Computer Science Department at The Royal Institute of Technology in Stockholm had done some research on computer-based text processing and computer graphics, and were interested in participation in the project, as were Morten Kyng and his colleagues at the Department of Computer Science at the University of Århus, Denmark. The DUE project, a Danish sister project to DEMOS, had given them experiences similar to ours, and a similar wish to participate in the design of skill-based alternatives. This became the interdisciplinary and Scandinavian academic environment for the project.

But the project web would have been most incomplete, and the research strategy most unsatisfactory, if there had not been active roles for the ultimate users in the research team. Since much of the design work had to be carried out in a research and development laboratory rather than at a specific workplace this was a real problem. Our organizational solution was to have skilled graphic workers with trade union experience participate directly in the design team. This was organized as a part time engagement, to allow the graphic workers to 'bridge' experiences between the UTOPIA project and the ordinary work practice at their workplaces. Besides graphic workers working directly in the project group, the Scandinavian graphic workers' unions followed and supported the project through a group consisting of representatives from Sweden, Denmark, Finland and Norway, all appointed by the Nordic Graphic Workers' Union. This Nordic trade union base for the UTOPIA project was due to the Nordic Graphic Workers' Union's wish to create a closer cooperation between the Nordic countries and a common proactive approach to new technology to prevent the loss of skill and jobs in the printing industry.

As project leader, and the only full time employee, one of my main tasks was to facilitate a common understanding between people who spoke so many different 'languages'. The difference between national languages was only a minor problem: we all pretty quickly learned to speak 'Scandinavian'. The real challenge was to establish the project as a language-game where all participants could make use of their professional language. This meant developing a research and design approach where researchers with as different backgrounds as computer science and systems design, ergonomics, organization theory, sociology, and history could not only speak with each other, but – just as importantly – with the users in the design team, i.e. skilled typesetters, page make-up persons, graphic artists, and experienced trade unionists.

(When we later on established cooperation with a vendor who was willing to try to implement our UTOPIAn specifications, the project as language-game also had to take into account the specific technical and financial language of a commercial producer. Finally, when we came to 'test site' implementation, the language at that workplace, as used not only by the local graphic workers, but also by journalists and management , also affected our UTOPIAn language).

From a design point of view the challenge was to develop really participative design methods that allowed both professional users and professional designers to be creative in the design process. To this end we came to focus on what we called 'design-by-doing' methods, using simulations like prototypes, mock-ups, and organizational games, which allowed the graphic workers to articulate their demands and wishes in a concrete way by actually doing page make-up or picture-processing work in the simulated future environment.

The UTOPIA project as a 'demonstration example' of conditions for designing new technology as tools for skilled workers, and as part of a strategy for democratization of working life, has doubtless contributed to the debate on alternative designs. Examples include a film made by an American movie team on this new Scandinavian approach,[19] an educational television program on computers in the workplace,[20] articles in the international press on UTOPIA, where workers craft new technology,[21] and all the invitations we still get to tell the story of UTOPIA.

It was certainly stimulating for us, and a deliberate practical aim of the project, to participate in the debate on

[19] The movie *Computers in Context* by Larry Daressa of California Newsreel and Jim Mayers of Ideas in Motion, 1986.

[20] The Danish television program *Ny Teknologi – UTOPIA* by Ulla Rønnow, 1984.

[21] See e.g. Howard, B.: 'UTOPIA – Where Workers Craft New Technology' in *Technological Review*, vol 88 no 3, Massachusetts Institute of Technology, 1985.

new technology and industrial democracy. However, a more fundamental communication problem for us was the dialogue with Scandinavian graphic workers, and the diffusion of project experiences in that context. The ways we handled this had great impact on the reporting from the UTOPIA project.

To make the project and our activities well known at Scandinavian graphic workplaces we created a (typographically well designed) magazine called *Graffiti* that was distributed via the trade unions. Our purpose with this publication was to report on the ongoing research, on problems and ideas, and to give background for our activities, while the project was still work in progress. Furthermore, we wanted to do this in a form that could encourage initiatives from graphic workers outside the research team. When the summary report *UTOPIA – alternatives in text and images*[22] was published as *Graffiti no 7*, UTOPIA was already well known at many graphic workplaces.

With *Graffiti* we could contribute to an open debate and provide some basic information on conditions for technical and organizational alternatives in newspaper production. But since the enhancement of professional graphic skills was one of the main ideas of the project, this was far from enough. Hence, the final UTOPIA reports on computer based page make-up,[23] image processing[24], work organization[25] and work environment[26] were written as

[22] The UTOPIA project group: *An Alternative in Text and Images,* Graffiti no 7, Swedish Center for Working Life, Stockholm 1985.

[23] Ehn, P. et al.: *Datorstödd Ombrytning,* Swedish Center for Working Life, Stockholm 1985.

[24] Frenckner, K. and Romberger, S.: *Datorstödd Bildbehandling,* Swedish Center for Working Life, Stockholm 1985.

[25] Dilschmann, A. and Ehn, P.: *Gränslandet,* Swedish Center for Working Life, 1985.

[26] Gunnarson, E.: *Arbetsmiljökrav,* Swedish Center for Working Life, Stockholm 1985.

textbooks to be used in graphic trade schools rather than as traditional research reports.[27]

We could certainly have done better with both *Graffiti* and the textbooks, but to me the effort to 'bridge' the gap between research and the ultimate users is fundamental to research that aims at supporting industrial democracy and quality of work and products.

## ACADEMIA

My working life seems to be divided into five year periods. The second half of the 1970s I spent in DEMOS, the first five years of the 1980s I lived in UTOPIA, and now I have moved to ACADEMIA (which is not another acronym but the land of theoretical reflection). This book is a preliminary report from that place.

But although in ACADEMIA I have not completely managed to keep away from practical research. It has been only all too tempting to join new projects, and I could not resist participating in the DIALOG project on human-computer interaction,[28] and in the establishment of a UTOPIA-like project on the office of the future,[29] and in developing our new interdisciplinary research program on computer support for cooperative design and communication.[30] But there has also been time for reflection. And

---

[27] However, several articles for research conferences and scientific publications as well as a Master's and a PhD thesis have been published based on the project.

[28] See e.g. DIALOG project group: *Årsrapport för 1984*, Department of Computer Science, Royal Institute of Technology, Stockholm 1985.

[29] The KNUT project or network is described in the first issue of the project newsletter *Bakom Knuten*, Swedish Center for Working Life, Stockholm, September 1987.

[30] Our program and the first projects are outlined in Andersen, P.B. et al.: *Research Programme on Computer Support for Cooperative Design and Communication*, Department of Information Science and Department of Computer Science, University of Aarhus 1987.

I have moved from the interdisciplinary and trade union oriented environment at the Swedish Center for Working Life to a university environment. First I moved to the Computer Science Department at the University of Århus in Denmark, where several colleagues from the UTOPIA project already were working, and later on to the Department of Information and Media Science at the same university.

My reasons for moving to ACADEMIA were not only scientific, but also personal and political.

Personally I really felt a need to step back and reflect upon a decade of practical research work that had been so intensive and involving that it was more like one long day. I needed some distance, and I wanted time to dig deeper into the question of design of computer artifacts, and especially I wanted to explore why 'design-by-doing' worked so well in practice and also to find out more about the meaning of regarding computer artifacts as tools. It was also hurting my personal ego that the work we had been doing in DEMOS and UTOPIA was looked upon by the academic world as interesting, but often more as politics than as 'real science' or good research. We were invited to give speeches at universities all over the world, but did not really seem to belong anywhere. Hence, I both wanted to reflect upon our experiences and to defend our approach as good research.

Politically it has for most of us at all times been important to do good research. However, the ways we have moved have often carried us away from the academic main stream, the reason being that this is not where our research subjects live. Our focus on democracy at work and quality of work and products has 'forced' us to use highly participative and interventionistic research methods and structures (instead of just objective observing), and to apply research perspectives on work and technology that highlight conditions for emancipatory change (instead of staying politically neutral). I find the academic legitimization of such research politically important.

Finally, a complementary scientific reason for entering
ACADEMIA had to do with a feeling that something was
fundamentally 'wrong' in rationalistic systems thinking.
There simply had to be theoretical alternatives.

One of my first activities in the academic world was to
participate in the organization of an international conference on the 'development and use of computer-based
systems and tools in the context of democratization of
work'.

The conference was organized at the Department of
Computer Science at the University of Århus, and was an
anniversary celebration of the first Scandinavian conference on the same theme ten years earlier at the same
place. That earlier conference was the first organized
meeting between researchers and trade unionists interested in discussing computers and industrial democracy.
It was an important step in the development of cooperation between researchers and trade unionists in the field,
and in the development of a research strategy based on
this cooperation.

Our purpose with the new conference was to open up
an international dialogue with researchers concerned
about the theme. We wanted to share our Scandinavian
experiences and perspective, which we named *the collective resource approach*, with other researchers, and we
wanted to listen to other researchers applying other perspectives and possessing other experiences. I think that
*Computers and Democracy – A Scandinavian Chal-
lenge,*[31] our anthology from the conference, gives a good
international overview of research in the field. I also think
it was a well chosen act of honor to dedicate the book to
Kristen Nygaard. He not only organized the first conference, but has also been a main contributor to the collective resource research strategy, and the most important
person for 'bridging' the gap between the academic world

[31] Bjerknes, G., Ehn, P., Kyng, M.: *Computers and Democracy –
A Scandinavian Challenge*, Avebury, 1987.

of computer science and the practical world of these artifacts in working life – in Scandinavia and internationally.

The main organizer of the conference was Morten
Kyng. It was to work with him and to jointly write a book
on work-oriented design of computer artifacts that I
moved to the Computer Science Department at the University of Århus. The conference was a good start for us.
Other joint activities that gave us opportunities to reflect
on our experiences, and forced us to read more, were de-
partmental courses which we developed and taught on
'computers and tools', 'computers and cognition' and
'computers and democracy'. However, as matters fell out
I came to be the only author of this book. But it is much
more than a polite gesture, when I state that especially
Morten, but also many of my other colleagues, researchers and practitioners that participated in DEMOS
and UTOPIA, also speak from these lines. It has all been a
cooperative effort. I only wish the lonely process of writing
this academic book on work-oriented design of computer
artifacts also could have been more cooperative.

## Position on the Map

Before surveying the content of this book I will spend a
few words on tentatively placing DEMOS, UTOPIA and
*work-oriented design of computer artifacts* in the atlas of
research.

To place our work in DEMOS and UTOPIA on the Scandinavian systems design research map is a relatively easy
task, since this map recently has been drawn by Jørgen
Bansler in his Ph.D. dissertation on the theory and history
of Scandinavian systems design research.[32] Bansler distinguishes three influential research traditions from the
late 1960s until today: *the infological approach, the socio-
technical approach, and the collective resource ap-*

---

[32] Bansler, J.: *Systemudvikling – teori og historie i skandinavisk
perspektiv*, Studentlitteratur, Lund 1987.

*proach.*[33] All three traditions are concerned with practical systems design in organizations. However, the different *knowledge interests* that motivate these traditions lead to different theoretical perspectives, focus on different problems, and result in the development of different methods.

The infological approach focuses on information flows in organizations understood as information systems. Good systems become a question of efficient use of information. The socio-technical approach focuses on the 'fit' between the technical and the social system of an organization. Organizations will be more efficient if 'human factors' and worker satisfaction are considered in the design. Neither this harmony view of organizations nor the focus on efficiency is shared by the collective resource tradition. Here focus is on the conflicting interests within an organization. Good systems design becomes a question of democratization of working life, of influential participation by workers and their trade unions. According to Bansler there are especially four research projects that have formed the collective recourse approach. Besides DEMOS and UTOPIA they are NJMF, the initial trade union oriented Norwegian project on planning, control and data processing, and DUE, the Danish sister project of DEMOS. I think the contributions from the PAAS project and its followers,[34] with their complementary focus on skill formation, definitely also should be situated as important places within the collective resource approach.

To elaborate a little more on the Scandinavian map I would as a fourth approach like to add *professional systems design.*[35] This approach grew out of the collective resource tradition, shares many of its research methods,

---

[33] Bansler calls them 'informationsteoretiske', 'socio-tekniske', and 'fagpolitiske'.

[34] See e.g. Göranzon, B. et al.: *Datorn som verktyg*, Studentlitteratur, Lund 1983, and Göranzon, B. (ed.): *Datautvecklingens filosofi*, Carlsson & Jönsson, Malmö 1984.

[35] Andersen N.E. et al.: *Professionel Systemudvikling*, Teknisk Forlag, Copenhagen 1986.

and overall theoretical perspective, but focuses on the interests of the systems designers and their working life.

Bansler concludes that all three (I would say four) systems design approaches today are well established at Scandinavian universities, both as research traditions and as types of education, but that there is very little communication between them. This book may hopefully contribute to a more open dialogue.

However, if we take an interdisciplinary look at the Scandinavian map the collective resource approach has many connections. Especially architects[36] but also engineers[37] have developed similar research projects, methods, and theoretical perspectives, and we have had close cooperation with these research groups.

To place the collective resource approach and *work-oriented design of computer artifacts* on an international map is more difficult.

As a political commitment our tradition shares many of the values and ideas of the *alternative production* movement; we have especially been influenced by the strategy of quality of work and product developed by workers and engineers at Lucas Aerospace in Britain.[38]

The best known of them, Mike Cooley, has also been most influential in establishing a research strategy for *human centered design*, the design of new technology based on the skill and qualitative judgements of workers and designers, and influential trade union participation. He is now coordinating an EEC project on a human centered computer integrated manufacturing system. Other

---

[36] E.g. the *Dairy Project*, which was conducted by architects, but used methods and a perspective similar to the DEMOS and DUE projects, See e.g. Steen, J. and Ullmark, P.: *De anställdas Mejeri*, Royal Institute of Technology, Stockholm 1982.

[37] E.g. the *Carpentry Shop* project, which worked with methods and a design perspective similar to the UTOPIA project but within a 'low tech' area. See Sjögren, D. (ed.): *Nyhetsblad från Snicke-riprojektet*, Swedish Center for Working Life, 1979–83.

[38] See e.g. Cooley, M.: *Architect or bee? – The Human/technology Relationship*, Langley Technical Service, Slough 1980.

early contributions to human centered design were the designs by Harold Rosenbrock[39] and his team at the Manchester Institute of Technology in Britain, both in the area of computer aided design and in the development of human centered lathes. In addition to the British tradition, there have been corresponding research developments in Germany. Peter Brödner,[40] in particular, has elaborated on the human centered production concept, and helped bring it out into actual design of computer-based systems, in cooperation with the metal workers' union.

The collective resource approach comes close to the central ideas of human centered design, and it was my intention to call the book *human centered design of computer artifacts*, since I essentially see it as theoretical reflections within that tradition. However, as friends have pointed out to me, there is more to human life than work, and since I only reflect upon computers in the workplace, I have restricted the title to *work-oriented design of computer artifacts*.

To place this book on the map of recent developments in theory of design in Information and Computer Science we have to go to the land where *language is action*. This is where many of our basic concepts in design of computer systems are rethought.

Geographically this place can be found at the American west coast, literally in the heart of 'Silicon Valley'. As the reader will soon discover, I find the new philosophical foundation in the tradition of *hermeneutics and phenomenology* proposed by Terry Winograd[41] and Hubert L.

---

[39] See e.g. Rosenbrock, H.: *Social and Engineering Design of an FMS*, CAPE 83, Amsterdam 1983.

[40] See e.g. Brödner, P.: *Fabrik 2000 – Alternative Entwicklungspfade in die Zukunft der Fabrik*, Sigma Rainer Bohn Verlag, Berlin 1985.

[41] Winograd, T. and Flores, F.: *Understanding Computers and Cognition–a new foundation for design*, Ablex, Norwood 1986.

Dreyfus[42] a most challenging place to visit. Neither do I mind learning more about the technical and artistic ways of designing human-computer interaction referred to as *user centered system design*[43] that also take place in this geographical environment. The land where language is action can also be found in Germany, and I am just as pleased to follow Christiane Floyd into the new *process oriented paradigm in software engineering* she is proposing.[44] Restricting myself to the Scandinavian region, I feel at home with dissertations like the ones based on *human activity theory* by Susanne Bødker[45], or Jens Kaasbøll's *rethinking of the information concept*.[46]

With the hope that the reader now has both an idea of the research lands of DEMOS and UTOPIA that I come from, and a sense of where on the research map I try to place myself, I will now turn to an outline of this book on work-oriented design of computer artifacts.

## Survey of Contents

This book is divided into four parts, in addition to this prologue and an epilogue with 'postmodern' reflections. Each

[42] Dreyfus, H. L.: *What Computers Can't Do – A Critique of Artificial Reason*, Harper & Row, New York 1972, and Dreyfus, H. L. and Dreyfus, S. D.: *Mind over Machine – the power of human intuition and expertise in the era of the computer*, Basil Blackwell, Glasgow 1986.

[43] See e.g. Norman, D. & Draper, S. (eds.): *User Centered System Design*, Lawrence Erlbaum, London 1986.

[44] See e.g. Floyd, C.: 'Outline of a Paradigm Change in Software Engineering' in Bjerknes, et. al (eds.): *Computers and Democracy – A Scandinavian Challenge*, Avebury, 1987.

[45] Bødker, S.:*Through the Interface – A Human Activity Approach to User Interface Design,* DAIMI PB–224, Department of Computer Science, University of Aarhus, 1987(dissertation).

[46] Kaasbøll, J.: *A Theoretical and Empirical Study of the Use of Language and Computers,* Institute of Informatics, University of Oslo, forthcoming (dissertation).

part begins with an introduction. In the four parts I reflect upon: philosophical foundations of design; perspectives on design as art and as science; design strategies and democratization of work; and skill based design of computer artifacts. Taken together, these four parts give my scholary views of *work-oriented design of computer artifacts*.

## Part I. Design Philosophy – On Practice and Reflection

This part concerns the philosophical foundation of design for computer artifacts. I argue the need for a more fundamental understanding of design than the one offered by the dominating rationalistic systems thinking based on the Cartesian dualism of the objective and the subjective, of body and mind. This need concerns knowledge in the design process, as well as knowledge in doing design research, and knowledge in theories of design. The direction outlined for theory and practice in work-oriented design is towards practical understanding of the games people play in design and use of computer artifacts. I argue that *human practice and understanding in everyday life should be taken as the ontological and epistemological point of departure in inquiries into design and use of computer artifacts*. Design becomes a concerned creative activity founded in our traditions, but aiming at transcending them by anticipation and construction of alternative futures.

The alternative design philosophy suggested is based on pragmatic 'interpretations' of the philosophies of existential phenomenology, emancipatory practice, and use of ordinary language. The approaches are here labeled *Heideggerian*, *Marxist*, and *Wittgensteinian*. Skill and democracy are at the core of my 'interpretations'.

With a Heideggerian approach focus is on how people use computer artifacts. The fundamental *difference between involved practical understanding and detached theoretical reflection* is stressed.

Emancipatory practice is emphasized in the Marxist approach. In addition to the cultural understanding of design and use of computer artifacts offered by a Heideggerian approach, this is *a social or political interpretation*. The emancipatory focus is on social relations, on the transcendence of conditions that prevent humanization of the world – theoretically and in practice.

The Wittgensteinian approach gives an 'untheoretical' way of understanding the practice of design and use of computer artifacts. Knowledge is understood in much the same way as in the earlier approaches, but with emphasis on competence as having learned to follow rules in practice. The suggestion is to think of *design and use activities as language-games* that people play in ordinary use of language.

## Part II. The Art and Science of Designing Computer Artifacts

This part concerns the academic activities of research and teaching in the field of designing computer artifacts. I start out with a critique of the academic division of labor, arguing that *the disciplinary boundaries between natural science, social science and humanities are dysfunctional* when we want to understand the subject matter. I relate this institutional critique to *a priori* interests of knowledge, arguing that *not only the knowledge interest of technical control but also of intersubjective communication and emancipation are fundamental* to the subject matter in design of computer artifacts.

In arguing a shift from the dominant rationalistic engineering systems approach towards work-oriented design I begin with some tentative qualifications of the subject matter. What are we really concerned about in a science of 'systems development' or an art of designing computer artifacts?

I then turn to a critique of the *science of design of the artificial* by Herbert A. Simon. His influence on psychology and organization theory, especially the interpretation of these disciplines into the context of computer science, has had far-reaching consequences for an interdisciplinary comprehension of 'systems development'. It goes without saying that this engineering approach to design with focus on formal methods for the analysis of complex systems fits badly with the kind of design philosophy that I advocated in the previous part.

The following chapters in this part are a search for *alternative paradigm cases* for a science or art of designing computer artifacts.

I first look for 'internal alternatives', internal in the sense that they either emanate from within computer science, or are more concerned with the development of systems thinking than with taking a non-system view. And there are alternatives. What I find is *social system design methods* that we can use right away. I also find a *new foundation for design*, and a *new potential for design in the use prototyping software and hardware*.

However, there are many other disciplines that are occupied with design of artifacts. Architectural and industrial design are the examples I use in an inquiry into the ways that other disciplines see and do in design.

Compared with information and computer science, architecture is a mature art searching for its scientific identity. Considerations that have been important to architectural design should be worth reflecting upon for a science or art of designing computer artifacts. After all, houses and 'computer systems' are both social artifacts that play an important role in many people's lives. A comparison gives insight into the social and political aspects of design. It also sheds light on the creative sides of design, and leads me to argue that *design of computer artifacts is just as much a craft or an art as a science*. The question of *style* becomes just as important as that of scientific theory and method.

Architectural and industrial design also play an important role in transdisciplinary attempts to establish a discipline of *design methodology*. I argue that a discipline for design of computer artifacts can gain a great deal of inspiration from reflections on 'generations' of design methodology. Why did for example eminent researchers and designers like the architect Christopher Alexander and the industrial designer Christopher Jones, though starting very much with just as rational approaches as Simon, develop their thinking about design in quite different directions?

In the concluding chapter of this part an alternative to Simon's approach in the field of design of computer artifacts is outlined. An alternative understanding of the subject matter and a curriculum for its study is discussed.

This is based on the supporting arguments that any discipline which deals with the subject matter of design of computer artifacts should be able to theoretically and methodologically treat design as including aspects like interventions into practice, as communication between users and professional designers, as a creative process, and as a concerned human activity. Any discipline dealing with such aspects of design will have to transcend a natural science foundation, no matter whether the discipline is called computer science, informatics or information science. The domain of the subject matter outlined is not primarily a theory of physical events or logical inferences in a machine, but of concerned human activity within a background of tradition and conventions in designing and using these artifacts.

I find this subject matter truly interdisciplinary, with relations not only to aspects of traditional computer science, but also to theories and methods from social and human sciences such as sociology, psychology, anthropology, linguistics and business administration. However, I also wish to take seriously the indications that what professional designers really do is more art than science.

## Part III. Designing for Democracy at Work

This part concerns *the collective resource approach* to design of computer artifacts – our attempt to widen the design process to also include trade union activities, and the explicit goal of industrial democracy in design and use. This is the democracy aspect of work-oriented design.

The main features of the collective resource approach are trade union activities. They occur locally, influencing new technology introduced at the workplace, and centrally improving the conditions for local work through national agreements, improved education, and design projects which aim at broadening the scope of available technical solutions.

As a background for understanding the role played by trade unions in relation to the collective resource approach some characteristic features of Scandinavian industrial relations are sketched. Then the origin and development of the collective resource approach is outlined. I start in the dominant research tradition in relation to industrial democracy in Scandinavia in the late 1960s and the beginning of the seventies: the *socio-technical* research tradition. The negative strategic implications of this tradition, in terms of no real worker influence, formed an important part of the challenge to develop an alternative research approach for participation, work organization, and democracy in design and use of computer artifacts. Then I continue, focusing on the original Norwegian Iron and Metal Workers' Union project, by describing some of the major *projects* in the collective resource tradition.

Next, I go into details of the DEMOS and UTOPIA projects, discussing them in the context of designing for democracy. As background, the history and research strategy of the projects are given. The *interplay between Marxist labor process theory and our understanding of concrete design* is also highlighted. I then exemplify its results in terms of *strategies and methods for democratization of design and use of computer artifacts.*

In the concluding chapter of this part I summarize some reminders on design for democratization based on experiences from the collective resource tradition. They include:

*A participative approach to the design process is not sufficient in the context of democratization.*

*The union investigation and negotiation strategy is a democratic and workable complement to traditional de-*

*sign strategies. But it is very resource-consuming for the local unions.*

*Local trade union design efforts have to be supplemented by central union design activities.*

*It is technically possible to design computer artifacts based on criteria such as skill and democracy at work.*

I claim that the practical impact on democratization of working life that fifteen years of research in the collective resource tradition in Scandinavia has resulted in has been considerable, also reaching beyond the borders of Scandinavia. This is important, since participating in changes for democracy and skill is a key aspect of this kind of research. However, there has not only been progress. Retreats from gained positions form a considerable threat in times of recession and a new political conservatism. Not only has the role of the unions in reshaping technology and work been questioned, but also the very idea of industrial democracy.

I also claim that the theoretical perspective of collective resource projects has contributed to a better understanding of and methods for designing for democracy at work. However, theoretically the approach is an even more fragile plant than it is in practice. The theoretical perspective is interdisciplinary, and the methods used are unorthodox. Much still has to be researched, rethought and developed.

## Part IV. Designing for Skill

In this part I consider opportunities for and constraints on the ideal of designing computer artifacts as tools for skilled work. This is the quality of work and product aspect of work-oriented design.

I start with a revisit to UTOPIA. I outline our *tool perspective* – the ideal of skilled workers and designers in cooperation designing computer artifacts as 'craft' tools for skilled work.

Then I investigate in what sense we can understand computers as tools. I discuss the human use of tools, what craft tools are, and how they differ from machines and

computer artifacts. I also look into different kinds of critiques of understanding computer artifacts as tools, as well
as into alternative suggestions, such as a media perspective emphasizing communication, and a 'postmodern'
perspective emphasizing pleasurable engagement. I also
discuss the tool aspects of computer artifacts in terms of
existing hardware and software, and in terms of design
principles like direct manipulation and the use of metaphors. The inquiry concerns whether properties of craft
tools and their use should be seen as essential aspects in
designing computer artifacts, and to what extent we can
realize such an ideal.

My conclusion is that *computer artifacts* in the general
sense of being deliberately designed means to an end *are
tools*; but that they on a more concrete level *are machines*,
in the sense that once started they perform automatic action, and hence they *are different from simple hand tools*;
that they, however, are machines that *can be designed
with the ideal of craft tools* for a specific craft or profession, utilizing interactive hardware devices and the capacity of symbol manipulation to create this resemblance.

I find the tool perspective, used with care, to be *one*
useful design ideal for work-oriented design of computer
artifacts. This is not to neglect the importance of other design views like a media perspective or a play perspective,
nor is it blindness to the prevailing situation in industry
today, where computer artifacts more often are designed
as machines, in the sense that they take control away
from the user and automate skill.

Associated with the ideal of craft tools is the ideal of
craftsmanship. The consequences of such a skill ideal in a
tool perspective are discussed, especially the problematic
character of *tacit knowledge*, as is the difference between
the skills of individual instrumental activity and of social
interaction. I suggest that our UTOPIAn tool perspective as
design ideal needs to be supplemented by ideals that help
focus on cooperative aspects in general and especially on
the tacit knowledge performed as social interaction competence at work.

Finally I investigate the ideal of computer artifacts as tools for skilled work from a sociological perspective. I try to position the tool perspective on design of computer artifacts in relation to empirical studies on changes of qualifications in working life. What comes out is *a scattered picture of qualification, dequalification, polarization, requalification, and segmentation*. I find support for a design ideal based on craft skills, but it is a support with many question marks.

## Epilogue

The *epilogue* to this book contains some concluding remarks on the future of work-oriented design of computer artifacts. This includes a possible contradiction between the tradition-based ideal of skill, and the modern rationalistic ideal of democracy. The ideal of designing for skill and democracy at work is revisited in the light of the contemporary 'postmodern' condition.

*Part I*

# Design Philosophy –
# on Practice and Reflection

*'All social life is essentially practical.*
*All the mysteries which lead theory*
*towards mysticism find their rational solution*
*in human practice and*
*in the comprehension of that practice.'*

Karl Marx in *Theses on Feuerbach*

# Introduction

We live in a world of systems. This is absolutely natural to us. Nevertheless, my point in this part on *Design Philosophy* is that it is exactly this fact which must be made a problem for a science of design and use of computer artifacts. Neither existing systems nor systems thinking as such should be taken for granted.

Computer and information science, and systems design, are based on an often implicit philosophical foundation that may have been adequate when the field of study was restricted to understanding computers as formal systems. Today computer artifacts have to be understood in a much wider sense — as social phenomena playing an increasingly dominant role in our everyday life. This leads to a questioning of the philosophical foundation of a science of design and use of the artifacts we call computers.

In a science of design and use of computer artifacts we have to be concerned with a *technical* interest, i.e. the purposive rational design of systems, and the technical functionality of these systems. This is at the core of such a science. However, the design and use of computer based systems are historical and social processes. As such they have to be understood with the research interest of the human and the social sciences. According to the well-known categorization by Jürgen Habermas in *Erkenntnis und Interesse* this means a *practical* and an *emancipatory* research interest.[1] The practical research interest is directed towards interpretation, human understanding and communication, towards the establishment and ex-

---

[1] Habermas, J.: *Erkenntnis und Interesse,* Suhrkamp, Frankfurt 1968.

pansion of action oriented understanding. The emancipatory research interest is directed towards emancipation from hypostatized forces of history and society, the goal being the contribution to conditions for independent individuals in a society of free cooperation and communication.

The point I want to make is that these interests should be integrated into a science of design and use of computer artifacts. Design processes as a social and historical phenomenon have characteristics that in research should be guided not only by the technical research interest, but also by the practical and emancipatorial research interest.

This cannot be abandoned to *a posteriori* studies by the human sciences and the social sciences, because the design process is 'where the action is'. Critique may help change the conditions for design and use, but not until integrated into theory and methods of design can these interests have any real impact on how people design and use computer artifacts. This integration is a theoretical challenge to Work-Oriented Design of Computer Artifacts. Hence this inquiry into the philosophical foundations of design in this part of the book.

## Detached Reflection and Practical Skill

We ask philosophical questions because they give clues to what and how we can know, and how we have acquired the knowledge that we claim to possess. These are the kind of questions I will discuss in this part. It will be argued that there is more to a science of design and use of computer artifacts than can be understood with mathematics and logic, especially if we are concerned about skill and democracy.

A distinction between two kinds of knowledge is important to the argumentation. The first is the *practical skill* of professional designers and professional users. This is knowledge in everyday practice and in ordinary language use. The second is *detached reflection* about design.

This is propositional, often theoretical or scientific knowledge.

What I am doing in this book, for example, is detached reflection about design. I take a step back and look 'objectively' at the research and design practice I have been involved in for the last fifteen years. How does this kind of knowledge relate to design skill? This is a philosophical inquiry to which one can try to find epistemological and ontological answers. Some of them will be considered below.

My point is that computer science and systems design has to a large degree been unsuccessful in relating design knowledge as detached reflection to design knowledge as practical skill. The latter has been made invisible. The scientific way of thinking and doing has been seen as superior to, and actually the norm for, practical design activities and use of computers. Hence, formal description is almost another label for computer science, and systems the epitome of design.

The foundation for this understanding is a rationalistic philosophy of mirror-images of objective reality. Admittedly, it is a gross generalization to suggest, as I do, that most contemporary theories and methods for design of computer artifacts, as well as theories and methods for research in the area, belong to a tradition of dualism and rationalistic reasoning – what I will label a *Cartesian approach*. It should, however, not be taken as a strict classification: the outline is much too sketchy for such a purpose. However, in order to include not only a technical interest in design, but also practical and emancipatory design interests, this rationalistic foundation is questioned here.

The alternative position argued is that there is much more knowledge in the practice of design and use than can ever be formally described or reflected as systems descriptions. Theoretical reflective knowledge is seen as important in design, but more as a supplement to practical understanding than as a substitute for it. Hence, in the detached reflections below on design and use of computer artifacts, I will focus upon the importance of knowledge as *practice, everyday understanding and ordinary language.* This is done in search of a philosophical foundation for design theory and methods that can enhance the capabilities of designers and users to develop their practical knowledge. What I am looking for is *theoretical knowledge about everyday understanding* in and about design.

Over the years, three philosophical traditions have especially influenced my understanding of, and research in, design of computer artifacts, and focused it on the importance of everyday practice. They are *existential phenomenology, emancipatory practice,* and *language-games* philosophy.

From West Churchman's philosophical investigation into *The Design of Inquiring Systems*,[2] I have adopted the idea of interpreting philosophical ideas to a form which fits a discussion about design. However, my concern is with interpretations of Heidegger, Marx and Wittgenstein, rather than with their predecessors Leibniz, Locke, Kant and Hegel, all of whom Churchman introduced to design philosophy.[3] The alternative design approaches I

---

[2] Churchman, C.W.: *The Design of Inquiring Systems – basic concepts of systems and organization,* Basic Books, New York 1971.

[3] Kristo Ivanov 'traces' in *Systemutveckling och ADB-ämnets utveckling,* Department of Computer and Information Science, Linköping University, Linköping 1984, the philosophical roots of contemporary schools of computer science and systems design in Sweden. Some of his philosophical 'labels' for different 'schools' are summarized below: The 'infological approach' (professor Börje Langefors) he finds inspired by the logical empiricists and, going backwards, Carnap, Martin, Bar-Hillel – 'the first' Wittgenstein (analytical philosophy) – Russell, Frege (logicism), Bretano (psychologism) – Mill (empiricism). The 'database and artificial intelligence approach' (Professor Janis Bubenko) is described as having similar roots. The 'pragmatic approach' (Professor Kristo Ivanov) is via Churchman, Singer (empirical idealism), Dewey, James and Peirce (pragmatism) traced back to Hegel (idealism), Kant, Mill (empiricism) and Bain. Still another tradition is the 'phenomenological approach' (Professor Hans-Erik Nissen): among its inspirations are Habermas, Heidegger

suggest are probably best placed as successors of his *Hegelian Inquiring Systems*, even if the philosophical roots constitute a complicated tangle.

## Structure of Part I

In chapters 2, 3 and 4, respectively, I outline basic features of design and use of computer artifacts according to an *Existential Phenomenology – a Heideggerian alternative*, *Emancipatory Practice – a Marxist alternative*, and *Language-Games – a Wittgensteinian alternative*.

In chapter 5, *With Alternative Glasses – conclusions on design philosophy*, I summarize and exemplify what I understand as the common implications for theory and practice of Work-Oriented Design of Computer Artifacts.

However, to begin the philosophical journey I will have to characterize the philosophical tradition of dualism and rational reasoning, on which most computer science and systems design theory is based. So as in Churchman's dialectical Hegelian Inquiring System I start with a brief discussion of the 'deadliest enemy' to a practice oriented design philosophy, the *Cartesian approach* to systems design. This is done in chapter 1, *Mirror, mirror on the wall ... – the Cartesian approach and beyond*.

The critique I present and the alternatives outlined may seem odd to a reader who for the first time is exposed to them. However, they are not all that unique. When a few years ago I started to look around for an alternative

---

(existentialism), Husserl (phenomenology), Dilthey (Geisteswissensschaften), Kant and Hegel (idealism); another path back to Dilthey goes via Berger/Luckmann, Schütz, Scheler and Weber, while still another one indicates a relation backwards to 'the first' Wittgenstein (analytical philosophy), Peirce (pragmatism) and Mill (empiricism). The 'path' I will follow in this book comes closest to that of the 'phenomenological approach', but it will also include Marxist successors (dialectical materialism) to Hegel like Lukács, Marcovic´, Freire, Kosik and Israel. Habermas will also be seen in this connection. Emphasis will also be on the influence from the ordinary language school originating from 'the second' Wittgenstein.

philosophical foundation for design of computer artifacts
that was more in line with our research experiences from
DEMOS and UTOPIA I was lucky enough to get hold of a
manuscript by Terry Winograd and Fernando Flores.[4]
From inside computer science a critique of the rationalistic Cartesian approach was formulated, and alternatives
in the direction suggested here were presented.[5] Later I
have seen several examples in the same direction. Recently I met with Ragnar Rommetveit. Discussing the
philosophical foundation of cognition he referred to a paper he just had written on convergent trends in current
social-scientific research.[6] What he suggests in that paper
is that we are today witnessing a clear trend in research
on cognition and communication away from the Cartesian analytical-rationalist model and towards a convergent hermeneutic-dialectical view, including elements
from a Heideggerian, a Marxist and a Wittgensteinian
approach. As I was making the final version of this
manuscript I received from Markku Nurminen a floppy
disk containing a book on perspectives for information
systems pointing in the same direction.[7] To me these examples, both inside and outside computer and information
science, are an important philosophical legitimization for
beginning to look for new and perhaps most important
aspects of design of computer artifacts.

[4] The manuscript was later published as Winograd, T. and Flores: *Understanding Computers and Cognition – a new foundation
for design*, Ablex, Norwood 1986.

[5] An indication of the challenge the book has been to the established computer science society is that the well known journal *Artificial Intelligence*, no 31, 1987, pp. 213–261, published no less than
*four* reviews of the book and a reply from the authors.

[6] Rommetveit, R.: 'Meaning, Context, and Control – Convergent
Trends and Controversial Issues in Current Social-scientific Research on Human Cognition and Communication', in *Inquiry*,
no 30, 1987.

[7] Nurminen, M.: *Three Perspectives to Information Systems*,
Studentlitteratur, (forthcoming).

To the reader who already knows what the design of computer artifacts is all about, and who needs no philosophy to reflect about this, I pass on as a challenge my favorite quotation from Ludwig Wittgenstein:

> The aspects of things that are most important to us are hidden because of their simplicity and familiarity. (One is unable to notice something – because it is always before one's eyes.) The real foundations of his enquiry do not strike man at all. Unless *that* fact has at some time struck him. – And this means: we fail to be struck by what, once seen, is most striking and most powerful.[8]

This is what I have been struck by.

[8] Wittgenstein, L.: *Philosophical Investigations*, Basil Blackwell, Oxford (1953) 1963, § 129.

## Chapter 1

# Mirror, Mirror on the Wall . . . – the Cartesian Approach and Beyond

When designing computer artifacts we are to a large extent occupied with descriptions, often formal ones. We make systems descriptions of computer based systems and of the surrounding organizations. We write programs to run on computers. We make models of machine configurations, etc. And as researchers in the field we make theoretical models that mirror and explain this reality. What we reflect about in systems design and in research are real systems in an outer world of natural and artificial objects. Our descriptions are models of these objects and their relations. Based on our maps or mirror-images of the world we reason about the world and draw conclusions. We try to make the maps or mirror-images as correct as possible, and our reasoning as rational as we can.

Here are three typical examples that I am familiar with.

## Three Examples

### Theory of Science

The first one concerns descriptions and models in research. As a Ph.D. student in computer science I attended a course on theory of science given by my professor Börje

Langefors. We were taught the relation between model and reality.[1] This is, in short, the idea:

One can make observations in the object field (i.e. reality). A model is a map or a mirror-image of some part of this reality. It is based on observations in the object field. All models are

'system models' in the sense that they are designed as a system of components in such a way that this system can be expected to have properties that mirror some of the properties of the object field. (...) When we want to make models that are not physically or geometrically identical with the object field we have to define system components with properties that *for our study* are similar to the corresponding components in the objects field, and that are related in a way that is similar to the corresponding relations in the object field.[2]

Models can than be used for forecasts and explanations of relations and properties of the object field.

By simulations with a model we get model experiences that can be formulated as hypotheses about the properties of the model. When tested in the model these model hypotheses can be formulated as hypotheses about the object field. To be verified they have to be tested in the object field.

If the model is theoretical, then we can deduce theorems (propositions about properties of the model) from its axioms and logical structure. The model together with the theorems forms a theory. The theorems can be formulated as hypotheses about properties of the object field.

This was an example of a view of reality, systems, models and theory in *the field of theory of science* in computer and information science.

[1] Langefors, B.: *Samband mellan modell och verklighet*, IB-ADB 66, no 1, (rewritten 1971-11-02).

[2] Ibid., p. 2 (my translation).

## System Description Languages

My next example comes from the field of *system description languages* in computer and information science. It concerns the view of Kristen Nygaard, my mentor for many years, and one of the best known computer scientists in Scandinavia in the field of programming languages as well as in social rethinking of systems design to include the interest of trade unions. In his view

> a *system* is a part of the world, *which we choose to regard as a whole*, separated from the rest of the world during some period of consideration, *a whole which we choose to consider as containing a collection of components*, each characterized by a selected set of associated data items and patterns, and by actions which may involve itself and other components.[3]

In short: A system exists in the real world as objects with specific relations, but it is a human choice to consider this part of the world as a system.

Furthermore, we have to distinguish between two types of systems, *mental* and *manifest* systems. The former are

> those existing in our minds as a result of our thought processes. Systems existing in the human mind, physically materialized as states of the cells of our brains, are called *mental systems*. Systems external to human minds are called *manifest systems*.[4]

The system studied is called the *considered system*.

> Our understanding of a considered system, manifest or mental (in some other person's mind) will always be based upon mental systems which we create and manipulate within our own minds, and which we try to make *similar to* the considered system in some sense. (...) We have to select a subset of the properties of the

[3] Holbæk-Hansen E., Håndlykken, P. and Nygaard, K.: *System Description and the DELTA Language*, Norsk Regnesentral, Oslo 1975, p. 15.

[4] Ibid., p. 18.

system for incorporation in our mental system portraying the considered system. The reason for this is that any considered system possesses too many properties. (...) The mental system created in this way, in order to portray a selected set of the considered system's properties, is called a *mental model system* (...) a model (mental or manifest) is always itself a system. When we say that some system is a model, it is being related to another system – the considered system.[5]

When information about a system is communicated in a language the information passed on may be said to be a *system description*. An example of a *transient system description* is a spoken description. Examples of *permanent system descriptions* are descriptions written on a blackboard or printed in a book. When receiving a system description we create a mental model system of the considered system to which the system description refers.[6]

*Practical Guidelines*

My third example is less sophisticated. Nevertheless, it may well be the most important one. It comes from the field of *practical guidelines* in systems design. Edward Yourdon is an internationally well-known systems design consultant, and one of the most successful writers in this field. Here is a hint of his view from a textbook on systems design methods.

A methodology, as we will use the term in this book, is a formal specification of the system for building systems. It defines the pieces, or components, of the system for building software systems – that is, the phases or activities that one finds in a software project; it also defines the interfaces between those components. You'll also find that this book makes a distinction between a *tech-*

---

[5] Ibid., pp. 19–21.

[6] Ibid., p. 23.

*nical* model of the system for building systems and a
*managerial* model.[7]

Furthermore, for the methods to work there is an important assumption:

> Virtually everything in this book assumes that you are
> a rational manager; that you have rational program-
> mers and analysts working for you; that you deal with
> rational users and customers; and that the environ-
> ment in which you determine your schedules and
> manpower estimates is not only rational, but also
> friendly and supportive.[8]

## Systems, Dualism and Rationalistic Reasoning

Though different, all three examples are similar in at least
two aspects. They all share an understanding of the world
in terms of systems, models and descriptions of reality, i.e.
of systems thinking for purposive rational action. And
they have all been most successful in their respective fields
of design of computer artifacts. The instrumental power
of systems thinking for purposive rational action seems to
be beyond doubt.

The use of 'the scientific method' (logical empiricism),
as in the case of Langefors, has generated new knowledge
for design of more effective computer-based information
systems. New powerful object-oriented programming
languages are the result of systems thinking, as in the
case of Nygaard. And many of the computer based systems designed today could not have been created without
rational systems design methods like the ones by Yourdon.

---

[7] Yourdon, E.: *Managing the System Life Cycle*, Yourdon Press,
New York 1982, p. ix.

[8] Ibid., p. xi.

With success stories like the above, why would anyone worry about systems thinking? For me, the reason was a feeling that:

- systems thinking has helped produce hierarchical computer based systems with increased division of labor and less planning as part of the job, rather than more democratic labor processes of design and use;
- systems design has helped reduce the job of many workers to algorithmic procedures, rather than enhanced their skill;
- objectifications and formalizations in systems descriptions have to a great extent locked the users out of the design process, rather than supported creative participative communication between professional users and professional designers.[9]

What if these 'anomalies' to some extent are *inherent* in contemporary systems thinking as exemplified above?

What if traditional theories and methods for systems design not only have been politically applied to deskill users, but more fundamentally, theoretically reduce the skills of users to what can be formally described? Then a *critique of the political rationality* of the design process, points at a *critique of the scientific rationality* of methods for systems design and description. It becomes important to reflect about the philosophical foundations of systems thinking, and the foundations of research in the field.

*The Cartesian Approach*

Returning to the three examples of systems thinking above, one can say that they share the philosophical assumptions of *rationalistic reasoning as epistemology*, and that *dualism as ontology* is taken for granted. This is not exceptional. These are philosophical assumptions that

---

[9] This is further developed in Ehn, P. and Kyng, M.: *A Tool Perspective on Design of Interactive Computer Support for Skilled Workers* in Proceedings of the Seventh Scandinavian Research Seminar on Systemeering, Helsinki, 1984.

have proved to work well, and the ideas have a long history in Western tradition. Philosophers will tell us that the roots go back at least to Plato, and that science and technology are to a great extent based on the version of rationalism given by René Descartes.[10]

Descartes had a background in the humanities, but found himself embarrassed with all the doubts and errors that he found. To find true knowledge he turned to mathematics and was delighted with the certainty of its demonstrations and the evidence of its reasoning. True knowledge was to be found in arithmetic and geometry because they alone were free from any taint of falsity and uncertainty. The objective is rational reason emancipated from bodily feelings and emotions. Craft, artistry, passion, love, and care became the subjective and unreliable aspects that have to be sacrificed in search for the truth.

The prototypical Cartesian scientist or systems designer is an observer. He does not participate in the world he is studying, but goes home to find the truth about it by deduction from the objective facts that he has gathered. The truth is found in detached reflection by use of the method of rationalistic reasoning. Simple objects are organized into more and more complex systems which expand our knowledge of the world.

The Cartesian philosophy is an epistemology and ontology of an inner world of experiences (mind) and an outer world of objects: Our body being perhaps the most significant object, and language our way of mirroring this outer world of real objects.

To make this philosophy somewhat more concrete, think of a person driving a nail with a hammer. In the outer objective world there is the person (body), the nail and the hammer, all with their given properties. With our language we can name all these objects, so we know what they are. The person's inner world (mind) reflects the outer world. He perceives the hammer, the nail etc. To

[10] Descartes, R.: *A Discourse on Method and Selected Writings*, (1637) J.M. Dent and Sons, London 1912.

drive the nail rationally he examines the properties of the hammer, the nail, and of other objects that might be of importance to the hammering. From this inspection and his former knowledge about these objects he determines how to drive the nail. When he has made this rational decision in his mind, the mind causes his body to grip the hammer and drive the nail the right way.[11]

This understanding of hammering corresponds well with the systems thinking in the examples above. I will refer to it as the *Cartesian approach* to systems design. Terry Winograd and Fernando Flores have summarized it in the following way:

• characterize the situation in terms of identifiable objects with well defined properties

• find general rules that apply to situations in terms of these objects and properties

• apply the rules logically to the situation of concern, drawing conclusions about what should be done.[12]

This is the epistemological assumption of *rationalistic reasoning*. With this goes the ontological *dualism* assumption, that is:

• We are inhabitants of a 'real world' made up of objects bearing properties. Our actions take place in that world.

• There are 'objective facts' about the world that do not depend on the interpretation (or even presence) of any person.

---

[11] The hammering example is chosen by reason of its popularity. It is used as a paradigm example by many of the authors I will refer to for other ontological or epistemological positions. It is also a good example because it facilitates reasoning about designing computer artifacts as tools for skilled work, which is one of the main purposes of this book.

[12] Winograd, T. and Flores, F.: *Understanding Computers and Cognition – a new foundation for design*, Ablex, Norwood 1986, p.15.

• Perception is a process by which facts about the world are (sometimes inaccurately) registered in our thoughts and feelings.

• Thoughts and intentions about action somehow cause physical (hence real world) motion of our bodies.[13]

Systems design is not a social and creative enterprise, but a process of rational decision-making. We need only make correct descriptions of the world; the rest is simply logic. The computer systems that are designed are not artifacts like hammers, but logical machines like our minds. Cartesian mind-body dualism paradoxically suggests that there is 'a ghost in the machine' [14](the ghost that artificial intelligence today wants to place in the artifacts we design).

## The Invisibility of Skill and Subjectivity

In spite of all the merits of the Cartesian approach and systems thinking, there also seems to be reason to be critical of these philosophical foundations. Given my interest in work-oriented design, the shortcomings I find most striking are that *practical skills and subjectivity are rendered invisible* – that *the social construction of reality is hidden in the background.*

What if we reject Cartesian dualism, i.e. that what we know about the world is a reflection or mirror image of that outer world of objects? What if we rather assume that we socially construct the world?

[13] Ibid., p. 30.

[14] An expression used about the Cartesian mind-body dualism by Ryle, G.: *The Concept of Mind*, Penguin Books 1949.

If we instead, as Wittgenstein, assume that:[15]

> What I see in the dawning of an aspect is not an attribute of the object, but an internal relation between it and other objects.

Then it does not become necessary to make assumptions of individual mental representations of an external Cartesian world independent of language. Aspects of objects, as opposed to attributes, become, as Ragnar Rommetveit has argued, theoretically anchored in the constructivist assumption.[16] The 'dawning of an aspect' takes place as situated cognition and communication by which we actively make sense of the world and 'bring it to language'. There is a shift from language as description towards language as action. And furthermore, for the sense I make of the world to be accepted by others as intersubjectively valid it must to some extent be a matter of social control and negotiation. The following chapters on design knowledge will be based on this *constructivist assumption*, rather than the dualism assumption.

Now to the invisibility of skills in the Cartesian approach. What are the consequences of giving priority to reflective purposive rationalistic thinking? After all, as the philosopher Peter Winch, has put it:[17]

> a cook is not a man who first has a vision of a pie and then tries to make it, he is a man skilled in cookery, and both his projects and his achievements spring from that skill.

---

[15] Wittgenstein, L.: *Philosophical Investigations*, Basil Blackwell, Oxford (1953) 1963, p.212.

[16] Rommetveit, R.: 'Meaning, Context, and Control – Convergent Trends and Controversial Issues in Current Social-scientific Research on Human Cognition and Communication', in *Inquiry*, no. 30, 1987, p.85.

[17] Winch, P.: *The Idea of a Social Science and its Relation to Philosophy*, Routledge & Kegan Paul, London 1958, p. 55 (quoted after Oakeshoot).

And when the cook *reflects-in-action*, as Donald Schön has labeled the professional skill of being a researcher in a practical situation,

> he does not keep means and ends separate, but defines them interactively as he frames a problematic situation. He does not separate thinking from doing, ratiocinating his way to a decision which he must later convert to action. Because his experimenting is a kind of action, implementation is built into his inquiry.[18]

Nevertheless, the Cartesian view of the cook is similar to the rationalistic assumption of a professional designer as a person who in advance makes detailed explicit plans of all future steps, and a user as someone whose skill can be reduced to and described as algorithmic procedures.

Or to continue Winch's argument,[19] what would even the best Cartesian mathematician be without the practical skill of *doing* something? Can he make sense of a logical formula, an expression of objective knowledge (i.e. something encoded in a written language) without having learnt a socially shared way of making special kinds of marks on paper, and understanding how to use them in inferring conclusions from a set of premises? Does not rationalistic reasoning lack all significance, without such practical skills which we come to embody when we become socialized into a certain culture?

If this is the case, do we not need a philosophy of design that does not, as the Cartesian approach does, reduce the practical skill of designers and users to what can be formally described and understood as rationalistic reasoning? The following chapters on design knowledge will focus on the role of practical knowledge of users and

[18] Schön D. A: *The Reflective Practitioner – How Professionals Think in Action*, Basic Books, New York 1983, p. 68.

[19] Ibid., p. 57, and further developed in Shotter, J.: 'Consciousness, Self-consciousness, Inner Games, and Alternative Realities', in Underwood, G. (ed.): *Aspects of Consciousness*, vol 3, Academic Press, London 1983.

designers. They will be based on the assumption that *practical skill is more fundamental than theoretical rationalistic thinking.*

In rejecting Cartesian dualism, the relations between objectivity and subjectivity must also be rethought. It is not by accident that especially female philosophers have focused on the need for such a rethinking. Evelyn Fox Keller argues that the division of the world in the knower (mind) and the knowable (nature), as well as rationalistic or objective reasoning as a relation between the two, is a genderized philosophy of the world. She writes:[20]

> Not only are mind and nature assigned gender, but in characterizing scientific and objective thought as masculine, the very activity by which the knower can acquire knowledge is also genderized. The relation specified between knower and known is one of distance and separation. It is that between a subject and an object radically divided, which is to say no worldly relation. Simply put  nature is objectified. (...) Concurrent with the division of the world into subject and object is, accordingly, a division of the forms of knowledge into 'subjective' and 'objective'. The scientific mind is set apart from what is to be known, that is, from nature, and its autonomy – and hence the reciprocal autonomy of the object – is guaranteed (or so it had traditionally been assumed) by setting apart its modes of knowing from those in which that dichotomy is threatened. In this process, the characterization of both the scientific mind and its modes of access to knowledge as masculine is indeed significant. Masculine here connotes, as it so often does, autonomy, separation, and distance. It connotes a radical rejection of any commingling of

[20] Fox Keller, E.: *Reflections on Gender and Science*, Yale University Press, New Haven 1985, p. 79. For an application of Fox Keller's gender analysis on systems design see Greenbaum, J: *The Head and the Heart – using gender analysis to study the social construction of computer systems*, Computer Science Department, Aarhus University, Denmark 1987.

subject and object, which are, it now appears, quite consistently identified as male and female.

Instead of rendering the bodily emotional subjective actors
in design and science invisible, in the name of objectivity,
why not participate in the practice of the concerned subjects and this way construct reality as objectively as we
can? At  the same time we can, as Ragnar Rommetveit
has suggested, ask as a critique of the Cartesian ideology
and the unequal distribution of knowledge and power in
society:[21]

> What is it that characterizes those persons who in our
> society thus manage to have their subjectivity endorsed
> by others and hence, in a way, accepted as 'objectivity'?
> Can we, by systematic investigation of such asymme-
> tries, perhaps start unravelling institutionalized pat-
> terns of dependencies and 'meaning monopolies' in so-
> ciety at large?

The following chapters will be based on the assumption
that *subjectivity is a valuable source in design and design
research,* not a factor that necessarily should be kept under control or reduced to a minimum. Under all circumstances subjectivity should be made visible.

## Beyond Cartesianism?

The fundamental question to be discussed in the following
chapters is if and how we can do better in design of computer artifacts, and in research about them, without the
Cartesian ontological and epistemological assumptions.

To speak of my own design experiences in the DEMOS
and UTOPIA research projects: Could other philosophical
positions help us understand our own shortcomings in the
use of traditional system description tools in design *with*
professional users? Could they shed some light on the
comparatively good results of applying 'design-by-doing'
methods like prototyping, experimental systems design,

---

[21] Rommetveit, op. cit., p.98.

the use of mock-ups, scenarios, etc., in design work with skilled users?[22]

In the languages of the coming sections: What new understanding is possible if we *break down* our *readiness-to-hand* of the Cartesian approach to design and use of computer artifacts? What are the consequences if design and design research are understood as *emancipatory practice* in an integrated social and historical context that is not taken for granted? And what if the Cartesian approach is just one out of many possible *language-games?* What if systems, instrumental rationality and dualism are no more than the historically and socially produced and intersubjectively accepted conventional rules of the game – no more real than any other rules produced this way? What other language-games can we then play in design and use of computer artifacts?

So far this may sound like odd ideas presented in alien languages. It is my hope, however, that the following chapters written in these languages will suggest to the reader some new and useful aspects on understanding design and use of computer artifacts.

Anyhow it should be worth mentioning that we are encouraged to a critique of the Cartesian approach by the author of the perhaps strongest contemporary arguments for it.[23]

[22] Ehn and Kyng, op. cit. and Bødker, S. et al.: 'A Utopian Experience' in Bjerknes et al. (eds): *Computers and Democracy – A Scandinavian Challenge*, Avebury, 1987.

[23] Ludwig Wittgenstein was not only the author of *Philosophical Investigations*, but also of *Tractatus Logico-Philosophicus*, Kegan Paul, 1923. *Tractatus* was a major contribution to the 'Cartesian approach' taken by the logical empiricists of the influential Vienna Circle. *Philosophical Investigations* may be seen as the mature Wittgenstein's critique of the position taken by the young Wittgenstein. This view will be referred to in a later chapter as the strongest support for the proposed understanding of design and use of computer artifacts.

*Practice as Reality – the Alternative Point of Departure*

In the following inquiry into design and use of computer artifacts I suggest as an alternative point of departure an ontological and epistemological position that focuses on human *practice* to replace the dualist mirror-image theory of reality. In short, this is what I understand as practice:

*Practice is our everyday practical activity. Practice is ontological. It is the human form of life. To be in-the-world is more fundamental than subject-object relations. In practice we produce the world, both the world of objects and our knowledge about this world. Practice is both action and reflection. But practice is also a social activity. As such it is being produced cooperatively with others being-in-the-world. To share practice is also to share understanding of the world with others. However, this production of the world and our understanding of it takes place in an already existing world. It is the product of former practice. Hence, as part of practice, knowledge has to be understood socially – as producing or reproducing social processes and structures as well as being the product of them.*[24]

In the following chapters of this part I will elaborate on the position that is taken and its consequences for work-oriented design of computer artifacts.

As mentioned in the introduction to this part three philosophical traditions in particular have, over the years, influenced my understanding of, and research in, design of computer artifacts, and focussed it on the importance of everyday practice. They are the philosophies of Martin Heidegger, Karl Marx and Ludwig Wittgenstein. This should not be taken literally.

By a *Heideggerian approach*, I do not mean a comprehensive account of *Sein und Zeit* (1927)[25], but rather an

---

[24] The background for this view of practice can be found among the many philosophers mentioned in footnote 28, below.

[25] In fact I have not really managed to read Heidegger, M.: *Being and Time*, Harper & Row, New York 1962.

interpretation of some ideas I find of interest to design in the wide tradition of *existential phenomenology*.

Neither is the discussion of the *Marxist approach* a thorough treatise on the theory of the capitalist mode of production in the three volumes of *Das Kapital* (1867, 1885, 1895)[26] or the philosophical writings of the young Marx, nor is it an account of the many different and conflicting 'Marxist' approaches to both epistemology and society. It is a reflection of some thoughts I find useful in understanding design and use of computer artifacts.

The *Wittgensteinian approach* is based on different interpretations of *Philosophical Investigations* (1953)[27], but is in no way an attempt to discuss the many sides of this 'untheoretical' philosopher, nor of the ordinary language school's position today.

Looking into the philosophical debate, the above mentioned philosophical positions are often seen as contradictory. However, there are also attempts made towards syntheses. Below, I will try to elucidate why these different traditions to me seem to converge and supplement each other in a useful interpretation and understanding of design and use of computer artifacts. In doing this I will be as truthful as I can to the different traditions. However, the context for the inquiries is a science of design and use of computer artifacts, not philosophy.[28]

---

[26] Marx, K.: *Capital – A Critical Analysis of Capitalist Production*, vol. I-III, Progress Publishers, Moscow 1953-1971 (first published 1867, 1885, 1895). This is the tradition in which I have my background. Hence, I am familiar with a great portion of 'Marxist' literature. However, in a two year study circle at the Swedish Center for Working Life we did not come much further than the first volume of *Capital*.

[27] Wittgenstein, L.: *Philosophical Investigations*. Not until a few years ago I did really read Wittgenstein. Since then *Philosophical Investigations* had more or less been my philosophical Bible, as the reader will soon find out.

[28] I am not thinking of any definite syntheses, but rather of inspiring examples of rethinking the different traditions. The Hegelian heritage shared by Marxists (M) and existential phenomenologists (P) is one obvious source for this transcendence.

The way the world comes into language in these approaches is quite different from the Cartesian world of
rationality, objectivity, planning, decision-making, etc.

The background for integrating the 'second' Wittgenstein (W)
seems more difficult to point at, perhaps as a dialectical transcendence of the analytic 'first' Wittgenstein. By mentioning some
names I will indicate the kind of syntheses I have in mind.
Among the 'classic' Marxists we find Georg Luka´cs (M, P) who
was inspired by Edmund Husserl (P). The Frankfurt School have
also been most important, from Max Horkheimer, Theodor
Adorno and Herbert Marcuse to Jürgen Habermas (M+P+(W)).
There is also the somewhat more pragmatic Jugoslav Praxis
group, e.g. Mihailo Marcovic´(M+P). Paul Freire's liberating pedagogy (M+P) and Jean-Paul Sartre's existentialism (P+M) are
truly transcendental to both traditions. Among contemporary
Marxists Karel Kosik's work is one of the most influential (M+P).
Influential existential phenomenologists with relations to Marxism are Maurice Merleau-Ponty (P+(M)) and, in the field of sociology of knowledge, Peter Berger (P+(M)+(W)). The computer scientist Terry Winograd (P+(W)) and the philosopher Hubert Dreyfus (P+(W)) have both given most important contributions to a new
understanding of design and of computers. In the contemporary
Scandinavian setting I especially want to mention the sociologist
Joachim Israel (M+W+P) and the psychologist Ragnar Rommetveit (M+W+P), who have suggested challenging eclectic contributions, the philosopher Tore Nordenstam (W+P+(M)), who
has integrated philosophical investigations into case studies in
the field of computer science and systems design, and the
architect Jerker Lundeqvist (W+M), who has contributed to a new
comprehension of design knowledge. Finally in the Scandinavian
context of computer science and systems design, I also want to
mention the work by Bo Göranzon and Ingela Josefsson
(W+P+(M)). Many other names could have been mentioned, as
well as the intergroup conflicts on e.g. idealism-materialism or
politics. However, this footnote hopefully give the philosophical
reader an indication of the direction of my inquiry.

*Chapter 2*

# Existential Phenomenology –
# A Heideggerian Alternative

In a *Heideggerian approach* we are thrown into a human world that exists before subject, objects, systems, and detached rational reflections.

Again, consider a carpenter driving a nail with a hammer. In his hammering activity the hammer does not exist for him as an object with given properties. It is part of the carpenter's world, but it is explicitly recognized just as little as the arm he holds the hammer with.

## Being-in-the-world

### Background – Ready-to-hand

According to a Heideggerian approach, an interpretation along the lines of *existential phenomenology* , the hammer belongs to the *background*, it is *ready-to-hand* ('zuhanden') without reflection in the carpenter's world. It must primarily be understood as a *practical artifact* ('Zeug') that he uses in his everyday life, not as a thing or an object external to him. The carpenter's world is not Descartes' world of objects given by nature. Nor is his mind a subjective reflection of it.[1]

---

[1] The basic inspiration for this section on a Heideggerian approach is Winograd, T. and Flores, F.: *Understanding Computers and Cognition – a new foundation for design*, Ablex, Norwood 1986 and Dreyfus, H. L. and Dreyfus, S. D.: *Mind over Machine – the power of human intuition and expertise in the era of the computer*, Basil Blackwell, Glasgow 1986. Another source that should be mentioned is an undated manuscript on Heidegger by

According to a Heideggerian approach, *human existence* is more fundamental than subject-object dualism. Human beings do not primarily come to an understanding of the world through philosophical, scientific or theoretical reflections. Humans beings, including researchers and scientists, are already in-the-world. Human existence is *Being-in-the-world* ('Dasein'). The subjective is already Being-in-the-world beforehand, before there can be any reflections about relations between subject and object or between objects. All these detached reflections are secondary. Rather than to say with Descartes that 'I think', we can with Heidegger say 'it thinks me', because human existence is a manifestation of Dasein.

Being-in-the-world is *thrownness*. We are always Being-in-the-world, in a situation, where we have to act one way or another. But Being-in-the-world is also a *projective* activity of *understanding*. We are always on our way towards understanding the situations we are thrown into.

Boje Katzenelson that we used in a seminar on computers and psychology. I can also clearly see the influence from the PAAS project at the Swedish Center for Working Life (Bo Göranzon, Ingela Josefsson and Tore Nordenstam). Of course the writings of Maurice Merleau-Ponty, Jean-Paul Sartre, Jürgen Habermas, Dag Österberg, Georg Herbert Mead, Peter Berger and Thomas Luckmann also belong in the background.

In addition I would like to make a comment on Heidegger and practice. Heidegger's world is the world of human beings-in-the-world. However, to Heidegger human beings are Beings for their own sake, always caring about this Being. Their possibilities are once and for all given in this Being. This aspect is certainly in contrast to the understanding of human practice as a possibility to historically and socially transcend the given world. However, contemporary 'philosophers' inspired by existential phenomenology like Jean-Paul Sartre, Peter Berger and Jürgen Habermas have demonstrated possibilities to overcome Heidegger's conservatism and replace it with a dialectical understanding of practice as the social construction of reality. In these interpretations not only the understanding of conditions for skill, but also for democracy, can be seen as fundamental. It is such 'interpretations' I have in mind in this chapter.

This understanding is not detached contemplation, but pre-reflective activity.

To use the hammer, our carpenter must in this sense understand what it is meant to be used for. Our use of artifacts is what they mean to us. They only have meaning within a social and historical background. The hammer can only exist within a background of e.g. 'hammering' or 'carpentering'.

This is the humanized and understood world that is ready-to-hand for us. The ready-to-hand matters are the artifacts we use in concerned activity. In the words of Winograd and Flores:

> In driving a nail with a hammer (as opposed to thinking about a hammer), I need not make use of any explicit representation of it. My ability to act comes from an understanding of *hammering*, not of a *hammer*.[2]

As a designer I might understand the artifact as a complex system, but that is not the meaning in use within the profession the artifact is designed for. Can I design useful artifacts without understanding use within the users' professional domain?

## Breakdown  – *Present-at-hand*

However, as in the Cartesian approach, we also relate as subjects in detached reflection to a world of objects and their relations., but now understood as a secondary phenomenon as compared to involved ready-to-hand use. For our carpenter, the hammer exists as a hammer only when it does not work or is not there – when it becomes unready-to-hand. Reflective, investigative, theoretical knowledge requires an *unreadiness-to-hand* of what before was ready-to-hand. A world of objects becomes *present-at-hand* ('vorhanden'). The present-at-hand are things as given by nature, what they are when they are not understood. This process of change from readiness-to-hand to present-at-hand is referred to as *breakdown*.

---

[2] Winograd and Flores, op. cit., p. 33.

This breakdown can only occur when for example our carpenter in practice has already understood 'hammering'. Again in the words of Winograd and Flores:

> The hammer presents itself as a hammer only when there is some kind of breaking down or unreadiness-to-hand. Its 'hammerness' emerges if it breaks or slips from grasp or mars the wood, or if there is a nail to be driven and the hammer cannot be found. (...) As observers, we may talk about the hammer and reflect on its properties, but for the person engaged in the thrownness of unhampered hammering, it does not exist as an entity.[3]

Hence, a main concern in design of computer artifacts must be to design for future situations of 'thrownness of unhampered' *use*. We should then aim at designing computer artifacts that are ready-to-hand for the users in their ordinary use situations.

However, the concept of breakdown is also fundamental to the design process. *Breakdown is both desirable and undesirable.*

On the one hand it is necessary to break down the everyday understanding and use within a specific tradition to create new knowledge and new designs.

On the other hand designs that are not based on the understanding and use within a tradition – the users' practical skills – are likely to fail. Breakdown of understanding of a well known situation is at the same time the opening to new knowledge and eventually an understanding of something new. The ability to deal with this contradiction between understanding of the ready-to-hand and detached reflection of the present-at-hand is fundamental to design. I shall later refer to this as *the dialectics of tradition and transcendence in design.*

---

[3] Ibid., p.36.

## Intentions

I have said that, in a Heideggerian approach, use and understanding are different aspects of the same activity by the user of an artifact. The same is the case with the users' *intentions* with that activity. Intentions or goals are not – as in the rationalistic tradition – prior to action. Of course, we make explicit plans and try to carry them out. However, the point to be made is that detached planning is not what we fundamentally do in everyday thrown situations of use of artifacts, nor is this how expert designers perform.

We have intentions, but the plan takes form during the activity. The intention determines the activity, but is also determined by it. There is no causal relation between intention and activity in thrown and projective everyday situations, because they are at this point not yet separate phenomena. It is not until afterwards, when reflectively looking back on the activity, that one can separate intention from execution and see them as different phenomena.[4]

This is also fundamental to design. Nevertheless it seems that reflections on design practice today, as part of the rationality of the Cartesian tradition, are based on the assumption that we can always separate plan and execution. Systems descriptions as well as the idea of formal requirement specifications are based on this assumption. It may be argued that this has proved to work well. The counter-argument is that this may be because design so far has mostly been for routine work. Or perhaps more accurately: it may be so because design of computer artifacts has meant routinization of work. This is 'Scientific Management' from the early principles of separation of planning and execution by Fredric Taylor to modern

---

[4] In Österberg, D.: *Metasociologisk essä*, Verdandi, Stockholm 1971, pp. 17-18, this aspect is discussed, as based on Sartre's *Critique de la Raison Dialectique*, Librairie Gallimard, 1960.

computer based planning and control systems.[5] The
political critique against the dehumanization that accom-
panies these principles has at all times been strong. The
philosophical argument given by the Heideggerian approach is that this separation is impossible, at least if we
want to design computer artifacts for skilled work.

## Understanding the Others

So far I have discussed the use and understanding of artifacts. What about human beings in a Heideggerian approach? Are they different from the artifacts? Yes they
are, because an *I* can only be thought of in relation to a
*You*. When *I* use artifacts *the others* are there, because the
artifacts and the background within which they have a
meaning to me are produced and communicated by them.
Hence, being-in-the-world is always being-in-the-world
together with other beings-in-the-world. My understanding of my self is my understanding of 'the others',
and vice versa.[6]

Communication, in a Heideggerian approach, is not
understood as conveying of information from me to the
other. It is an *act of interpretation*. The interpretation that
the other triggers off in me has a meaning to me only
within my background of understanding. This background is social and historical. Only when this background is shared can we understand each other.[7]

Language, according to a Heideggerian approach, is
not only a medium to share understanding of the world. It

[5] Fredrick Taylor's principles of separation of planning and
execution at work, as a means for managerial control over workers, were formulated in 1903. I will in detail discuss this kind of
division of labor in the later part: *Designing for Democracy at
Work*.

[6] See Mead, G.H.: *Mind, Self and Society*, University of Chicago
Press, Chicago 1934.

[7] Social division of labor and the possibility of planning according
to common goals is not emphasized in a Heideggerian approach.
This aspect will be discussed under the Marxist approach in the
next chapter.

also in itself contains implicit assumptions about it –
language is in itself as social and historical as other artifacts. Imagine the professional language that our carpenter uses when communicating with his apprentice.
There is a world of 'hammering' that is taken for granted.

However, even more important: In using language we
do not describe the world, we create it. Just as we do with
other artifacts. The carpenters' world is continuously re-
produced in ready-to-hand use of language, and eventually recreated in situations of breakdown.

Certainly the understanding that, *language as action* is
more fundamental than *language as description*, takes us
far away from the Cartesian approach and the world of
systems. The consequences are fundamental to design and
to the use of descriptions in design – *the thrown and projective ready-to-hand everyday practice and ordinary
language of the users come into focus, not detached reflection of present-at-hand systems of related objects.*

## Acquisition of Skill

So far the discussion of a Heideggerian approach to design
and use of computer artifacts has focused on the the importance of understanding the fundamental character of
everyday use and understanding. But how do humans
acquire practical skills? For an elucidation I will turn to
an interpretation given in *Mind over Machine* by Hubert
and Stewart Dreyfus.[8] In their critique of artificial intelligence they develop a five stage categorization of skills acquisition, to facilitate an understand of what humans can
do, while computers cannot. Their categorization is based
on observations of everyday practice in professional
learning and interpreted along the lines of existential
phenomenology.[9] Here I relate the categorization to the
question of design.

[8] Dreyfus and Dreyfus, op. cit. chapter 1.

[9] In fact the approach to design taken by Winograd and Flores is
in its existential phenomenological aspects influenced by Hubert

Dreyfus and Dreyfus see two basic procedures for skill acquisition. Especially during childhood we acquire skill through *trial and error,* often guided by imitation of those that are more experienced. But we also acquire skill by written or verbal *instructions.* Both are important in professional training or education when we learn a craft. This latter categorization is, however, limited to situations of learning by instructions.

The five stages are: *novice, advanced beginner, competence, proficiency* and *expertise.* I will illustrate them with examples from the activities of car driving and relate this to design and use of computer artifacts, and research in the field.

## *Novice*

In learning new skills by instructions we do not start out as novices, but as experts. In a Heideggerian approach, this is not a paradox. We always start from a situation of expert understanding of thrown and projective activities in our everyday life. Learning by instructions means breakdown of this understanding, but also an opening for new expert understanding. However, there may be a long way to go from detached novice reflection to expert understanding.

What we do as *novices,* according to Dreyfus and Dreyfus, is to apply *context-free rules* to objective facts and features in a relevant domain. This is theoretical knowledge based on detached reflection that others can write down for us to follow.

The novice car driver operating a shift-stick car shifts gears at speeds he has been told (a context-free rule), ignoring context like a steep hill or the sound of the engine. He does not know when to violate these rules. In fact, to the novice improvement is a question of how well he manages to follow the learned rules.

Dreyfus' interpretation of these aspects. The approach taken by Dreyfus and Dreyfus is also related to the Wittgensteinian approach which I will take a closer look at later in this part.

These are the kind of rules we see in most textbooks on design.[10] The novice designer follows these rules in trying to master a specific description tool, a sequence of design phases, a way of organizing the project work, etc. But following these rules he will never be able to professionally design computer artifacts. Not surprisingly, skilled designers do not follow them.

What you can learn this way is theoretical knowledge, but this do not make you professional.

An inexperienced design researcher can conduct a good experiment according to the 'method book', but that does not make him or her a professional researcher.

### *Advanced Beginner*

However, our performance improves when we get considerable practical experience coping with real situations. This is not only due to the fact that we get better in using the learned rules, and that we also learn to use more complicated ones. The *advanced beginner* starts through practical experience to be able to recognize important context dependent *situational elements* that cannot be defined by others as explicit and context-free rules. This knowledge is practical. He begins to understand the new situation.

The advanced beginner car driver not only judges when to shift gear from the car's speed, but also from situational elements like the sound of the engine. The advanced beginner does not know when to violate rules, but from experience with earlier cases or examples he can also act according to situational elements.

This is probably the level where we find designers that have a few projects behind them. They begin to have a 'feeling' for different design situations. This is likely to be the level of design skill of many computer science researchers, too. If this is true, then practical designers have a reason for skepticism towards design advice from re-

---

[10] See e.g. Yourdon, E.: *Managing the System Life Cycle*, Yourdon Press, New York 1982.

search. An advanced beginner car driver might be a good teacher in the theory of driving, but most of us would probably prefer to take advice from a somewhat more experienced driver.

## Competent Performance

*Competent performance* is the next level of skill acquisition. The competent performer knows in practical situations how to deal with the overwhelmingly increased number of both context-free rules and situational elements he can distinguish. He improves and simplifies his performance by knowing how to *choose and organize a plan*, which makes it possible for him to concentrate on the set of factors he has learned are the most important ones. He also learns the outcome of chosen plans, an experience that is different from that of recognizing situational elements.

The competent car driver may choose and organize a plan to drive a certain distance as quickly as possible. Given this plan, he will concentrate on the most important context-free rules and situational elements, like the condition of the car and the traffic situation at that time of the day. And he may certainly, if necessary, violate rules to fulfill the plan.

One can think of competent designers and researchers with a similar characterization.

## Proficient and Expert Performance

Performance on the *proficient and expert* levels is characterized by *involved, rapid, fluid, intuitive* performance rather than the more detached, reflective, deliberative and sometimes agonizing following of rules and selection among alternatives that has been considered at the earlier levels. Though complex, the situation remains ready-to-hand for the expert. There are no regular breakdowns of his understanding. Breakdowns occur, but afterwards as a deliberate means for detached reflection and improvement.

Proficient and expert performance is far from extraordinary. Acquisition of skill is more like an expanding circle than as a ladder. Think for example of the experience most of us have from situations in our everyday life where we are experts. When we talk and walk we seldom 'choose our words' or 'place our feet'. From long practical experience we simply know how to do it. The point is not that we cannot reflect when we act as experts, but that we do it only when the spell of involvement is broken, and this is secondary to the expertness.

However, some design experts have, as Donald Schön has noticed, in addition to their involved and fluid ready-to-hand performance, the competence of a complementary reflective conversation with the situation, developing on-the-spot theory. Schön calls this *reflection-in-action*.[11]

Proficient or expert performance is *arational* rather than rational, but it is not irrational. It is neither a performance contrary to logic or reason, nor is it an analytic decomposition and recombination of objects to a whole, as in the Cartesian approach. As Dreyfus and Dreyfus put it:

> In general, when everything is normal, experts don't solve problems and they do not make decisions: they simply do what works.[12]

I have pointed out that expertness is something we all possess in our everyday practice in some domains. Here the emphasis is on everyday practice in professional domains. We can nevertheless still say that every designer and user is an expert on his or her life, and that it is this expertness that breaks down in the design process.

There is also expertness in use and understanding of artifacts – for example a systems description tool in design of computer artifacts or a word processor in typing.

However, by professional expertise we more often think of really experienced understanding of the whole situa-

[11] Schön D. A: *The Reflective Practitioner – How Professionals Think in Action*, Basic Books, New York 1983.

[12] Dreyfus and Dreyfus, op. cit. p.30.

tion – be it car driving, design of computer artifacts or research. In this view expertness in a professional domain is
something that may require a lifetime to acquire, and
many of us still would not reach that level of skill.

Proficiency and expertness are the skill levels of a professional car driver. He drives without effort and understands without reflection when and how to perform an act
like slowing down, and he will not have to evaluate and
compare alternatives. But of course this pre-reflective
understanding breaks down if the conditions for the expertness changes. Many skilled drivers in Sweden were
for some time transformed into non-experts in 1967 when
there was a shift from driving on the left to the right side
of the road.

## Related Skills

Using Dreyfus and Dreyfus's skill categorization we can
make some interesting reflections about relations between
user skills, designer skills, and research skills in the field of
design of computer artifacts.

Suppose a designer wants to use Cartesian systems descriptions methods to describe user skills as a basis for a
new computer-based system. This may in principle be
possible according to the categorization as long as he
designs for users on the levels below proficiency and
expertness. Their skills can in principle be described as
algorithmic procedures and routinized (though most
professions contain skills on the proficient or expert level,
skills that will then be lost).[13]

However, the designer runs into problems as soon as he
tries to capture the rules an expert follows. He can make
algorithmic descriptions, but these descriptions will be
something different than the rules of an expert, since
what counts as expertness is exactly the competence to

---

[13] Here I am not discussing the political impact involved. That
will be done in the part on *Designing for Democracy at Work*.

break rules in creative ways or to follow rules in unforeseen, yet correct ways.[14]

Are we doomed to design to replace unskilled work or just to support skilled work with artifacts for routine work? Principally, there seems to be two ways out of the dilemma.

By acquiring proficiency or expertness in the domain we are designing for we may be able to understand how to design computer artifacts as skill enhancing tools for the experts, without having to make the skill explicit, formalized and routinized. The designer becomes involved in thrown ready-to-hand activity *both as design and as use.*

The complementary way to surpass breakdown by formal descriptions may be to create conditions for skilled users to utilize their professional skills in the design process. The proficiency and expertness we are looking for in design may be mastery of methods that let the user participate in design as if it was his or her thrown ready-to-hand use activity.[15]

Finally, the categorization can shed some light on our knowledge as design researchers.

We can certainly develop theories about design and use of computer artifacts without knowing much about practical design and use of computer artifacts. As unskilled designers and users, but skilled researchers we can still create systematic breakdowns in users' and designers' traditional knowledge. As theoretical knowledge we can propose to users and designers that the tradition they have taken for granted is problematic and suggest other ways of seeing. This is an important critical function of design research that can support better design and use.

But if we as researchers also want to creatively support the development of better designs and a better design

[14] This will be further developed in chapter 18, *Skills and the Tool Perspective.*

[15] The philosophical foundation for such 'design-by-doing' methods will be discussed in chapter 4, *Language-Games – A Wittgensteininan Approach.*

practice we seem to be in the same dilemma as the practical designer, and to have at our disposal similar ways out of it.

If we acquire proficiency or expertness as designers we should be able to understand design and use without having to make the skills of designers and users explicit, formalized and routinized. The researcher becomes involved in thrown ready-to-hand activity as *research, design and use*. If we look at design research fields other than computer science, like architecture, we find that really skilled researchers often also are excellent designers.[16]

As in the designer case, a complementary alternative might be to create conditions allowing skilled users and designers to utilize their professional skills in the research process. To master such methods and let users and designers participate in research as if it were their thrown ready-to-hand use activity might well be the proficiency and expertness we are looking for in research.[17]

## Research, Design and Use

### *Research*

A science of design and use of computer artifacts must according to a Heideggerian approach, be able to deal with everydayness, with the practical understanding and use of ready-to-hand artifacts as concernful activity in the world.

This is not to say that practical understanding is superior to detached theoretical knowledge. However, the point that has been made is that thrown and projective understanding is *prior* to detached theoretical reflection. It is also what is typical of skilled activity in use as well as in design.

---

[16] This will be developed in chapter 9, *Other Ways of Seeing and Doing — External Alternatives.*

[17] Actions research and psychoanalysis seem to be good prototypical examples.

Theoretical reflective research about design can be *illuminating of what is not understood – make the ready-to-hand present-at-hand*. This is the process of breaking down. However there is also a need to gain *knowledge about how to design artifacts that can be understood and ready-to-hand to the users in thrown use activity*.

To acquire knowledge about this it seems that we as researchers have to understand the everydayness of the specific activities that we research. After all, what we can reflect upon is what we already have understood and been able to use.

## Design

A Heideggerian approach also creates openings for a new understanding of the process of designing computer artifacts. What we want to design is computer artifacts that are ready-to-hand for the users in their everyday activity. To do this we must have technical design qualifications. But we also must be able to deal with the following contradiction:

On the one hand, to design so as not to breakdown or make obsolete the understanding and readiness-to-hand the users have acquired in the use of the already existing artifacts. The new artifacts should be ready-to-hand in an already existing practice.

On the other hand, to break down the understanding of the already existing situation and make it present-at-hand, is to make reflection about it possible, and hence to create openings for a new understanding and alternative designs.

This is the contradiction between *tradition* and *transcendence* in design and use of artifacts that will be a main theme in my further discussions about design in this book. Here I relate it to breakdown and readiness-to-hand.

This may be exemplified with what Kim Halskov Madsen[18] calls literal versus metaphorical design. He gives an illustrative example from a library.

In the first case the users' normal understanding of a library is taken for granted. The design aims at supporting the circulation department's lending and retrieval of books etc. The library is a place from which books are supplied. This emphasis is on how to find books quickly, their retrieval, registration of lending, etc. This may be the way it always has been understood.

In the alternative approach a metaphor is used suggesting that the library staff should see the library as a meeting place for people interested in conversations about books and other subjects related to books. This creates a breakdown of the library staff's traditional understanding of their library work, but may provoke a new understanding, and some very fruitful designs, e.g. for better communication between borrowers, and between borrowers and the library staff.

Ideally it seems that *we should be aiming at design processes that primarily make it possible for the users (and the designers) to utilize their practical understanding, in design of the new situation. But the design process should also incorporate breakdowns as a means for detached reflections on what is already understood among the users as well as among the designers.*

A design process which does not break down the user's understanding and readiness-to-hand in the given situation requires that the designer also understand the situation and/or that he or she has access to design methods that help avoid undesirable breakdowns. To share the users' practice for a long time and to use 'design by doing' methods like prototyping, experimental systems design, mock-ups etc., seems to be a way to overcome some of the

---

[18] Madsen, K.H.: 'Breakthrough by Breakdown – Metaphors and Structured Domains' in Klein, H. and Kumar, K. (eds.): *Information Systems Development for Human Progress in Organizations*, North-Holland (forthcoming).

constraints.[19] It goes without saying that it helps if designers and users are the same persons or share background
for understanding – if they have a shared practice.

The other aspect, i.e. to create breakdown, is at least at
first glance much easier. It may be argued that it is an
advantage if the designer is not too familiar with the everydayness of the situation and the users' understanding
of it. He may then be able to come up with some really
creative new alternatives. However, since he only has
limited understanding of the users' situation he will have
to deal with this situation as objects for rationalistic reflection. In this way he cannot possibly understand the
skills of professional users. His new designs may be ever so
clever, but they will lack the quality that comes from understanding the users' profession. Fundamental knowledge is lost in such a design.

How should he be able to design the computer artifacts
ready-to-hand for the users, when he does not understand
the profession? Here he may create most undesirable
breakdowns.

In a similar way it can be understood why traditional
systems descriptions do not work in communication with
users. The users cannot understand the systems descriptions because their ready-to-hand situation has been
made present-at-hand. The descriptions may be useful for
the designer's detached reflection, but they are not mirror
images of the users' situation. All they represent to the
users is breakdown of traditional understanding.

However, if we do not look upon them as descriptions,
but as pragmatic methods for breaking down everyday
understanding of a given situation, as artifacts to contribute to new and richer designs they may be very useful
also to the users. A good example is the systems approach
by West Churchman.[20]

---

[19] This will be developed in the part on *Designing for Skill*.

[20] Churchman, C. W.:*The Systems Approach*, Delta, New York
1968.

In forcing us to think about a situation, not only in terms of related components (as most systems methods do), it also draws our attention to teleological , environmental, control, and not least resource aspects. This breaks down the everydayness of our carpenter's hammering, but might also help him find out new aspects of driving nails, perhaps without hammers, or even with computers. It might also suggest that hammering and driving nails are not at all appropriate activities in the kind of building activity he is involved in. But Churchman is fully aware of the conditions for progress in this enterprise.

> The designers are everyone – in the ideal. Progress can be measured in terms of the degree to which the client, decision maker, and designer are the same.[21]

And this brings us back to the Heideggerian approach and the importance of shared background for understanding.

## Use of Computer Artifacts

In design of computer artifacts we also have to anticipate future breakdowns in relation to the artifact itself.

Most obvious is the support for the user in situations of software or hardware mal-functions. A ready-to-hand computer artifact understood as a word processor should not suddenly become present-at-hand and only possible for the user to understand as metal and plastic.

However, as in the discussion of the design process, there is also the other side of the coin. When the user gets more and more experienced with the artifact, breakdown of its readiness-to-hand might well be desired. The word processor above might to begin with function well as a computer-based typewriter. However, without a breakdown in the understanding of it as a typewriter, the user will never have the possibility to fully utilize its word processing capabilities. Hence, this is a reverse, but just as important aspect of the artifact to anticipate in the design.

[21] Ibid., p. 201.

# Summary

In summary, I think that a Heideggerian approach provides us with some admittedly unconventional concepts hard to digest, concepts that at the same time greatly enrich our understanding of design and use of computer artifacts. These are concepts that help focus on the importance of everydayness of use as fundamental to design. They are also concepts that provide a philosophical base for dealing with human understanding and use of artifacts. Practical skills of users and designers, and computer artifacts understood as their use become the key, rather than detached reflections and logic machines.

What we have to be concerned about in design of computer artifacts is a world of human practice, a practice that in essence is pre-reflective involved everyday use and understanding of artifacts. This may seem obvious, but it carries us far away from Cartesian systems thinking.

With this in mind let us now turn our attention to the next approach to design knowledge – *the Marxist alternative of emancipatory practice.*

*Chapter 3*

# Emancipatory Practice – A Marxist Alternative

In the discussion of a Heideggerian approach emphasis has been placed on how via *thrown* and *projective* everyday practice we understand our world. In particular I have considered what kind of skills are essential in design and use of artifacts. These aspects will also be essential in the following discussion of a *Marxist approach*. However, this time emphasis will rather be on the social and historical conditions for our creation of the world. So rather than to introduce the Marxist approach as one being in complete opposition I will introduce it as basically complementary, and in addition illuminative of the power aspect of design. Hence, it will hopefully be possible to theoretically reflect not only on the skills aspect but also on the democracy aspect of design – the other basic aspect of Work-Oriented Design of Computer Artifacts.

Let us once more consider our carpenter: The activity of 'hammering' or 'carpentering' is still understood as in the Heideggerian approach. But which are the social and historical conditions for this activity? How is labor divided between the journeyman and the apprentice? And why is it so? Which commodities do they craft and why? What are the conditions for changing this practice, and for their reflection on this everyday practice in a way that make it possible for them to change it? If we see design as a process of changing practice, these questions are important too in understanding the design process.

A Marxist approach to design and use of computer artifacts can be seen as an attempt to understand the conditions for social and technical change. In contrast to the Heideggerian approach emphasis is not on individual understanding but on social critique and emancipation. However, everyday life and practice, especially labor activity is just as much emphasized as before.

Philosophy in a Marxist approach is not merely a question of knowledge, but just as much a question of practical change. As Marx expressed it in the famous thesis on Feuerbach: [1]

> The philosophers have only interpreted the world in different ways; the point is to change it.

The focus of this transcendence, both in theory and in practice, is on those conditions that constrain humans socially and individually to form a free cooperation of equal men and women. In a Marxist approach this includes the constraints imposed by modern capitalism. In the words of *The Communist Manifesto*:[2]

> In place of the old bourgeois society, with its classes and class antagonisms, we shall have an association, in which the free development of each is the condition for the free development of all.

Marxist design philosophy, as I see it, is an integration of philosophical (ontology and epistemology), and sociological (e.g. labor process theory) aspects. Below I will try to illus-

[1] Marx, K.: *Thesis on Feuerbach*, (first published in 1845), (translated in Bottomore, T.B.: *Karl Marx – Selected Writings in Sociology and Social Philosophy*, Penguin Books, Harmondsworth 1971, p. 84).

[2] Marx, K. and Engels F.: *The Communist Manifesto*, (first published 1848), Penguin Books, Harmondworth 1980, p. 105.

trate both aspects.³ What I am aiming at is to introduce
concepts that are important to an understanding of design
and use of computer artifacts, not a comprehensive presentation of Marxist traditions.

³ The Marxism I refer to is not the orthodox interpretations in the
tradition of Marxism-Leninism and the interpretations of dialectical materialism in this tradition. Neither is it the structuralist
school in the Marxist tradition of Lois Althusser. What I have in
mind are philosophical interpretations in the Marxist tradition of
Georg Lukács, Anatoli Gramsci, the Frankfurt school, the Yu-
goslavan praxis philosophers etc. Here the links to Hegelian philosophy are strong, as well as the parallels to existential phenomenology. On Marxist epistemology I have especially been inspired by Joachim Israel's *The Language of Dialectics and the
Dialectics of Language*, Harvester Press, London 1979. His work
has also been most challenging since it intellectually brings together a convincing eclectic synthesis of the three philosophical traditions I outline as a basis for design philosophy in this book. I
also want to mention Karel Kosik's *Die Dialektik des Konkreten*,
Suhrkampf, Frankfurt 1967, on Marxist epistemology with relations to Heidegger's existential phenomenology. Paulo Freire's
*Pedagogy of the Oppressed*, Herder & Herder, New York 1971,
should also be specially mentioned. Jürgen Habermas, Jean-Paul
Sartre and Peter Berger are perhaps not 'real' Marxists; nevertheless their works are certainly important to the kind of Marxism I am thinking of. However, I also regard Marxism as theory
on social and technical change at work, in the labor process tradition emerging from Marx's three volumes of *Capital*. See e.g.
Dahlkvist, M.: *Att studera kapitalet* , Bo Cavefors, 1978 (dissertation), for an introduction, and Helgeson. B.: *Arbete, teknik,
ekonomi*, Högskolan i Luleå, 1986 (dissertation), for an overview of
trends in modern industrial sociology and, for cases e.g. Björkman, T. and Lundqvist, K.: *Från Max till Pia* , Arkiv, Malmö 1981
(dissertation), and Ekdahl, L.: *Arbete mot kapital*, Arkiv, Lund
1983 (dissertation). Internationally I refer to books like Braverman, H.: *Labor and Monopoly Capital – The Degradation of Work
in the Twentieth Century,* Monthly Review Press, New York 1974,
Edwards, R.: *Contested Terrain*, Heinemann, London 1979, Projektgruppe Automation und Qualifikation (PAQ): *Widersprüche
der Automationsarbeit, Argument Verlag*, West-Berlin 1987,
Noble, D.: 'Social Choice in Machine Design ' in Zimbalist, A.
(ed.): *Case Studies on the Labor Process*, Monthly Review, New
York 1979. This will be further referred in the part on *Designing
for Democracy at Work* and in chapter 18, *Skills and the Tool
Perspective.*

# Practice

Practice is a fundamental concept in my interpretation of a Marxist approach. Practice is both our producing the world and the product of this process. It is always the product of historically specific conditions, produced by former practice as well as the production of the conditions for future practice. In the words of Marx

> society itself stands out as the ultimate result of the societal process of production, i.e., man himself in his societal relations. Everything which has solid form, e.g., products, etc., appears only as a moment, a vanishing moment in this movement. The conditions and objectifications of this process are themselves at the same time moments of it and as the subjects of this process appear not only the individuals, but individuals being in relation with each other, relations which they produce in the same way as well as in a new way. It is their own continuous moving process (Bewegungsprozess) in which they renew themselves as well as they produce the world of richness.[4]

Compared to a Heideggerian approach everyday practice is still the point of departure, that which is essential to design and use, but now emphasis is on transcendence of the given as emancipatory practice. In the context of design of computer artifacts, emphasis changes from the users' everyday understanding and use of artifacts to possibilities and constraints hindering transcendence of this practice. But this emancipatory practice is the practice of the users. A design process and methods that support the users to emancipatorily transcend the given practice comes into focus. This is also the position we took in DEMOS and UTOPIA.

---

[4] Marx, K.: *Grundrisse der Kritik der politischen Oekonomie*, Diets Verlag, Berlin 1953 (quoted after Israel 1979, p. 118).

*Aspects of Practice*

In grasping practice as a process of transformation and transcendence we can view *work, language* and *morals* (Sittlichkeit) as the fundamental aspects of practice. The Marxist sociologist Joachim Israel argues in accordance with Habermas as follows:

> In work man's dependence on nature is manifested, and through labor, used in the Marxian sense of the 'material' process of production, man and society are produced and reproduced. Language signifies man's dependence on man. Through language human inter-action is instigated and made possible. Work and inter-action are indissolubly related to each other. Through morals as manifested in politics and power, finally, man's dependence on common goals and the means to reach them are manifested.[5]

We must relate the design of computer artifacts to all three aspects of practice: In *practice as work*, this is to the transformation of a given labor process and to the users' participation in the design process. In *practice as language*, it is to the professional language and the interaction in a given labor process as well as the associated design process. In *practice as morals*, it is to the politics and power of the different groups or classes involved in a given labor process as well as in the associated design process.

In this chapter I will focus on practice as work, especially the labor processes of design and use of computer artifacts under 'the capitalist mode' of production. But first I will consider Marxist epistemology and emancipatory practice in the context of design and use of computer artifacts.

---

[5] Israel, op. cit. p. 46, with reference to Habermas J.: *Erkentnis und Interesse*, Suhrkampf, Frankfurt 1968.

## Marxist Epistemology

As mentioned, practice is a central notion for Marxist epistemology. The Czech Marxist philosopher and nonconformist politician, Karel Kosik, points out that 'for man to be able to recognize how things are independently of himself, he has to subject them to his practice; in order to determine how they are without his intervention he has to intervene into them.'[6]

This intervention, rather than Cartesian detached reflection, is fundamental to Marxist epistemology. This is not to deny the importance of Cartesian reflection. According to Kosik human consciousness has to be understood both as theoretical or reflective knowledge and as intuitive understanding. To deny or understate the importance of theoretical knowledge leads to irrationalism and 'vegetative thinking', and to deny or understate the importance of everyday practice and understanding leads to rationalism, positivism and scientism.[7]

The two kinds of knowledge form a dialectical unity. Theoretical reflection is based on everyday involved practice and understanding, and may also change it by transcendence. However theoretical knowledge is not the truth of what was already practically understood, nor is everyday practice and understanding more than, in Kosik's terminology, 'pseudo-concrete' knowledge. This 'pseudo-concrete' knowledge has to be transcended by 'a revolutionary-critical practice of humanity, which is identical with the humanization of man (...) the decisive steps of which are social revolutions.'[8]

In *The Language of Dialectics and the Dialectics of Language* Israel discusses a Marxist epistemology of practice in the direction indicated.[9] Hence, his point of departure is everyday practice. This practice is the human

[6] Kosik, op. cit. p.21 (quoted after Israel).

[7] Ibid, pp. 50.

[8] Ibid., p. 19 (quoted after Israel).

[9] Israel, op. cit.

production of the world, a process of production through which that which exists is transformed. It is in practice that the world of objects is produced, as well as our knowledge of this world, and of our selves as subjects in it.

Israel's and Kosik's point is that our pre-reflective *understanding* in everyday dealings with phenomena in the world, as discussed in the Heideggerian approach, is fragmented knowledge, is 'pseudo-concrete'. In a Marxist approach essential knowledge is *produced knowledge*: it is *understanding mediated by reflection to theoretical understanding*. However, knowledge acquisition is a dialectical relation between two different process of knowledge production. One is insight and new understanding as the result of breakdown and active *theoretical production of knowledge*. The other is *acquisition of competence*.

Below I will relate Israel's account of a Marxist epistemology to design and use of computer artifacts.[10]

*Understanding*

The first category or stage of knowledge that Israel distinguishes is what I earlier have called *understanding*. This is to be acquainted with something, without necessarily reflecting about why we know or can do it. We know both how to do the activity in a 'routine manner' and how to talk about it. This could be how one knows how to drive a car, ride a bike etc., or how a carpenter knows how to use a hammer, and talk about 'hammering' so that other carpenters can understand him. Or think of a Cartesian designer using rationalistic description methods – it is all natural.

---

[10] Ibid., pp. 211–222. An interesting conceptual analysis of systems design processes and methods along the lines of Israel's theoretical framework is Mathiassen, L.: *Systemudvikling og Systemudviklingsmetode*, DAIMI PB-136, Department of Computer Science, University of Aarhus 1981 (dissertation).

## Awareness of Understanding

A second stage of knowledge is when we for some reason start to reflect upon what earlier has been natural, self-evident or obvious.

The carpenter finds that the hammer slips, or the nails are of a new kind with which he is not familiar; the car engine sounds strange to the driver, etc. In short we are facing a non-normal situation, or view a familiar situation from a new angle. These are examples of the breakdown situations discussed in the Heideggerian approach. We can call this breakdown knowledge, or in Israel's terminology, *awareness of understanding*.

This is the kind of knowledge our carpenter acquires when forced to describe 'hammering' in terms of a system of related objects. This creates a breakdown of his understanding of 'hammering', but not necessarily better understanding. Or think of a rationalistic designer who for the first time is confronted with trade union demands for active participation and design methods and goals in accordance with these demands. The ready-to-hand becomes present-at-hand, to speak the language of the Heideggerian approach. However, this knowledge is not only different from traditional understanding, but also different from active production of new knowledge.

## Insight

Transcendence of former knowledge as awareness or as understanding is Israel's third stage of knowledge. This is a *process of active production of knowledge*, and of changing practice, not an activity that passively reflects the world within a tradition. The result of this process is *insight*.[11] By actively treating well-known situations as if they were something else, or by actively approaching them from a different point of view than the normal, we

[11] I will not go into details of the terminology of the Hegelian dialectics of negating a negation, as Israel does. But the presentation will hopefully illustrate the concept sufficiently for the present discussion.

may produce new knowledge about them. To obtain insight you have to know the practice you are reflecting about. To produce insight requires the competence to reframe something well known in the light of of something else. For example, the dramatist Bertolt Brecht explicitly used his theatric method of *Verfremdungseffekt* to make well-know situations appear as something new to the audience, something worth reflecting on, in the light of Marxist theory of capitalism. This is done in science as development of new theories and new scientific practices. In skilled work it can be done as development of new tools and working procedures. In all cases it is a competence close to what we normally understand as artistic performance.

Think of the library example from the previous chapter. New knowledge about library work may be produced by regarding a library as a meeting place for people interested in books, rather than as a place to input, store and output books. This new knowledge may suggest completely new designs. New knowledge as insight is based in understanding, but produced by actively negating this understanding as a means of transcending it in artistic or theoretical reflection. Hence, our Cartesian designer can suggest alternatives that among the users create an awareness of their understanding and ultimately new insight for them; but for the designer to also acquire new insight about library work, he or she will have to have understood it, and that is not possible through just external theoretical detached reflection.

*Skill and Creativity*

Insight is not the end of the process. When we get acquainted with this new knowledge as insight it may be incorporated into our everyday knowledge as new practice and understanding. Knowledge is brought back to the first stage, but is not the same. This is the other related process of knowledge production – *the acquisition of new knowledge in the sense of competence or skill.*

Carpenters who understand hammering may start to reflect over hammers and nails if they meet trouble in their everyday hammering activity. This may lead to a process of active production of new knowledge about hammering by negating and transcending former understanding. This detached theoretical reflection may result in new insight into hammering and new design of hammers, nails or work methods. When carpenters get acquainted with this new design their understanding and practice of hammering may change. They may have acquired new skills or competence.

However, to really master 'hammering' requires *the ability, in involved practice, to transcend the unaware and given routine rules and create new ones within the frame of social interaction.* Israel calls this *creativity*. It is based on deep understanding and considerable practice, but it is different from theoretical knowledge produced by detached reflection.

Israel's Marxist reflections on acquisition of competence seems to be close to Dreyfus and Dreyfus's five stage characterization discussed under the Heideggerian approach. They also both relate to the understanding of what it means to 'follow a rule', which will be discussed under the Wittgensteinian approach in the next chapter. Hence, I will not go into details here. Instead I wish to point at a potential contradiction between the two processes of production of knowledge discussed, i.e. between theoretical production of knowledge and skill acquisition. This is a contradiction of importance to design.

According to a Marxist approach new insight requires theoretical reflection. But this is at the same time a breakdown of the user's everyday understanding and use, a neglect of fundamental conditions for creativity and of the importance of skilled performance as unbroken involved activity.

This is the contradiction between tradition and transcendence in design that I already discussed in connection with the Heideggerian approach. However, in the Marxist approach it also has another dimension. What has to be transcended theoretically and practically is an oppressing situation. The challenge to design is to identify such situations and to actively participate in the emancipation from them.

## Emancipatory Practice

So far I have been discussing a Marxist approach as epistemology, and I have been concentrating on individual skill and understanding. Using an example, I will try now to illustrate a wider meaning of emancipatory practice.

The systems approach by West Churchman mentioned in the previous chapter is a good example of a design method that helps produce new knowledge about something normal and well known by actively supporting not only breakdown of former understanding (as do most systems description methods), but also by suggesting useful questions to be asked to transcend it.[12] Churchman gives an illuminating example of a transportation system.

When asked to describe a car, we might start by saying that it has four wheels and an engine. A second question would be if we can accept a car with only three wheels. A third question if two is enough, etc. By now our understanding has broken down. Churchman's systems approach suggests that instead of the already understood structure we take, as the departure for our description, what a car is to be used for, which resources are then needed, what the environment of the car looks like, and what the meaning of driving a car is. This way we may produce insight. We may find out that the need for wheels is one of the truly big problems in the transportation system we call a car. Maybe it would be a much better transportation system, creating fewer accidents and less traffic jams, if it had no wheels at all. We may even come up with new interesting designs of flying cars, new planning of towns, etc.

---

[12] Churchman, C. W.: *The Systems Approach*, Delta, New York 1968.

The systems approach suggests a dialectical method for transcending the understanding we take for granted, but is it also a Marxist approach? Not necessarily, because to a Marxist approach it is of great importance which questions are asked. As expressed by Kosik the Marxist dialectical reason is not only a process of dialectical thinking, but also a process in which the world is designed for reason, that is, in which freedom is realized. This reason must in a Marxist approach be seen as a historical process. The questions that must be asked are questions that support actions to overcome historically and socially produced oppression. This is why in a Marxist approach the epistemology at the same time has to be a social theory. In Kosik's words:[13]

> Dialectical reason does not exist outside the world, and does not leave the world outside itself. It only exists by realizing its own reason, that is, it will take the form of dialectical reason only to the extent that it designs a reasonable world in the historic process.

The problem with the systems approach, despite all its merits, is – from a Marxist position – that it is ahistorical. It may be used by workers to fight back against a computer based planning and control system that deprives them of skill and control of their own work,[14] but also used equally well by managers designing such systems.

A good example of integration of the dialectical epistemology and social theory as emancipatory practice is Paulo Freire's *Pedagogy of the Oppressed*.[15] His method takes the form of a pedagogy to be used with and by oppressed people in their own emancipatory practice. His basic concept is *conscientization*. The dialectical method of reflection focuses on the practical understanding that 'students', 'users', etc. have of social, political and eco-

---

[13] Kosik, op. cit. p. 108 (my translation).

[14] For an example see Ehn, P. and Erlander, B.: *Vi vägrar låta detaljstyra oss*, Swedish Center for Working Life, Stockholm 1978.

[15] Freire, op. cit.

nomic contradictions, and their discovery of ways for acting in oppressing situations. Though developed for the situation of poor Brazilian peasants, the method was in the mid-seventies a great source of inspiration for us in the DEMOS project and in general for the emerging research cooperation in Scandinavia between trade unions and computer and social scientists on design and use of computer artifacts.[16]

The method is based on 'students' and 'teachers' forming investigating groups. The teacher, researcher, designer etc. share everyday life with the members of the group for some time. From what they see and understand they help formulate *generative themes* i.e. a complex of questions that can be useful in the groups' reflection over their own understanding of their situation. These questions are grounded in the practice of the workers but also contain a theoretical understanding of the situation grounded in social and historical reflection of the situation.[17]

The dialogue between e.g. workers and designers is based on these generative themes, and in the breakdown process that follows they learn from each other, and participate jointly in the integrated process of change. For example a generative theme on 'new technology' might contain questions about skills, cooperation between workers, control of the work, the work environment, quality of the product etc. Typically they will be formulated as contrasting effects – craft-skill versus deskilled work, etc.

These questions may be formulated in terms of a discussion of a computer based planning and control system that management has announced will be introduced. But they will also be based on theoretical knowledge of managerial strategies, division of labor, technological development, power structures, trade union resources, etc.

The systems approach can admittedly be a useful part of this knowledge production, but it is then integrated the-

---

[16] See the part on *Designing for Democracy at Work*.
[17] For an example see Ehn and Erlander, op. cit.

oretically into a context of social and historical knowledge, and practically in a strategy for emancipation based on reflection and practical change by and with those concerned.

Emancipatory practice as epistemology is identification with oppressed groups and support of their transcendence in action and reflection. In research as well as in actual design the interest in emancipation is the moral core of the Marxist approach to design knowledge. It is *not* external to this approach.[18]

What then might be oppressing in design and use of computer artifacts according to a Marxist approach? To discuss that question I now turn to a Marxist social and historical theoretical understanding of the labor processes of design and use of computer artifacts. What kind of social and historical processes and structures are they?

I see such an analysis in a Marxist approach as a social critique to support emancipation. As in the case of Marx's and his *Das Kapital. Kritik der politischen Oekonomie*[19] it can be a social and historical critique of the forces of production of the capitalist mode of production, or as in the case of the Marxist Rudolf Bahro and *Die Alternative. Zur kritik des real existierenden Sozialismus*[20] it can be a critique of bureaucratic-centralistic organization, lack of freedom, alienation of the workers, and detailed division of labor in those societies that according to their official doctrine have 'implemented' a Marxist approach.

---

[18] How this aspect of emancipatory practice in a Marxist approach in practice can have an  influence on research strategies and design methods in design and use of computer artifacts is something I will return to in the concluding chapter of this part. For a more developed Marxist psychological theoretical framework on 'tools for transcendence' see Engeström, Y.: *Learning by Expanding*, Orienta-Konsultit, Helsinki 1987 (dissertation).

[19] Marx, K.: *Capital – A Critical Analysis of Capitalist Production*, vols. I-III, (first published 1867, 1885, 1895), Progress Publishers, Moscow 1953 -1971.

[20] Bahro, R.: *Die Alternative – Zur kritik des real existierenden Sozialismus*, Europäische Verlagsanstalt, Köln 1977.

# Design and Use as Labor Processes

Here I can only indicate a few aspects derived from Marx's theoretical framework in the volumes of *Das Kapital* and of importance to design philosophy and our understanding of the labor processes of designing and using computer artifacts.

Keeping in mind Marx's thesis that the philosophers have only interpreted the world in different ways, and that the point is to change it, we can say that what practically has to be transcended in emancipatory practice is the capitalist mode of production – in theory and practice.

According to a Marxist approach this is the mode of production in which our carpenter friends do not produce chairs for themselves or for their usefulness, but for wages. These wages are paid by possessors of capital who, to enlarge this capital, converts most of it into wages, machinery and materials. What such a capitalist buys from the workers is their labor power, their productive capacity, their competence, over a period of time, not an agreed amount of labor. This labor power is what is put into work in the production process. The historical and social requirements for this mode of production are in summary exchange relations, commodities, money, and especially purchase and sale of labor power – a class society that has separated the means of production from the producers, and transformed them into hired laborers, whose only property is their capacity to work.

The carpenters and their building activity are part of a social division of labor and cooperation characteristic of all developed societies. When involved in the labor process of building their *labor* power is put into work to refine *objects* into new use-values e.g. wood, nails etc. into a chair. In doing this they utilize hammers, saws, etc. – the *artifacts* or the instruments of labor, which Marx describes as:

a thing, or a complex of things, which the labourer interposes between himself and the subject of his labour, and which serves as the conductor of his activity.[21]

At this level of abstraction the labor process is not specific to the capitalist mode of production. It could be a description of producing with stone axes as well as with computer artifacts. Only a definition of artifacts, nothing new to our understanding of design and use of artifact has been added.

However, if, with Marx, we understand the production process not just as labor process to produce use-values, but also as a *valorization process* to produce surplus value, in short a process for the expansion and accumulation of capital and the creation of profit, then there is a clear difference.

As values, to be used in the valorization process to expand capital, the carpenters' competence, their hammers and the materials they work with will change for this purpose, not for the purpose of the usefulness of the products produced. Or to paraphrase Marx: A carpenter is a man who builds. Only under certain conditions does he become a wage worker. A hammer is a tool to hammer with. Only under certain conditions does it become capital.[22]

## Rationalization

These changes of the labor process understood as valorization process may be called *rationalization*, and can be directed towards the worker's labor, the artifacts he uses

---

[21] Marx, op. cit., p. 174.

[22] 'A negro is a negro. Only under certain conditions does he become a slave. A cotton-spinning machine is a machine for spinning cotton. Only under certain conditions does it become capital.' Marx, K: *Wage Labour and Capital*, (first published in 1848), (translated in Bottomore, T.B.: *Karl Marx – Selected writings in Sociology and Social Philosophy*, Penguin Books, Harmondsworth 1971, p. 155).

or the objects of labor. *Division of labor* and *design and use of new artifacts* are means for this change.

This form of division of labor is not the necessary social division of labor characteristic of all societies, but a form specific to the capitalist labor process, as is the human productivity gained by design and use of new artifacts.

Detailed division of labor in an assembly plant, or programming of CNC-machines at a special planning department are, according to a Marxist approach, not technical necessities, but expressions of rationalization to increase profits, the capitalist subsumption of the production process as valorization process. A division of labor that gives the workers cooperative control over the assembly work, or shop floor programming that develops the workers' skill are both technical possibilities. These technical possibilities will in practice only be designed and used under the condition that they do not violate the production process as valorization process. However, ultimately the conditions for these changes are expressed as *class struggle*. Not only market conditions and available technology are conditions for the valorization process, but also the organized strength of labor and capital.

Rationalization actually affects the *process of design of computer artifacts* in a double sense.

Not only is *the form of division of labor between the labor processes of design and use* an expression of this capitalist rationalization, but also *the aim of design is rationalization of the labor process being designed for.*

An example could be systems designers that develop a production control system to be used by a planning department and that takes away planning activities from the shop floor. This is an illustration of the often applied classical method of 'scientific management' by Fredrick Taylor.[23] This is in no way the only way of capitalist rationalization, but it has historically often proved to be a type of rationalization supporting the valorization process, the production of profits. Which rationalization strategy sup-

---

[23] Taylor, F.W.: *Principles of Scientific Management*, 1911.

ports the valorization process in a given historic situation has to be found out by analysis of the concrete conditions.[24]

To the extent that this rationalization, by division of labor, means a separation of human reflective thinking and imaginary understanding from the actual execution of the work, it is not only epistemologically a tendency to destruction of human knowledge, but also literally a tendency to dehumanization.

As pointed out, the rationalization process not only transforms and changes skill and control by changes in cooperation and division of labor, but also does so by the change of the artifacts themselves. Marx remarked in *Capital* that:

> Though a use-value, in the form of a product, issues from labour-process, yet other use-values, products of previous labour, enter into it as means of production. The same use-value is both the product of a previous process, and a means of production of a later process. Products are therefore not only results, but also essential conditions of labour.[25]

In the capitalistic subsumption of the labor process the workers' own capacity, *via design objectified in the artifacts*, becomes a hostile power. This is not only because the artifacts are owned by others, the possessors of capital, but because its capitalist genesis and design, is inherent in the structure of the artifact.

To the use of computer artifacts this becomes true in a double sense. Not only are they artifacts that can be designed for deskilling automation of competence, but also for alienating planning and control of the labor process. This is confused as neutral or general principles for increasing human productivity. *The capitalist genesis and design is all hidden in the technically objective rationality of the artifacts.* The development of numerical controlled

---

[24] I will return to such concrete analyses in the part on *Designing for Democracy at Work*.

[25] Marx, op. cit., pp. 176–177.

machines, and how skill based alternatives were rejected, is a good example that is well documented by the historian David Noble.[26]

The computer as artifact is certainly a technically complex machine. However it is not primarily this fact, but rather its social form that distinguishes it from the tools of the individual handicraft trades of the guilds.

Taken as a whole this means that *emancipatory practice must not only aim at changing the use of artifacts, but also their technical design, the design process, and the relation between the design process and the labor process the artifacts are designed for.* When these changes violate the production process as valorization process there are social conflicts inherent in the capitalist mode of production. To identify with oppressed groups and to actively participate in their struggle is an essential aspect in a Marxist approach to the labor processes of design and use of computer artifacts.

In a Marxist approach trade unions involved in class struggle at work are today the most clear example of an emancipatory practice that strives to counteract or transcend capitalist rationalization, not only when wages are concerned, but increasingly more as a struggle over the artifacts to be designed and used, and the constraints to skill and democracy.[27]

To regard the actual use of computer artifacts in modern industry and in offices as just artifacts for production of use-values is, in a Marxist approach, misleading. It is just as misleading as to understand the division of labor between design and use of computer artifacts as natural or given. Certainly it is all rational, but in the sense of capitalist rationalization.

---

[26] Noble, op. cit.

[27] I will return to a discussion of concrete rationalization strategies, trade union responses and the theoretical framework in the later parts on *Designing for Democracy at Work* and *Designing for Skill*.

A science of design and use of computer artifacts that has no theory for understanding the social and historical character of what is studied may have seen the technical side of the artifacts, but not really understood it. Division of labor is not only social but also technical; design and use of artifacts is not only technical but also social. These are the objectifications of social relations that produce us, and that we reproduce in our everyday practice. Regarding the computers of today, this is more true than ever. Social relations are inherent in them. A science of design and use of computer artifacts should not reject this as a fundamental aspect of its field of study.

## Summary

Above I have discussed design philosophy in a Marxist approach as epistemology, as transcendental practice, and as labor process theory. In comparison with the Heideggerian approach to design philosophy there is a common point of departure in everyday practice and understanding. Less is said about the individual use of artifacts, but more about the social content of design and use of artifacts, and about the social relations inherent in the artifacts. And rather than finding *Dasein* by transcendence of our everyday understanding of the world, we are advised to *dialectical emancipatory practice*, which not only transcends our everyday understanding of the world, but also the practical world itself. Interaction and use of language in design and use of computer artifacts could very well have been discussed within a Marxist approach, especially the cultural-historic tradition of human activity.[28] Instead I now turn to the *language-games* people play when they

[28] See e.g. Vygotsky, L.S.: *Thought and Language*, The MIT Press, Cambridge 1962 and Leontiev, A.N.: *Problems of the Development of the Mind*, Progress, Moscow 1981. For an application in the field of human computer interaction see Bødker, S.: *Through the Interface – A Human Activity Approach to User Interface Design*, DAIMI PB – 224, Department of Computer Science, University of Aarhus, 1987(dissertation).

design and use computer artifacts, and a Wittgensteinian approach to design philosophy, an approach that also is based on everyday practice and understanding, or rather on ordinary language use.

## Chapter 4

# Language-games –
# A Wittgensteinian Alternative

I will introduce my third complementary interpretation of an approach to design philosophy as a treatise in language, interaction and communication. This time the interpretation will be in accord with the later philosophy of Ludwig Wittgenstein, the author of *Philosophical Investigations*.[1] As with the earlier approaches there is no attempt made to give a full account of the philosophical richness of the ideas involved, but hopefully I will be able to demonstrate the usefulness some of these ideas have when understanding design and use of computer artifacts.

Once again I return to the carpenter and his hammering activity, but now emphasizing on language, interaction and communication. In the professional language of carpenters there are not only hammers and nails. Say our

[1] Wittgenstein, L.: *Philosophical Investigations*, Basil Blackwell & Mott, Oxford 1953. I have no clear relation to the Wittgenstein reception. However, the group around the PAAS project at the Swedish Center for Working Life, including the philosophers Tore Nordenstam and Allan Janik, have been important for my understanding of the 'second' Wittgenstein, as has the architect Jerker Lundeqvist, whose PhD thesis I especially want to mention: *Norm och Modell – samt ytterligare några begrepp inom designteorin*, Department of Architecture, Technical University of Stockholm, 1982, in which he develops the basis for a Wittgensteinian design theory. The influence from Joachim Israel's interpretation has been mentioned before. A philosopher as original as Peter Winch should also be mentioned.

carpenter is making a chair.[2] Other artifacts used would
be a draw-knife, a brace, a trying plane, a hollow plane, a
round plane, a bow-saw, a marking gauge, chisels, etc.
The objects or materials that he works with are elm
planks for the seats, ash in the arms, and oak for the legs.
He is involved in saddling, making spindles, steaming etc.

Are we as designers of new artifacts for chair making
helped by this labeling of artifacts, materials and activities? In a Wittgensteinian approach the answer would be:
Only if we know the practice in which these names make
sense, the point being the following: To label our experiences is to do this deliberately. To do it deliberately we have
to be trained to do so. Hence, the activity of labeling has to
be learned. Language is not private but social. The labels
that we come up with are inherent in our social meaning
constituting practice. We cannot learn without learning
something specific. To understand and to be able to use is
the same.[3] Understanding the professional language of
chair making, as any other *language-game*, is to be able to
master practical rules which we did not create ourselves.
They are techniques and conventions for chair making as
part of a given practice.

To master the professional language of chair making
means to be able to act in a correct way together with
other people that are familiar with chair making. To
'know' this does not mean that you explicitly have to know
the rules you have learned, but it means, e.g. for a chair
maker to know when someone utters 'saddling', or is saddling, in an incorrect way. To have a concept is to have
learned to follow rules as part of a given practice. *Speech
acts* are, as a unity of language and action, part of prac-

---

[2] The example is based on Seymour, J.: *The Forgotten Arts – A
practical guide to traditional skills*, Dorling Kindersley, London
1984, pp. 65.

[3] Wittgenstein, op. cit. §264 'Once you know *what* the word stands
for, you understand it, you know its whole use.', §421 'Look at the
sentence as an instrument, and at its sense as its employment.'

tice. They are not descriptions, but actions among others in a given practice.

Artifacts and objects in a given language-game also play a fundamental role. A hammer is in itself a sign of what you can do with it in a certain language-game. And so is a computer artifact. These signs remind you of what you can do with it. In this light, an important aspect in the design of computer artifacts is that its signs remind the users of what they can do with the computer artifact in the language-games of use, just as a hammer does so.[4] This sheds some light on the popularity of 'what-you-see-is-what-you-get' and 'direct manipulation' interfaces.[5]

Below I will elaborate on language-games, focusing on the design process, descriptions in design, and knowledge in design and use of computer artifacts.

## Language-games

To use language is to participate in *language-games*, the Wittgensteinian notion of practice. In discussing how we in practice follow (and sometimes break) rules as a social activity Wittgenstein asks us to think of games, how they are made up and played. Why games?

We often think of games in terms of a playful, pleasurable engagement. I do not think that this aspect should be totally denied, but a more important aspect of the games children play is that they are most concerned activities, as are most of the common language-games we play in our ordinary language.

We do not understand what counts as a game because we have an explicit definition, but because we are already familiar with other games. There is a kind of *family resemblance* between games. Similarly, professional lan-

---

[4] This 'sign' aspect of objects and artifacts in language games have been pointed out by Brock, S.: 'Wittgenstein mellem fænomenologi og analytik' in Brock, S. et al.: *Sprog, Moral & Livsform*, Philosophia, Århus 1986.

[5] See chapter 17, *The 'Toolness of Computer' Artifacts*.

guage-games can be learned and understood because of their family resemblance with other language-games which we know how to play. Even professional language-games of e.g. systems designers, carpenters or typographers, complicated as they may be, are grounded in our everyday ordinary language.

Language-games, like the games we play as children, are social activities. To be able to play these games we have to learn to follow rules, rules that are socially created, but far from always explicitly existing. The rule-following behavior of being able to play *together with others* is more fundamental to a game than explicit regulative rules. Playing is interaction and cooperation. It is intersubjective practice. To follow the rules in practice means to be able to act in a way that others in the game can understand. These rules are 'embedded' in a given practice from which they cannot be distinguished. They are this practice. To know them is to 'embody' them, to be able to practically apply them to a principally open class of cases.

Language-games are performed both as speech acts and as other activities, as practice with 'embodied' meaning within societal and cultural institutional frameworks. To be able to participate in the practice of a specific language-game one has to share the *form of life* within which that practice is possible. This form of life includes our natural history as well as the social institutions and traditions we are born into. This is prior to agreed social conventions and rational reasoning. Hence intersubjective consensus is more a question of shared background and language than of stated opinions. Wittgenstein put it like this:[6]

'So you are saying that human agreement decides what is true and what is false?' – It is what human beings *say* that is true and false; and they agree in the

---

[6] Wittgenstein, op. cit., §241, §242.

*language* they use. That is not agreement in opinions but in form of life.

If language is to be a means of communication there must be agreement not only in definitions but also (queer as this may sound) in judgements. This seems to abolish logic, but does not do so. – It is one thing to describe methods of measurement, and another to obtain and state results of measurement. But what we call 'measuring' is partly determined by a certain constancy in results of measurement.

This seems to make us prisoners of language and tradition, which is not really the case. Being socially created, the rules of language-games, as those of other games, can also be altered.

There are, according to Wittgenstein, even games in which we make up and alter the rules according to which we play, as we go along.[7] The design process is a good example.

Creative transcendence of traditional behavior is also possible in a language-game. With mastery of the practice of a certain language-game comes the freedom to follow the rules in totally unforeseen but still 'correct' ways.[8]

I see the Wittgensteinian notion of language-games as a most fruitful elaboration of understanding human practice as the product of, and the same time producing, the world and our understanding of it; of the ontological and epistemological point of departure for the inquiry into design philosophy in this part of the book.

I also find it striking how much Wittgenstein's view of *language* resembles the view of artifacts in general in the Marxist design approach. Being social, as the product of others, and as something we use to change the world,

---

[7] Ibid., §83; see also §23, §67, §75.

[8] This will be further discussed in chapter 18, *Skills and the Tool Perspective*.

ourselves, and our understanding of it, language is not only an expression of social relations, but contains them.

The idea of language-games entails an emphasis on how we linguistically discover and construct our world. However, language is understood as our use of it, as our social, historic, and intersubjective application of linguistic artifacts. As I see it, this is not a neglect of how we also come to understand the world by use of other artifacts. As with the use of other artifacts we are, however, bound to tradition, a practice that in principle can be transcended.

In the following I will concentrate on the labor processes of design and use of computer artifacts as language-games (not forgetting what has been said about them in the Heideggerian and Marxist approaches).

## The Language-games of Design and Use

As designers we are involved in reforming practice, in our case typically computer artifacts and the way people use them. Hence, the language-games of design changes the rules for other language-games – those of use of the artifacts. What are the conditions for this interplay and change?

To design new artifacts that are useful for people, designers have to understand the language-games of the use activity, or users have to understand the language-game of design, or the users must be able to give complete explicit descriptions of their demands. The latter seems, as discussed in the chapter on a Cartesian approach, to be the common assumption behind most design approaches. Hence, the emphasis is on methods to support this explication by means of requirement specifications, system descriptions etc.[9] Earlier I have argued that this means to make professional users express their knowledge on a level much below the knowledge they possess. One can say

---

[9] See e.g. widely used methods like Jackson, M.: *System Development*, Prentice Hall, 1983, or Yourdon, E.: *Managing the System Life Cycle*, Yourdon Press, New York 1982.

that they follow rules, but these are open-ended rules, and many of them have never been made explicit. Having acquired the knowledge of when to break the given rules is exactly what counts as skilful and creative activity. This possibility of radical innovation is the logical limit of description.[10]

## Design Artifacts

In a Wittgensteinian approach, the emphasis is not on the 'correctness' of systems descriptions in design, on how well they mirror the desires in the mind of the users, or on how 'correctly' they describe existing and future artifacts and their use. Systems descriptions are design artifacts, typically linguistic artifacts. The crucial question is how we use them, what role they play in the design process.

The rejection of emphasis on 'correctness' of descriptions is especially noteworthy: In this we are advised by the author of the perhaps once strongest arguments for a picture theory and the Cartesian approach to design – the young Wittgenstein in *Tractatus Logico-Philosophicus*.[11]

Nevertheless, we know that systems descriptions are useful in the the language-game of design. The new orientation suggested in a Wittgensteinian approach is that we see these linguistic artifacts as a special kind of artifacts that we refer to as 'typical examples' or 'paradigm cases' when we describe something, or when we 'inform' each other. That does not, however, make them models in the meaning of Cartesian mirror-images of reality.[12] In the language-game of design we use these artifacts as *reminders* and as *paradigm cases* for our reflections on

[10] This will be further discussed in chapter 18, *Skills and the Tool Perspective*.

[11] Wittgenstein, L: *Tractatus Logico-Philosophicus*, Kegan Paul, 1923.

[12] This aspect of models and descriptions in a Wittgensteinian approach is argued by Nordenstam, T: 'Två oförenliga traditioner' in Göranzon, B. (ed.): *Datautvecklingens Filosofi*, Carlsson & Jönsson, Malmö 1984, pp. 58–60.

future computer artifacts and their use. The use of design
artifacts brings earlier experiences to our mind and it
'bends' our way of thinking of the past and the future. I
think that this is how we should understand them as *representations*.[13] And this is how they 'inform' our practice.
If they are good design artifacts, they support good moves
within a specific design-language-game. As such they can
be intended to create breakdowns (to use the language of
the Heideggerian approach) as well as help avoiding
them, depending on what kind of reminders or paradigm
cases they are in the learning process of design.

Consider the following example of an application of a
popular systems descriptions method in the Cartesian
tradition:[14]

The users of a future page make-up system are presented with a *data flow diagram*. This is a graphic means
of *modelling* the flow of data through a *system*. The basic
objects are *sources (or sinks) of data, data flows, processes*,
and *data stores*. Typical *processes* may be 'copy editing'
and 'make up'. They are represented by *circles*. 'Ad department' and 'news room' might be examples of *data
sources*. They are represented by *rectangles*. Example of
*data flows* are 'article' and 'ad'. They are represented by
*arrows* between the other objects, etc.

In the proposed language of Cartesian systems descriptions this may be a *model* of a *system* in which e.g. the
copy editor Joan may tell Martin the composer that the
article on the life of that strange philosopher Ludwig
Wittgenstein is delayed at least half an hour, but that he
can place the display ads and make-up the rest of the
page.

Does the system description really shed any light on the
users' understanding of making-up of newspaper pages,
with or without computer artifacts? Which arguments

[13] This has been suggested by Kaasbøll, J.: *A Theoretical and Empirical Study of the Use of Language and Computers,* Department
of Informatics, University of Oslo, forthcoming (dissertation).

[14] Yourdon, op. cit. pp. 9–35.

can be made that support the idea that Joan and Martin necessarily should think about their situation in terms of systems, with objects and relations like sources (or sinks) of data, data flows, processes, data stores, circles, rectangles, arrows, etc?

If we focus on system descriptions as linguistic artifacts that designers and users can use as reminders or paradigm cases in the language-games of design, linguistic artifacts like the one above are probably close to useless; literally they make non-sense.

What if the description above instead was done in the professional and situational language of Joan and Martin? Nor is this done to make a mirror-image of their situation, but by e.g. a metaphorical twist transforming it into a linguistic artifact which may help both users and designers to be struck by something familiar as the most striking aspect of the situation. Why are for example Joan and Martin working in different departments, when they could do their cooperative work much better if they shared offices and used available technology that makes this possible? The acquisition of this understanding could for example be triggered by use of scenario methods. One basis for development of these scenarios could be methods for studying the users' use of their professional language as speech acts in real professional language-games.[15]

Given this example, there are two aspects of design artifacts that I will consider a little further. One is the question of tradition and transcendence. The other is language and design artifacts.

If we see the design artifacts from the example above as reminders or paradigm cases are we not then caught in the tradition, without support to transcend it? Not really. As referred above, in language-games we not only follow rules, but we also make up and alter rules as we go along.

---

[15] For such an approach see Andersen, P.B.: 'Semiotics and Informatics: Computers as Media' in Ingwersen et. al.: *Information Technology and Information Use*, Taylor Graham, London 1986.

In my view this is typical of the language-games of design. In a Wittgensteinian approach transcendence is, however, understood differently than in a Marxist approach.

In a Marxist approach focus is on producing new knowledge by demonstrating practical transcendental possibilities. It could for example mean utilizing something like the Marxist Bertolt Brecht's theatrical *Verfremdungseffekt* to highlight emancipatory untried possibilities in everyday practice by presenting a well known practice in a new light. Practice enlightened by theory, one could say. It could for example mean a play about the composer and copy editor in the example above by which the users come to insight about how the division of labor between them is a result of the capitalist mode of production, a rational means for accumulation of capital as analyzed by Marx.

Also in a Wittgensteinian approach design artifacts can shed new light on a well-known situation, since, as earlier quoted:[16]

> the aspects of things that are most important to us are hidden because of their simplicity and familiarity. (One is unable to notice something – because it is always before one's eyes.) The real foundations of his enquiry do not strike man at all. Unless *that* fact has at some time struck him. – And this means: we fail to be struck by what, once seen, is most striking and most powerful.

However, as Peter Winch put it, in a Wittgensteinian approach

> the only legitimate use of such a *Verfremdungseffekt* is to *draw attention* to the familiar and obvious, not to show that it is *dispensable* from our understanding.[17]

Design artifacts, linguistic or not, may in a Wittgensteinian approach certainly be used to create breakdowns,

[16] Wittgenstein, *Philosophical Investigations*, § 129.
[17] Winch, P.: *The Idea of a Social Science and its Relation to Philosophy*, Routledge & Kegan Paul, London 1958, p. 119.

but they must make sense in the users' ordinary language-games. If the design artifacts are good, it is because they help users and designers to see new aspects of an already well-known practice, not because they convey a theoretical interpretation.

With a Wittgensteinian approach there is a focus on the *language-games* of design. Hence, it is almost paradoxical that it was this approach that best helped us in the UTOPIA project to understand our relatively successful use of non-linguistic design artifacts like prototypes, mock-ups and role plays. The point is that, since design artifacts understood as reminders or paradigm cases do not linguistically mirror a given or future practice, they can even be *experienced* beyond language, e.g. as practical use of a prototype or mock-up, or as participation in a role play, an experience that can be further reflected upon in the language-games of design in ordinary language or in an artificial one. This does not, however, change the fundamental role of non-linguistic design artifacts as soon as we forget about the picture theory of reality.

On the other hand this focus on non-linguistic design artifacts is not a rejection of the importance of linguistic ones. Understood as triggers for our imagination rather than as mirror-images of reality, they may well be our most wonderful human inventions.

## Practical Understanding and Propositional Knowledge

There are many actions in a language-game that cannot really be explicitly described in a formal language. What is it that the users know, i.e. what have they learned, that they can express in action, but that they are not able to state explicitly in language? Wittgenstein asks us to

> compare knowing and saying: how many feet high Mont Blanc is – how the word 'game' is used – how a clarinet sounds. If you are surprised that one can know something and not be able to say it, you are perhaps

thinking of a case like the first. Certainly not of one of the third.[18]

In the UTOPIA project we were designing new computer artifacts to be used in typographical page make-up. The typographers could tell us the names of the different artifacts and materials that they use e.g. knife, page ground, body text, galley, logo, halftone, frame and spread. They could also tell when, and perhaps in which order, they use specific artifacts and materials to place an article, e.g. they could say, 'First you pick up the body text with the knife, and place it at the bottom of the designated area on the page ground. Then you adjust it to the galley line. When the body text fits you get the headline, if there is not a picture, etc.' What I, as designer, get to know is equivalent to knowing the height of Mont Blanc. What I get to know is very different from the practical understanding of really making up pages, as knowing the height of Mont Blanc tells very little of the practical understanding of climbing the mountain.

Knowledge of the first kind has been called *propositional knowledge*. It is what you have 'when you know that something is the case and when you also can describe what you know in so many words'.[19] Propositional knowledge is not necessarily more reflective than practical understanding. It might be something that I just have been told, but have neither practical experience, nor theoretical understanding of.

The second case, corresponding to knowing and saying how the word 'game' is used, was more complicated for our typographers. How could they for example tell us the skill they possess in knowing how to handle the knife when making up the page in paste-up technology? This is their *practical experience* from language-games of typographic design. To show it they had to do it.

---

18 Wittgenstein, op. cit. § 78.

19 Nordenstam, T.: *Technocratic and Humanistic Conceptions of Development*, Swedish Center for Working Life, Stockholm 1985.

And how should they relate what counts as good layout, the complex interplay of presence and absence, light and dark, symmetry and asymmetry, uniformity and variety? Could they do it in any other way than by giving examples of good and bad layouts, examples that they have learned by participating in language-games of typographical design? As in the case of knowing how a clarinet sounds, this is *typically sensuous knowing by familiarity with earlier cases* of how something is, sounds, smells, etc.

Practical understanding in the sense of practical experience from doing something and having sensuous experiences from earlier cases defies formal description. If it is transformed to propositional knowledge, it becomes something totally different.

The practical understanding that remains unarticulated is often referred to as tacit knowledge.[20] It should be observed that it is not tacit in the sense that no one else can understand expressions about it. One typographer can very well communicate about the layout of a page with another typographer, or someone else who knows how to play the language-games of typography. However it is subjective in the sense that it requires a human subject to possess it. 'Objective knowledge' is knowledge that has been objectified as signs in a medium, e.g. a museum, a book, a film, or a computer. Objective knowledge is accessible and useful for us only via our subjective knowledge. Subjective knowledge or practical understanding is carried by the participants of specific language-games. You cannot learn typography entirely from books. Only in interaction with others skilled in the trade is it possible.[21]

---

[20] Polanyi, M.: *Personal Knowledge*, Routledge & Kegan Paul, London 1957. This will be further discussed in chapter 18, *Skills and the Tool Perspective*.

[21] These aspects of objective and subjective knowledge in a Wittgensteinian approach are discussed by Lundeqvist, J.: 'Ideological och teknologi' in Göranzon, B. (ed): *Datautvecklingens filosofi*, Carlsson & Jönsson, Malmö 1984. He discusses objective knowledge in relation to Karl Popper's position.

It is typically propositional knowledge that we make objective in systems descriptions (though the use of e.g. video film as a design artifact make it possible to also make objective tacit aspects of practical understanding).

However, it is hard to see how we as designers of computer artifacts for page make-up could manage to come up with useful designs without understanding how the knife is used or what counts as good layout. For this purpose we had to have access to more than what can be stated as explicit propositional knowledge. This we could only achieve by at least to some extent participating in the language-games of use of the artifacts. Hence, participation is not just a question of users participating in the language-game of design, but perhaps more fundamentally of designers participating in use. It may be repeated again that it of course helps if the designers and the users are the same persons.

Nevertheless, I think that we to some extent must accept that *design is a language-game of its own*, it has its own professionals, so that it is now time to ask: What do we as designers have to do to qualify as participants in the language-games of the users? What do users have to learn to qualify as participants in the language-game of design? And which means can we develop in design to facilitate these learning processes?

## Design-by-doing – New 'Rules of the Game'

*If* designers and users share the same *form of life* it should be possible to overcome the gap between the different language-games. It should at least in principle be possible to develop the practice of design so that there is enough *family resemblance* between a specific language-game of design and the language-games the design of the computer artifact is intervening in. A mediation should be possible.

But what are the conditions for this 'if'? To Wittgenstein it makes no sense to ask questions beyond a given form of life. In a famous quotation he says:[22]

If a lion could talk, we could not understand him.

To a Marxist approach the 'if' can in practice only be achieved by emancipatory practice in class struggle, as activities that transcend existing forms of life and create new ones within which it is possible. In the arguments below, I have assumed that the conditions for a common form of life are possible to create, that the lions and sheep of industrial life can live together. This is more of a normative standpoint of how design ought to be, a democratic hope rather than a reflection over political conditions for its realization.[23]

To possess the competence required to participate in a language-game requires a lot of learning within that practice. But in the beginning, all you can understand is what you have already understood in another language-game. You understand because of the family resemblance between the two language-games. (It should be observed how close this is to what can be said in a Heideggerian approach about conditions for understanding.)

What kind of design artifacts may be applied to support this interplay between language-games, and to make this mediation from the one to the other possible? I think that what we in the UTOPIA project called design-by-doing methods, e.g. the use of prototyping, mock-ups, scenarios etc., are good examples.[24]

---

[22] Wittgenstein, op. cit. p. 223.

[23] I shall return to this in the part on *Designing for Democracy at Work*.

[24] See Ehn, P. and Kyng, M.: 'A Tool Perspective on Design of Interactive Computer Support for Skilled Workers' in *Proceedings of the Seventh Scandinavian Research Seminar on Systemeering*, Helsinki, 1984, Ehn, P. and Kyng K.: 'The Collective Resource Approach to Systems Design' and Bødker, S. et al.: 'A Utopian Experience' in Bjerknes, G. et al. (eds.): *Computers and Democracy – A Scandinavian Challenge*, Avebury, 1987. This is

The language-games played in design-by-doing can be viewed both from the point of view of the users and of the designers. This kind of design becomes a language-game in which the users learn about possibilities and constraints of new computer artifacts that may become part of their ordinary language-games. The designers become the teachers that teach the users how to participate in this particular language-game of design. In order to set up these kind of language-games the designers have to learn from the users.

However, paradoxical as it sounds, users and designers do not really have to understand each other in playing language-games of design-by-doing together. Participation in a language-game of design and the use of design artifacts can make *constructive but different sense*, to users and designers. Wittgenstein notes:

> When children play at trains their game is connected with their knowledge of trains. It would nevertheless be possible for the children of a tribe unacquainted with trains to learn this game from others, and to play it without knowing that it was copied from anything. One might say that the game did not make the same *sense* as to us.[25]

As long as the language-game of design is not a nonsense activity to any participant, but a shared activity for better understanding and good design, mutual understanding is desired but not really required.

*User Participation and Skill*

The users can participate in the language-game of design, because the design artifacts applied give their design activities a family resemblance with the language-games that they play in ordinary use situations. An example from the UTOPIA project is a typographer sitting at a

further developed in chapter 15, *The 'Tool Persspective' – An Example*.

[25] Wittgenstein, op. cit. §282.

mock-up of a future workstation for page make-up, actually doing make-up on the simulated future computer artifact.[26]

The family resemblance is only one aspect of the methods. The other is what can be expressed. I think that it is reasonable to say that in design-by-doing the user will be able express both propositional knowledge and practical understanding. Not only could e.g. the typographer working at the mock-up tell that the screen should be bigger because then it would be possible to show a full spread, something which is important in page make-up. He also could show what he meant by 'cropping a picture', by actually doing it, as he said it. It was also possible for him to express practical understanding in the sense of sensuous knowledge by familiarity. He could e.g. while working at the mock-up, express the fact that, when the artifact is designed one way he can get a good balanced page, but not when it is designed another way.

*Designer Participation and Skill*

For us as designers it was possible to express both propositional knowledge and practical understanding about design and computer artifacts. Not only could we express propositional knowledge like 'design-by-doing design artifacts have many advantages as compared with traditional systems descriptions' or 'bit-map displays bigger than 22 inch and with a resolution of more than 2000 x 2000 pixels are very expensive'. In the language-game of design–by–doing we could also express practical understanding of technical constraints and possibilities by 'implementing' them in the mock-up, prototype, simulation, experimental situation etc. Not least simulations of the user interface, the sign aspect of the future artifacts discussed above, the reminders of what they are for, were important in this language-game of design.

---

[26] See Ehn, P. et al: *Datorstödd Ombrytning*, Swedish Center for Working Life, Stockholm 1985, Bødker et al., op. cit.

However, as designers, our practical understanding will most of all be expressed as *the ability to construct specific language-games of design in such a way that the users can develop their understanding of future use by participating in design processes.*

Family resemblance with the users' ordinary language-games is an important aspect of these language-games of design, but there is also, as mentioned above, another important aspect of language-games: we make up the rules as we go along. To assist in such transcendental rule breaking activities should be an important competence of a skilled designer. Perhaps this is the artistic competence a good designer needs?

I have argued that in design-by-doing language-games users can express both propositional knowledge and practical knowledge. From both these kinds of activities there is much that will prove useful in the design process for the designers. But it should be observed that most of the items that can be learned are examples of correct and incorrect moves in the language-game of use, not formal descriptions of this practice.

However, in language-games of design based on participation and design-by-doing, much can also be learned from the users by the practice that is shared in the design activity. To take some examples from the UTOPIA project, activities such as joint visits to work places, with situations in some aspects similar to the ones being designed for, may be a kind of 'design artifact' from which both designers and users can learn and create the language-game of the specific design they both are involved in.[27] To really learn the language-game of the use activity by fully participating in that language-game is of course an even more radical attempt by the designer. Less radical but perhaps more practical would be that the designer concentrates the design activity to just a few language-games of use,

----

[27] See chapter 15, *The 'Tool Perspective' – An Example.*

and for them develops a practical understanding of useful specific language-games of design.[28]

## The Language-games of Design Research

This brings me to some reflections about a science or an art of design and use of computer artifacts in a Wittgensteinian approach. What if researchers lack practical experience about actual language-games of design, and of the language-games which the design is aimed for, and in which the computer artifacts are used? What kind of knowledge will our reflections produce if we do not understand design and use of computer artifacts practically?

These questions could be put to any science, and the answer would be: theoretical propositional explicit knowledge, but also considerable practical understanding of these theories as language-games, as they are being played within the scientific community. They may be interesting language-games in their own right, games with intricate moves and complicated explicit and implicit rules that it may take a lifetime to master.

However, in the language-games of an art or a science of design and use of computer artifacts we are not only reflecting, but also proposing new designs, and methods to be used in design. Our purpose is not only to reflect, but also to advocate change. We do not leave things as they are, as according to Wittgenstein, philosophy does.[29] This doubleness we share with other design sciences.[30]

This makes the initial questions more crucial. As a Wittgensteinian inquiry we can also reformulate the questions in the following way: How can we as researchers in design and use of computer artifacts learn from the actual language-games of design and use, and

---

[28] See Ehn and Kyng 1987, op. cit.

[29] Wittgenstein, op. cit. § 126.

[30] This has been pointed out by Lundeqvist, op. cit.

how can we teach designers and users our theoretical design knowledge? Participation and family resemblance seem to be just as important aspects of the language-games of design research as in the language-games of design and use. After all, we are not only following the rules of science or reflecting those of practice; we also make up the rules as we go along. And we even alter them – as we go along.

## Summary

In my discussion of the Wittgensteinian approach to design philosophy, focus has been on communication and interaction in the design process. Less has been said in general about the acquisition of knowledge, and of how artifacts, including computer artifacts, have to be understood as their use, though much could have been said. However, it should be obvious that the view of skilled work as rule following and eventually creative rule breaking activities that must be achieved in practice, through practical experience, has great similarities to the understanding of acquisition of skill in both the Heideggerian and the Marxist approaches.[31] Hence, I will not go into details on these aspects now, but turn to a summary of and some conclusions on what might have been learned from all three intertwined 'interpretations' of design philosophy in the context of an art and a science of design and use of computer artifacts, and the experiences from DEMOS and UTOPIA.

[31] Wittgensteinian aspects of 'tacit knowledge' and of 'creativity' will be further developed in chapter 18, *Skills and the Tool Perspective*.

*Chapter 5*

# With Alternative Glasses – Conclusions on Design Philosophy

In this part of the book I have tried to weave an intertwined web of three philosophical languages for understanding design and use of computer artifacts. In pragmatic interpretations of Heidegger, Marx and Wittgenstein I have argued that an emphasis on *human practice* is a possible philosophical foundation serving as an alternative to the Cartesian design philosophies of rationalism and dualism.

## Beyond Systems Thinking

In opposition to the Cartesian approach which dominates computer science and systems thinking today, I have argued that human practice and understanding in everyday life should be taken as the ontological and epistemological point of departure in inquiries into design and use of computer artifacts.

In the Heideggerian approach there was an emphasis on how people *use* the artifacts that we call computers. Concepts like *ready-to-hand, breakdown, present-at-hand* and *thrownness* were important for this interpretation. A conceptual framework for understanding the *skill* people acquire and possess in design and use of computer artifacts was introduced as well. The fundamental difference between *practical understanding* and *theoretical reflection,* as well as their relation in the process of skill acquisition, was demonstrated. Without the development of theories and methods based on people's practical understanding and use of artifacts rather than just detached representations of it, 'knowledge acquisition' in systems design is in serious trouble, practically as well as theoretically. That was a message for the science of design and use of computer artifacts. Furthermore, the use of artifacts is something very fundamental to human beings. In fact, in designing computer artifacts there is much to learn from the use of stone axes. A science of design and use of computer artifacts is advised to learn from the Humanities. For practical design, the message was that the users' real competence cannot be formally described, and that design should aim at computer artifacts that do not break down the users' understanding in ordinary use situations.

*Emancipatory practice* was emphasized in the Marxist approach. This was understood both epistemologically and socially. In addition to the cultural understanding of design and use of computer artifacts that was offered by the Heideggerian approach, the Marxist approach points at the need for social or political interpretations. The emancipatory focus was on social relations, on the transcendence of conditions that prevent humanization of the world – theoretically and in practice. A message to a science of design and use of computer artifacts was that the labor process of design and use must be understood socially. This does not only mean that such a science must understand the social relations (and the oppression) in the division of labor between design and use, or the social relations within the design process. *The artifacts themselves must be understood as social relations. Especially an understanding of the rationalization processes in design and use of computer artifacts in our contemporary societies* was seen as necessary. A science of design and use of computer artifacts is advised to learn from the Social Sciences. Not only are theories in design to explain these relations necessary, but also relations to emancipatory practice to practically, not only theoretically, transcend oppressing relations. One message addressed to practical design was that it is a political process, in our society often a process of rationalization, and as such neither neutral nor rational as a mean for humanization. Hence, to participate in the design process, is to take a stand one way or another.

With the Wittgensteinian approach an 'untheoretical' way of understanding the practice of design and use of computer artifacts was introduced. However, knowledge was understood in much the same way as in the earlier approaches, with emphasis on competence as having learned to *follow a rule* in practice. The suggestion was to think of design and use activities as *language-games* that people play, i.e. how we learn to participate, interact and communicate in games, how we *use our ordinary language in shared activities*. No concepts were introduced that could not be understood with ordinary use of language. If a science of design and use of computer artifacts in the two former approaches was advised to learn from the Humanities and the Social Sciences, I think the complementary lesson here rather should be formulated as: learn from the games people play in their ordinary use of language and artifacts in their everyday lives. This may also have been said about the other approaches, but here it is the essence. This is also the Wittgensteinian message to practical design.

Throughout the discussion of the Heideggerian, Marxist and Wittgensteinian approaches they have been compared, and family resemblances between them have been pointed out.

Certainly I could also have discussed major differences between a philosopher that found the conditions for human existence once and for all given, another who saw philosophy as a way 'not only to explain the world but also to change it', and a third one that tells us that philosophy 'leaves everything as it is'.

I could also have gone deeper into existential phenomenology and Heidegger's cultural conservative relation to Nazism, into relations between Marxism as philosophy and Gulag as reality, or even into the understanding of social interaction as language-games and Wittgenstein's socially deviant behavior.

Some might find this 'blindness' unacceptable. Others might find it inappropriate to 'interpret' philosophical traditions in such an instrumental way as has been done above. Philosophers could say that what has been interpreted above is not really Heidegger, Marx, Wittgenstein, or Descartes. They could also point out that the relations between the philosophical traditions are much more complicated than indicated. From a philosophical point of view they are right.

In the same way different schools in phenomenology could claim that this is not really existential phenomenology, as could hundreds of Marxist schools argue that this is not the right Marxism, and the same probably goes for those engaged in the analytic ordinary language school of philosophy.

As stated in the introduction of this part, my purpose here has been a different one. The interpretations are an attempt to explicitly state my understanding of what aspects in the different philosophical traditions discussed are especially important to *design and use of the artifacts we call computers*, as practice, as science, or even as art, but not as philosophy in general. This is done with my own practice as a researcher and designer in the field as background. The labels attached to the different approaches are not what is important here; instead, it is whether the approaches can be instrumental in design research and in practical design.

## Some Consequences

I have neither the philosophical competence nor the intention to present a great synthesis of the three approaches, a consistent conceptual framework that transcends the discussions on design philosophy so far. For the time being I find it wiser to see them as partly convergent trends, while still philosophically very different. Openness to eclectic 'bridges' and a transcending 'dialogue' between approaches focusing on the role of human practice seem to me to be more fruitful than a proclamation of the one and only new design philosophy.

Instead of that new design philosophy I will give some examples as illustrations or paradigm cases, in which I try to apply design philosophy from the three approaches to actual research and design situations I have been involved in.

However, a few more general comments on the philosophical foundation for the main topic of this book on *work-oriented design of computer artifacts* should be made, before considering the examples.

In the *Prologue* I singled out two aspects as fundamental – *conditions for skill* and *conditions for democracy*.

I think all three philosophical approaches have contributed to an epistemological foundation for understanding the role of skill, both in the design process and in the use of computer artifacts. This will be utilized in the part on *Designing for Skill*.

When it comes to democracy, their contributions are more unclear. Only the Marxist approach suggests radical emancipation, since its epistemology also includes transcendence of whatever might socially oppress humanization of the world. The Marxist approach offers an understanding of oppressing aspects in the labor processes of design and use, as well as in the computer artifacts themselves. And methods for emancipation by and with those oppressed are focused on.

However, methods for establishing a democratic dialogue in design and use of computer artifacts are perhaps better supported by the more conservative approaches of Heidegger and Wittgenstein. With the Heideggerian interpretation of computer artifacts, and with the Wittgensteinian interpretation of the language-games of design and use, philosophical suggestions arise for useful means for a practice towards democracy both in design and use – a democratic dialogue based on participation by and competence of the users.

But there also seems to be an inherent conflict between democracy and skill. I have focused on the character of professional skill as knowledge that cannot be made fully explicit nor fully communicated to or understood by others than humans with similar competence or background. It is, for example, a well-known phenomenon that professional groups use this to escape democratic control and participation by others in what they are doing. One of the foundations in the democratic tradition is not only equal participation by all concerned, but also a demand for arguments to be, in principle, made explicit in a way that can be understood by all involved.[1] No doubt, this is close to a Cartesian rationalistic ideal. This will be kept in mind in a following part on *Designing for Democracy at Work*.

I also think that all three philosophical approaches show that *work-oriented design* must transcend theoretical reflection and be involved in the practice of practical design and use. This is true whether we see it as conditions for interpretation, emancipatory practice, or family resemblance between language-games. Given the Marxist approach it is also obvious that its moral stance must be not only to be participative, but also to take a stand whenever it finds situations that are oppressive of the development of skill and democracy at work.

Finally, if I should single out one aspect that to me seems to be the most crucial to design philosophy, it must be the contradiction that has run through all three interpretations above, and also between them and the Cartesian approach. This is *the dialectics of tradition and transcendence in design and use*. Emphasis has mostly been placed on the utilization of involved practical competence by interaction in design, which has been seen as fundamental, compared to detached theoretically produced insight. However, breakdown of traditional knowledge, as a process of transcendence by finding out new aspects of

[1] See e.g. Vedung, E.: *Det rationella samtalet*, Aldus, Stockholm 1977, Abrahamsson, B.: *Varför finns organisationer*, Norstedts, Stockholm 1986.

what already has been understood, has also been seen as important to design.

During the discussion several dimensions of the contradiction between tradition and transcendence have emerged. One can focus on tradition or transcendence in the *artifacts* to be used. Should a word processor be designed as a traditional typewriter or as something totally new? Another dimension is *professional competence.* Should the 'old' skills of typographers be what is designed for or should 'new' knowledge replace these skills in future use? Along the same dimension is *division of labor and cooperation.* Should the new design support the traditional organization in a composing room or suggest new ways of cooperation between typographers and journalists? There is also the contradiction between tradition and transcendence in the objects or *use values* to be produced. Should the design support the traditional services a library has produced or should it support completely new services and even new clients? Tradition or transcendence, that is the question in design.

Not an answer, but an illustration of the dialectics between traditional competence and new knowledge is given in *The Name of the Rose* by Umberto Eco. We enter the story at a meeting between his rational hero William of Baskerville and Nicholas of Morimondo, master glazier of the abbey.

> 'It's hopeless,' he (the master glazier) went on. 'We no longer have the learning of the ancients, the age of the giants is past!'

> 'We are dwarfs,' William admitted, 'but dwarfs who stand on the shoulders of those giants, and small though we are, we sometimes manage to see farther on the horizon than they.'

> 'Tell me what we can do better than they were able to do,' Nicholas exclaimed. 'If you go down to the crypt of the church, where the abbey's treasure is kept, you find reliquaries of such exquisite craftsmanship that the little monstrosity I am now cobbling up – he nodded to-

ward his own work on the table – 'will seem a mockery of those!'

'It is not written that master glaziers must go on making windows, and goldsmiths reliquaries, since the masters of the past were able to produce such beautiful ones, destined to last over centuries. Otherwise, the earth would become filled with reliquaries in a time when saints from whom to take relics are so rare,' William jested. 'Nor will windows have to be soldered forever. But in various countries I have seen new works made of glass which suggest a future world where glass will serve not only for holy purposes but also as a help for man's weakness. I want to show you a creation of our own times, of which I am honored to own a very useful example.' He dug inside his habit and drew out the lenses, which dumbfounded our interlocutor.

With great interest, Nicholas took the forked instrument William held out to him. 'Oculi de vitro cum capsula!' he cried. 'I had heard tell of them from a Brother Jordan I met in Pisa! He said it was less than twenty years since they had been invented. But I spoke with him more than twenty years ago.'

'I believe they were invented much earlier,' William said, 'but they are difficult to make, and require highly expert master glaziers. They cost time and labor. Ten years ago a pair of these glasses ab oculis ad legendum were sold for six Bolognese crowns. I was given a pair of them by a great master, Salvinus of the Armati, more than ten years ago, and I have jealously preserved them all the time, as if they were – as they now are – a part of my very body.' [2]

I think that it is in a transcendence of the contradiction between Nicholas and William that the design philosophy

[2] Eco, U.: *The Name of the Rose*, Pan Books Ltd, London 1984, pp. 85.

of the future should be looked for. In design of computer artifacts we can neither do without traditional competence nor without new knowledge that challenges and transcends what already has been understood. We can create breakdowns of traditions. But that is not necessarily production of new knowledge. We can produce new transcendental knowledge and practice. But that is not done by neglect of traditional competence and understanding.

## Design Knowledge – Three Illustrations

To conclude this part I will in a few examples apply the design knowledge argued in the three philosophical approaches above. These examples or illustrations of design knowledge are reflections on situations which I already have understood, in the sense that they all have been ready-to-hand to me. The illustrations are reflections on practice I have been involved in.

One illustration is of design philosophy applied to production of *theoretical knowledge* on design and use of computer artifacts. The example is this book on *Work-Oriented Design of Computer Artifacts*. The second illustration is design philosophy applied to *strategy and methods in research* on design and use of computer artifacts. The examples will be based on DEMOS and UTOPIA, the two research projects that have given me most of the understanding that I reflect in this book. The third illustration is of design philosophy applied to *strategy and methods in actual design* of computer artifacts. As my example I will choose to reflect upon how we designed computer-based tools for skilled graphic workers in the UTOPIA project.

The illustrations are just examples, not extensive treatments of what has been studied; at best they will work as 'paradigm cases'. I will begin with the application to an actual design case.

*UTOPIAN Design – on Design Strategy and Methods*

The UTOPIA project was both a research and a development project. Actual design of alternative computer-based page make-up and image processing were part of the project. To this end a design strategy and methods had to be applied. The strategy that was chosen meant cooperation with the ultimate users of the design, i.e. graphic workers. To begin with, requirement specifications and the systems descriptions were based on traditional methods like interviews and graphical representations of existing and future systems. This was not very successful. The situation improved when:[3]

- we started to understand traditional tools as a design ideal for computer artifacts – the design of tools for skilled work,
- we made joint visits (designers and graphic workers together) to interesting plants (and discussed with users there), trade shows, vendors, etc.,
- we dedicated considerable time for learning from each other: designers about graphic work, and graphic workers about design,
- we started to use design-by-doing methods and descriptions in the language of graphic work, i.e. mock-ups, work organization games etc.

From all three philosophical approaches the usefulness of these changes may be understood in the way that they help utilize the practical understanding of both designers and graphic workers, not just their detached reflections of what they already had understood.

Interpreted as Heideggerian design knowledge, the mock-ups as design artifacts helped the graphic workers express their practical knowledge by doing design on the simulated equipment. This helped to some extent avoid breakdown of their practical understanding, and even if

[3] This will be further discussed in chapter 13, *Case II: The UTOPIA Project*.

they were simulations the mock-ups supported ready-to-hand experiences.

Interpreted as Wittgensteinian design knowledge the methods may be understood as supporting integration by family resemblance between the language-games of newspaper production and design of computer artifacts. Most activities can be understood as creating conditions for participation in these language-games. Especially there is the creation of a language-game that designers and graphic workers have in common when designing for graphic work by doing it.

As Marxist design knowledge the design strategy can be understood as emancipatory practice. The graphic workers' existence as skilled workers was threatened by capitalistic technological development. To show the possibility of skill based alternatives by actually designing them was seen as essential to counteractions. The work was carried out with graphic workers and their organizations. The purpose was to support actions like negotiations on new technology and professional training. The design process was seen in its total context of industrial relations. The UTOPIAN design was not a general methodology, but methods applied as part of a strategy for emancipation.

The designs produced were quite new as compared with how computer-based page make-up and image processing generally was understood at that time. Though technically advanced, our designs were, however, less new as compared with traditional paste-up and graphic arts technology.[4]

What could have been achieved with more drastic breakdowns, and what would have been lost? This is again the contradiction between tradition and transcendence, which seems to be at the heart of design.

[4] See Ehn, P. et al.: *Datorstödd ombrytning*, Swedish Center for Working Life, Stockholm 1985.

### DEMOS and UTOPIA – on Research Strategy and Methods

In my work as a researcher in the field of design and use of computer artifacts the DEMOS and the UTOPIA project have been the cornerstones.

As outlined in the *Prologue*, the DEMOS project was an attempt to develop knowledge on planning, control and use of computers at work. The study was conducted jointly with workers and trade unions in order to find acceptable democratic alternatives to the then dominant practice and theory. The research work was based on the practice of investigative groups that the project helped establish in local unions at four enterprises: a department store, a steel mill, a newspaper and an engine repair shop. The groups investigated problems at the plant where they worked. As researchers we participated as resource persons in this work. We contributed with practical investigations, as well as with teaching our knowledge in computer science, organization theory etc. Our other role in the project was reflection over the practice in the investigation groups as a basis for contributions to scientific knowledge in our field of research, and to research methodology.

As described earlier, the UTOPIA project concentrated on one industry – newspaper production. It was based on the experience from the DEMOS project and other similar research, namely that the supply from the vendors had to be influenced if new technology that in practice supported a democratic work organization and skilled work was to be implemented. Hence, our emphasis was on actual design of technological alternatives for text and image processing. These alternatives were not only to include the technology, but also professional training. Quality of work and product were the design goals. Both technical and social prerequisites, as well as obstacles and limitations, were part of the research analysis.

Strategically, the project was supported by the Nordic Graphic Workers' Union. The actual research and development work was done jointly by a group of researchers and graphic workers (skilled workers and at the same time experienced trade unionists).

The researchers participated both in the actual design work, and in the analysis of the conditions for the approach taken, and in theoretical reflection on the practical experiences.

Both the DEMOS and the UTOPIA projects were action research based – gaining understanding by participation in actual change, an understanding that could be theoretically reflected. The projects' grounding in participation in the practice investigated seems well anchored as a research strategy in all three philosophical interpretations of design knowledge used here.

Interpreting the research strategies and methods via Heideggerian design philosophy, I will only point at the hermeneutic aspect. To understand other human beings, and what they are doing, we must have a shared background. All we can do is interpretations, which are always done within the horizon created by our background of understanding. Interpretation based on participation does not seem to be such a bad idea, at least when compared with just Cartesian reflections based on collected data.

With Wittgensteinian design philosophy both projects can be interpreted as developing knowledge by learning the rules of the language-games of use, by creating design artifacts that support the users' acquisition of new understanding, and at the same time teaching the rules of the academic knowledge about design and use of computers. If successful, the projects also changed the language-games for design and use, or at least some of the rules, in a democratic direction. The 'negotiation model'[5] for system design developed in the DEMOS project is an example that to some extent changed both the practice of systems design, and the theoretical understanding of the rules of that

---

[5] This will be discussed in chapter 12, *Case I: The DEMOS Project.*

game. 'The tool perspective'[6] of the UTOPIA project has had a similar effect.

It is also possible to understand the methods applied as means to create family resemblance between the language-games of research and what is researched (as above with design and use). This way it would to some extent be possible for researchers to understand the language-games of use, e.g. graphic work, an understanding that later can be reflected in the language-games of research.

Interpreted via Marxist design philosophy the DEMOS project is a clear case. Workers seen as oppressed by capitalist technology and division of labor are the subjects of this research. The aim is emancipatory practice, and this is the practice of the workers themselves at the plants investigated. It is not only the researchers that are supposed to reflect, but also the other subjects involved. And it is reflection of changes in their practice that is emphasized. If successful, these changes are in a more democratic direction or at least some limits to such a development are understood. These experiences can also be theoretically reflected upon and help produce new theoretical knowledge as understanding of, e.g., limits to democratization at work, the labor processes of design and use of computer artifacts, or trade union organization theory.

Interpreted via Marxist design philosophy the research strategy and methods of the UTOPIA project can be understood as follows: It aimed at practical knowledge about the impact of new technology in newspaper production. This knowledge was to be used by graphic workers and their organizations in emancipatory practice to transcend the dehumanizing aspects of the existing capitalistic technology. But to develop alternatives requires not only resources, but also new knowledge of design possibilities with the new technology. Hence, the research strategy was on the one hand based on strong institutional

---

[6] This will be discussed in chapter 13, *Case II: The UTOPIA Project*, and chapter 15, *The 'Tool Perspectie' – An Example.*

support (the trade unions of the graphic workers in the Nordic countries). This way the market conditions for the new technology could be influenced, since only technology that fulfills certain demands would be accepted by the unions. On the other hand these alternatives had to be developed and made concrete. This required new design principles that made it possible for graphic workers to express their practical knowledge in the design process, and to think creatively about alternatives. These are requirements for the practical change, but also for theoretical reflection. The activities performed and the understanding achieved can be broken down and reflected upon in a theoretical context. This may produce new knowledge about, e.g., strategies for and limits to technological change, or design methods that utilize users' practical understanding.

Interpreted via Marxist design philosophy one more aspect common to the research approaches of the two projects should be mentioned. With its emphasis on emancipatory practice the results of the projects had first of all to be communicated to the subjects of this transcendence – the workers and their trade unions. Hence an important aspect of the research strategies was to find forms in which the theoretically reflected and produced knowledge could be returned to the practice it grew from. The textbook on design, planning and computers from the DEMOS project is an example of this.[7] Examples from the UTOPIA project are the summary report distributed to graphic workers in all the Nordic countries,[8] and the textbooks for professional training of graphic workers.[9] The intellectual challenge of writing these kind of

[7] Ehn, P. and Sandberg, Å.: *Företagsstyrning och löntagarmakt*, Prisma, Stockholm 1979.

[8] UTOPIA project group: *An Alternative in Text and Images,* Graffiti no 7, Swedish Center for Working Life, Stockholm 1985.

[9] See e.g. Ehn et. al., op. cit., and Frenkner, K. and Romberger, S.: *Datorstödd Bildbehandling*, Swedish Center for Working Life, Stockholm 1985.

research reports is by no means smaller than in trying to communicate with an academic audience.

## *Work-Oriented Design – on Theory*

My purpose in writing this book is to theoretically reflect upon and hopefully transcend what I already have understood in my practice as researcher and designer. I am involved in Cartesian reflections on the kind of experiences that have been exemplified above. I want to contribute to theoretical understanding of *Work-Oriented Design of Computer Artifacts*. What I have in mind are reflections about conditions and strategies or methods in designing for democracy at work and for skill-enhancing computer-based tools.

An interpretation of the practice of contributing to theoretical knowledge of work-oriented design, along the lines of all three philosophical approaches, may run as follows:

My understanding of design from the involvement in research projects and actual design has to be broken down and transcended by reflections. This breakdown may be created by framing my understanding in a philosophical context, e.g as a Heideggerian approach, as a Marxist approach, or as a Wittgensteinian approach to design philosophy as in this part of the book.

My understanding may also be broken down by relating it to other approaches to designing for democracy and skill. An example of alternative theory of design and democracy is the socio-technical approach.[10] An example of alternative theory for skill and design is the approach taken by cognitive science.[11] Such breakdowns will be considered in the appropriate parts of this book.

---

[10] See e.g. Mumford, E.: 'Sociotechnical System Design – Evolving Theory and Practice', in Bjerknes, et al. (eds.): *Computers and Democracy – A Scandinavian Challenge*, Avebury, 1987.

[11] See e.g. Norman, D. & Draper, S. (eds.): *User Centred System Design*, Lawrence Erlbaum, London 1986.

Another way of reflecting on my understanding is by relating it to other design disciplines and approaches like architecture or industrial design, as will be done in a later chapter.[12]

However, the point of these breakdowns is to produce new knowledge of what was already understood. The questions have to be asked in ways that allow new aspects to be seen, e.g. so that practical knowledge can be brought into focus. Only then is new theoretical knowledge produced. If successful, this can be understood by others as new insight and in the long run as new practice and understanding. This is the most general interpretation. However, *the fundamental point is the practice and understanding that is being reflected*, what has already been understood. Philosophically there seems to be a strong case for action research, and participation in actual design, as the instance for this practice and understanding. This is true whether we call it hermeneutics, dialectics, or ordinary language.

The paradox is that my rejection of a Cartesian research approach itself is being argued as Cartesian reflections, though explicitly grounded in a practice. Even when taking a Heideggerian, Marxist, or Wittgensteinian approach, Cartesian reflections seem to be a necessary beginning for developing design philosophy. To interpret philosophers one has in a way to be a Cartesian one. The point is, however, as Hans Skjervheim has put it, not to try to escape this dilemma (which is impossible), but to be in it in a *proper* way. Ultimately it is a question of being with others in the world in a proper way.[13] The alternative philosophical approaches to design argued in this part of

---

[12] See e.g. Lundeqvist, J.: *Norm och Modell – samt ytterligare några begrepp inom designteorin*, Department of Architecture, Royal Institute of Technology of Stockholm, 1982 (dissertation), Cross, N. (ed.): *Developments in Design Methodology*, John Wiley & Sons, Bath 1984, Mayall, W.H.: *Principles in Design*, Design Council, London 1979.

[13] Skjervheim, H.: *Deltagare och åskådare*, Prisma, Halmstad 1971, pp. 79-80.

the book can shed some light on what that means. Transcending a tradition while being in it; that is the dialectics of design as well as of design research.

Now to some more specific interpretations. For a Marxist inquiry one can ask what kind of emancipatory practice this book on work-oriented design is part of. A negative answer could be that it is part of no such practice; its academic conception of design even makes it harmful to emancipatory practice. But there are also possible positive answers: production of new knowledge is not a bad thing, especially if it is supportive of emancipatory practice; academic legitimacy of work-oriented design is of importance; understood and used by other academics, this theoretical knowledge might even contribute to better conditions for work-oriented design as emancipatory practice.

Finally, with a Wittgensteinian approach the writing of this book can be seen as a move in the the academic language-game of a science of computer and information science. Can I demonstrate that I have learned the rules of the game? This means not only mastering a set of theories and research methods, but also for example a style of writing, or more generally, the conventions of being a researcher in the field of design and use of computer artifacts in the Scandinavian academic world in the late 1980s. What counts is whether the move is a proper one or not. To play the academic game according to the rules is what is done in what Thomas S. Kuhn calls *normal science* in his well-known book *The Structure of Scientific Revolutions*.[14]

In normal science there is an established practice of exemplary cases that define the paradigm. However anomalies may begin to occur within this paradigm, e.g., observations that cannot be explained; theories that do not fit but still get spread; other researchers entering the game and claiming superiority of their rules (research

[14] Kuhn, T.S.: *The Structure of Scientific Revolutions*, Chicago 1962.

methods and theories from another discipline), etc. Then we enter a phase of revolutionary science in which the old paradigm withers away and a new one is established.

Whether or not this book is part of such a new paradigm in computer and information science remains to be seen, and is up to others to judge. However, I think there are enough anomalies in the existing language-games of computer science, and enough researchers that have begun to play according to changed rules, for us to understand the current state as unstable. Not only are philosophers and scholars in other disciplines engaged in a fundamental critique of the Cartesian orientation of rationalism and dualism in computer science, but even rationalization as such in society (to which computer science makes a major contribution) is being more and more questioned.[15] These alternatives have their emphasis on a dialogue between the people concerned.

Tore Nordenstam calls the existing paradigm the *technocratic* conception of development.[16] The opposing alternative he labels *humanistic*. I can only hope to have made a correct move or broken a rule or two in that direction. My point is that this humanistic conception of development not should be external to, but a paradigm case *in* the language-games of a science or art of design and use of computer artifacts.

With these reflections on design philosophy as background I now turn to an inquiry into *The Art and Science of Designing Computer Artifacts*.

---

[15] The Environmentalist movement all over the western world is perhaps the strongest practical evidence of this critique. The theoretical critique typically develops ideas from Karl Marx or Max Weber. See e.g. Habermas, J.: *Theorie des Kommunikativen Handelns*, I, II, Suhrkamp, Frankfurt 1981 or Offe, C.: *Disorganized Capitalism*, Polity Press, Oxford 1985.

[16] Nordenstam, T.: *Technocratic and Humanistic Conceptions of Development*, Swedish Center for Working Life, Stockholm 1985, p. 8.

# The Art and Science of Designing Computer Artifacts

*'Both art and design at last seem like meeting,*
*across the Cartesian split of mind from body,*
*to enable us to find a new genius collaboration*
*not in the making of*
*products and systems and bureaucracies*
*but in composing of contexts that include everyone,*
*designers too.*
*To be a part.*
*To find how to make all we do and think*
*relate to all we sense and know,*
*(not merely to attend to fragments*
*of ourselves and our situations).*
*It was a question of where to put your feet.*
*It became a matter of choosing the dance*
*Now its becoming*
*No full stop '*

J. Christopher Jones in
*How My Thoughts about Design Methods*
*have Changed During the Years*

# Introduction

In this part I will be concerned with the art and science of designing computer artifacts, and with finding an academic 'home' for work-oriented design. I am not concerned with the name of this place, be it computer science, information science, informatics, or whatever, but with what should be *done* there.

## Disciplinary Boundaries

What is computer science? Not long ago this question was addressed by Paul Abrahams, president of the Association for Computing Machinery, in *Communications of the ACM*.[1]

As a first conclusion he suggests that any definition whose scope strays too far from the pragmatic answer that computer science is what is taught by computer science departments is unlikely to meet much acceptance. I would guess he is right. Nevertheless I agree with him that the question is worth discussing.

I agree with Abrahams that computer science is *not* the study of Vaxes or Macintoshes, not even of Connection Machines or Turing Machines, though such studies may be part of it. However, I am afraid that this is where the agreement might stop. At least when he suggests that 'most of the interesting questions in theory are special cases of two general types: what can we compute, and what resources do we need in order to compute it?' I can imagine many other theoretically interesting questions

[1] Abrahams, P.: 'What is Computer Science' in *Communications of the ACM*, vol 30, no 6, June 1987.

for an art and science of designing computer artifacts. These questions concern designing computer artifacts for concernful human use. The disagreement may be due to a different emphasis, but I think it goes deeper.

It is not a disagreement on the belief that theory of computer science includes such specialities as algorithmic analysis, computational complexity, and formal language theory, but perhaps on the scope of what we are studying, and what other theories we need.

It is not a disagreement on the position that pragmatic computer science has a flavor of engineering (or is concerned with design of computer artifacts, as I would put it) but perhaps on the theoretical consequences of this position.

Finally, it is not a disagreement on the position that the microstructure of computing is inherently mathematical, and that the macrostructure may not be, but maybe on what it may be.

Leaving Abrahams for the Scandinavian scene I think what has to be challenged is what is understood as normal science[2] in computer science.

I have neither competence nor reason to challenge the mathematical and natural science base of computer science when the subject matter is efficiency of algorithms, semantics of programming languages, computability, etc. However, I will have to consider it problematic as soon as any kind of human use of computers is involved, or when any social or organizational setting for its design ought to be taken into account. Here I am primarily thinking of specialities such as 'systems design', or design of computer artifacts, i.e. the subject matter I am concerned about. I also think matters become problematic in subject areas such as knowledge-based systems, human-computer interaction or design of programming environments.

In fact, the idea of mathematics and natural science as normal science for a science of designing computer arti-

[2] Kuhn, T.: *The Structure of Scientific Revolutions*, University of Chicago Press, Chicago 1962.

facts is due to history, tradition and coincidence, rather than fundamental reflections of the subject matter. Here, I have the history of these academic institutions in Scandinavia in mind.[3]

When the first departments were established in the late sixties it was typically around people with a mathematics or natural science background. They were people that either had participated in constructing computers or had used their computational power in their academic work. The focus on natural science and the neglect of other scientific perspectives may have been reasonable then. Today they are not, especially if the speciality of 'systems design' is to be part of what is studied at such departments. One obvious reason is the tremendous expansion in use of computers during the two decades departments for computer or information science have existed in Scandinavia.

Let me consider two major objections to my conclusion that the scientific base for computer science is too limited:

• The first objection is based on *the need for division of labor*. The objection is that computer science only deals with the *natural science and mathematical aspects of computers*, the rest being left to other disciplines in the human and social sciences.

I think that this objection holds in so far as the effects of using computers are studied by many other disciplines. However, there is, to my knowledge, no computer science department in Scandinavia that does not at least have something like knowledge-based systems, human-computer interaction, design of programming environments, or 'systems design' in their curriculum for the students. Is the study of these subjects true natural science? I question the fruitfulness of such an assumption. I will also, at least in the case of 'systems design', argue against the fruitfulness of the prevailing division of labor between academic disciplines.

---

[3] See Bansler, J.: *Systemudvikling – teori og historie i skandinavisk perspektiv*, Studentlitteratur, Lund 1987 (dissertation).

One of my arguments against this academic division of labor, an argument that can be raised as a critique from inside computer science, is that many researchers and teachers in the human and social sciences base their statements on too limited an understanding of computers.

My other argument against the prevailing division of labor is more fundamental. Social and human sciences play an important role in the study of effects, or long range social consequences of adaptation of computers in society, etc. However, their role *in design* of computer artifacts is so far very limited and certainly constrained by the existing division of labor between the disciplines. When it comes to 'systems design' I see this as a major obstacle.

• Now to the second major objection to human and social science approaches in computer science. It is theoretical. It is the idea of *a science of design of computer artifacts as engineering based on natural science theories and methods.* Historically I see this as the main approach to 'systems design'. Though a lot of criticism has been raised over the years, this approach seems stronger than ever today. A good example is the recent plea for real systems engineering by Janis Bubenko, a leading Scandinavian computer science professor.[4]

In this part I will take the foundation of such engineering approaches to design as a challenge for reflections on the subject matter of design of computer artifacts. However, in search for fundamental theories and methods of the subject matter I will argue that we must

---

[4] In a plea for a real engineering approach the theme was formulated like this in a conference invitation recently: 'Information Systems Engineering represents an approach to information systems development that is based on an 'engineering' way of coming to grips with the different tasks to be solved in large systems development projects. (...) Information Systems Engineering represents work carried out by 'engineering' analysts and constructors in a rigorous, methodological way of coming to grips with every sub-problem, no task in the systems development being solved by capricious approaches' (my translation), Invitation to conference in Åre, April 6–8, 1987.

transcend the prevailing division of labor between academic disciplines, focusing instead on the subject matter itself, reconstructing it so we can grasp *use* as a fundamental aspect of design.

## Knowledge and Interest

By returning to the scientific *interests of knowledge* that Jürgen Habermas has been investigating, I think that some light can be shed on the dilemma for a subject matter of designing computer artifacts.[5]

Habermas traces the base for every science to the *a priori* imperatives of our sociocultural form of life that I earlier have discussed in connection with Wittgenstein's ordinary language philosophy.

Labor takes place in 'the functional sphere of *instrumental action*' where we, as human beings, encounter objects as things, events, and conditions which in principle can be manipulated. The knowledge interest of technical control concerns instrumental action.

In language and interaction we encounter speaking and acting subjects. This is where understanding in principle is possible. The practical knowledge interest of *intersubjective communication* concerns language and interaction.

According to Habermas these a priori anthropological everyday procedures and interests of knowledge determine the conditions under which every science objectifies reality. Typically the technical control interest leads to focus on observation, empirical analyses, and instrumental control, as in the technical and natural sciences, whereas the practical interest in intersubjective communication leads to focus on dialogues, participatory relations, and understanding, as in the hermeneutic sciences.

---

[5] These *knowledge interests* were referred in the introduction to the part on *Design Philosophy*. Here they are elaborated with reference to Habermas, J.: *Technik und Wissenschaft als 'Ideologie'*, Suhrkamp, Frankfurt 1968.

The dilemma in determining the subject matter for an art and science of designing computer artifacts is, as I see it, that *both the technical knowledge interest in instrumental control, and the practical knowledge interest in intersubjective communication, seem just as fundamental.*

Design of computer artifacts is an activity of determining these artifacts so that they can be constructed and implemented. Hence the technical interest in instrumental control. But it is also a dialogue and a participatory relation between those concerned about the computer artifact being designed. Hence the practical interest in intersubjective communication.

Considering the use situation designed for, there is the same doubleness. Computer artifacts may be designed to support control of objects as well as to facilitate dialogues and intersubjective communication.

This doubleness I see as the fundamental condition under which design of computer artifacts must be objectified as a scientific subject matter. Hence, in studying this subject matter we must transcend the disciplinary boundaries between the natural sciences, the social sciences and the humanities, to be able to deal with the different interests of knowledge that constitute the subject matter.

As mentioned in the first part Habermas also distinguishes a third scientific interest of knowledge, the *emancipatory interest*. This is a consciously incorporated interest in science that directs knowledge towards emancipation going beyond the other interests of knowledge. As paradigm examples Habermas mentions the critique Marx developed as a theory of capitalism, and Freud as a metapsychology. This is the interest in the process of critique as a means to reveal power relations embodied in our sociocultural form of life as systematically distorted communication – the interest of liberation and a dialogue free from coercion through knowledge. Hence the fundamental relations to political practice in Marxist theory and to therapy in Freudian theory.

I am not proposing that the emancipatory interest of knowledge must be constituent to all aspects of the subject matter of designing computer artifacts, though the fundamental relation between such a science and changes in work and language is an obvious argument. However, for *work-oriented design of computer artifacts* this interest should be cardinal.

## Structure of Part II

In this part of the book I will investigate the theoretical possibilities for establishing an art and science of designing computer artifacts. I will sketch a complementary program of the subject matter and a curriculum for its study, a program that if institutionalized can be a base or a 'home' for further studies of *work-oriented design of computer artifacts*. As mentioned above, my emphasis is not on the names of such departments, whether they should be called computer science, information science, information processing, informatics, datalogy or whatever, but on the 'spaces' for doing research and teaching on the art and science of designing computer artifacts.

Part II has the following structure:

In chapter 6, *From Systems Design to Design of Computer Artifacts* I relate the subject matter to some existing positions on systems design in Scandinavia and outline a frame of reference in line with the discussions in the part on *Design Philosophy*.

I will then (chapter 7) turn to a critique of the *science of design of the artificial* by Herbert A. Simon, since the problematic influence of his scientific program on computer science is mandatory, not only for artificial intelligence and the understanding of complex hierarchical systems, but also for computer science as an empirical discipline.

In chapter 8, *Other Ways of Seeing and Doing I – Internal Alternatives*, I discuss contributions to an art and science of designing computer artifacts from 'within' computer and information science. The contributions discussed are: 'social system design methods', 'a new foundation of design', and 'a changing paradigm in software engineering'.

In chapter 9, *Other Ways of Seeing and Doing II – External Alternatives*, I investigate contributions from other 'design disciplines' than those focusing on computer artifacts. Developments in the 'design methodology movement' are introduced, and a 'catalogue' of paradigm examples from architectural design are considered.

Finally, in chapter 10, *Conclusions: A Subject Matter and a Tentative Program* for the art and science of designing computer artifacts is outlined.

*Chapter 6*

# From Systems Design to Design of Computer Artifacts

The purpose of this chapter is to 'define' the subject matter for an art or science of designing computer artifacts.

I will relate my understanding of the subject matter to approaches in the field of 'systems design', and I will relate 'definitions' of design and design science to the approaches discussed in the part on *Design Philosophy*. In particular, I will consider the conceptualization of design, the means used in design, and the artifacts and use situations designed.

The chapter expresses a frame of reference, to be used later in this part, when I discuss the different contributions to a curriculum in design of computer artifacts.

## 'Systems Design'

'The proper study of mankind is the science of design'[1] Herbert Simon concludes in his well-known book, *The Sciences of the Artificial*. That may or may not be true. My inquiry is much more constrained. I will try to distinguish important features of an art or a science of design of computer artifacts. What I have in mind is a subject matter close to what goes under such names as 'systems design', 'systems development', and 'systemeering'. This is the study of the kind of production and creation processes that typically contribute to new or changed computer ap-

[1] Simon, H.: *The Sciences of the Artificial*, The MIT Press, Cambridge 1969, p. 83.

plications in organizations, e.g. 'a production control system' or 'tools for desktop publishing'.

Historically, the field borrowed its concepts from engineering in general and from early experiences of developing computer applications.[2]

'Systems design' was typically seen as a step-by-step method, starting with a phase of *analysis* of problems, needs, requirements, etc., then a *design* phase resulting in formal requirement specifications, then (based on these) a phase involving *construction* of the computer application, and finally *implementation* of the system.[3] The emphasis was on the technical system running on the computer and on techniques for formal specifications of this system.

When developed as an academic discipline in Scandinavia, both the phase or step-by-step approach, and the inability to deal with organizational and environmental aspects of the design were criticized, as was the lack of user participation in the development process. Especially the need for a theory of systems design was stressed, as opposed to just a collection of practical and normative principles.[4]

The state of art in the beginning of the 1980s in systems design as an academic discipline in Scandinavia can be seen in two dissertations.

In the tradition of Börje Langefors and Mats Lundeberg, Göran Goldkuhl defined *systemeering* as people's work with analysis and design of computer-based or

[2] For an overview see e.g. Boguslaw, R.: *The New Utopians – A Study of System Design and Social Change*, Prentice-Hall, Englewood Cliffs 1965.

[3] See e.g. Sveriges Standardiseringskommission: *Riktlinjer för administrativ systemutveckling*, SIS-Handbok 113, Stockholm 1973 (English version: *Systems Development –A Constructive Model*, SIS handbook 125, Stockholm 1975), and Andersen C. et al.: *Syskon – en bog om konstruktion af datamatiske systemer*, Gads Forlag, Copenhagen 1972.

[4] See e.g. Bansler, J.: *Systemudvikling – teori og historie i skandinavisk perspektiv*, Studentlitteratur, Lund 1987 (dissertation), and the coming part on *Designing for Democracy at Work*.

manual information systems. Prior to systemeering there has to be a decision in an organization to develop an information system. An information system

is intentionally arranged by certain people and the purpose of its utilization is to inform certain people of something. An information system is always part of a larger interpretation and action field. A formalized and computer-based information system can consist of the following functions: deduction of messages; transportation of messages; storage of messages. (...) This process can be supported by the aid of methodology. I define such a methodology as consisting of: concepts (definitions); division into problem areas; method steps, order and contents; description techniques.[5]

To Goldkuhl, systemeering does not include construction in the sense of writing computer programs or manual instructions. However it is construction in the sense of design of models of future information systems.[6]

Lars Mathiassen,[7] in the tradition of Kristen Nygaard, suggested that *systems development* should be understood as a labor process. The term systems development process was advocated partly for historical reasons, but at the same time because programs and computers are essential parts of systems development and that it is relevant to understand them as systems.[8]

Mathiassen distinguished between the *functions* and the *methods* of the systems development labor process.

---

[5] Goldkuhl, G.: Framställning och användning av informations-modeller, TRITA–IBADB–4099, University of Stockholm, 1980 (dissertation), p. 288 (my translation).

[6] Ibid., p. 289.

[7] Mathiassen, L.: *Systemudvikling og Systemudviklingsmetode*, DAIMI PB–136, Department of Computer Science, University of Aarhus 1981 (dissertation).

[8] Mathiassen, op. cit., pp. 45–48.

The continuously ongoing *functions* (as opposed to stages ordered in time) that he used to characterize the content of systems development are:

- *change* of an organization
- based on iterative *decision-making*
- with prior *investigations*
- as the basis for *construction* of computer applications that via the change function are integrated into the organization
- and a precondition for these functions is the function of *communication* between individuals and groups with relation to the system development process.

As systems development *methods* he characterized principles for how to carry out systems development, including tools, techniques, and principles for organization of the labor process. Methods are based on an understanding of the functions of systems development. *Descriptions* are important sub-functions of investigation, communication, construction and change. They are used both in communication about changes and as complete formal descriptions in a programming language to be automatically executed by a computer.

With the Marxist inspired approach by Mathiassen and the phenomenologically inspired approach by Goldkuhl steps were taken towards a reformulation of the engineering approaches to the subject matter for a science of design of computer artifacts in Scandinavia. The users had become visible in the design process. Human and social sciences, just as much as natural sciences, received emphasis.

Professionally I grew up within the same traditions that formed the above approaches, and my way of thinking about the subject matter has family resemblance with the examples.

However, though computers and information systems are central to the subject matter I find it far from obvious that concepts like systems, descriptions, models, information, and data should be fundamental to our thinking about design of computer artifacts.[9]

Hence, I will now take a broader view of the subject matter, putting questions like: What do we mean by design and design methods? What are the characteristics of using computers as compared with other artifacts? What does it mean to design these artifacts and their use? I will provide, and elaborate on, arguments I have found in design literature that fit with the understanding suggested in the part on *Design Philosophy*.

## Design

Let us start with some 'definitions' of design and design science found in the literature.

My dictionary suggests that to design is to:[10]

* make preliminary sketches of; sketch a pattern or outline for; plan
* plan and carry out, especially by artistic arrangement or in a skillful way
* form (plan, etc.) in the mind; contrive
* plan to do; purpose; intend
* to intend or set apart for some purpose

The second point, 'to plan and carry out by artistic arrangement or in a skillful way', comes closest to my understanding of design.

In defining a science of design Herbert Simon has suggested not only, as mentioned, that 'the proper study of mankind is the science of design' , but also that 'everyone

---

[9] This does not imply that I understand technical aspects of computers, programs, systems, data, information etc., as external to the subject matter. Professional designers will need this kind of competence to be good designers. They will need it to be able to design according to technical possibilities and constraints. Many of them will also be good programmers. This is not very different from an architect's knowledge of building techniques, materials etc.

[10] *Websters New World Dictionary*, 1982, p. 382.

designs who devises courses of action aimed at changing existing situations into preferred ones.'[11] Or a bit more elaborated:

> Engineering, medicine, business, architecture, and painting are concerned not with the necessary but with the contingent – not with how things are but with how they might be – in short, with design. The possibility of creating a science or sciences of design is exactly as great as the possibility of creating a science of the artificial.[12]

I will return to Simon's position in a later chapter. Here I will only remark on the problem of knowing what a 'preferred situation' is. Preferred by whom? Under what social and historical conditions? Such questions – typically posed by the social and human sciences – have, I think, to be an integrated aspect of a science of design. Furthermore, why a science of the artificial? Why not of the practical, of changes and reforms in the practice of using computer artifacts? Such a position comes closer to my arguments in the part on *Design Philosophy*, and the foundation for a science of design suggested by Terry Winograd and Fernando Flores. In 'defining' design they argue that :

> it constitutes an intervention in the background of our heritage, growing out of our already-existent ways of being in the world, and deeply affecting the kinds of beings that we are. In creating new artifacts, equipment, buildings, and organizational structures, it attempts to specify in advance how and where breakdowns will show up in our everyday practices and in the tools we use, opening up new spaces in which we can work and play. Ontologically oriented design is therefore necessarily both reflective and political, looking backwards to the tradition that has formed us but also forwards to as-yet-uncreated transformations of

[11] Simon, op. cit., p. 54.
[12] Ibid., p. xi.

our lives together. Through the emergence of new tools, we come to a changing awareness of human nature and human action, which in turn leads to new technological development. The designing process is part of this 'dance' in which our structure of possibilities is generated.[13]

Such a 'definition' of design goes beyond a rationalistic conception of design restricted to methodology for conscious design. As Winograd and Flores put it:

> We address the broader question of how a society engenders inventions whose existence in turn alters that society. We need to establish a theoretical basis for looking at what the devices do, not just how they operate.[14]

I agree with this position. As one of the consequences I see the need for two kinds of theories in a science of design. We need *instrumental* theory on how to do design. This aspect is characteristic to design science as opposed to natural, social and human sciences in general. But as in any other science we also need *substantial* theory about the phenomenon of design, about e.g. what kind of social, historical, scientific, artistic, and technical activity design is.[15] Especially, we need approaches that integrate instrumental and substantial theories.

Winograd and Flores's 'definition' of design is in line with the approaches discussed in the part on *Design Philosophy*. In many way it constitutes the Heideggerian approach. In a similar way the Marxist and Wittgensteinian approaches have been developed by the architect Jerker Lundequist.

---

[13] Ibid., p. 163.

[14] Winograd, T. and Flores, F.: *Understanding Computers and Cognition – a new foundation for design*, Ablex, Norwood 1986, p. 4.

[15] The distinction is due to Bunge, M.: *Scientific Research. The Search for System. The Search for Truth*, Springer 1967, who talks about operational and substantial theories.

In contributing to a general design theory he defines design as a product determining process.[16] There are, in society, social labor and production processes in which commodities and services, or in general, artifacts are produced. Before realizing or constructing these products they have to be determined as to form, function, and in terms of economic and social consequences. This is done in the design process. I agree with Lundequist, but rather than focusing on the artifacts themselves, I think we should emphasize their use. And I also think that it should be stressed that the design process very well can take place during the use of the artifacts, not just before.

Lundequist distinguishes four aspects of the design process that ought to be studied and related, in an art and a science of design. They are design as:[17]

- an *artistic and creative process*;
- an *information and decision-making process*;
- one of many *societal planning processes*;
- one of many *socially determined labor processes*.

Pursuing this, he goes on to argue that design is a special form of knowledge production. In short:

> Design is an activity that arises in the intersection between politics and economy, art and technology.[18]

And he concludes that in trying to develop general design theory we must start from the following two questions: What is a designer really *doing* ? What is really the *skill* of a designer?[19] The question of *who* the designer really is could have been added. What are different groups of people doing in the process of designing computer artifacts? Which are their skills? Who are they?

[16] Lundeqvist, J.: *Norm och Modell – samt ytterligare några begrepp inom designteorin*, Department of Architecture, Royal Institute of Technology, Stockholm, 1982 (dissertation), p. 10.

[17] Ibid., p. 11.

[18] Ibid., p. 21.

[19] Ibid., p. 27.

These questions relate to the understanding of *practice* discused in the previous part. The philosophical discussion also gave rise to the Wittgensteinian idea of design as a language game, to be played as a language-game with family resemblance to the language-games of the users, and to a Marxist understanding of design as a social and historical labor process characterized by a fundamental division of labor. The division of labor lies between the activities of planning and execution, in the sense that design interacts with and sets conditions for the process of use. Furthermore the Heideggerian approach gave rise to the idea of design as a concerned activity, a process of interpretation and breakdown, and anticipation of further breakdowns. I also concluded that the main dilemma or a fundamental characteristic of design is the dialectics between tradition and transcendence.

With the above 'definitions' as a background, I suggest, in summary, that *design* should be understood as *a concerned social and historical activity in which artifacts and their use are anticipated; an activity and form of knowledge that is both planned and creative, and that deals with the contradiction between tradition and transcendence.*

So far I have tried to outline design without taking the specific artifacts and their use into account, i.e. design of computer artifacts. Hence it is high time to ask: How can we understand the changes anticipated in design of computer artifacts and their use?

## Computer Artifacts

Thinking of computers and their use we often take for granted ideas from the domain of causal events in a physical artifact or the domain of computing in a logical artifact. The languages of systems and logic from natural science are used. Typically, we talk about logical aspects of software and physical aspects of hardware. However, as pointed out above, the design and use of computers takes place in practical situations, in domains of concerned and conventional human activity. I take the position that computers, in these domains, may be seen as the material or media from which we make artifacts. What is then an artifact?

My dictionary 'defines' *artifacts* as objects made by human work, especially primitive tools. In the Marxist approach discused in the previous part, it was pointed out that artifacts not only reflect social relations, but are social relations. According to the Heideggerian approach, *use* of artifacts (or rather of 'Zeug', including the tools that we use as well as the clothes we wear and the houses we live in) was to be understood as fundamental to human existence. A carpenter's understanding of a hammer in ordinary hammering is its use. Only in breakdown does the hammer as handle and head become present-at-hand to him.

Deliberately or not, in design of artifacts we design not only the artifacts but also conditions for their use. Hence, in design of artifacts the situation of the users and their understanding of it should be anticipated and included, rather than seen as external to the design of the artifact.

Now to some characteristics of artifacts understood as their use:[20]

Artifacts can support both *communicative* and *instrumental* activities. Artifacts can *mediate* our activity towards other humans or towards 'objects'. A telephone or a book are examples of artifacts mediating communication; they are used to e.g. coordinate activities in time and space. *Language* is important in this aspect. A hammer or an electric drill are examples of artifacts mediating instrumental activities: they can typically be used to refine 'products'. Human *work* is important in this aspect. However, many artifacts are designed to support both

[20] These aspects are further developed with special reference to computer artifacts in Bødker, S.: *Through the Interface – A Human Activity Approach to User Interface Design,* DAIMI PB–224, Department of Computer Science, University of Aarhus, 1987 (dissertation).

communicative and instrumental activities. Think, for example, of a house.

Another aspect of artifacts understood as their use is the *degree and character of externalization* of human activity. An artifact can *augment* a human activity more or less. It can also *replace* it more or less. A telephone may augment the communicative side of a human activity. We can talk over a longer distance. A telephone answering machine may replace the communicative side of the human activity of taking a message. Automatic dial numbers on a telephone may replace the instrumental side of the activity of calling another person. An electric drill may augment the activity of drilling, whereas a drilling machine may replace it. An assembly robot for automobiles may replace both the communicative and instrumental side of the activity of assembling. Degree and character of externalization are closely related to questions of *skill and competence.*

Furthermore artifacts can to a varying degree augment or replace *individual* or *cooperative* human activities. For a hammer the individual aspect may be most important. For a conference room the cooperative aspect may be in focus. Cooperative and communicative aspects of use of artifacts are closely related to the questions of *participation, decision-making* and *democracy.*

In the use of an artifact the users' activity is both augmented and constrained by the artifact. On the one hand the artifact is concernfully and purposefully used, because it is thought of as something that can be useful to carry out the intention – like killing an animal, typing a letter or communicating an idea. On the other hand, in use the artifact also stands in the way of carrying out the intention. For what and how an artifact can be used depends on the material it is made out of.

The fundamental characteristic of *computers as the material or medium* to design artifacts from, as opposed to e.g. wood or clay, is that it has a capacity for symbol manipulation. This is what is utilized when *computer artifacts* are designed, even when we use them as e.g. a word processor, a spreadsheet, a mail handler, a coordinator, etc. Alan Kay has put it this way:

> One feels the clay of computing through the 'user interface': the software that mediates between a person and the programs shaping the computer into a tool for a specific goal, whether the goal is designing a bridge or writing an article. The user interface was once the last part of the system to be designed. Now it is the first. It is recognized as being primary because, to novices and professionals alike, what is presented to one's senses *is* one's computer. [21]

This *user interface* of a computer artifact should be understood in relation to intentions of the use activity. Hence, functionality of a computer artifact is a relation between the user and the artifact, something that is found in the use activity, not just a property of the artifact. The user interface is both form and function, in the sense that it from the user's point of view conditions not only *how* but also *what* can be done through the artifact. The functionality comprises the remaining possible actions when the user's intentions have been constrained by the user interface.

In designing computer artifacts emphasis should be on concernful design of *signs* that make sense in the language-game of use. We design signs to be used as *reminders* of the user's earlier experiences, to speak in the Wittgensteinian language. The signs remind us of what we can do with the artifact. They can remind the user of earlier use of the artifact, but often they are used metaphorically. A user interface of a computer artifact to be used for document preparation can remind the user of earlier use of this specific artifact, but it can also be designed to remind the user of experiences from typewriting. Then metaphorical signs are used to create a family

---

[21] Kay, A.: 'Computer Software' in *Scientific American*, vol 251, no 3, September 1984, p. 42.

resemblance with the use of a typewriter in a well known language-game of document preparation.

It may be true that in the beginning we understand all artifacts, not only computer artifacts, metaphorically, as something already familiar. However, computer artifacts are in many use situations relatively new phenomena, and they are often redesigned. Hence, a stable use tradition, in which the computer artifact has a conventional meaning, frequently does not exist. To design computer artifacts metaphorically, as something new but with family resemblance with something well known, becomes a way of avoiding breakdowns for the user.

However, the sign aspect is far from the only aspect of importance in designing computer artifacts. As with other artifacts we may e.g. be interested in:[22]

- *physical* aspects
- *handling* aspects, i.e. conditions for operating or controlling the artifact
- *subject/object directed* aspects i.e. conditions for activities towards 'objects' or with 'others' via the artifact
- *ergonomic* aspects
- *aesthetic* aspects.

In summary I have suggested that in designing artifacts we should consider them as mediating instrumental and/or communicative activities; as supporting individual and/or cooperative activities; as augmenting and/or replacing human activities; as function and form that are irrevocably interconnected

All these characteristics apply to computer artifacts. However they are based on a material or medium – computers having a specific capacity for symbol manipulation – that can be shaped quite flexibly with regard to the different activities and aspects summarized above. Thus, a special characteristic of computer artifacts

---

[22] For a human activity approach to the physical, handling, and subject/object directed aspects of computer artifacts, see Bødker op. cit.

seems to be the kind of reminders they can be designed to be. These reminders may be in the tradition of the use of artifacts in a specific use activity, or they may transcend it.

In any case, a computer artifact is fundamentally what it is to the user in practical use and understanding, not what we find in detached reflection about its properties. If we focus on computers as their use, they must primarily to be understood as practical artifacts that are designed for and used in practice, not as objects that are related in a system. It is this practice that we must understand.[23]

I will now turn to some characteristics of how we design artifacts.

## Norms, Rules and Design Artifacts

The means we apply in design typically go under names such as *methods, models, descriptions, prototypes, mock-ups* and the like. Earlier I referred to some 'definitions' of these means in design of computer artifacts.

To Mathiassen methods may be characterized by principles for how to do systems development, including tools, techniques, and principles of organization of the labor process. Methods are based on an understanding of the functions of systems development. But there is a relation between methods and models too: 'a method may be seen as a model for a subset of system development processes'.[24] Mathiassen also sees descriptions as important sub-functions of investigation, communication, construction and change. Descriptions are both used in communication about changes, and as complete formal descriptions in a programming language to be automatically executed by a computer.

To Goldkuhl a methodology consists of concepts (definitions); division into problem areas; method steps

---

[23] In chapter 17 on *The 'Toolness' of Computer Artifacts* the arguments in this section will be further developed.

[24] Mathiassen, op. cit., p. 99.

and their order and content; description techniques. Information models are made according to certain rules of description techniques. The design process can also be guided by certain method rules (i.e. prescriptions for action).

Below, I will reinterpret these means used in design as *norms , rules* , and *design artifacts* in a language closer to that in the part on *Design Philosophy*.

In design of computer artifacts methods are typically understood as some kind of prescriptions (based on theory and/or practical experiences) of how to conduct some aspect of the design process. They prescribe how to think about design and computer artifacts, how to organize the design work, which tools and techniques to use, etc. In the Wittgensteinian approach, the methods in design may be understood as *norms* or *rules* governing specific language-games of design.[25]

In suggesting that methods are norms and rules, I think of how they are used in practice. I think of norms and rules that professional designers follow, and sometimes transcend, often without being aware of them. Methodological prescriptions are explicit rules that can be used in learning a practice or reflecting about it, but they are not to be mistaken for actual rule following in a language-game. To master the norms and rules of design in practice also requires learning by examples passed on from more experienced designers and users, since there is more to design than can be captured as propositional knowledge.[26]

Norms and rules on how to manage and control a design activity as an organizational arrangement typically take the form of *project* administration. These norms and rules include who the actors in design ought to be, their relations and commitments, and most importantly, how the design process is to be managed and controlled. Man-

---

[25] This has been suggested by Lundequist, op. cit.
[26] This is further developed in chapter 18, *Skills and the Tool Perspective.*

agement and control concerns distribution of resources, coordination of activities, handling of practical deadlines, etc. Norms and rules for project administration are basically a subject matter of business administration, but have also been developed with special reference to design of computer artifacts.[27]

However, one of the problems in understanding the language game of design as a project to be administrated, is that we tend to have historically and technologically too specific types of projects in mind. There is the risk of only taking as paradigm cases design projects like: development of new large administrative computer based systems, with a special design organization distinct from the use organization, using more or less formal techniques for program specification and testing, and third generation programming languages.

Factors that may change this view of the design process include new programming environments like application generators, explorative programming, prototyping, adaption of standard software rather than development of new systems, new domains of application, etc. Projects may be carried out as individual activities, as part of and within the use activity, as redesign of existing artifacts and their use, etc. No matter which form the design process takes, design is an intervention in the practice of ordinary use activities, an intervention based on norms and rules in a social, historical, and technological setting.[28]

Now to descriptions, models, prototypes, etc. I call these means *design artifacts*. My interactive computer-based thesaurus defines 'artificial' as:

---

[27] A good practice based example is Andersen, N.E. et. al.: *Professionel Systemudvikling*, Teknisk Forlag, Copenhagen 1986.

[28] I will not discuss aspects of management, control and planning of design any further in this part, but return to the subject in the part on *Designing for Democracy at Work*. Here my emphasis will be on design as a creative process and the design artifacts we use to this end in design.

- taking the place of something else and especially of something finer or more costly
- lacking in spontaneity and genuineness
- formed or developed by human art, skill, or effort and not by natural processes
- typical synonyms are: affected, assumed, dummy, ersatz, factitious, false, feigned, imitation, man-made, mock, sham, simulated, spurious, substitute.

I regard the above as a good characteristic of what design artifacts are. The role of design artifacts in the language-game of design is as *reminders* and as *paradigm cases* for our reflections on existing and future computer artifacts and their use.[29] The use of design artifacts brings earlier experiences to our mind and it 'bends' our way of thinking about the future. I think it is in this sense we should understand them as *re*-presentations.[30]

I see descriptions or models as design artifacts to objectify experiences, visions, and ideas relevant for communication in the design process. This may be communication between designers, between users, or between designers and users. Typically they are textual or graphical reminders. They have names like data or information flow diagrams, descriptions of existing and future labor processes, models of computer system architecture, information system models, program specifications etc. These kind of artifacts support *reflection*.

Another category of design artifacts is prototypes, mock-ups, scenarios with role playing, etc. They differ from descriptions and models in the sense that they also allow for involved practical *experience*, not just detached reflections. Since these kind of artifacts support both detached reflection and involved experience, they can be used as reminders or paradigm cases, not only of proposi-

---

[29] See chapter 4, *Language-Games – A Wittgensteinian Approach* for a further discussion.

[30] This has been suggested by Kaasbøll, J.: *A Theoretical and Empirical Study of the Use of Language and Computers,* Department of Informatics, University of Oslo, forthcoming (dissertation).

tional knowledge but also of practical understanding. They give better support to the ideal of design to be played as a language-game with family resemblance with the users' ordinary language-games.

However, textual and graphical reminders may also be used beyond detached reflection. A good example is the design artifacts called maps. Maps are intended for reflection-in-action, on-the-spot diagnoses of what is happening in a design situation. With reference to theory of action[31] Lanzara and Mathiassen[32] have developed design artifacts as means for active intervention in design situations themselves, as well as in the use situation designed for.[33]

Often, but far from always, the material or medium out of which we make design artifacts is computers. This is for instance the situation in prototyping. Hence, the design artifact is made out of the same material as the computer artifact that we are designing. I have heard the argument that this is what is specific about design of computer artifacts, as opposed to e.g. architectural design. However, no matter how efficient the code in the prototype is, a piece of correct code is not the same thing as the final computer artifact. The computer artifact should be understood as its use. Hence, as long as the design situation does not entirely overlap the use situation, the design artifact is not identical with the anticipated computer artifact.

[31] Argyris, C. and Schön, D.A.: *Organizational Learning: A Theory of Action Perspective*, Addison-Wesley, Reading 1978.

[32] Lanzara, G.F. and Mathiassen, L.: 'Mapping Situations Within a System Development Project' in *Information & Management* 8, 1985.

[33] The design artifacts discussed by Lanzara and Mathiassen are *diagnostic maps, ecological maps, virtual maps* and *historical maps*.

## Summary

In this chapter I have outlined some fundamental characteristics of designing computer artifacts.[34] I have tried to do this in a language closer to the philosophical positions argued in the preceding part than the often taken for granted rationalistic understanding of what design is all about.

I have argued that we should understand *design of computer artifacts* as a concerned social, historical, creative, and planned activity in which we try to anticipate computer artifacts and their use.

I have chosen to regard computers as the material or medium out of which *computer artifacts* can be designed. When designing computer artifacts we utilize the capacity for symbol manipulation in this material, in order to design them as signs that remind the users of earlier experiences. *Use* is emphasized in my 'definition' of computer artifacts. Design concerns the practical rather than the artificial. What we design is not primarily artifacts, but a changed or reformed practice.

I have used concepts such as *norms* or *rules* and *design artifacts (reminders* or *paradigm cases)* rather than *methods, descriptions* and *models,* to avoid the rationalist conception of design that such concepts come from. However, in the following chapters I will often use the 'old' terms to avoid too strange a language, even though the intended meaning will be the 'new' one.

I have also suggested that in the search for a science of design of computer artifacts we should look for *instrumental* theories proposing design norms or rules to be followed, and for *substantive* theories giving better understanding of what we do in design of computer artifacts.

I do not think that the position taken here on what design of computer artifact is all about, is very different from the positions of Mathiassen and Goldkuhl, referred ear-

---

[34] Most of them will be further developed in the part on *Designing for Skill.*

lier. But by discussing the language-games of systems design and system design methods in a language free from systems, data, information models, and methods, an understanding is offered that transcends the Cartesian rationalistic conception of what design is all about.

With the above discussed concepts, and those from the more philosophical part on design philosophy, I will now take a closer look at some of the candidates for forming a basic program for the art and science of designing computer artifacts, and a curriculum for its study. Such programs and a curriculum for its study already exist in the rationalistic tradition. Hence I start out with a critical note on the rationalistic foundation of the science of design of the artificial by Herbert Simon.

## Chapter 7

# 'The Science of Design' – A Note on Herbert Simon's Program

In a famous lecture at M.I.T. in 1968, Noble Prize winner Herbert A. Simon outlined a program for a science of design, and a curriculum for training of professional designers. He did this with engineering as an example, but argued that it was just as relevant for e.g. management science or computer science, fields from which he himself had experience. In fact he argued that[1]

> everyone designs who devises courses of action aimed at changing existing situations into preferred ones. (...) Schools of engineering, as well as schools of architecture, business, education, law, and medicine, are all centrally concerned with the process of design.

In a broader perspective he concluded, as earlier mentioned, that[2]

> the proper study of mankind is the science of design, not only as the professional component of a technical education but as a core discipline for every liberally educated man.

Simon based this latter statement on his experiences from having lived close to the development of the modern computer and the growing communication among intellectual disciplines taking place around the computer. The

---

[1] Simon, H.: *The Sciences of the Artificial*, The MIT Press, Cambridge 1969, pp. 55.

[2] Ibid., p. 83.

ability to communicate across fields does not come from the computer as such, he argues, but from the need to 'be explicit, as never before, about what is involved in creating a design and what takes place while the creation is going on.'[3] With the philosophical investigations in the previous part as background, some skepticism towards this interpretation should be recommended. What kind of design knowledge can be communicated by being explicit as never before? Is this really the essence of the language-games of design?

However, his theory for, and curriculum in, design should indeed be most relevant to discuss in the context of designing computer artifacts. After all, computer science and management science are two disciplines which he has a great deal of experience with, and they both deal with our subject matter. Furthermore, few scientists have been as influential in our field as he has.

Before looking at his program, let us see how he poses the problem. It may sound paradoxical that he is proposing that something is wrong with the natural science based education in the design disciplines. He observes that in order to gain academic respectability e.g.:

> engineering schools have become schools of physics and mathematics; medical schools have become schools of biological science; business schools have become schools of finite mathematics. The use of adjectives like 'applied' conceals, but does not change, the fact.[4]

He argues that this way of acquiring a scientific subject matter has moved the design disciplines away from their real subject – design of the artificial. Simon takes the position that what was traditionally known about design was 'intellectually soft, intuitive, informal, and cookbooky'[5], and that this is scientifically unsatisfactory. However, at the same time he claims that design of the artificial is re-

[3] Ibid., p. 83.

[4] Ibid., p. 56.

[5] Ibid., p. 57.

ally what most professions are about. Thus it cannot be replaced by mathematics, physics etc. This understanding of a fundamental dilemma for design sciences is an important observation by Simon.

The alternative that Simon suggests is *a science of design of the artificial*, a genuine science of its own. His elegant solution is to *pose the problem* of design of the artificial in such a way that we can apply methods of logic, mathematics, statistics etc., just as we do in the natural sciences. Let us proceed to the scientific alternative to the traditional 'cookbooky' knowledge about design – to the science of Herbert A. Simon.

## The Program for a Rationalistic Science of Design

> The proper study of those who are concerned with the artificial is the way in which adaption of means to environments is brought about – and central to that is the process of design.[6]

Such a science of design of the artificial did, according to Simon, already exist in the late sixties, 'particularly through programs in computer science and 'systems engineering''.[7] Management science was also included among the systems or design sciences that had started to develop 'a body of intellectually tough, analytic, partly formalizable, partly empirical, teachable doctrine about the design process.'[8]

To Simon the natural sciences are concerned with how things are, whereas design is concerned with how things *ought to be* – we devise artifacts to attain goals. However, Simon sees no need for a new logic to deal with the normative character of design. The problem of design can be

6 Ibid., p. 58.
7 Ibid., p. 58.
8 Ibid., p. 58.

reduced to declarative logic. We can, according to Simon, achieve this by:

*1. Utility theory and statistical decision theory – a logical framework for rational choice among given alternatives.*[9]

This is the field of optimization methods, and the first topic in Simon's curriculum in design. In a design there exists a set of alternative actions, *command variables*. The environment which we design in can be represented by a set of *fixed parameters* and perhaps a number of *constraints*. Command variables are linked to the given constraints by a *utility function*.

> The optimization problem is to find an admissible set of values of the command variables, compatible with the constraints, that maximize the utility function for the given values of the environmental parameters. (In the probabilistic case, we might say, 'maximize the expected value of the utility function,' for instance, instead of 'maximize the utility function.')[10]

When a design problem is formalized in this way, 'it is evident that the logic used to deduce the answer is the standard logic of the predicate calculus on which mathematics rests.'[11] According to Simon no special logic of imperatives is needed because we are dealing with sets of *possible worlds* – the worlds that meet the constraints in the environment and maximize the utility function.

> We simply ask what values the command variables would have in a world meeting all these conditions and conclude that these are the values the command variables should have.[12]

Simon's approach is an elegant way of dealing with the normative character of design, but far from useful for

9 Ibid., p. 62.
10 Ibid., p. 60.
11 Ibid., p. 62.
12 Ibid. p. 62.

most situations of design for concerned human use of computer artifacts. In design, designers typically do not know the alternatives – *that* is what they have to find out about. Furthermore, in design many groups with different and often conflicting interests participate. They will typically neither agree on constraints nor a relevant utility function. Besides, if we accept that there is more to design knowledge than detached reflection over what can be formally described (as the philosophical inquiry has suggested), then a great deal of knowledge relevant to design is excluded by this way of representing a design situation.

However, Simon also saw problems for the rationalistic approach, e.g. that finding the optimum is a computational problem. Even if we can easily define an optimal strategy the computations required may be astronomical and even beyond the capacity of prospective computers. Hence, a curriculum in the science of design should include:

*2. The body of of techniques for actually deducing which of the available alternatives is the optimum.*[13]

What Simon has in mind is linear programming theory, dynamic programming, geometric programming, queuing theory, control theory, etc.

But rationalistic reasoning logically faces another practical problem. It requires full knowledge of the outerworld being investigated. This is impossible, since in a given practical situation we cannot anticipate all future consequences. We are forced to operate with what Simon called 'satisficing' solutions and 'bounded rationality'.

> We satisfice by looking for alternatives in such a way that we can generally find an acceptable one after only moderate search.[14]

As designers we have to search an enormously extensive problem space for combinations of given elements that

[13] Ibid. p. 62.
[14] Ibid., p. 65.

give a satisfactory solution to the problem. To this end we can use heuristic problem solving methods. By dividing the search into steps, directions of further search can be based on the information gained from earlier steps – design becomes a process of learning and adaption in a given but not completely known problem space. The problem is of course which steps – how to 'factorize' the problem space. To Simon, as well, this 'factorization' is a problem from the point of view of 'logic' in the design process.

However, more unsatisfactory from my point of view is the still implied reduction of the design process to individuals making rational decisions, hiding which people participate in the design process or are affected, what they know, what different interests they may have, etc. This cannot be understood with the (bounded) rationalistic approach, no matter how successfully it deals with heuristics or satificing problem solving methods.

The formal logic of design and the search for alternatives, are matters Simon develops further into three more topics in his curriculum of design. I will not comment upon them here, but add them for completeness. They are:

*3. Adaption of standard logic to the search for alternatives.*[15]

*4. The exploitation of parallel, or near-parallel, factorizations of differences.*[16]

*5. The allocation of search resources to alternative partly explored action sequences.*[17]

[15] Ibid., p. 69.
[16] Ibid., p. 69.
[17] Ibid., p. 69.

Now to Simon's view of hierarchical systems and the topic of:

*6. The organization of complex structures and its implication for the organization of the design process.*[18]

Simon's systems engineering approach is so well known that it is often taken for *the* systems approach, though we know that there are many alternatives. The basic idea is that in design of the artificial we often design complex systems. A complex system is 'made up by a large number of parts that interact in a nonsimple way.'[19] A complex system can be biological, social, physical etc. To design complex systems we have to understand them as a hierarchy of levels, or as boxes-within-boxes down to the lowest level of subsystems. The 'inner environment' of the whole system as well as of the different subsystems may be defined by describing the different systems' functions without detailed specification of the sub mechanisms in them. As a flying system, a bird and an aeroplane may have the same functionality independent of their different inner structures and processes, Simon argues.

According to Simon, the method we can apply in design of complex systems is

> to discover viable ways of decomposing it into semi-independent components corresponding to its many functional parts. The design of each component can then be carried out with some degree of independence of the design of others, since each will affect the others largely through its function and independently of the details of the mechanisms that accomplish the function.[20]

However, decomposition can be performed in many ways, including the question of how to organize the design process – the precedence and sequence of steps to take. To

---

[18] Ibid., p. 76
[19] Ibid., p. 86.
[20] Ibid., p. 73.

this end Simon saw a need for new principles to be developed and included in a theory of design.

This systems approach has had a major influence theoretically as well as practically on 'systems design' in the design of computer artifacts.[21]

I have no intention of arguing against the power of this systems approach for *controlling* complex hierarchies, whether they are design projects or computer-based systems. However, I will argue, referring to our philosophical inquiry, that this is not primarily how professionals design in areas which they really understand. Actually, an understanding of a design situation as decomposition of complex systems may destroy their creative competence. Furthermore, from my point of view there is a big difference between applying a systems perspective to artifacts like computers and to social and concerned human use of these artifacts. This leads me over to the question of representation of systems in design and Simon's last topic.

*7. Alternative representations for design problems.*[22]

Simon is much more humble in proposing solutions when it comes to representations, though he finds it a central topic of design. Actually, he poses the problem pretty close to the non-rationalistic *seeing as* that was proposed in the Wittgensteinian approach. Nevertheless, the fundamental difference is that to Simon the problem is *given* and a new representation is only a question of making it transparent. There is no doubt that Simon saw the possibilities of a rationalistic scientific theory in this domain as well, at least as a theory of properties of representations. Especially in theories of machines and programming languages he saw the basis for a theory of representations.

---

[21] Good examples of theoretical approaches are Langefors, B.: *Theoretical Analysis of Information Systems*, Studentlitteratur, Lund 1973, Lundeberg, M.: *Some Propositions Concerning Analysis and Design of Information Systems*, TRITA-IBADB-4080, Royal Institute of Technology, Stockholm 1976 (dissertation).

[22] Simon, op. cit., p. 79.

This rationalistic view takes us far away from the Wittgensteinian notion of language-games.

To sum up: The propositions from Herbert Simon's science of design of the artificial are that computers are complex hierarchical systems, as are the users and the use organizations, and as is the design process – together they are subsystems of a bigger system, and we can define their various functionalities separately. In designing these systems we can use many scientific methods (based on theory in formal logic, mathematics and statistics) for evaluation of designs and in the search for alternatives.

However, to do this it seems that we have to assume that design is a process of problem-solving by individuals making decisions among sets of possible worlds. It may be that this transforms the question of design into the rationalistic scientific vein, but at the same time most essential aspects of design are lost. I am thinking of the creativity of professional designers and users that cannot be reduced to formalized decision-making. I am also thinking of the social and historical character of the design process – the conflicting interests, the differences in skill, experiences and professional languages. Given such aspects, but little in the science of design of the artificial seems useful in organizing the design process, and in developing reminders, paradigm cases, etc., in the design process.

About computer artifacts, the science of design of the artificial, informs us that computers are systems

> of elementary functional components in which, to a high approximation, only the function performed by those components is relevant to the behavior of the whole system.[23]

Scientifically they can be studied both as abstract objects by mathematical theory and as objects in an empirical science of the behavior of computers as complex systems. At the same time the computer artifact is also seen 'as a tool for achieving a deeper understanding of human be-

[23] Ibid., p. 18.

havior.'[24] This is argued because of its similarity in organization of components with the 'most interesting of all artificial systems, the human mind'.[25]

The science of design of the artificial leads us in the direction of what we today know as the discipline of artificial intelligence. And even though computer artifacts are in the center of most of Simon's examples of a science of design of the artificial, we are not told how to design computer artifacts that can be skillfully used by concerned users.

No matter how 'intellectually tough, analytic, partly formalizable, partly empirical, teachable [a] doctrine about the design process'[26] Herbert Simon's rationalistic science of design of the artificial is, it answers very few questions about the design of computer artifacts as I have formulated the inquiry. We are forced to question Simon's argument that since we have explicit knowledge of the design process in computer programs running optimizing algorithms, search procedures, etc., there is no need to retreat to 'the cloak of 'judgment' or 'experience''.[27] Yet the practical understanding that we cannot formally describe and put into the computer may well be the most essential experience and judgement in professional design. In his rationalistic perspective Simon has very little to suggest on principles for organizing the design process, and on theory of descriptions. Is it more than a coincidence that exactly these questions are seen as the most crucial ones, when attempting to understand the subject matter of design of computer artifacts that I have outlined?

In the search for an art and a science of design of computer artifacts and a teachable doctrine about it we will have to look for further alternatives about what professional designers should do and know. Are there alterna-

[24] Ibid., p. 22.
[25] Ibid., p. 22.
[26] Ibid., p. 58.
[27] Ibid., p. 80.

tives to rationalistic 'systems engineering' to be included
in our own curriculum?

*Chapter 8*

# Other Ways of Seeing and Doing I – Internal Alternatives

In this chapter I will discuss 'internal alternatives' to be used as *paradigm cases* for an art and science of designing computer artifacts. I call them internal because they either emanate from within computer and information science, or are more concerned with the development of systems thinking than with taking a non-systems view.

My first examples are *social system design methods* like those proposed by C. West Churchman, Russel L. Ackoff and Peter B. Checkland.

The next example is a *new foundation for design* proposed by computer scientists like Terry Winograd and philosophers like Hubert Dreyfus.

My last example of internal alternatives is a changing paradigm – *from product-orientation to process-orientation* – within software engineering, as outlined by Christiane Floyd. I will especially stress the *new potential for design in the use of prototyping software.*

## Social System Design Methods

My first alternative approaches to Simon's systems engineering I have called social systems design methods, and I have labeled them as internal alternatives. By this I indicate that they have their origins in natural science, mathematics and logic oriented environments like operations research and systems analysis. They still argue the importance of systems thinking as detached rationality, but counter in many respects the view of Simon on the role of subjectivity in social systems design.[1]

## The Systems Approach

*The Systems Approach*[2] and *Design of Inquiring Systems*[3] by C. West Churchman is a challenging alternative to systems engineering. The philosophical richness of the alternative is beyond what can be summarized here – it grasps almost the entire history of modern western philosophy.

To Churchman a designer is engaged in detached reflection over the possibilities for developing and implementing good systems. In this he is guided by the *systems approach*. This is a special development of ideas from American pragmatism, especially Churchman's philosophical mentor E. A. Singer. The systems approach is a methodology the designer can apply. When the designer sees something as *related components in a system* he does this for pragmatic reasons – there is a *purpose* to the system. This purpose is the purpose of the *client*. Who the client is, is not given. To find out is part of the inquiry. If the purpose of the system changes, the designer has chosen another client. It is also part of the inquiry to find the

[1] For the arguments in this section I am very much indebted to a dialectical debate in *Journal of Applied System Analysis*, vol 9, 1982 and vol 10, 1983. The debate was initiated by Michael C. Jackson and addressed *The nature of 'soft' systems thinking* by C. West Churchman, Russel L. Ackoff, and Peter B. Checkland. It should be clear that I share with Jackson admiration for their methodological contributions to design, as well as criticism from a social theory point of view of their idealism. Later in the part on *Designing for Democracy at Work* I will make it clear how this position has guided my practical actions research work with trade unions since 1974.

[2] Churchman, C. W.: *The Systems Approach*, Delta, New York 1968.

[3] Churchman, C.W.: *The Design of Inquiring Systems–basic concepts of systems and organization*, Basic Books, New York 1971.

*decision-maker*. Like the client, the decision-maker is also a user of the system; he controls the *resources* of the system. The *environment* of the system is what is of importance, but beyond the control of the decision-maker. In designing systems the designer also needs a *measure of performance*. Otherwise there is no way to express improvement – that some situation appears to be clearly better than it was before. Ideally this is improvement of human conditions.

But who really does apply the systems approach? Not the ordinary designer, the one we know as a consultant who accepts the goals of the system as given by the decision-maker, without reflecting about whether these are the right purposes, taking the right clients into account, or the right decision-maker, etc. Nor is it the objective planner, the designer who tries to model the system objectively and simulate possible implementations. Only the *ideal designer,* the one that derives objectives and goals from

> the ethics of the systems approach, where a dialectic will emerge between the ideal of human well-being and the ideal that no one be forced to lead a life that others choose for him. In the first ideal, experts play an important role; especially those who perceive the larger system; in the second, everyone is an expert.[4]

In the ideal situation the designer, client and decision-maker are the same group or person.

As I understand the systems approach applied to the processes of designing computer artifacts and their use, it is a humanistic ethical ideal. Churchman's humanistic designer does not, as Simon's scientific designer, solve given problems, but tries first to identify the problems to be solved in the interest of humanity. In ordinary practice of design most of the crucial aspects of the system may be given, but should be challenged. To this end the systems approach can be instrumental. How far from Simon's ap-

[4] Churchman C.W.: *The Systems Approach and its Enemies*, Basic Books, New York 1979, p. 94.

proach this takes us may be illustrated by the following reflections in a recent paper by Churchman.

> Over the years I've asked my students to look at various systems, and among other things, to use their own ethical intuitions and judgement to decide whom the system is serving and whom the system should serve.

> With one exception among hundreds of such systems studies, the students judged that these two classes are different, often seriously different. In other words, the systems being studied served the ethically wrong client.

> From the point of view of the systems designer, this is another shocking result. What's the point of designing a system by an elaborate model and impeccably collected information in order to maximize a performance measure which serves the wrong people?[5]

Another difference compared with Simon's systems engineering approach is the view of objectivity in descriptions. Instead of transforming the normative *ought* into the scientific *is* of mathematics and logic, Churchman suggests that the *is* is always an *ought*. It is a social convention. The meaning of the description 'X is P' is 'the object observed is to be taken as having the property P plus or minus *epsilon*.' [6] As a consequence the quality of a description depends on how different views it captures. Objectivity is gained by representation of as different and divergent views as possible from subjects with different interests, background, etc.[7]

As a remarkable blend of mathematical and logic professionalism, philosophical wisdom, and religious spirit

---

[5] Churchman C.W. 'Who Should Be the Client of Systems Design', IIASA International roundtable on *The Art and Science of Systems Practice*, IIASA, November 1986.

[6] Churchman, 1971, op. cit., p. 202.

[7] This idea is developed in Ivanov, K.: *Quality Control of Information*, Royal Institute of Technology, Stockholm 1972, (dissertation).

Churchman's systems approach is certainly a serious humanistic alternative in design. As such it is a clear candidate to appear in the curriculum for design of computer artifacts. And at many institutes this is already the case.

However, given the way I have 'defined' design, I must have critical comments on this approach, as well.

To a great extent the design process is reduced to inquiring and detached reflection by the designer. Users as clients and decision-makers are certainly involved, but it is the designer that, via reflection, identifies and describes the problems. Hence, he tends to neglect the non-explicit, practical understanding of the clients in the design process. How much creativity is wasted in this way? In terms of the philosophical inquiry in the previous part Churchman's designer only considers what is present-at-hand, while the ready-to-hand practice of skillful users must be neglected. The systems approach works in the world of ideas with breakdown and transcendence, but not with practice and understanding.

Certainly Churchman's designer learns from experience, but in his idealistic conception of design (deeply rooted in the history of ideas) he foresees the social history of the labor process to be redesigned. Though humanistic in spirit, the systems approach provides no means for understanding the social and historical conditions for emancipatory design. Hence, in practice it may foster heroic designers to whom no one listens, as well as narrow goal oriented designers that follow the methodology instrumentally, but leave the humanistic ethics behind. Socially, both are tragic results of a great idea.

## Participation and Consensus

Another of the pragmatist philosopher E. A. Singer's disciples who has had a major influence on social systems thinking in operations research is Russell L. Ackoff. As with Churchman, he includes subjectivity in objectivity. But whereas Churchman is basically interested in ideas, Ackoff argues the crucial role of *participation*. To him objectivity in design 'is the social product of the open inter-action of a wide variety of individual subjectives'.[8] Ideally the design process involves as participants all those who can be directly affected by the system, its stakeholders. Ackoff's designer does not like a doctor identify or solve organizational messes by diagnoses, or prescriptions. He

> is more like a teacher than a doctor. Teachers know they cannot learn for their students; students must learn for themselves. But teachers can enable students to learn more, and more rapidly, than they can without the teachers' help.[9]

The designer is someone that through encouragement and facilitation enables the participants and stakeholders to deal more effectively with their organizational messes.

Successful participation, according to Ackoff, requires that

- it makes a difference for the stakeholders to participate,
- participation is fun, and
- implementation of the results are likely.

The first point requires equal voice in decision-making, that decisions are based on consensus, and that it can be understood how consensus will be sought and how decisions will be made if this is not possible – a surely democratic but rarely seen situation in design of computer artifacts in corporate business today.

However, Ackoff argues that in his practice such consensus has mostly been possible to achieve. By testing alternatives on which consensus cannot be reached one might find consensus on goals and then a new way of seeing the problem, he argues. If this is not possible the responsible decision-maker should make the choice. This

---

[8] Ackoff R.L.: 'The Social Responsibility of OR' in *Operational Research Quarterly*, 25, 1974.

[9] Ackoff R.L.: 'A Theory of Practice in the Social Systems Sciences' IIASA International roundtable on *The Art and Science of Systems Practice*, IIASA, November 1986.

tends, according to Ackoff, to create consensus, since conflict means that the participants lose their influence on the decision.

*Idealized redesign*[10] makes participation fun, according to Ackoff. It is 'a design of that system with which its designers would replace an existing system if they were free to replace it with whatever they wanted.' [11] The only restrictions imposed on the design are that the system should be technically feasible and capable of survival if it were brought into existence. However, there is no requirement that the system designed be capable of being implemented. It should be an ideal-seeking system designed so that it is capable of learning and adapting effectively. Ackoff argues that since the conditions assumed are so unrealistic, the design work is treated as play.

> To design is to imagine and create, and these activities are challenging and fun. Participation in idealized design enables the participants to raise their intrinsic and extrinsic values, especially their ideals, to consciousness. When the process is described to potential participants before it is initiated, it tends to invoke their curiosity. Once started, it usually generates excitement because it expands the participants' conception of what is possible. They find the process 'liberating' as well as fun.[12]

Finally, to make an implementation seem likely, Ackoff argues that the responsible decision makers have to pay for the work, that there has to be a widespread commitment to the design work being done, and that there has to be trust in the professional designers. He finds participative idealized design a good way of achieving this.

From my own research experience I find the question of *resources to unprivileged groups* just as crucial and important in design, as to *organize a consensus* despite of the risk of a genuine conflict in which there in practice is

[10] Ackoff, R.L.: *Redesigning the Future*, John Wiley, 1974.

[11] Ackoff, 1986, op.cit., p. 9.

[12] Ibid., p. 10.

no equality in decision making. In fact Ackoff himself argues in other places the importance in design of developing resources for unprivileged groups, to be controlled by the groups themselves.[13]

Churchman basically develops his understanding of design from the philosophy of knowledge, whereas Ackoff's understanding rather is supported by practical experience. However, the practice that he refers to is not the practice that I discussed in the part on philosophy of design. His practical experiences indicate that consensus between the stakeholders can and should be reached in design. It does take into account the ability and existential condition of human beings to create the world, but not the other side of practice, that their world is objective in the sense that it is created by others as institutions as well as ideas. This sets conditions for their thoughts, resources, interests, etc. With this view of practice, only theory that can help us understand the social and historical character of specific design processes can legitimate the designer's effort to create consensus among the stakeholders.[14]

There is no doubt that Ackoff's designer is a theoretical idealist, no matter how practical he is. However, this is not a neglect of the importance of Ackoff's contributions to methodology of social systems design, but a quest for theory that helps us understand when, in a humanistic perspective, the methodology should be used, and when rather to shift client or decision-maker in Churchman's terminology. Whether we want it or not, social systems design is politics, a fact which is also obvious for our third contributor to *soft systems thinking*.

[13] Ackoff, R. L.:, 'A Black Ghetto's Research on a University' in *Operations Research* , September 1970.

[14] In the part on *Designing for Democracy at Work*, I will return to this problem.

# 'Soft' Systems Thinking

Peter Checkland, like Ackoff and Churchman, started out in the tradition of rationalistic systems engineering. Like them he found that systems engineering simply was not appropriate for practical intervention in the complex and ambiguous 'soft' problem situations in social practice. His systems methodology developed in the direction of Hegelian and Singerian inquiring systems (in the terminology of Churchman[15]) – focusing on the importance of the dialectics between the many and different world views involved. With Checkland a step is also taken away from rationalistic systems thinking towards interpretation and phenomenology and the Heideggerian approach from the discussion in the part on *Design Philosophy*.

Checkland's methodology includes the following considerations:[16]

To begin with, a *rich picture* is given of how different participants may perceive various aspects of a situation to be problematic. However, there is no definition of the problem at this stage.

Out of the rich picture *root definitions* of some purposeful human activity systems are made. They are condensed representations of the system in its most fundamental form, reflecting specific ways of looking at the problematic situation – specific *Weltanschauungen.*

These root definitions are the basis for construction of *conceptual models*. They give accented one-sided views of the minimum activities which are necessary to produce a system according to a specific Weltanschauung.

The conceptual models are then compared with the rich picture, and used to structure the debate about change. The now elucidated Weltanschauungen are

[15] Churchman, *The Design of Inquiring Systems.*

[16] Checkland, P. B.: 'Systems Thinking in Management: the Development of Soft Systems Methodology and its Implications for Social Science' in Ulrich, H. and Probst, G.J.B. (eds.): *Self-organisation and Management of Social Systems,* Springer Verlag, 1984.

compared and contrasted. They are held up for examination, exploring conflicts and possible changes. By this process of breakdown and reflection the participants gain new insight.

On this basis the designer helps the participants to find possible changes that are both systematically desirable and culturally feasible. This is an iterative process. Rather than a 'solution' to the original problem it creates new problem situations in a never ending learning process.

To Checkland it is obvious that this kind of rational intervention in a problematic situation is political. It is in itself a political act, and it is acting in a situation where the participants have different amounts of power and different interests. To this end Checkland, in a recent paper, suggests a process of political analysis to be part of the initial stage of the soft systems approach.[17]

The political analysis first includes the definition of the roles of:

- the *client* causing the intervention to happen,
- the *would-be problem solver,* who will bring about improvement in the problematic situation, and
- the *problem owner*, i.e. the person the would-be problem solver takes to be the problem owner.

Secondly, the existing and changing roles, values and norms in the problematic situation are analyzed.

Finally, the *abstract commodities of power,* like formal authority, intellectual authority, personal charisma, access to information, external reputation, membership of various committees etc. are analyzed.

The reason for the analyses is as a basis for reflection by the different participants. This kind of analyses, Checkland argues, 'open up issues crucial to achieving change in

[17] Checkland, P. B.: 'The Politics of Practice' , IIASA International roundtable on *The Art and Science of Systems Practice*, IIASA, November 1986.

real situations. They lead to a clearer vision of what changes are culturally feasible.' [18]

Doubtless, this kind of analysis can bring about new important insight. One can only ask, who will be powerful enough to benefit from it?[19]

To this end we will need a theoretical understanding of the social, cultural and historical conditions that shape the practice in which a given methodology can or cannot support communicative competence and undistorted communication in a framework free of domination – the emancipatory ideal set up by Jürgen Habermas and Critical Social Theory. This humanistic ideal I share with Checkland. But in order not to just remain idealists in good faith, we then also, like Habermas,[20] must relate to theory of the kind of social structures that bring about distorted communication.

## *Lack of Social Theory and of Computer Artifacts*

To sum up: All the alternative approaches above point at important aspects in the design of social systems. By realizing and including the role of subjectivity in systems design and systems descriptions they have blown new life into the concept of system. However, it is a systems concept that basically means system in the sense of a systematic approach or a methodology. As such the approaches

---

[18] Ibid.

[19] In two papers from 1973 and 1974 I argued a similar approach for trade union participation in design of computer artifacts and their use, based on a critique of Churchman's Hegelian inquiring system. However, rather than primarily emphasizing consensus formation, I argued for the development of resources on behalf of the weaker part in the dialectical confrontation between the basic assumptions of different *Weltanschauungen*. The consequences of this approach to the politics of design will be discussed in the part on *Designing for Democracy at Work*. There I will also discuss the problem of participation and the role of the designer in that social context.

[20] Habermas, J.: *Theorie des Kommunikativen Handelns*, I, II, Suhrkamp, Frankfurt 1981.

are candidates for a curriculum in an art and science of designing computer artifacts. However, to that end I see two problems with them.

Firstly, the methodologies of social systems design need to be supplemented with explicit substantial social theory that can help us understand the social, cultural and historical conditions for their practical application in different problematic situations.[21] If not they may be reduced to nothing but instruments for manipulation of social organizations, even more effective than systems engineering, despite their humanistic spirit.

Secondly, the above approaches to social systems design tell us very little about the special characteristics of designing computer artifacts.[22] To this end I now turn to another vein of internal alternatives and a new foundation of design in computer science.

## Computers and Understanding

My second internal alternative to an art and science of designing computer artifacts emphasizes on the human use of computer artifacts. It is developed by people in close contact with the field of artificial intelligence. It is not just a critique of Simon's rationalistic approach, nor an attempt to extend it to enable the design of computer artifacts in social systems. It is philosophically and practically a fundamentally different tradition. As 'founders' of this

[21] An example for developments in this direction may be the methods of *future work shops* as developed by Jungk R. and Müllert, N. R.: *Zukunftwerkstätten, Wege sur Wiederbelebung der Demokratie*, 1981, and the application of such methods in design of computer artifacts, Kensing, F.:' Generation of Visions in Systems Development' in Docherty, P et. al. (eds.) *Systems Design for Human Development and Productivity – Participation and Beyond*, Elsevier Science Publishers, North Holland, IFIP 1987.

[22] The design artifacts called *maps* are an example of possible ways in this direction. See Lanzara, G.F. and Mathiassen, L.: 'Mapping Situations Within a System Development Project' in *Information & Management*, no 8, 1985.

tradition two persons have been especially important, philosopher Hubert L. Dreyfus and computer scientist Terry Winograd.

Hubert Dreyfus argues for the relevance and importance of skill and everyday practice, in understanding the use of computers. His investigations are based on the philosophical positions of existential phenomenology in the tradition of philosophers like Heidegger and Merleau-Ponty, and the positions on ordinary language and language-games taken by Wittgenstein.

His arguments have been put forward in *What Computers Can't Do*[23] from 1972, and recently, together with his brother, operations researcher Stuart E. Dreyfus, in *Mind over Machine – The Power of Human Intuition and Expertise in the Era of the Computer*.[24]

In *Understanding Computers and Cognition – A New Foundation for Design,*[25] another recently published book, Terry Winograd together with Fernando Flores, former minister of Economics and Finance in the government of Salvador Allende in Chile, brings this view into computer science and the design of computer artifacts for human use.

Rather than proposing a systems view for understanding the artificial in general, Winograd and Flores focus on the *differences* between concernful human activity within a tradition, and computer performance. In doing so they take as their point of departure what people *do* with computers, how in cooperation with each other they are using computers, and what might be done better with them.

---

[23] Dreyfus, H. L.: *What Computers Can't Do – A Critique of Artificial Reason*, Harper & Row, New York 1972.

[24] Dreyfus, H. L. and Dreyfus, S. D.: *Mind over Machine – The Power of Human Intuition and Expertise in the Era of the Computer*, Basil Blackwell, Glasgow 1986.

[25] Winograd, T. and Flores, F.: *Understanding Computers and Cognition – A New Foundation for Design*, Ablex, Norwood 1986.

It is in involved practical use and understanding, not in detached reflection, that we find the origin of design. To them design is the interaction between understanding and creation.

What they propose is not just another design methodology, but an attempt to create a new foundation for an art and science of design.

Here I will not go into details of their theoretical framework, because it comes very close to what I already, strongly inspired by them, have outlined in the part on *Design Philosophy*, as a Heideggerian approach, and partly as a Wittgensteinian approach. What I have in mind are concepts like *thrownness, background, tradition, interpretation, ready-to-hand, present-at-hand, breakdown,* and *language as action.*

However, below I will give a short account of their approach in comparison with the rationalistic science of design.

As pointed out in an earlier chapter, in Simon's rationalistic science of design a computer artifact as well as the surrounding organization are seen as complex hierarchical systems of related components. From a systems point of view they are the same kind of phenomena. In designing such artifacts we emphasize redundancy, and on the outer functionality of subsystems in the hierarchy. This makes it possible for us to design complex systems. Furthermore, the design process is a process of rationalistic and objective (though in practice often 'bounded') problem-solving, decision-making, and choosing between alternatives. The objective of the design is to meet given specifications and design efficient use.

To Winograd and Flores, design is conceived quite differently. Computer artifacts are what they are concernfully used for. In a domain of writing documents a 'word processor' is not an assembly of electronic and mechanical devices, as it might be for a manager of a factory that builds word processors. Neither is it a collection of software, as it might be for a person who programs word processors. By emphasizing functionality in terms of issues of layout, type fonts, and the integration of text with illustrations we may be closer to the answer, but are still missing the point. The word processor exists to the user not just as a means for creating a document. The user is involved in writing e.g. a letter or a book, which is a concerned activity that takes place in a complex social and technological network within a tradition of conventions. To the user the word processor is what it is within this background. It is only in breakdown of concernful use of the word processor that it becomes present-at-hand as pieces of hardware or software, or fonts and layout.

> The computer, like any other medium, must be understood in the context of communication and the larger network of equipment and practices in which it is situated.(...) One cannot understand a technology without having a functional understanding of how it is used. Furthermore, that understanding must incorporate a holistic view of the network of technologies and activities into which it fits, rather than treating the technological devices in isolation.[26]

A computer artifact is what it is being used for in practice. In designing computer artifacts we should not primarily be concerned with meeting technical specifications for efficient use, but with understanding conditions for the future user's readiness-to-hand in using the artifacts being designed. In doing this our concern should be to anticipate the breakdown that will occur in use. This anticipation means both designing to avoid breakdowns, and support to the user to recover from breakdown situations that will occur regardless. The breakdown in question is not seen with focus on breakdown in hardware or software, but in the larger context in which the artifact becomes present-at-hand to the user.

Furthermore, with this approach to design, the point of departure in design must be that the different participants enter the process acting in situations of 'normal resolu-

---

[26] Ibid., pp. 5-6.

tion'. They understand the situation they come from. This goes for users as well as designers. This understanding includes the blindness created by the tradition they come from. The design process is characterized by a breakdown of this understanding, which creates a 'situation of irresolution'. Design is the resolution of these situations of ir-resolution, based on commitments between the participants. This is neither objective problem solving nor rationalistic decision-making. It is concerned human activity, where different traditions and backgrounds meet.

Turning to Dreyfus and Dreyfus, they are basically concerned with the difference between on the one hand human practical understanding and expertise, and on the other hand computers as 'logic machines' or 'inference engines'. One of their fundamental remarks is – as discussed in the part on *Design Philosophy* – that human knowledge on proficient and expert levels cannot be captured in formal descriptions.

In design this gives a new role to the skilled user, and a new orientation in design methodology. In the design process we should concentrate on norms, rules and design artifacts that facilitate the use of this competence. These norms, rules and design artifacts are obviously not formal descriptions, but rather support for involved activity in the design process.

It is somewhat paradoxical that those most critical to the rationalistic approach and especially its developments in artificial intelligence are those that may have the most challenging theoretical foundation for really designing skill enhancing tools in the era of the computer. This will be examined in Part IV on *Designing for Skill*.

However, I also see differences between the new foundation of design by Winograd and Dreyfus, and the direction outlined in the part on *Design Philosophy*.

There is a difference in emphasis in understanding language as action by Winograd and Flores on the one hand, and my understanding outlined in the 'definitions' in earlier chapters. This is not a difference in focus on the need for considering language as action and concerned activity based on commitment within a tradition. Nor is it a difference in subordinating the rationalistic tradition's understanding of language as description.

However, Winograd and Flores emphasize *descriptions of these speech acts* in the tradition of John Searle.[27] My focus on language as action is a more literal interpretation of Wittgenstein's language-games. Emphasis is on the design process. I propose that design should be organized as language-games of concernful playing or doing in ways that support design by experience and interaction, instead of design by description. This position is close to that of Winograd and Flores, but one that they basically develop in the Heideggerian theoretical context and less in the ordinary language context. However, this is more a question of different emphasis, and I see these views as complementary rather than as conflicting.

Being fundamentally ontological, the design approach discussed in this section does not explicitly relate to social theory supporting an understanding of the social, cultural and political conditions for a realization of the design approach advocated. However, with the emphasis on the spell of tradition and background, as well as the concern with conditions for future breakdowns in the application domain of use of computer artifacts, the approach is certainly open for such extensions.

It should also be obvious that a methodology for design, as in the social systems approaches discussed in a previous section, still remains to be developed.

However, the remarks above should not be understood as major objections to the approach to computers, understanding and design now being discussed. On the contrary I see this approach as a major breakthrough for an art and science of designing computer artifacts. It gives us a foundation for understanding both what kind of phenomenon the design process is, and how to organize it, and for understanding what kind of phenomena computer

[27] Searle, J.: *Speech Acts*, Cambridge University Press, Cambridge 1969.

artifacts are, their human use and directions for their design.

In finding that the functionality of a computer artifact must be understood as how it is being used, we also have a basis to reformulate the demands for design artifacts. What is most urgently needed, is not better linguistic notations for a more or less formal description of the functionality of a system. Instead 'descriptions' should be *reminders or paradigm cases for experiences and reflections on the use of the anticipated computer artifacts*. This points in the direction of design artifacts to support *concerned involvement*, rather than *correct description*. This may be achieved by the use of scenarios, prototypes, mockups, etc. For support for such methods I now turn to some recent theoretical and technical developments in the field of 'software engineering'.

## Software Engineering and Prototyping

Software engineering is a field of computer science where the rationalistic Cartesian systems approach really has had an influence. Its emphasis has, since the founding conference of the discipline in 1968,[28] been on computer programs as formal mathematical objects derived by formalized procedures from an abstract specification. This development was very much a reaction to the software crisis of the late 1960s caused by the advent of powerful third generation computers with complex operating systems, and numerous new sophisticated applications in many fields. The old methods and approaches were simply insufficient.

> By insisting on program and specification texts as the basis of human understanding and of proofs for program correctness, it was provided a starting-point for the task of dealing with errors in programming. By as-

[28] Naur, P. and Randell, B.: *Software Engineering*, report from a conference sponsored by the NATO Science Committee, Brussels 1969.

sociating successive development stages with the controlled transition between increasingly formalized defining documents leading eventually to computer-executable code, it offered a means of structuring software production in a way that could be controlled, the defining documents taking the place of intermediate results. By providing guidelines on how to subdivide programs into parts, it supported the division of work in large development teams.[29]

These are remarks by Christiane Floyd on the still dominant paradigm in software engineering. However, having been active in the field since its very start, she notices many 'anomalies' in this *product-oriented* paradigm.

The product-oriented view leaves the relationship between programs and the living human world entirely open:

- There is no way of checking the relevance of the specification.

- Learning and communication between developers and users can only be accommodated in the earliest stages.

- Questions pertaining to the use of programs are deferred until the program is delivered.

- The interface between users and the computer as a tool is treated locally (within one program component), and often late (the functionality of the program being determined first, and is subsequently being made more 'user-friendly' to increase acceptance). This attitude is characterized by the wide-spread use of 'syntactic sugar', referring to the attempt at improving input-

---

[29] Floyd, C.: 'Outline of a Paradigm Change in Software Engineering' in Bjerknes, et. al (eds.): *Computers and Democracy – A Scandinavian Challenge*, Avebury, 1987, p. 197.

output formats by purely syntactic means as a side-issue in programming development.[30]

As a remedy to these anomalies Floyd sees a new *process-oriented* paradigm in software engineering. It is intended, not entirely to take the place of the first, but to be the *primary point of view*. This new primary point of view in software engineering focuses on software in connection with human learning and communication in both use and development of the software. The *product* of this process is not a piece of code or an abstract software system, but tools or working environments for people. Hence, the *quality* of the product is primarily a question of e.g. its relevance, suitability or adequacy in practical use situations, which cannot be reduced to just features of the product like reliability and efficiency of programs.

Viewed as a learning process software development cannot in a process-oriented approach be reduced to a linear model of phases, ordered in time, leading to increasingly formal defining documents with the software system as the final step. By contrast software development has to be an ongoing process of cycles of re-design, re-implementation, re-evaluation in the context of the labor process where the software is used. In such design and evaluation, *design artifacts* are primarily used to support communication and cooperation in gradually discovering the product, not to make software development less dependent on people by formal specification of the product. It follows that focus in design is on discussions between users and designers and that the former should have good opportunities for trial use of early versions of the software in real life like situations.

In fact, Floyd's view of software engineering is supported by that of Peter Naur, one of the founders of the software engineering tradition. In a paper commenting on the importance of practical understanding (intuition in Naur's terminology) in software development he writes:

[30] Ibid., p. 197.

The claim is often made that certain forms, or formalizations, will guarantee the absence of flaws of arguments. What seems to lie behind such claims is the fact that by use of certain kinds of formalizations it is possible to formulate the connections between statements corresponding to a proof in terms of rules for manipulating the statements. While this property is of great interest as a matter of principle, and also is the necessary basis for mechanical proof construction and verification, and occasionally is used in the reasoning carried out by people, it provides no guarantee for the absence of flaws in the arguments used in software development making use of formalizations. (...) However what is the most suitable form or language for any situation will depend not only on degree of formalization of the description, but equally on the character of the aspect of the world to be modelled and the background experience of the programmer who has to establish the description. Thus to claim, for example, that mathematical properties of a form of notation have to be decisive in choosing it for software development, implies a gross disregard for the importance of human intuition.'[31]

Naur concludes that programmers' experience is more important than their use of formal methods; these latter, he writes

appear to be useful primarily by providing check lists that may help programmers to avoid flaws of omission, why the rules of methods in the areas of form of expression and ordering of activities are of doubtful utility.[32]

[31] Naur, P.: 'Intuition and Software Development' in *Formal Methods and Software Development*, Lecture Notes in Computer Science no. 186, Springer Verlag, 1985, p. 77.

[32] Ibid., p. 78.

Or put in a more literary way:

> what is the role of semantics in software development? Answer: neither that of the composer, nor of the librettist, the conductor, the hero, or the heroine, but that of the prompter, who does nothing but tell the actor things they know already, but that momentarily have slipped from their minds.[33]

Naur also argues against the idea of 'correctness' of a program as the matching with strictly defined specifications of user requirements, simply because such specifications are beyond what is practically possible. We do no say that a car works correctly, but perhaps that it is in working order. We can have a practical understanding of what that means. Similarly with programs: the users cannot once and for all specify what is meant by it being in working order; it is a matter of practical experience with using it in many situations which cannot all be anticipated in a specification. Hence, we here, too, have a strong argument for process-orientation with user participation and experimentation.

In this sense the new paradigm is also related to another development in contemporary software engineering – the emergence of powerful computer-based design artifacts for *prototyping* in design of computer artifacts.

Again there is far from one perspective on what prototyping is or should be.[34] Is it a 4th generation tool (typically with a database, a query language, a screen editor and a report generator), a specific prototyping environment (also including special programming languages, interaction with other programming languages, a data dictionary, etc.), or an exploratory programming environment

---

[33] Ibid., p. 79.

[34] For some classifications see Floyd, C.: 'A Systematic Look at Prototyping' in Budde, R. et al. (eds.) *Approaches to Prototyping*, Springer-Verlag, Berlin 1984, Bansler, B. and Bødker, K.: *Experimentelle teknikker i systemarbejdet*, DIKU report no 83/7, 1983, and Flensburg, P.: *Personlig databehandling*, Studentlitteratur, Lund 1986 (dissertation).

on powerful workstations (like *Smalltalk-80* or *Lisp /
Loops*)? Is prototyping a design artifact for early sketches
of a future system, or for realization of small and incomplete but still running first versions of the computer artifact
to be used? Does a prototype include just a few functions of
the future use, but in full detail, or does it rather include all
functions, but with limited functionality?

All of these are important aspects, but the crucial question, given my theoretical understanding of design artifacts, is whether prototyping design artifacts allow the
users *by involvement in experiments with different prototypes to gain experience as a basis for design requirements*? It is the *use* of prototypes as paradigm cases and
reminders, as in the Wittgensteinian approach, that is of
importance. The question is how well a prototyping design
artifact can support the creation of imaginative paradigm
cases of future use situation, and what efforts it takes to
create these prototypes.

As powerful design artifacts in this respect, prototypes
can be used as alternatives or complements to traditional
textual or graphic more or less formalized detached descriptions. Integrated with scenarios of future use, the experimental use of prototypes in design may be an important technique in playing the language-game of design, a
game of involvement and by doing, that defeats some of
the limits of formalization.

Obviously we here have a paradigm that opens up for
creativity and user participation in design of computer
artifacts, but that does not automatically make it a democratic approach. Who decides which users are going to
participate? When will the process stop, and which prototypes will be implemented? I will return to such question
in Part III on *Designing for Democracy at Work*.

To sum up: I conclude that there are developments in
software engineering, both *theoretically* towards a new
process-oriented humanistic paradigm, and *technically*
towards some powerful design artifacts and environments for prototyping. They may not be main trends, yet, I

find them fundamental to a future curriculum in design of computer artifacts.

This is not an argument that the former kind of formal knowledge in software engineering has become obsolete. As Christiane Floyd emphasizes, the new paradigm is not a rejection of mathematically based methods, but *a shift of primary point of view*. Doubtless, we still need correct and efficient programs. But what is the value of these programs if they not are relevant, suitable and adequate to the user in the use situation?

## Summary

I think that the paradigm examples discussed in this chapter are good indications, not only of the existence of theoretical movements within computer and information science that go beyond rationalistic systems thinking, but also that they together form an already quite developed theoretical base for an alternative art and science of designing computer artifacts. How this alternative can be further developed by inspiration from more mature design disciplines, such as architectural and industrial design, I will try to illustrate in the next chapter.

*Chapter 9*

# Other Ways of Seeing and Doing II – External Alternatives

In this chapter I will consider the inspiration we can get by going outside the boundaries of computer or information science in looking for *paradigm cases* for an art and science of designing computer artifacts.

In the first section I will reflect upon the multi-disciplinary attempts to establish a science of *design methodology*. It will be argued that in an art and science of designing computer artifacts we can learn a great deal from reflections on 'generations' of design methodology. Why did e.g. eminent researchers and designers like architect Christopher Alexander and industrial designer Christopher Jones, though starting very much with just as rational approaches as Simon, develop their thinking about design in quite different directions?

Compared with computer and information science, architecture is *a relatively mature art searching for its scientific identity*. Questions of style, artistic competence, and social responsibility in architectural design are , in the next section, related to our own field, and a 'catalogue' of paradigm examples to learn from is discussed. Considerations that have been important to architectural design should be worth reflecting upon for a science of designing computer artifacts. After all, houses and 'computer systems' are both social artifacts that play an important role in many peoples' lives.

# The Design Methodology Movement

*Design methodology* in general is a 'movement' or research field that has been dominated by architectural and industrial design. Leading theorists in architecture like Christopher Alexander or in industrial design like J. Christopher Jones have contributed to the movement, but important contributions have come from the field of computer science and management science as well, not least from Herbert Simon.

In *Developments in Design Methodology*[1] architect and design researcher Nigel Cross has brought together major contributions of the movement since its beginning in the early 1960s. This collection of papers covers design methodology conferences between 1962 and 1982, and contributions in the major design journals. Cross 'defines' design methodology as:[2]

> the study of the principles, practices and procedures of design in a rather broad and general sense. Its central concern is with how designing both *is* and *might be* conducted. This concern therefore includes the study of how designers work and think; the establishment of appropriate structures for the design process; the development and application of new design methods, techniques, and procedures; and reflection on the nature and extent of design knowledge and its application to design problems.

As Cross sees it, the movement has progressed from an initial interest in *prescription* of an ideal design process, via *description* of the intrinsic nature of design, into *observation* of the reality of design, and on to *reflection* on the fundamental concepts of design. Cross sees this development as a process of maturation, from which design methodology today can return to its origins, to the pre-

---

[1] Cross, N. (ed.): *Developments in Design Methodology*, John Wiley & Sons Ltd, Bath 1984.

[2] Ibid., p. vii-viii.

scription of realistic ideals. However, the understanding of design methodology has changed dramatically during this development. Many of the contributors have by practical experience, and subsequent theoretical reflection, come to abandon their early rationalistic Cartesian positions.

The design methodology debate has been chronicled in three generations.[3]

*First Generation*

The *first generation* design methods (up to the early 1970s) are Cartesian approaches, breaking the problem down into fragments and solving them separately before assembling them to a well functioning system.

Some very important contributions were Jones' *A Method of Systematic Design*[4] with emphasis on factors; Alexander's *Notes on Synthesis of Form*[5] and the misfit variables; and Simon's *The Sciences of the Artificial*[6] and the structure of ill-structured problems.

However, in practice these systems engineering techniques did not prove adequate to the 'wicked' problem of design. This was not accepted by Simon, who tried to show how 'wicked' or 'ill-structured' problems could be transformed into problems that could be solved with methods from operations research, systems theory etc. In contrast, Alexander had in the early 1970s become totally disillusioned with his own approach based on mathematics, logic and a step-by-step process. He claimed his original motive for becoming involved with design methods was because he wanted to design beautiful buildings. Since design

[3] Rittel, H.: 'Second-generation Design Methods' , and Broadbent, G.: 'The Development of Design Methods' in Cross, op. cit.

[4] Jones, J. C.: 'A Method of Systematic Design' in Jones, J. C. and Thornley, D. (eds.): *Conference on Design Methods*, Pergamon Press, Oxford 1963.

[5] Alexander, C.: *Notes on Synthesis of Form*, Havard University Press, Cambridge 1964.

[6] Simon, H.: *The Sciences of the Artificial*, The MIT Press, Cambridge 1969.

methods in no way had contributed to this his advice now was to 'forget it; forget the whole thing'. He was at that time moving in the direction of a more anti-expert participatory approach. Jones, too, radically changed his perspective on design methods in the beginning of the 1970s. He reacted strongly against 'the machine language, the behaviorism, the continual attempt to fix one's whole life into a logical framework'. In an attempt to resolve the apparent conflicts between rationality and intuition, logic and imagination, order and change, he began experimenting with art in design (like the music of John Cage). Hence, his writings also became more poems than articles.

Researchers have found it hard to demonstrate examples of 'successful' application of first generation design methods. However, architect Geoffery Broadbent has found an illustrative example of what goes 'wrong' when these methods are successfully applied.

> I am referring to the most carefully *calculated* piece of architectural and urban design that has ever been built; Disney World at Orlando, Florida. (...) Among other things, Disney World represents the most comprehensive application of queuing theory anywhere in the world. On first arrival, having parked one's car, one is picked up almost immediately by a motorized train and transferred to the monorail systems–where a system of ramps, barriers, and chains ensures that waiting passengers are distributed evenly along the station platform *before* the train arrives. From this, through the whole vast system of interrelated 'people movers' to the simple act of queuing for a meal (one walks to a counter, to be served immediately by a Disney-programmed girl, rather than walking *along* a counter and thus being delayed by other hesitant customers), one is conscious of being subject to the most subtle manipulation. (...) There is much more to it than that, but the crucial point is that in terms of techniques, and more particularly in terms of those attitudes in which the 'expert' knows best, Disney World represents the

most complete realization of first-generation design methods applied to the built environment anywhere in the world.[7]

*Second Generation*

When the design approach that gave rise to (Brave) New Disney World was abandoned it was to a great extent to open up the design process to include users and lay people. In these anti-expert *second generation* design methods (as they were chronicled by architect Horst Rittel) participation was a key element, and the designer was thought of as a midwife or a teacher, rather than as one who designs or plans for others. This was based on the assumption that expertise in design is distributed among all participants, and that the design process had an argumentative structure in which one had to make up one's mind in favor of, or against, various positions on each issue. From the mid 1970s such participative design approaches were the center of design methods debate, and the arguments were theoretical, as well as practical and political. Both existentialism and Marxism had an influence on the formation of the design methods of this generation.

To demonstrate that there also are problems associated with the second generation design methods, Broadbent gives an example of what can go 'wrong' with this approach, as well. The example is Lucien Kroll's buildings for the University of Louvain. The design methods used really allowed medical faculty and students as future users to participate in the design, and to have fun doing so.

The resultant buildings are amazing collages of rubble, brick, tile, asbestos sheeting, glass, and glass-reinforced plastics, whose random appearance obviously *expresses* the ideal of participation. Visually they are most exciting, but at a more objective level they present a great many problems. The study/bedrooms themselves are inordinately small, the circulation is extremely com-

[7] Broadbent, G.: 'The Development of Design Methods' in Cross, op. cit., pp. 338–339.

plex and, above all, the building fabric itself is perversely opposed to any concept of sensible environmental control. One section of La Meme is covered with Miesian curtain wall (is called – for that reason – Les Fascists), but it faces south-west, the worst possible orientation for such a facade in terms of solar heat gain. The famous 'solid' wall of l'Ecole has almost exactly the right amount of glazing for a south-facing facade in these latitudes, yet it actually faces due north! All this results in gross discomfort for those who have to use the buildings.[8]

Broadbent sees this as a result of insisting on total participation and neglecting to insist on exercising the necessary expertise possessed by a well-informed and skilled designer. Hence, in the late 1970s he argues the need for a *third generation* of design methods.

## Third Generation

As an approach that draws upon the better aspects of both first and second generation design methods he suggests (inspired by the philosophy of Karl Popper) that the role of the designer is to make expert design conjectures. However, these conjectures must be open to refutation and rejection by the people for whom they are made.

This brings the design methodology debate to the question of what design really is, what designers really do and know, and what they should do and know.

In this debate not only the philosophical position of social piecemeal engineering with reference to Popper is suggested. Others argue in accordance with the American pragmatist philosopher Charles Sanders Peirce the importance of 'abduction' as the logic of design.[9] Abduction suggests that something *may be*, as opposed to deduction, which proves that something *must be*, and induction, which shows that something *actually is* operative. A de-

[8] Ibid., pp. 341–342.
[9] March, L.: 'The Logic of Design' in Cross, op. cit.

sign proposal is not a logical proposition. Design initiates
novel forms: its interest is neither in the abstract forms of
logic nor in the extant forms that an empirical science in-
vestigates.

There is also the rethought position that what is wrong
with the mathematical and logical design methods is that
they are the product of a mode of reasoning alien to design.[10] The point is that there is a *designing way of thinking* that is quite different, but appropriate to the ill-defined,
untamed problems of everyday life that designers tackle.
This 'innate capability of cognitive modelling', as expressed through sketching, drawing, construction, acting
out, etc., is thought of as as fundamental to thought and
reasoning as the human capacity for language.

Still others argue the importance for design of the philosophy of ordinary language-games, as developed by
Wittgenstein.[11] This concerns the limits of verbal descriptions in design and the creativity of designers. The point is
that only a relatively small and perhaps insignificant part
of design knowledge can be expressed in verbal descriptions as *propositional knowledge* (as opposed to *practical
understanding*).[12] Hence, what designers (and users, I
would like to add) do and know, to a great extent has to be
experienced in practice, not for some romantic or mystical
reason, but because it is literally indescribable in linguistic
terms.[13]

Today, participative and creative approaches to design
are championed as candidates to replace systematic or
rationalistic design in the movement of design methodology. This is a critique that comes from inside, from some

[10] Archer, L.B.: 'What Became of Design Methodology?' in Cross,
op. cit.

[11] Daley, J.: 'Design Creativity and the Understanding of Objects'
in Cross, op. cit.

[12] See chapter 3 on *Language-Games – A Wittgensteinian Approach*.

[13] This is further developed in chapter 18, *Skills and the Tool
Perspective*.

of the most important contributors to a Cartesian design approach. Theory and practice in architectural and industrial design have moved away from the early ideas of design as decomposition of complex hierarchical systems, towards an understanding of the participative and creative character of the design process, and towards a qualitative understanding of what good design is. How, is it possible that in computer science the early rationalist systems engineering approach and the program of Herbert Simon is still alive? Should the practical failures of rationalistic design methodologies in other design fields not be taken as an indication of a need for a new paradigm for an art and a science of design of computer artifacts, as well?

I find that the disciplinary critique and alternatives proposed within computer and information science (as outlined in the previous chapter), definitely find strong support in theoretical and practical experiences from the research field of design methodology. The direction for an art and science of designing computer artifacts that I have suggested seems to be well in accordance with the development in other more mature design fields.[14]

---

[14] Another reason for why I find the developments in the three generations of design methodology as striking is how well this agrees with how my own research has developed. As outlined in the *Prologue* my first interest was in rationalistic systems analysis and systems description methods (1969-1972). Partly as a critique of this approach I then worked theoretically and in actions research with participatory approaches with the aim of supporting democracy at work (1973-1979). From then until now, my research, theoretically and in empirical research projects, has concentrated on skill and creativity in participative design with the aim of supporting quality of work. However, this development took place in a Scandinavian social and historical environment different from that of the design methodology debate. I will return to this Scandinavian research situation and political environment in the following parts of this book.

## Architectural Design

During the years when I have done research on design of computer artifacts I have often had the pleasure of cooperating with, and receiving inspiration from research colleagues in the field of architectural design.

In my research in Scandinavia on democratization of design of computer artifacts in industrial organizations in the mid 1970s I had close contacts with researchers in the field of architecture. They worked with a participative, local activity, trade union perspective on design of work environment in industrial sites. Inspired by Alexander, some developed a 'pattern language' on work environment solutions, a tool-kit of prototypical examples to be used locally.[15] Others developed design strategies and methods for the work environment, in much the same way as we did action research together with local trade unions on design of computer artifacts.[16] Academically this design perspective resulted in several dissertations.[17]

When my research focus also shifted in the early 1980s towards design of computer based tools for skilled work, colleagues from the field of architecture were able to contribute with useful inspiration. In particular, I learned a lot from the approach taken in a Ph.D. dissertation on design theory by Jerker Lundequist.[18] Maintaining a Marxist approach as a basis for understanding the social and political dimensions of the design process, he transcended it by incorporating into design theory the thoughts of the 'second' Wittgenstein. Hence, it became

[15] Ahlin, J.: *Arbetsmiljösanering – förnyelse genom demokratisering av planeringsprocessen*, Royal Institute of Technology, Stockholm 1974 (dissertation).

[16] See for example Steen, J. and Ullmark, P.: *En egen väg – att göra fackliga handlingsprogram*, Royal Institute of Technology, Stockholm 1982 (dissertation).

[17] See e.g. the examples above.

[18] Lundeqvist, J.:*Norm och Modell – samt ytterligare några begrepp inom designteorin*, Department of Architecture, Royal Institute of Technology, Stockholm, 1982 (dissertation).

conceptually possible to grasp the practical skills of professional designers and users, and to reframe the design process and the labor process designed for, as language-games.

I think that by being concerned with the more mature discipline of architectural design as a mirror for reflecting research and education in design of computer artifacts we could well gain deeper insight and new ideas for our own field of design. This is, as will be demonstrated, a position shared by several researchers in our own field.

## Styles and Movements in Architectural Design

In design of buildings as well as computer artifacts a primary consideration is of course that they will fulfill the purposes they are intended for. In architectural design this assessment is articulated in a design program, which gives the general goals and constraints for the design. Within these frames, and sometimes beyond them, the design to a great extent depends on the individual designers as well as the prevailing social conditions and cultural climate. And styles have changed in Western architecture, as we all can notice. From historicism at the beginning of this century, via functionalism beginning in the 1920s, to modernism in the 1950s and post-modernism in the early 1970s, buildings have been like grand statements, transparent functions, and on to postmodern playfulness and even cynicism. The focus on buildings as objects which express grand or small, international or local statements, versus the view of buildings as artifacts and elements for human interaction, has shifted several times in the modern history of architecture, a situation we can observe, both as amateurs in architecture and as experts in using and living with these artifacts.

In particular two very different styles, schools or movements in modern architecture may be of special interest in an analogy with design of computer artifacts – *Bauhaus* and *Postmodernism*. They both represent design concepts that go far beyond the architectural domain, and they both deal with fundamental aspects of design in society today.

The Bauhaus movement had its origin in Germany in the 1920s. This was a movement with strong belief in progress for the new world that industrialism opened up. They wanted form and function to be one. Artifacts should be transparent as to their *functionality*. Forms should be appropriate to the kind of material that was being used. The program was a fusion of the fine arts with the crafts. But it was also a social and revolutionary program. Buildings and other artifacts should be designed to engender social change. *By design of progressive social and cultural values into the artifacts, these were thought of as vehicles for change by creating the necessary conditions.* This is socially a grandiose program from which we can learn a great deal of conscious proactive design of computer artifacts for a better world.

Early functionalistic Bauhaus designs like the experimental school-house built at Am Horn in Weimar in 1923 are good examples of the attempt to integrate artistic competence and craft skills with industrial production and user participation.[19] And products from the design program for industrial production of functional high quality furniture for ordinary people are far from outdated.

But too analytic a utopian design of the future can also lead to severe mistakes, when the actual social context is not taken into account. A warning example is the Pruitt-Igoe low-income buildings in St Louis,[20] designed in the

---

[19] The design was based on a draft by the painter Georg Muche, chosen by representatives for the students, designed by architect Fred Forbat, with the interiors being made in the school's workshop. See e.g. Schädlich, C.: *Bauhaus i Dessau 1925–932*, Catalogue from Randers Art Museum, 1985.

[20] For a further discussion see Jencks, C.: *The Language of Postmodern Architecture*, Rizzoli, New York 1984, and Bannon, L. 'Issues in Design – Some Notes' in Norman, D. A. and Draper, S. W. (eds.): *User Centered System Design – New Perspectives on*

'international' style by Minoru Yamaski in the early 1950s. They did away with traditional streets, gardens and semiprivate spaces. Instead they were designed in a purist style, based on a clean salubrious hospital metaphor, meant to instill the corresponding virtues in the inhabitants. This was an award winning design of good form as a means for good content or at least good conduct. The problem was that it was totally inappropriate for its inhabitants. Many of them were Southern migrants without experience of living densely packed in compartments with little room for expression of individuality and traditional social activity. In short time the covered walkways became the site for vandalism, drug abuse and crime. Hence, people started to move out of this nightmare. Attempts to rehabilitate the complex were in vain. Ultimately, in 1972, the authorities literally blew the thing up after recommendations from the residents. Do we have similar positive and negative functionalistic examples in design of computer artifacts? That should be worth investigating.

Postmodernism in architecture is a quite opposite program or set of trends first developed in the USA in the late 1960s. The emphasis is no longer on internationalism or social revolution, but on small stories, narratives and language-games. Buildings are seen as sign artifacts. Bricks looking like bricks are no more real than bricks looking like marble, and a department store that looks like a department store is no more real than one reminding us of a church (of mammon). Instead buildings are *deliberately designed as signs reminding us of something else*. These signs may be e.g. history of, or traditions in, the place where a house is built, or bits and pieces from the history of architectural design. They might be very personal reminders of the architect's own development as well as cultural reminders for whole ethnic groups. The artifacts

*Human-Computer Interaction*, Lawrence Erlbaum Associates, London 1986, p. 28.

are not intended to be true to any tradition, but playful and stimulating.

Interesting examples include Andrew Derbyshire's design of Hillingdon Civic Centre in London. The place is a veritable collision of low-pitched roofs and brick all over, reminding the users of the vernacular and traditional building types they know and enjoy. The architect set out

> to design a building that spoke a language of form intelligible to its users (its occupants as well as the citizens of the borough) and used it to say something they wanted to hear.[21]

And a study asking if postmodernism communicates showed that the form of the building really was perceived as welcoming by its users.[22]

A well known warning example might be Ricardo Bofill's housing project in a Parisian suburb. Thousands of families live in a palace-like complex. But the inhabitants are neither royal nor rich, but ordinary low-paid families with a bunch of kids. The whole palace is just a facade, which becomes even more cynical when there is no outdoor place for the children to play in. Have we corresponding good and bad postmodern designs of computer artifacts? That should also be worth investigating.

I find both Bauhaus and Postmodernism in architecture relevant for design of computer artifacts. Bauhaus because of its proactive approach, the insight that design of artifacts is design for future conditions of living, a vehicle for change – with all the responsibility and moral questions that this incorporates. Postmodernism because computer artifacts even more than buildings lend themselves to this kind of semiotic design. What are represented on the screen are signs or metaphors that remind

---

[21] Derbyshire, A.: 'Building the Welfare State' in *Architecture: Opportunities, Achievements*, p. 29 (quoted after Jencks, C.: *Current Architecture*, Academy Editions, London 1982).

[22] Groat, L and Canter, D.: 'Does Post-Modernism Communicate' in *Progressive Architecture*, December 1979.

the users of experiences and support the imagination. Hence we had better use this capacity consciously, using metaphors and signs that make sense to people in their ordinary lives, and that are fun to play with, artifacts that remind the users of their own local stories, and sometimes support imaginary transcendence of them.

But are these kind of examples really relevant for design of computer artifacts? Maybe not for such a *science* in a narrow sense, but certainly for extending it to, and incorporating in it, an *art* of designing computer artifacts, and for our understanding of what kind of enterprise design of computer artifacts is socially. Style might not be scientific, but it certainly plays an important role in design of computer artifacts too.

Today the 'desktop metaphor' is à la mode in interface design, and 'object orientation' is very popular in programming. What is style or art in this, and what is purely scientific? Ten years from now other styles may be in vogue. It should be worth reflecting about what was science and what was art in the ideas that Alan Kay had, and before him Douglas Engelbart, that today are manifested as Macintosh style workstations?[23] Why did Kay and the people at Xerox PARC design SMALLTALK-80 as they did, and which ideas led Kristen Nygaard and Ole Johan Dahl to design SIMULA and basic concepts of what today is known as a school of object oriented programming?[24] To my mind these innovations are just as much artistic creations of new design styles as new scientific approaches, but that does not make them less important. On the contrary they show the importance of artistic competence in the field of designing computer artifacts.

[23] See e.g. Kay, A.: *The Reactive Engine*, University of Utah, 1969 (dissertation), and Engelbart, D. C.: *Augmenting human intellect – A conceptual framework*, Stanford Research Institute, Menlo Park 1962. This will be further referred to in chapter 17, *The 'Toolness' of Computer Artifacts*.

[24] Actually the first conference on the history of programming languages was held in Los Angeles as late as in June 1978.

By becoming aware of the importance of style, one finds new questions arising. Is, for example, the systems approach in practice more of a design style, one that requires artistic creativity to perform, than a scientific method? What was science and what was style in the Management Information Systems of the 1960s, in the large database approaches of the 1970s, and which are the scientific versus artistic ideas behind the approaches of networked workstations of the 1980s? Finally, we can also reflect upon what might neither be science nor art, but simply marketing by large vendor corporations.

Certainly an awareness of style, the history of schools and their programs, and experiences with different styles is important in a curriculum in design of computer artifacts. Style may not be scientific in a rigorous sense, but it is professionally important to be able to master different styles. Furthermore, to reflect about styles and schools in design of computer artifacts, as well as to investigate analogies to architectural and industrial design, is a most rational endeavor. After all, design styles and artistic ones live and die as scientific paradigms do. We had better be aware of both, both as tradition and for creative transcendence that can lead to better designs.

Furthermore, examples like the architectural ones discussed above also tell us something about the contradiction between on the one hand artistic or design freedom, and participation and control by the future users on the other. Both the functionalistic socially oriented Bauhaus enterprise, and the playfulness suggested by the postmodern designers may end up in a dehumanizing chaos despite opposite intentions. Participation might constrain design freedom and it might be hard to recognize the future users. Nevertheless this seems to be just as important as individual artistic creativity. And future users of computer artifacts are easier to identify than future inhabitants in buildings. The life cycle of computer artifacts is after all shorter than for example that of churches.

In the *Epilogue*, I will return to Bauhaus and Postmodernism relating the socially and culturally proactive enterprise of *work-oriented design* to the postmodern conditions of our contemporary Western culture and state of capitalism.

# A 'Catalogue' of Paradigm Examples

I will end this section on inspirations from architectural design with a 'catalogue' of paradigm examples. In one way or another they all show how experiences from architectural design may be helpful for understanding design of computer artifacts, and for designing more useful and perhaps even more beautiful computer applications.[25]

## *User Interface – Facade or Entranceway?*

The first paradigm example, concerning the design of user interfaces, is due to Kristina Hooper.[26]

In architecture there has often been emphasis on the facade of a building as a principle element. Some architectural theorists see the facade as the membrane between the outside and the inside, with the purpose of articulating the relation between the two. Others argue that the facade should contain information about the structure of the building. What if we, as in current postmodern design, focus on the interface as a false facade, delighting in the lack of necessary relationship between exterior facade and interior design, Hooper asks? She concludes that:

> no matter how beautiful a screen display is, an interface will not be effective unless the functionality of the

[25] A primary source from which several of the examples have been drawn is Norman, D. A. and Draper, S. W. (eds.): *User Centered System Design – New Perspectives on Human-Computer Interaction*, Lawrence Erlbaum Associates, London 1986, where several of the authors draw analogies between the design of computer artifacts and architectural design.

[26] Hooper, K.: 'Architectural Design – An Analogy' in Norman and Draper, op. cit.

system is revealed, preferably directly. In contrast to the architectural domain where one can walk into a building and then evaluate the informativeness of the facade, one is stuck on the screen, using the tracings presented there to infer the structure of the computer system.[27]

An important critique, but is not the crucial point in fact how useful reminders (postmodern or not) we manage to design the screens to be, rather than how well these portray the structure of the computer system?

Hooper goes on to consider the architectural analogy of an interface as an entranceway rather than as a facade. Again there are strong architectural traditions:

> Consider European cathedrals and formal Japanese gardens: The viewpoint of a visitor is carefully planned to reveal the whole place in a very systematic way. In the design of interfaces one must also consider carefully how one selectively informs a user about a particular system, providing well-chosen bits and pieces that constitute a general understanding of the system. Some of the metaphors of entranceways may be useful in addressing this issue of selective disclosure to new users of a particular computer system.[28]

I quite agree that the metaphor might be useful, but not primarily in relation to the structure of the computer system, which is another metaphor, but in relation to the work or communication the user is involved in via the artifact.

### Participation and Long-Term Effects
The next example concerns the 'distance' between designers and users.

---

[27] Ibid., p. 14.
[28] Ibid., p. 14.

Based on the Pruitt-Igoe story, referred to above, Liam Bannon[29] notices that the 'vision' of the designer, and the needs and desires of the people designed for, can be dramatically different. He relates this to the circumstances that the designer often works for a client with different values than those of the ultimate inhabitants of a building.[30] He also relates the differences to the situation that design teams often perform their work far away from the physical and cultural context in which the buildings are to be useful. He concludes that:

> obviously, fault does not lie at the door of the designer alone, as that person is but one element in a complex socioeconomic system that makes decisions about features of artifacts, but it behooves the designer to display a thorough understanding of the needs of the people that will ultimately live and work around these artifacts, be they houses or computers.[31]

The lesson to be learned from architecture is that a socially concerned approach to the design of computer artifacts has to be based both on active involvement by the people that will be affected by the design and careful attention to the longer-term effects our designs have on work and society.

### 'Seed of New Cultures'

The third example, by John Seely Brown, concerns the Bauhaus approach and 'how we might design computational artifacts – that is, to create artifacts that can act as the seeds of new perspectives or 'cultures'.[32]

---

[29] Bannon, L. 'Issues in Design – Some Notes' in Norman and Draper, op. cit.

[30] In the terminology of the *systems approach* by Churchman discussed in the previous chapter, we can say that the client is *not the client but the decision-maker*.

[31] Bannon, op. cit., p. 29.

[32] Brown, J. S.: 'From Cognitive to Social Ergonomics and Beyond' in Norman and Draper, op. cit., p. 480.

One of Brown's examples of design as a proactive tool for social change emerged out of an idea of transferring a new perspective on interfaces to designers of copiers. The actual computer-based artifact he has in mind is a proto-typing design artifact called *Trillium*.[33] Rather than spending months on individual designs, the designers could, with the help of this tool, in a few days progress from a design idea to a functioning artifact. Hence, he argues, the designers were likely to have invested less ego in a particular product, and to be more willing to criticize it and change it.

*Trillium* as a proactive means of social change did have an effect on the subculture of designers of copiers. However it can be questioned if the changes were all foreseen. As reported by Blomberg, in different sites *different* organizational and professional structures emerged when these computer-based artifacts were implemented in the organizations.[34]

Another concrete example where Brown sees great possibilities of a Bauhaus-like approach is to open up cooperation and learning in groups in organizations. And he concludes that:

> building tools that enhance collaboration can bring about the development of community support structures that more effectively tap individual resources and increase group learning. In order to realize this potential, we need to be aware of the subtle ways in which computational artifacts function as cultural artifacts.[35]

This proactive 'vision' from one of the people that contributed to the computer workstation so commonplace today should be worth reflecting about. We know that computer workstations have drastically changed the indivi-

---

[33] Trillium was designed by Austin Henderson of Xerox PARC.

[34] Blomberg, J.: 'The Variable Impact of Computer Technologies on the Organization of Work Activities' in *Proceedings of CSCW '86*, Austin 1986.

[35] Norman and Draper, op. cit., p. 486.

dual work assignments for many users. Will the new tools have a similar effect on cooperative work? Which 'visions' should then be guiding, and who should participate in the design?

## Social and Political Process

The fourth example, due to Rob Kling, concerns how we can utilize experiences from the branch of architecture dealing with urban planning to understand design as a social and political process.[36]

According to Kling urban artifacts shape the social terrain in which we live much as computer artifacts shape the 'information terrain' in organizations. The planning of neighborhoods, urban centers, and buildings has much in common with the design of computer artifacts. He argues that we can learn a great deal from analogies with designers of buildings as complex as universities or whole cities – not that they always have been successful, but because there is a long history of traditions and examples to study. How do they think about the interplay between the artifacts and the people that are encouraged to live with these artifacts?

Another aspect of the analogy is the social and political means society and communities have developed to plan and control urban design projects. The point is that the planning and design of computer artifacts, just like buildings, takes place in complex, conflicting and pluralistic social settings. These are settings which urban planners have considerable experience with explicitly designing pro-social artifacts for.

With this analogy we can also reflect over our own practice. We have all worked or played in hundreds of buildings designed by architects and urban planners. What can we infer from this to the comparatively fewer computer artifacts most of us have had practical experi-

---

[36] Kling, R.: 'Computerization as an Ongoing Social and Political Process' in Bjerknes, et al. (eds.): *Computers and Democracy – A Scandinavian Challenge*, Avebury, 1987.

ence of? How do we make explicit the presumptions of social life, the ethical and aesthetic considerations, made by planners and designers of computer artifacts, so that they become as visible to us as the choices made by architects and urban planners?

## The Reflective Practitioner

My last example in arguing for the usefulness of paradigm cases from architecture for an art and science of designing computer artifacts is more theoretical, and relates back to the philosophical discussion in the part on *Design Philosophy*. It concerns what designers really *do*, and is drawn from *The Reflective Practitioner – How Professionals Think in Action* by Donald A. Schön.[37]

I think that Schön's perspective can be described as closely related both to the Wittgensteinian approach to language-games, practical knowledge and knowledge by familiarity, and to the Heideggerian approach to understanding proficient and expert knowledge in thrown and projective situations.

However, according to Schön, what is typical of professional practice is *reflection-in-action*. This is neither completely detached reflection nor all-absorbing involved and thrown activity. It is the kind of research professionals do as reflections or breakdowns while they act in thrown situations. To Schön this is a major aspect of how professionals develop new insight.

One of his cases on reflection-in-action is of special interest to us here. It is from architectural design. He studies a situation in a design studio at a school of architecture where a student is undertaking a design project under the supervision of a master designer. His claim is that the kind of generic design process architects follow is shared by other design professions.

What is typical of the design process is designing as a *conversation with the materials of a situation*. A designer

---

[37] Schön D. A: *The Reflective Practitioner – How Professionals Think in Action*, Basic Books, New York 1983.

works in particular situations, uses particular materials, and employs a distinctive medium and language. Every *move* in the language-game of designing is a local experiment, where the initial moves often must be *reframed,* as the changed situation most often deviates from the initial appreciation. Hence, it is also a global experiment in reframing the whole situation, which might lead to the appreciation of completely new ideas. The professional designer responds to the situation's *back-talk.* This is reflection-in-action as breakdown of the understanding of the situation, the strategies of action, the modeling, etc., that have been implicit in the initial moves.

The *language of designing* that is used for communication and learning in design is a parallel process of drawing and speaking about the design. The verbal dimension is full of deictic utterances like 'here', 'this' or 'that'. They refer to pointing at drawings, making new sketches, etc. It is *a language of doing*, in creating images or visions of the future.

It should be obvious that this language is not constrained to the use of drawings. In our context of designing computer artifacts, prototypes, mock-ups, scenarios, or even role plays are just different complementary media for the language-game of design, and different triggers for reflection-in-action. They may have the advantage of making it easier for users to participate in the design process, since they are less abstract and less alienated from practical use situations.

In teaching or giving examples of design there is also an intertwined *meta-language about design.* This is how a designer describes features of the design process as he designs, typically as detached reflection about design principles.

According to Schön the dimensions of language-games of designing typically include:

> the domains of language in which the designer describes and appreciates the consequences of his moves, the implications he discovers and follows, and his

changing stance toward the situation with which he converses.[38]

A professional designer masters a repertoire of *design domains* which he draws upon to fulfill constructive, descriptive and normative functions in designing.

These design domains contain names of elements, features, relations, and actions, and of norms used to evaluate problems, consequences, and implications.[39]

In architectural design these domains may be siting, building elements, form, organization and space, scale, structure/technology etc. In design of computer artifacts to be used in a specific activity we could certainly find similar domains.

The design domains contain the ordering principles or rules that the designer uses in early moves in the design. However, as the materials of the situation talk back the professional designer knows how to 'soften' or transcend these rules to get a good design.

In the conversation with the materials of the situation, the designer can never make a move that has only intended *implications*. The design material is continually talking back to him. This causes him to apprehend unanticipated problems and potentials, which become the basis for further moves.

Both the repertoire of design domains and the situations' back talk seem to be what causes the designer to make the right or at least good moves.

As the professional designer spins out a web of moves he also *shifts stance* toward the design situation. He oscillates between involved design of details and detached reflection on the totality of the design. This detached reflection of the totality may be seen as a global reframing of the whole situation. As the design proceeds, the designer also economizes the designing by shifting stance from explorative

[38] Ibid., p. 95.
[39] Ibid., p. 97.

adaption of tentative strategies to involved commitment to a specific design.

Though emphasizing the specific role of reflection-in-action in design, Schön has to admit that there is more to it. Commenting on the masterful way in which the observed architect 'zeroes in immediately on fundamental schemes and decisions which quickly acquire the status of commitments'[40] he concludes that the designer 'seems to have developed a feeling for the kind of conversation which the design situation sets in motion.'[41] Hence, reflection-in-action is just one of the designing ways of thinking the professional practitioner performs. Other fundamental ways of thinking and doing professional design come closer to the arational, involved, rapid, fluid, and intuitive performance described as typical for proficient and expert knowledge in the chapter on the Heideggerian approach.

A science of design does not have to be based on the assumption that the practice of professional designers is an activity congruent with the activity of natural scientists. At least the competence of professional architects seems to stem from many other sources, and it seems to be better understood within other epistemological and theoretical domains. I see no reason why this should not also be the case with design of computer artifacts. And I think we have some inspiring paradigm examples to follow from the more mature design arts.

## Summary

I find that the 'external alternatives' from the design methodology movement and from architectural design discussed in this chapter are most inspiring paradigm examples for rethinking computer and information science and developing an art and science of designing computer artifacts. Hence, in the concluding chapter on a program

[40] Ibid., p. 104.
[41] Ibid., p. 104.

for, and a curriculum in, the art and science of designing computer artifacts, they will play an important role.

## Chapter 10

# Conclusions: A Subject Matter and a Tentative Program

This part of the book has been a search for the subject matter of design of computer artifacts. I have tried to outline the subject matter in relation to theory of what in computer and information science more commonly is known as the field of systems design, in relation to theory of design in a wider context of other design sciences, and in relation to the philosophical positions argued in the preceding part on *Design Philosophy*.

In doing this, I have tried to demonstrate the fruitfulness of an understanding of design of computer artifacts in a language that transcends the rationalistic natural science based language of systems, objects, information, and data. I have also tried to argue that with such an understanding of the subject matter, there already exist well elaborated and teachable theories and doctrines.

## The Subject Matter

To sum up I will recapitulate the outline of some fundamental characteristics of the subject matter (designing computer artifacts), as discussed in a language close to the philosophical positions argued in the preceding part.

It was suggested that we should understand design of computer artifacts as a concerned social and historical activity in which artifacts and their use are anticipated, an activity and form of knowledge that is both planned and creative, and that deals with the contradiction between tradition and transcendence.

In designing computer artifacts we should consider them as mediating instrumental and/or communicative activities; as supporting individual and/or cooperative activities; as augmenting and/or replacing human activities; as function and form that are irrevocably interconnected, and where aesthetic and ergonomic aspects may be just as relevant as instrumental functionality.

I have chosen to regard computers as the material or medium out of which *computer artifacts* can be designed. When designing computer artifacts we utilize this material's capacity for symbol manipulation, to design them as signs that remind the users of earlier experiences. These reminders may be in the tradition of the use of artifacts in a specific use activity, or they may transcend it as paradigm cases for new ways of seeing and doing. *Use* is fundamental to my understanding of designing computer artifacts. Design concerns the practical rather than the artificial. What we design is not just artifacts, but – by intervention – a changed or reformed practice.

I have also suggested that rather than focusing on methods as prescriptions, we should be concerned about *norms* or *rules* governing specific language-games of design. These are the norms and rules which professional designers follow, and sometimes transcend, often without being aware of them. Methodological prescriptions, on the other hand, are seen as explicit rules that can be used in learning a practice or reflecting about it, but they are not to be mistaken for actual rule following in language-games of design. To master the norms and rules of design in practice also requires learning by examples passed on from more experienced designers and users. Hence, the practice of design should be emphasized.

I have referred to descriptions, models, prototypes, etc., as *design artifacts*. The role of design artifacts in the language-game of design is seen as *reminders* and as *paradigm cases* for our reflections on existing and future computer artifacts and their use. The use of design artifacts brings earlier experiences to mind and it 'bends' our way of thinking about the future. I think it is in this sense we should understand them as representations. Design artifacts are used to create reminders that we can *reflect upon*, and sometimes *experience* (e.g. by using a prototype).

I have preferred to talk about *norms or rules, and reminders or paradigm cases* rather than *methods, descriptions and models,* to avoid falling back into Cartesian dualism and the trap of an epistemology of mirror-images.

It has also been suggested that an art and science of designing computer artifacts should include not only instrumental theories espousing design norms or rules to be followed and design artifacts to be used, but also substantial theories giving better understanding of what design of computer artifacts is all about. Especially we should be interested in theories relating instrumental aspects to substantial ones.

# A Program in Design

Given such an understanding of design of computer artifacts, I outlined the following candidates for inclusion in a curriculum to be taught in disciplines dealing with the subject matter:

## 1. Social System Design Methods

This topic covers methods which include the role of subjectivity in design of systems. Theoretically the different approaches to social systems design have their origin in rationalistic systems thinking, but transcend this framework philosophically by including the subjectivity of the users. The different approaches are well developed and they are based on extensive practical experience. However, these approaches are fundamentally 'pure' methodology. Hence a challenge will be to investigate how they can be integrated with, or supplemented by, substantial theory of the social situations in which they are to be used. Another challenge is how they can be refined to more specifically deal with design of computer artifacts and their use.

## 2. Theory of Designing Computer Artifacts

This topic covers fundamental theory of what kind of phenomenon the design of computer artifacts actually is. It reframes the rationalistic understanding of computer artifacts. The point of departure is what people do with computers in concerned human activity within a tradition. This also means an emphasis on differences in kinds of knowledge between on the one hand human practical understanding and experience, and on the other, knowledge representation in computers understood as 'logic machines' or 'inference engines'.

In design, focus is on concerned involvement rather than on correct descriptions. Design becomes a process for anticipation of possible breakdowns for the users in future use situations with the computer artifacts being designed. This is anticipation both to avoid breakdowns, and to recover from them.

Being a new and fundamentally ontological approach to design of computer artifacts, not much instrumental design methodology has as yet been developed. Neither has its relation to substantial social theory been extensively investigated. In both respects there are challenging possibilities.

## 3. Process-Oriented Software Engineering and Prototyping

This topic is a paradigmatic rethinking of the process of designing software much along the lines of the first two topics. The paradigmatic shift of primary point of view is from design of software as formal mathematical objects derived by formalized procedures from abstract specifications, towards a process-oriented view. In this new paradigm, the software engineering focus is on human learning and communication in the design process, and the relevance, suitability and adequacy in practical use situations of the software being designed, not just on the correctness and efficiency of the piece of code being produced.

The relevance of this view is also accentuated by the development in software engineering of powerful computer-based design artifacts for prototyping, which make it possible for prospective users to get experience of future computer artifacts by *using* these design artifacts as a basis for design requirements. A challenge is to develop programming environments for prototyping that can be integrated with full scenarios, role plays etc., of future use situations, and to use these prototypes as design artifacts in playing language-games of design as games of involvement and doing that defeat some of the limits of formal descriptions. Another challenge is to support the emergence of democratic environments for the utilization of this approach.

## 4. History of Design Methodology

Another topic for the curriculum in design of computer artifacts is general reflections on design methodology. Computers are not the only artifacts that are designed. How has design methodology developed in more mature design fields such as architectural and industrial design? Why has there e.g. been a shift from rationalistic, formal and mathematically oriented approaches towards both more participatory approaches and more 'design-like ways of thinking'? Why have theoretically influential designers reacted so strongly against their own rationalistic approach 'to fix the whole of life into a logical framework' (industrial designer Christopher Jones) that they now even advise us to 'forget the whole thing' (architect Christopher Alexander) and start to experiment with art in the design process? It should be important to every well educated designer in our own field to reflect upon the relation between design methodology for computer artifacts and the experiences with different generations of design methodologies in other fields.

## 5. Architectural and Industrial Design as Paradigm Examples

Still another relevant topic for our curriculum is how design is carried out in other design disciplines like architectural and industrial design. We can use design experiences from these disciplines as paradigm examples to reflect over theory, methods and practice in our own field. This includes reflections over the relations between science and art in design, on styles or 'schools' in design, on the relation between science and styles in design, and on the social relations of designing in complex conflicting and pluralistic social settings.

Styles or schools like Bauhaus (as a proactive approach based on the insight that design of artifacts is design of future conditions of living, a vehicle for change) and Postmodernism (as the use of signs and metaphors that are joyful to play with) are good examples of such paradigm cases for reflections over the relations between science, art and society in design. The examples may also help us to focus on the styles used in design of computer artifacts, and they may themselves furnish some inspiration for design of computer artifacts.

## 6. Philosophy of Design

Philosophy, especially theory of knowledge, and its relation to design is a topic for a curriculum in design of computer artifacts that is inherent in many of the other topics, but that also should have a place of its own. The relevance of, and some directions for, such studies were hinted at in the preceding part on *Design Philosophy*. A topic like this can be argued for any science, but it is crucial to a science of design of computer artifacts, since this subject matter, as conceived here, is both interdisciplinary and concerned with basic conditions for knowledge production in practice.

## 7. Practical design

With the program outlined it is obvious that a reduction of
a curriculum in design of computer artifacts to what can
be taught and learned as detached theoretical reflections
is contradictory. Both the philosophical investigation and
the examples from architecture and industrial design
point at the importance of practical understanding as
knowledge by experience, by familiarity, and as reflection-
in-action in design. Hence practical design taught by professional designers of computer artifacts and their use,
both as experimentation in a master-apprentice relation
and as investigations into real cases, seems most fundamental to our curriculum.

This practical education should include examples of,
and experimentation with, both a wide variety of application domains, and a wide range of design artifacts and
norms and rules for their use. Hence, application domains
should not be restricted to traditional administrative systems, but include new domains e.g. computer support for
graphic arts, or cooperative work in small groups. Neither
should design artifacts and methods be restricted to more
or less formal system description techniques. A new focus
should be on design artifacts that support involvement
and experience, like the use of prototypes and mock-ups,
exploratory programming environments, scenarios,
maps, and even role playing.

# A Disciplinary Base for
# an Interdisciplinary Subject Matter

I do not see these topics of a curriculum in design of computer artifacts as a replacement of what is already taught
in computer and information science. But any discipline
that teaches and does research on the subject matter of
design of computer artifacts is strongly encouraged to let
it take its place by the side of what is already taught, because it covers some of the fundamental aspects of what
design of computer artifacts is really about.

It has been my intention with this part to provide arguments that any discipline that deals with the subject matter of design of computer artifacts should be able, theoretically and methodologically, to treat design as including aspects like interventions into practice, as communication between users and professional designers, as a creative process, and as a concerned human activity. And I have argued that any discipline dealing with such aspects of design will have to transcend a natural science foundation, regardless of whether the discipline is called computer science, informatics or information science.

The domain of the subject matter outlined is not primarily theory of physical events or logic inferences in a machine, but of concerned human activity within a background of tradition and conventions in designing and using these artifacts.

I find this subject matter truly interdisciplinary, with *relations not only to aspects of traditional computer science, but also to theories and methods from social and human sciences such as sociology, psychology, anthropology, linguistics and business administration*. Such relations have only marginally been touched upon in this part, though the role of substantial theories and methods from these disciplines in a curriculum in design of computer artifacts is evident. I will return to some of these relations in the coming chapters where the social setting and the practical situation are more defined.

Neither have I discussed *research methods for a science of design of computer artifacts*, another obvious topic for our curriculum. However I think that many research situations bear a family resemblance with the design approaches discussed here. What I have in mind is participatory actions research, explorative experimentation, and case studies – not as a replacement for detached theoretical reflection in one or another theoretical context, but as their practical and empirical foundation. I will return to the topic of research methods in connection with my empirical cases in the coming chapters.

Instead I have tried to focus on *a disciplinary base for the interdisciplinary subject matter of designing computer artifacts*. In doing this I have tried to benefit from developments in other more mature design disciplines, particularly the theoretical and methodological discussions in architectural and industrial design as paradigm cases. However, recent developments in computer science have provided valuable contributions, as well.

There have also been indications that what professional designers really do is more art than science. This challenge to an art and science of designing computer artifacts particularly deserves further investigation. A first step could be to explore *the traditional master-apprentice relation* as one form for education in design of computer artifacts. A second is to consider *the arts* as paradigm cases for the design of computer artifacts.

However, the different contributions discussed in this part indicate that we already have an intellectually sound and teachable disciplinary base for an art and science of design of computer artifacts. Much still remains be developed, especially when it comes to methods. And in many respects we have to understand 'the design process [as] hiding behind the cloak of 'judgment' and 'experience'[1], that Herbert Simon once started his rationalistic crusade against, and for which he has had so many followers. But this retreat to practical understanding is for theoretical reasons, not because of intellectual softness. Simon's rationalistic systems engineering approach may be an ever so elegant 'intellectually tough, analytic, partly formalizable, partly empirical, teachable doctrine about the design process',[2] but I see no reason for us to retreat to it as a paradigm case for an art and a science of design of computer artifacts.

As compared with the rationalistic approach the outlined program may be a step backwards on the road to-

---

[1] Simon, H.: *The Sciences of the Artificial*, The MIT Press, Cambridge 1969, p. 80.

[2] Ibid., p. 58.

wards instrumental theory and methodology, but by being more fundamental, this may also allow us to take two steps forward in designing powerful computer artifacts to augment the skill of users rather than replacing them by artificial intelligence.

By taking this road, we will certainly also need to make extensive use of many of the theoretical and methodological findings in the natural science based research tradition in the design of computer artifacts. By understanding computers as the material we use in design of computer artifacts, the importance of computer science knowledge to design is obvious. An architect that has no understanding of building materials and techniques may design aesthetic and socially useful houses, but no one will be able to live in them, if they cannot be physically constructed. The same holds for designers of computer artifacts.

The question is not whether the one kind of knowledge or the other is needed. Both the research-guiding interest in technical control, and the interest in intersubjective communication are fundamental to an art and science of designing computer artifacts. The problem is that the interest in intersubjective communication has – hitherto to a great extent – been neglected in research and education of our subject matter. There are good theoretical and practical reasons for changing this.

## Work-Oriented Design

With the outlined art and science of designing computer artifacts an academic setting for *work-oriented design of computer artifacts* has been established.

However, as earlier pointed out, work-oriented design is also a practical normative enterprise. As such it has the complementary immanent research-guiding interest in emancipation.

Firstly, the question of participation must normatively be reframed as a question of *designing for democracy at work*.

Secondly, the question of what kind of artifacts computers are must normatively to be reframed as a question of conditions for *designing for skilled work.*

In the coming parts I will turn to my experiences with such designing.

# Part III

# Designing for Democracy at Work

*'Therfore when I consider and way in my mind*
*all these common wealthes,*
*which now a dayes any where do florish, so god help me,*
*I can perceave nothing*
*but certein conspiracy of riche men*
*procuringe theire owne commodities*
*under the name and title of the common wealth.*
*They invent and devise all meanes and craftes,*
*first how to kepe safely, without feare of lesing,*
*that they have unjustly gathered together,*
*and next how to hire and abuse the worke and laboure of*
*the poore for as little money as may be.'*

Thomas More in *Utopia*

# Introduction

The democratic ideal is a beautiful human invention, stating the right for every human to equally participate in decisions concerning his or her life. In practice, however, this freedom has always been limited. The first democrats, the ancient Greeks, constrained it to free men, excluding women and a class of slaves. The modern democratic state in capitalistic societies has in theory, and in many practical affairs, removed these constraints. The representative democracy is a formal arrangement for securing decisions in the interest of the majority, and often for securing some discretion for minority groups. Still, in many sectors of human life the democratic rights remain merely formal, without a real content for those concerned, and many sectors are excluded from the practice of this ideal. Here I am concerned with democracy inside the factory gates and office doors – i.e. *industrial democracy*.

I have earlier identified work-oriented design of computer artifacts not only with the technical and practical research guiding interests of instrumental control and intersubjective communication, but also with the research guiding interest of emancipation. This interest focuses on knowledge and understanding for emancipation from hypostatized forces of history and society and is directed towards creating conditions for independent individuals in a society of free cooperation and communication. This comes close to the democratic ideal, but there is a supplementary emphasis on the *process of democratization*.

Taking this ideal seriously, questions of the following kind arise: Why does democracy stop at the factory gate, and how can it be developed to also include our working life? What are the practical constraints and possibilities for democratic design and use of computer artifacts at work? How can research contribute in this direction?

I have earlier argued for an understanding of design of computer artifacts as a concerned social, historical, creative and planned activity in which we try to anticipate computer artifacts and their use. How is this related to the emancipatory democratization ideal and the questions above? In this part I will discuss research efforts to deal with these questions. In particular, I will reflect upon our experiences from the DEMOS and UTOPIA research projects.

## Industrial Democracy

The author and researcher Sven Lindqvist once described the relation between the scientific community and people at the workplaces in the following way:[1]

> The modern society is completely dependent on science. There is no sector of society that is not affected by progress in research and technology. This is certainly also true for the Swedish working class. (...) We must seek contacts and intermediate links between the researchers and the representatives of society and the workers, and this communication net must be traveled in both directions. We must know the needs of the working class, and the working class must know our resources. It is this double function that the university will try to fulfil through its contact secretariat. (...) The trade unions are best acquainted with the workers' needs. Therefore, the contact secretariat regards cooperation with the trade union movement as absolutely natural. However, there is of course no impediment to individual workers or groups of workers directly contacting the secretariat. (...) This way even a small local

[1] Lindqvist, S.: *Gräv där du står – Hur man utforskar ett jobb*, Bonniers, Stockholm 1978, pp. 267–268 (my translation).

union, without resources for their own applied research, can fulfil their research needs.

The document Lindqvist based his vision on really exists. His description was taken from a pamphlet from the venerable University of Uppsala, signed by its president. As a researcher Lindqvist was aware of the document; but as an author he used his 'licentia poetica', changing just a few words. Where the original document said 'corporate business', Lindqvist wrote 'working class', while 'employer federations' was replaced by 'trade unions', and 'management' by 'workers'. The *Verfremdungseffekt* he in this way created shed some light on the real relation between research and democratization of working life.

The research work that we (at the Swedish Center for Working Life) carried out together with trade unions in the DEMOS and UTOPIA project programmatically approached Lindqvist's version of the pamphlet. The 'oddness' of our *collective resource approach* did not come from the close contacts with users and their organizations, but from who these users and their organizations were. It is by no means exceptional that research is directed towards e.g. technological problems at workplaces and the interests of people there. However, with few but important exceptions (the Swedish Center for Working Life perhaps being the most significant one) the established research world does not direct its resources to the interests of workers and their trade unions, and the emancipatory ideal of industrial democracy. Not even in Scandinavia.

## The Trade Unions as Vehicles for Industrial Democracy

In Marxist theory the relations between on the one hand workers and their trade unions, and on the other hand management and capital owners has its origin in the *labor contract*. This is an exchange relation between two kind of commodity possessors – capital that owns the means of production and the workplace, and labor that owns its labor power. To produce a profit the capital owner needs to buy labor power; to earn a living the worker needs to sell his or her labor power and work at a workplace.

Due to the labor contract differences in interests are fundamental. To make a profit capital has an interest in lowering the price of labor and to exercise the right to control and divide work. These 'managerial prerogatives', often supported by laws, run counter to workers' interests both in term of wages and in terms of working conditions. Hence, the conflicting interests concerning industrial democracy.

The *workers' collective* is a concept developed by the Norwegian sociologist Sverre Lysgaard.[2] By this he refers to the informal defense organization of workers at a workplace. The workers' collective is manifested as shared norms concerning how an individual worker should behave in relation to the management or the rationality of technical-economic organization, e.g. in relation to the managerial interest in intensification of work, control of the labor process, and rationalizations by use of new technology. As labor power, the workers are also part of the technical-economic organization at the workplace, but the workers' collective is based on the workers' *subordinated* position in the technical-economic organization at the workplace. The degree of strength in the workers' collective comes from the 'we-feeling' created by shared experiences. The basis for this 'we-feeling' is physical nearness at the workplace – which makes interaction possible; similarity in working conditions – which makes the workers identify with each other; and a similar problem situation which they interpret in a similar way. The norms of the workers' collective outline what it means to be a 'good work mate' as well as what it means to be a 'traitor'. The workers' collective is a 'buffer'

2 Lysgaard, S.: *Arbeiderkollektivet*, Universitetsforlaget, Stavanger 1961. For a case discussion of the relation between the workers' collective and local trade unions see Svensson, L.: *Arbetarkollektivet och facket – en lokal kamp för företagsdemokrati*, Studentlitteratur, Lund 1984 (dissertation).

between the individual worker and managerial interests in the technical-economic organization of the work place.

However, the workers' collective has two major weak points in relation to industrial democracy. Firstly, the workers' collective can only informally defend the individual worker, meaning that it has no formal organizational power for achieving structural changes at the workplace. Secondly, as a defensive organization responding to 'managerial prerogatives' it lacks the ability to formulate and carry through an offensive strategy for changes in the direction of industrial democracy.

The trade union movement, and especially local unions, is a formal organization through which such interests can be developed and implemented. This does not mean that trade unions always represent the interests of the workers' collective, and indeed there can certainly be contradictions. How well can the trade unions represent the interests of the workers' collective, and how well is this formal organization suited to uphold the interests of democracy at work, especially when design and use of computer artifacts are concerned?

In a historic perspective, trade unions have served the interest of the workers' collective in two ways that are important in our context. They have been a strong support in negotiating wages for workers, and they have been a most active instrument for furthering the interest of democracy in society as a whole.

However, it seems that the design and use of new technology requires new trade union activities. The reasons for this are many. Traditionally trade unions have focused on what Åke Sandberg[3] calls *distribution issues* such as wages, working hours, and general terms of employment. Such issues are characterized by:

• relatively well developed union objectives
• clearly formulated demands, often quantified

[3] Sandberg, Å.: *Technological Change and Co-determination in Sweden – Background and analysis of trade union and managerial strategies*, Temple Press (forthcoming).

- demands based on the workers' own practical experience
- clearly delimited, short negotiation situations.

The design and use of computer artifacts are in Sandberg's terminology typical *production issues*. They are, on the other hand, characterized by:

- only vaguely formulated union objectives
- demands that are difficult to quantify
- practical on-the-job experiences that must be supplemented by more theoretical, technical/scientific knowledge
- the design processes stretch over long periods of time, and it is hard to distinguish clearly defined negotiation situations.

Several of the prerequisites for traditional wage negotiations do not exist here. As Sandberg puts it:[4]

> Constructive problem solving and the design of new models for work seem to require more deep-seated and qualitative aspects to be considered than can be easily fitted within the traditional trade union strategy. Of course, this is deeply problematic for the trade unions.

How to prepare and conduct negotiations? How to build up knowledge and formulate demands? How to ensure internal union democracy, i.e. that the demands put forward are in the interest of the members and have their support? These are questions which will have to be addressed in new ways.

Obviously decentralization of decision-making and participation in the design process give more influence and access to important information. But is decentralization of decision-making at work, and participation in the traditional systems design process, really the answer to the questions? The position we took in DEMOS, UTOPIA and other collective resource projects was that decentraliza-

---

4 Ibid.

tion of decision-making and a participative approach to the design process are not sufficient. Fundamentally this position goes back to the labor contract, and the different interests of management and workers concerning industrial democracy.

Hence, we rejected the *harmony view* of organizations, according to which conflicts in an organization are regarded as pseudo-conflicts to be dissolved by good analysis, and consequently we also rejected an understanding of design as a rational decision-making process based on common goals. Instead our research was based on a *conflict view* of industrial organizations in our society. In the interest of emancipation we deliberately made the choice of working together with workers and their organizations, supporting the development of their resources for a change towards democracy at work.[5] We found it necessary to identify with the 'we-feeling' of the workers' collective, rather than with the overall 'we-feeling' that 'modern management' dedicates its resources to creating,

in order to gain more productivity out of the work force. In short: Trade unions were seen as organizations with a structure that was problematic when functioning as vehicles for designing for democracy at work at the same time they were seen as the only social force that in practice could be a carrier of this ideal.

## What Does Democratization of Design and Use of Computer Artifacts at Work Concern?

Fundamentally, industrial democracy concerns freedom, another value-laden concept. It concerns *freedom from* the limits to democratization manifested by the market economy and the power of capital, but it also concerns *freedom to* in action and reflection practically formulate

[5] See Sandberg, Å.: *The Limits to Democratic Planning – knowledge, power and methods in the struggle for the future,* Liber, Stockholm 1976 (dissertation), and with special reference to the design process Ehn, P. and Sandberg, Å.: 'God utreding ' in Sandberg, Å. (ed.): *Utredning och förändring i förvaltningen,* Liber förlag, Stockholm 1979.

and carry out this ideal. Attempts towards industrial democracy can address e.g:[6]

- the *power of capital owners to control how resources are used* for economic goals, structural changes in the company, investments in new technology, choice of business idea, product assortment, etc.
- the *organizational and technological power* to decide how the production process in general is organized, how technology is designed and used, etc.
- the *power over the workers to decide how work is to be organized, planned and controlled*
- the *power over the individual's autonomy at work*, e.g. choices concerning which tools to work with, and at what pace to work.

The projects of the collective resource approach that I will discuss in this part of the book concerned industrial democracy in all these aspects. Furthermore, they aimed both at a better understanding of freedom from 'managerial prerogatives' and at an active process of freedom to develop and implement strategies for democratization at work. Design of computer artifacts was seen in the context of democratization at work.

## The Scandinavian Setting

Scandinavian countries have, for quite some time, been well known for their industrial relations. The following should be counted among the more distinguishing aspects:

- high level of unionization,
- strong national trade union federations,
- centralized negotiation systems,
- large social democratic parties with strong links to the the national trade union federations of blue (and some

---

[6] See e.g. Dahlström, E.: *Bestämmande i arbetet – Några idékritiska funderingar kring arbetslivets demokratisering*, Department of Sociology, University of Gothenburg, Gothenburg 1983.

white) collar workers, parties which for long periods of
time have led the governments,
- relations between trade unions and employers are to a
large extent regulated by laws and central agreements,
- positive attitude to new technology from the central
trade union federations, at least since World War II,
based on the assumption that jobs lost by introduction of
new technology would be compensated by active labor-
market policies from the governments (there has,
however, been some opposition at the local level).

These factors have probably contributed to the relative
stability of Scandinavian labor relations.

Another distinguishing fact, at least when foreigners
look at Scandinavian labor relations, is the high degree of
democratization. The following remark after a tour of
Scandinavia is a typical outsider's view:[7]

> Democracy [in the U.S.A.] stops at the office door and the
> factory gate. (...) Western Europe is extending democ-
> racy into working life. Democratization of work has
> gone further in Scandinavia than elsewhere in Europe.
> Job redesign projects, (...) Codetermination arrange-
> ments, (...) Health and safety legislation (...) Employee
> representatives on corporate boards (...)

These are important historical prerequisites for understanding the DEMOS and UTOPIA projects and the emergence of the collective resource approach. But just as important is the other side of the coin. The Scandinavian
countries are themselves advanced capitalist economies,
and also an integrated part of international western capitalism. Hence, even if the historical situation is different
in Scandinavia, the forces of rationalization of work and
technology that workers and their trade unions meet are
basically the same as in other capitalist economies.

[7] Einhorn, E. and Logue, J. (eds.): *Democracy at the Shop Floor –
An American Look at Employee Influence in Scandinavia Today*,
Kent Press 1982, pp. 5,11,12.

*Laws on Democratization of Work*

The 1970s were the decade when democracy at work truly appeared on the agenda, an intensive debate took place in trade unions, and a number of new labor laws were enacted.[8]

In Norway employees obtained the right to elect one third of the members of the so-called 'company assembly'. In 1975 the first collective agreement on development and introduction of computer-based systems was concluded, giving the trade unions the right to appoint so-called data shop stewards. In 1977 the Norwegian Work Environment Act gave workers extensive rights to stop production that was dangerous to their health. New codetermination procedures for work environment issues were established, and a system of sanctions was defined for when an employer did not fulfil the new work environment requirements.

The Swedish 'work democracy package' in the 1970s also contained several new acts, and existing legislation was revised. The work democracy package included the Act concerning Labor Representatives on Company Boards (LSA), the Companies Act (ABL) concerning financial information, the Act concerning the Status of Shop Stewards (FML), and the Work Environment Act (AML).

Finally, and most important, the Joint Regulation Act (MBL) concerning the workers and their trade unions' right to codetermination in production issues such as design and use of new technology and work organization was enacted in January 1977. It was this law that Prime Minister Olof Palme described as the greatest reform in Swedish society since the introduction of the universal right to vote. In practice, however, there turned out to be no such dramatic change, and hence there was great disappointment among many active union members that

[8] For an overview and several perspectives see e.g. Fry, J. (ed.): *Towards a Democratic Rationality – Making the Case for Swedish Labour*, Gower, Aldershot 1986.

had received the impression that this was the decisive step towards democracy at work.

However, MBL meant new conditions for design and use of computer artifacts. Article 11 stipulates that the employer has to negotiate with the local union before making major changes in production. Article 12 give the union the right to initiate negotiations on any production issue. Articles 18 and 19 stipulate the right for unions to have access to documents management refers to in negotiation, and to receive continuous information on production issues, financial situation, and guidelines for personnel policy.

These were really important changes in the conditions for introduction and use of new technology, but there was also drawbacks. When trade unions and management cannot reach an agreement in negotiations the employer has the exclusive right to make decisions. Furthermore, what 'major changes' meant turned out to be a most disputable issue, as did whether the obligation to give information also included early plans for e.g. the introduction of a computer-based system.

Finally, Article 32 should be mentioned. This article concerns the right for trade unions to negotiate agreements on 'the management and assignment of working duties, and the conduct of the operation at large'. The number of this article was by no means random, since it concerned the same fundamental issue as Article 32 in the Swedish Employers' Confederation (SAF's) Statutes requiring its members to retain the right of decision when entering collective agreements. If collective codetermination agreements (MBA) have been achieved the unions have 'priority of interpretation' of issues covered by the agreement until a dispute is settled in negotiations. This gives the trade unions a possibility to postpone decisions. However, the main idea with Article 32 was that central agreements should be negotiated, and on the basis of these agreements local agreements should be developed. In 1978 the first central collective agreement on codetermination (MBA-S) was reached in the public sector, but not until 1982 was an agreement reached in private industry.

By this time the forms of codetermination had certainly been developed and made more concrete, but at the same time the trade unions democratization offensive had to a significant extent faded out. What started as a trade union response to local demands for democratization in the late 1960s, often expressed as 'wildcat' strikes concerning work environment and introduction of new technology, had received a form sanctioned by parliament, national trade union federations, and national employers' federations.

The 'wildcat' strike by the workers' collective of iron miners at the LKAB mines in the north of Sweden was the starting point for these democratization reforms, reforms that not only concerned democratization of the work place, but also internal trade union democracy. The DEMOS and UTOPIA projects took place in the midst of the practical implementation of these reforms.

## Structure of This Part

In this part I will discuss my two empirical cases, the DEMOS and the UTOPIA project, focusing on them as approaches to designing for democracy at work.

In chapter 11, *From Socio-Technical Satisfaction to Collective Resources*, I will sketch the background for the research strategy chosen, and the emergence of the collective resource approach.

In chapter 12, *The DEMOS Project*, and chapter 13, *The UTOPIA Project*, the projects themselves are presented. I will outline the research objectives, the theoretical foundations, the research approaches, and give examples of activities and results. For each of the projects I will also provide some *post hoc* 'evaluations'.

Finally, in chapter 14, *Reminders on Designing for Democracy at Work*, this part is concluded with a number of 'theses' on design of computer artifacts in the context of industrial democracy.

*Chapter 11*

# From Socio-Technical Satisfaction to Collective Resources

'The socio-technical approach as created by members of the Tavistock Institute aims to provide a set of precise guidelines for creating democratic organizations that are excellent in both human and production terms,' Enid Mumford stated in a recent paper.[1] And in a research overview of design of computer artifacts for, by and with users it was not without reason concluded that 'without exaggeration it can be said that the work of Enid Mumford has greatly influenced the discussion about user participation in the behavioral sciences in the seventies.'[2] Furthermore, the socio-technical approach was at the beginning of the seventies often also connected with attempts to attain industrial democracy in Scandinavia.

Not only did the socio-technical approach address the issue of industrial democracy in Scandinavia; it was also developed with special reference to design and use of computer artifacts. Hence, it may appear as a paradox that some Scandinavian researchers and trade unions in the early 1970s developed *the collective resource approach* to democratization of design and use of computer

[1] Mumford, E.: 'Sociotechnical System Design – Evolving Theory and Practice', in Bjerknes, et al (eds.): *Computers and Democracy – A Scandinavian Challenge*, Avebury, 1987, p. 70.

[2] Kubicek, H.: 'User Participation in System Design' in Briefs et. al. (eds.): *Systems Design for, with, and by the Users*, North-Holland, Amsterdam 1983, p 4.

artifacts as an alternative in opposition to the socio-technical tradition, rather than within that tradition. In this chapter I will try to explain why. I will also outline the emergence of this alternative collective resource approach, focusing on the pioneering research work by Kristen Nygaard and other researchers from the Norwegian Computing Center in cooperation with the Norwegian Iron and Metal Workers Union.

# The Socio-Technical Approach

## *Origin of the Socio-Technical Approach*

The origin of the socio-technical tradition is one of the best known social science experiments after the Second World War. Researchers from the Tavistock Institute of Human Relations in London 'rediscovered' an old work tradition in the North West Durham coal fields. The transformation of this tradition into a new type of work group organization,[3] and the later theoretical reflections in which the socio-technical approach was outlined, suggested an alternative more productive and human way of organizing work and technology than the Tayloristic detailed division of labor. Notably, Bamforth, one of the researchers, 'had been a coal miner before joining the Tavistock Institute and it was through a visit which he made to his old pit in South Yorkshire that the notion of autonomous groups brought itself to the attention of the researchers.'[4]

This *practical* background, it seems, was a good base for understanding the role of the workers' collective and of trade unions in democratization of the work place. However, in the later *theoretical* development the Tavistock researchers came to focus on ideas from general systems theory, especially the biological notion of organic wholes. However, applying this organic view to organiza-

---

[3] Trist, E. and Bamforth, K.: 'Some social and psychological consequences of the longwall method of coal getting' in *Human Relations*, no 4, 1951.

[4] Mumford, op. cit., p. 63.

tions, using analogies drawn from the human body, rather seems to imply that trade union demands for radical organizational changes must be seen as diseases threatening a healthy organizational system, than as a healthy democratic sign.

The basis for the socio-technical analysis is simply to regard work as a socio-technical whole. In designing the production system one has to investigate both *the technical system* and *the social system* and their *interrelations on work group level*. The four stages of the original socio-technical analysis are:[5]

- tracing the outlines of the technical and social system and identifying key variances (a variance is defined as a deviation from some standard or from some specification),
- analysis of the systems' mutual dependencies, focusing on the key variances,
- a description of the company and its environment,
- proposals for change.

In design the fundamental criterion is to control variances as close to their point of origin as possible.[6]

Quite early the socio-technical approach was taken up and further developed in Norway[7], and from there spread to Sweden in different kinds of codetermination experiments.[8]

In the Norwegian version of the socio-technical approach the researchers developed the well-known *psy-*

---

[5] Emery, F. (ed.): *The Emergence of a New Paradigm of Work*, Centre for Continuing Education, The Australian National University, 1978.

[6] Cherns, A.: 'The principles of socio-technical design' in *Human Relations*, no. 29, 1976.

[7] Thorsrud, E. and Emery, F. E.: *Mot en ny bedriftsorganisation*, Tanum, Oslo 1970.

[8] For an overview see Sandberg, T.: *Work Organization and Autonomous Groups*, Liber Förlag, Uppsala 1982 (dissertation).

*chological job requirements* and the *group autonomy criteria*.

The psychological job requirements were:[9]

1. The need for the content of the job to be reasonably demanding (challenging) in terms other than sheer endurance and yet providing some variety (not necessarily novelty).

2. The need for being able to learn on the job and go on learning (which implies known and appropriate standards, and knowledge of results). Again it is a question of neither too much nor too little.

3. The need for some area of decision-making that the individual can call his own.

4. The need for some minimal degree of helpfulness and recognition in the work place.

5. The need to be able to relate what he does and what he produces to his social life.

6. The need to feel that the job leads to some sort of desirable future.

The criteria of group autonomy were:[10]

1. The group can influence the formulation of its goal, including: a) qualitative aspects (...) and b) quantitative aspects (...)

2. Provided that established goals governing relationships to the subordinate system are satisfied, the group can govern its own performance in the following way: a) the group can decide where to work (...) b) the group

[9] Emery, F. and and Thorsrud, E.: *Democracy at Work: The Report of the Norwegian Industrial Democracy Program*, Martinus Nijhoff, Leiden 1976, p. 14.

[10] Gulowsen, J.: 'A measure of work-group autonomy' in Davis, L. and Taylor, J. (eds.): *Design of Jobs*, Penguin, Harmondsworth 1972, pp. 376-378.

can decide when to work (...) c) the group can decide which other activities to engage in.

3. The group makes the necessary decisions in connection with the choice of the production method.

4. The group makes its own internal distribution of tasks.

5. The group decides on its own membership.

6. The group makes its own decisions with respect to two crucial matters of leadership: a) the group decides whether it wants to have a leader with respect to internal questions, and – if it does – who this leader shall be; b) the group decides whether it wants a leader for the purpose of regulating boundary conditions, and – if it does – who this leader shall be.

7. The group members decide how the work operations shall be performed.

These criteria obviously address questions of democratization of work, but their relations to the theoretical foundation of the socio-technical approach are far from obvious. Was the socio-technical approach really a strategy to implement these criteria? And if so, would they form the first steps in a process of continuing democratization of work?

## The Socio-technical Approach in Scandinavia

The Norwegian Industrial Democracy Project was a joint project between the Norwegian Federation of Trade Unions (LO) and the Norwegian Employers' Confederation (NAF). It was initiated around 1960, approximately ten years after the initial Tavistock socio-technical experiments, based on the Tavistock experiences and conducted in cooperation with researchers from Tavistock. The leader of the experiments, Einar Thorsrud, summarized the background in the following way:[11]

[11] Thorsrud and Emery, 1970, op. cit., p. 9 (my translation).

At the end of the fifties the growth in many areas
seemed to come close to the limits set by the natural resources. Matters were quite otherwise for the resources
which depend on human initiative and creativity (...)
Both economic considerations (...) and a growing unrest
in the left wing labor movement contributed to the
creation of strong interests (...)

Between 1964 and 1967 four experiments on work organization were carried out.[12] The new work organization
solutions were all of group production type. They included
some planning activities, but were primarily concerned
with changes in job distribution and wage systems.

However, the experiments did not create much interest
among the workers involved. From one of the four companies Thorsrud reported that the workers 'lost interest in
all of it'[13] when it turned out that management was not
interested in going into further discussion on the more
important issues. And in another company the attitude of
the workers 'gradually turned into resignation, since no
important improvement in their situation seemed to come
about.'[14] The socio-technical ideas did not really disseminate in Norwegian working life.

Though developed in Norway, the real diffusion of the
socio-technical approach in industry happened in Sweden.
Thoralf Qvale, in one of the evaluations of the socio-
technical approach to democratization in Norway, gives
the following explanation:[15]

Apart from the researchers there are very few persons
trying to convey experience from one company to another. In Sweden 'job satisfaction and productivity' have
been the slogans, and a network of employers/pro-

[12] These four experiments are described in Emery and Thorsrud,
1976, op. cit.

[13] Thorsrud and Emery, 1970, op. cit., pp. 72-74, (my translation).

[14] Ibid., p. 99 (my translation).

[15] Qvale, T.:'A Norwegian strategy for democratization of industry' in *Human Relations*, no 5, 1976, p. 468.

duction engineers have taken care of the diffusion. In Norway the slogans were 'industrial democracy and participation', and the union networks were expected to play a central part. As explained, ideological support has come from the top of LO, but the practical involvement from the individual unions' officials has systematically been lacking.

In the late 1960s in Sweden, the rapid technological and structural change was conceived as a problem both by the trade unions (dequalification of work, lack of influence, safety and health problem) and by the employers as personnel problems (recruitment, turnover, absenteeism) and as production problems (efficiency, planning and quality problems due to the Tayloristic organization of production). Especially problematic for the Swedish Employers' Confederation (SAF), but also for the Swedish Federation of Trade Unions (LO), were 'wildcat' strikes at many workplaces, demanding not only higher wages but also democratization.[16] Given this background the socio-technical experiments in Norway seemed most interesting to both parties on the labor market.

Experiments were initiated by the central unions and employer organizations jointly both in the private and the public sectors. Increased job satisfaction and higher productivity were seen as equally important goals. Several of the experiments that started in the late 1960s came up with interesting ideas on work organization and democratic participation. But the practical implementation was a different story, as summarized by Åke Sandberg:[17]

> However the second phase of deciding upon an actual program of change made manifest differences of interest: management was primarily seeking solutions to personnel problems and possibilities for better control of

[16] See e.g. Dahlström, E. et. al.: *LKAB och demokratin*, W & W, Stockholm 1971.

[17] Sandberg, Å.: *From Satisfaction to Democratization – On sociology and working life changes in Sweden*, Swedish Center for Working Life, Stockholm 1982, p. 6.

the wages, whereas unions viewed the experiments as part of a strategy for democratization and union influence at various levels. After conflicts between management and researchers in several of the experiments, the interest of employers in socio-technical changes with participation of sociologists of work was very limited.

Instead most of the Swedish socio-technical experiments were carried out without involvement of independent researchers. The projects were controlled by local management and coordinated by the Technical Department of SAF. The employers were obviously satisfied with the socio-technical approach, but not with the joint experiments. LO was also skeptical to the joint work, as expressed in a program document:[18]

> This method of working proved difficult to implement. Later, when the conflict of views between the two sides with regard to industrial democracy development became more manifest, the problems grew greater. Within the private sector SAF (the Swedish Employers' Confederation) drew its own conclusions from this fact and set up its own development projects with the aid of its Technical Department. In its development projects, SAF stressed the individual, in a form which complicated collective solutions and the possibilities available to the trade union movement.

In 1975 SAF launched a new socio-technical strategy. The Technical Department of SAF coordinated the 'new factory' project, which aimed at more stable production systems based on the principle of *coordinated independence of small sub-systems.*[19]

---

[18] LO: *Codetermination on the Foundation of Solidarity*, Prisma, Stockholm 1977, p. 61.

[19] For a summary see Aguren, S. and Edgren, J.: *Annorlunda fabriker – Mot en ny produktionsteknisk teori*, The Swedish Employers' Confederation, Stockholm 1979.

This principle was not new – it really came from basic socio-technical theory – but the strategy was a different one. The production technology was not taken as given, but as something that should be designed to fit the control of semi-autonomous groups rather than individuals. Specifically, the changes were restricted to the shop floor production level. The vertical division of labor was not at all altered. Management's overall control was rather strengthened. The world-wide known production technology at the Volvo Kalmar plant is as good an example as any.[20] Participation for democracy was in no sense included in the aims of the design.[21] This is one of the reasons why in the late 1970s LO refused to accept a joint socio-technical program for 'new factories'.

In summary it can be concluded that the socio-technical tradition in Scandinavia was theoretically developed in Norway, but practically diffused in Sweden. When the socio-technical approach was diffused to industry it was under the control of management and in forms that fitted managerial interests. Thomas Sandberg found, in comparing the diffusion in Norway and Sweden, that there are two important criteria for success: the projects must be initiated and carried out locally, and they must be planned and managed entirely by management.[22] If these are the prerequisites for diffusion of the socio-technical approach its importance for industrial democracy must be questioned.

---

[20] See e.g. Ehn, P. and Sandberg, Å.: *Företagsstyrning och löntagarmakt – planering, datorer, organisation och fackligt utredningsarbete*, Prisma, Stockholm 1979.

[21] For a more detailed critique of SAF's 'new factory' concept see e.g. the contribution by Jan Kronlund in *Produktionslivets förnyelse – teknik, organisation, människa, miljö*, conference in Uppsala, The Swedish Work Environment Fund, 1978.

[22] Sandberg, T., op. cit., p. 173.

## Socio-Technical Design of Computer Artifacts

When the socio-technical approach, in the early 1970s, was introduced in Scandinavian systems design research it was neither as a diffusion from the Norwegian theoretical development nor from the Swedish practical industrial experiments. Once again it was imported from England, this time in the form developed by Enid Mumford and other researchers at Manchester Business School. [23]

The socio-technical approach certainly had a challenging impact on research on design of computer artifacts in Scandinavia,[24] but there was also an early critique of ideology from the emerging collective resource tradition. For example, the socio-technical systems design method, as presented in an early paper by Mumford,[25] was regarded as anti-trade union and even anti-democratic.[26]

In the paper by Mumford it was suggested that union power and influence was to be measured in order to construct organizational profiles, and how 'indications will come from examining the group's past behavior and from noting the degree of militancy of the union to which its members belong.'[27] Given this knowledge 'the levers of manipulation which are at the planners' disposal for altering attitudes and behavior are as follows: *education, information, participation, compensation, negotiation,*

[23] Mumford, E and Ward, T.B.: *Computers: Planning for People*, Batsford, London, was published as early as 1968.

[24] The tradition was developed in Scandinavia by e.g. Bo Hedberg (Sweden), Niels Bjørn-Andersen (Denmark) and Rolf Højer (Norway), who all had contacts with Enid Mumford.

[25] Mumford, E.: *A Comprehensive Method for Handling the Human Problems of Computer Introduction*, Manchester Business School, 1970(?), mimeo.

[26] For a more detailed critique of the report see Ehn, P.: *Bidrag till ett kritiskt social perspektiv på datorbaserade informationssystem*, Department of Information Processing, Stockholm 1973, pp. 29–32.

[27] Mumford, 1970, op. cit., p. 8.

*command.*'[28] 'Good fit' between management demands and employee expectations is accomplished by changes of the employees' understanding, attitudes and behavior. This version of the socio-technical approach seemed to have very little to do with industrial democracy.

The first academic 'confrontation' between the socio-technical approach and the emerging collective resource approach to design and use of computer artifacts in Scandinavia occurred at an international conference on alternative organizations that took place outside Gothenburg in 1974.[29] In a report evaluating the conference we concluded that there clearly were two different approaches to the social aspects of design of computer artifacts, based on different political perspectives:[30]

> According to [the socio-technical] approach, one should, on the one hand, try to convince management and designers that it is necessary to consider 'human factors' when designing information systems, and on the other hand provide them with useful 'tools' for this aim. Differently phrased, the intention seems to be that directions for humanized information systems are to be given by socio-technical experts. The problem, given this approach, can be summarized in the following question: *How do we design systems to fit people?*

> The attending representatives favoring trade union interests opposed this approach. They emphasized the importance of the employees themselves having the right to determine the content of humanization by real and meaningful participation in the systems design process. In other words: What is aimed for are not gifts

[28] Ibid., p. 10.

[29] Alternative Organizations: The Impact of Computers and Automation on Management, Structure and Work Design, Hindås, July 1974.

[30] Ehn, P. and Göranzon, B.:*Perspektiv på systemutvecklingsprocessen*, Department of Information Processing, University of Stockholm, 1974, pp. 15-16 (my translation).

from management and designers, but participation in and influence over the process. For this aim 'tools' have to be developed. The problem, given this [collective resource] approach, may be summarized in the following question: *How do we make it possible for people to design their own systems themselves?*

*Theory and Practice*

However, the critique of the socio-technical approach should not be seen as a complete dissociation from all aspects of the socio-technical approach. Many of the 'tools' that have been developed are extremely useful in analyzing work organization and production technology; and the job requirement and group autonomy criteria are, when taken seriously, really a challenge to design for democracy at work. The problem is that these requirements seem to have disappeared in the practical application of the approach. In theory and practice this can be understood in terms of questionable harmony assumptions concerning the social forces of production and the distribution of power. The critique is basically not one of design methods, but one of theory and practice in the context of democratization of work.

The main features of the socio-technical approach have indeed changed in a much more participatory and less manipulative direction during the last decade,[31] hence making it more instrumental for democratic design. However, this is – in theory and practice – how we met the socio-technical approach in the early seventies when trying to formulate a research approach for democrati-

---

[31] Se e.g. Gustavsen, B.: 'Workplace Reform and Democratic Dialogue' in *Economic and Industrial Democracy*, vol 6, Sage, London 1985. Concerning design of computer-based systems see e.g. Hedberg, B.: 'Using Computerized Information Systems to Design Better Organizations' in Bjørn-Andersen, N. (ed.) *The Human Side of Information Processing*, North-Holland, Amsterdam 1980, and Mumford, E.: *Designing Human Systems*, Manchester Business School 1983.

zation of design and use of computer artifacts in the workplace.

As we understood it, democratization of design and use of computer-based systems in the Scandinavian setting had to be based on strong local union involvement. In practice the socio-technical approach had failed to support this. This position was also gaining terrain within the trade unions. In the first *action program on industrial democracy and computers from LO* (the Swedish national trade union federation) the situation and the strategy were outlined in the following way:[32]

> The workers and the trade unions are not satisfied with managers and their experts who say they develop systems for planning and control which take human beings into consideration, by paying attention to needs for self-realization and the social impact of technical systems, etc. On the contrary, the unions must work for a situation that makes it possible for workers to develop their own organizational and knowledge resources. This creates the capability to scrutinize and influence, via negotiations, the various aspects of corporate planning and control, and, by extension, to develop worker controlled systems. Thus, the present situation in organizations makes increasing demands upon the commitment and knowledge of the workers. The crucial point is whether these demands become absorbed in an employers' strategy for decentralization and so-called autonomous groups, or whether they will be developed within a workers' strategy for democratization, transcending the level of the work organization.

We had to look for an alternative based on a historical, social and political understanding of the Scandinavian situation, an alternative where the trade unions could play a

---

[32] LO – *Handlingsprogram för företagsdemokrati och data,* Swedish Federation of Trade Unions, Stockholm 1975, p. 30-31 (my translation).

major role. These were basic assumptions in the emerging *collective resource approach*.

# The Collective Resource Approach

## *Origin of the Collective Resource Approach*[33]

By the end of the sixties a new platform for industrial democracy was established in Norway: a new law stated that in all companies with more than 250 employees a company assembly should be established, where one third was elected by the employees and two thirds by the shareholders. This assembly should then elect the company board by proportional vote. This legislation was seen by the unions as a necessary supplement to the socio-technical industrial democracy experiments, about which the Norwegian Iron and Metal Workers Union (NJMF) in 1970 said:[34]

> The codetermination experiments, (...) show that opportunities exist for the development of a new and better work situation for the individual human being. But if one fails to make this kind of initiatives part of a whole they will not contain the opportunities for creating a real democratic situation.

The unions wanted to be accompanied by the new legislation intense educational activities, and, based on the experiences from the first trade union courses dealing with the impact of computers, it was concluded that planning, control and data processing were key areas in this context. Furthermore, it seemed to the unions that the existing knowledge in the area did not reflect workers'

---

[33] This introduction to the collective resource approach is based on Ehn, P. and Kyng K.: 'The Collective Resource Approach to Systems Design' in Bjerknes G. et al. (eds.): *Computers and Democracy – A Scandinavian Challenge*, Avebury, 1987.

[34] Quoted after Nygaard, K. and Bergo, O. T.: *Planlegging, Styring og Databehandling*, part 1, Tiden Norsk Forlag, Oslo 1973, p. 171.

interests, and it was believed that workers would run the risk of acquiring a management perspective, if educational activities in this area were entirely based on existing knowledge.

## The NJMF Project

In 1970 the Norwegian Iron and Metal Workers Union (NJMF) decided to initiate research of their own. In cooperation with researchers from a governmental research institute (the Norwegian Computing Center) who had taught the abovementioned courses on the impact of computers, an application was prepared for the Royal Norwegian Council for Scientific and Industrial Research. After some initial resistance to this 'political' application, money was granted from January 1971, and the project was completed in August 1973.

When the NJMF project was first set up the design was quite traditional: A steering committee, a project group and associated local unions at four different work places. The associated local unions were to act as reference groups. The project group consisted of two researchers and two staff members from the national union, and according to the research plan the researchers were to carry out a number of investigations in close cooperation with the two other members of the project group. These investigations included:

- a study of two or three computer-based planning and control systems,
- a survey of the goals of the union in areas such as working conditions and control of organizations,
- formulation of demands on computer-based systems based on the survey, and finally
- an evaluation of the need for knowledge within NJMF in the areas of planning, control and data processing, and possibly development of teaching material.

However, as the project progressed it turned out to be impossible for the union people involved to actively use the project in the daily work at the factories, the local unions, or the national unions. There was no connection between the work in the project and the action possibilities of the workers and the union. The original project design had to a large extent been copied from traditional research used by managers and management consultants in a context where the goals are clear and means have been discussed for decades. For the unions the situation was different. There had been no extensive discussions on planning, control and computer artifacts and there were no established or clear goals. If the project was not redesigned it seemed likely that it would fail for much the same reasons as the socio-technical codetermination experiments, from a union point of view, had failed: there was no strategic whole in which the partial results from the project could be applied.

### A New Strategy

In the fall of 1971 a new research strategy was developed. This happened at the same time as, and under influence of, the development of the highly successful strategy of the Norwegian anti-European Economic Community (EEC) movement. An important aspect of the new strategy was reflected in the new definition of result:[35]

> as a result of the project we will understand actions carried out by the Iron and Metal Workers' Union, centrally or locally, as a part of or initiated by the project.

In this strategy knowledge was acquired when actions had made the need for new knowledge clear. It was realized that successful initiatives at the national level had to be based on discussions and actions at the local level. The revised strategy towards design and use of computer artifacts aimed at creating a process which would build up

[35] Nygaard, K.: 'The Iron and Metal Project: Trade Union Participation' in Sandberg, Å. (ed.) *Computers Dividing Man and Work*, Swedish Center for Working Life, Malmö 1979, p.98.

knowledge and activities at all levels, with the main emphasis at the local level.

The steering committee played a central role in the discussions leading to the revision of the strategy, and from then on the committee was instrumental in developing the strategy as well as in diffusing the ideas of the project within the trade union movement.

The new strategy was finished and presented in a report in January 1972, and the spring was used to produce a first version of a textbook presenting a union view on planning, control and computer artifacts based on the experiences gained so far.

Probably the most important change was the new role to be played by the local unions. It was decided, as a part of the project, to try out the work practices that the people in the project believed would become commonplace in the future: that the local unions themselves investigate their important problems at the workplace and in the relation between the workplace and the local community, and that in this work they use external consultants as well as consultants and other resources provided by the company. At each of the four work places a number of investigation groups, consisting of union members, were formed. These groups began a process of

- accumulating knowledge about planning, control and data processing,
- investigating selected problems in this area, which were considered to be of special importance by the local unions, and
- taking actions directed at management in order to change the use of new technology.

All the local unions internally chose the problems they wanted to work with. The groups always began with discussions of practical workplace problems, problems which everybody was familiar with. Attempts to analyze and to solve these problems led to requirements for new knowledge and an educational process was started.

The groups met regularly, 2–3 hours at least twice a week, and between the meetings the members did a lot of 'homework', in preparing proposals, discussing with fellow workers, etc. In addition to this the groups participated in different kinds of educational activities. The work of the researchers now concentrated upon supporting these groups.

One investigation group made evaluations of some of the computer-based planning and control systems in the company, including an on-line production information system under development. The other investigation groups evaluated experiences from participation in the planning of a new plant, made proposals for reorganization of one of the main assembly lines, and a company policy action program for the local union.

*Some Results*

A few examples from Kongsberg Våpenfabrikk can illustrate the content of the work in the investigation groups:

- In their analysis of the computer-based planning system CLASS from IBM, the investigation group showed how the use of CLASS inevitably led to overtime.
- A number of proposals were made for a new planning system under development at the factory. These included how to use display terminals for shop floor planning, as opposed to the data entry terminals of the IBM system.
- Changed work organization in connection with numerically controlled machines, including shop floor programming, was also investigated.[36]

As an important part of their work the researchers produced the previously mentioned textbook on planning, control and computer artifacts. The first version was used in the initial knowledge-gathering process in the local investigation groups, and experiences from their work were

[36] Nygaard, K. and Bergo, O.T.: *En vurdering av styrings- og informasjonssystemet KVPOL*, Tiden Norsk Forlag, Oslo 1975.

used in the revision of the book.[37] The book was a key source in developing trade union courses on planning, control and data processing in the Scandinavian countries.[38]

One of the most tangible, and certainly the most widely studied and publicized outcome of the NJMF project was the *data agreements*. These agreements primarily regulate the design and introduction of computer-based systems, especially acquisition of information. The first agreement , a local one, was signed at the beginning of 1974. It was followed in April 1975 by a central agreement between the Norwegian Trade Union Federation and the Norwegian Confederation of Employers. The central agreement was soon followed by a large number of local agreements and the election of numerous so-called data shop stewards, a new kind of shop steward introduced in the central agreement. Among other things the central agreement stated:[39]

> Through the shop stewards the management must keep the employees orientated about matters which lie within the area of the agreement, in such a way that the shop stewards can put forward their points of view as early as possible, and before the management puts its decisions into effect. The orientation must be given in a well-arranged form and in a language that can be understood by non-specialists. It is a condition that the representatives of the employees have the opportunity to make themselves acquainted with general questions concerning the influence of computer-based systems on matters that are of importance to the employees. The

[37] Nygaard, K. and Bergo, O.T.: *Planlegging, Styring og Databehandling*, part 1, Tiden Norsk Forlag, Oslo 1973.

[38] The project is not very well documented, but in addition to the above mentioned reports and books a good English reference is Nygaard, K. and Bergo, O.T.: 'The Trade Unions – new users of research' in *Personal Review*, no 2, 1975.

[39] *General agreement on Computer Based Systems*, Norwegian Employers Federation and Norwegian Federation of Trade Unions, 1975.

representatives must have access to all documentation
about software and hardware within the area of the
agreement.

## The Collective Resource Approach in Scandinavia

The NJMF project inspired several new research projects
throughout Scandinavia, and the development of a research tradition of cooperation between researchers and
workers and their trade unions – *the collective resource
approach*. In Sweden the DEMOS project on 'trade unions,
industrial democracy and computers' started in 1975.[40] A
parallel project in Denmark was the DUE project on
'democracy, education and computer-based systems'.[41] As
the NJMF project these projects emphasized democratization of the design process.

Although growing, the extent and impact of these activities did not meet the initial expectations. It seemed that
one could only influence the introduction of the technology, the training, and the organization of work to a certain
degree. From a union perspective, important aspects like
the opportunity to further develop skill and increase
influence on work organization were limited. Societal
constraints, especially concerning power and resources,
had been underestimated, and in addition the existing
technology constituted significant limits to the feasibility of
finding alternative local solutions which were desirable
from a trade union perspective.

As an attempt to broaden the scope of the available
technology we decided to try to supplement the existing
elements of the collective resource approach with union
based efforts to *design* new technology. The main idea of

[40] See chapter 12, *Case I: The DEMOS project*.

[41] The DUE project is described in Kyng, M. and Mathiassen, L.:
'Systems Development and Trade Union Activities', in Bjørn-An-
dersen, N. (ed.) *Information Society, for Richer, for Poorer*,
North-Holland, Amsterdam 1982. For practical use the DUE pro-
ject group wrote the textbook: *Klubarbejde og EDB*, Fremad,
Copenhagen 1981.

the first projects, to support democratization of the design process, was complemented by the idea of *designing tools and environments for skilled work and good use quality products and services*. To try out the ideas in practice, the UTOPIA project was, in 1981, started in cooperation between the Nordic Graphic Workers' Union and researchers in Sweden and Denmark with experiences from the 'first generation' of collective resource projects.[42]

The NJMF, DEMOS, DUE and UTOPIA projects are by no means the only projects of the collective resource approach, nor is it restricted to the design and use of computer artifacts. Some other projects within or related to this Scandinavian tradition are:

- The Dairy Project, which was conducted by architects, but used methods and perspectives similar to the DEMOS and DUE projects.[43]
- The PAAS project, which besides contributing to a theoretical understanding of changes of skills when computer artifacts are used, also contributed to methods for trade union design work.[44]
- The Bank Project, which was conducted by researchers originally from the socio-technical tradition, although they worked closely with trade unions and with methods and perspective very similar to the collective resource projects.[45]
- The TIK-TAK project worked with local trade unions in the public sector to develop union resources in relation to 'office automation'.[46]

---

[42] See chapter 13, *Case II: The UTOPIA Project*.

[43] See Steen, J. and Ullmark, P.: *De anställdas Mejeri*, Royal Institute of Technology, Stockholm 1982.

[44] See e.g. Göranzon, B.: *Datautvecklingens Filosofi*, Carlsson & Jönsson, Malmö 1984.

[45] See e.g. Hedberg, B. and Mehlmann, M.: *Datorer i bank*, Swedish Center for Working Life, Stockholm 1983.

[46] See e.g. Foged, J. et al.: *Håndbog om klubarbejde, edb-projekter og nye arbejdsformer*, HK kommunal, Århus 1987.

- The Carpentry Shop project, which worked with methods and a design perspective similar to the UTOPIA project but within a 'low tech' area.[47]
- The Florence project, focusing on the work situation of nurses, is another 'second generation' collective resource project designing computer-based environments for skill and quality production.[48]

These are examples of different, but by far not the only collective resource projects. Nor is the approach limited to Scandinavia today. Especially in Britain, despite a very different trade union structure, there are several projects working with similar perspectives and methods.[49] In the coming two chapters I will discuss our contributions to the collective resource approach via the DEMOS and the UTOPIA projects.

[47] See e.g. Sjögren, D. (ed.): *Nyhetsblad från Snickeriprojektet*, Swedish Center for Working Life, Stockholm 1979–83.

[48] See e.g. Bjerknes, G. and Bratteteig, T.: 'Florence in Wonderland – Systems Development with Nurses' in Bjerknes, G. et al. (eds.): *Computers and Democracy*, Avebury, 1987.

[49] See e.g. Williams, R.: 'Democratising Systems Development– Technological and Organisational Constraints and Opportunities' in Bjerknes, G. et al. (eds.): *Computers and Democracy*, Avebury, 1987.

## Chapter 12

# Case I: The DEMOS Project

The DEMOS project (Democratic Planning and Control in Working Life – On Computers, Industrial Democracy, and Trade Unions) began in July 1975, with a duration of four years. It was financially supported by the Bank of Sweden Tercentenary Foundation, The Swedish Work Environment Fund, and at the end by the Swedish Center for Working Life. The Swedish Trade Union Confederation (LO) supported the project, with its 'data-council' acting as an advisory group for the project.

The project was carried out by an interdisciplinary research team (with competence in computer science, sociology, economics and engineering) in cooperation with workers and their trade unions at four different enterprises (a daily newspaper, a locomotive repair shop, a metal factory, and a department store).

This cooperative effort concerned the unions' possibilities to influence design and use of computer artifacts at the local level in the companies. The emphasis was on what the unions could do to safeguard and promote its members' interests in having meaningful work when the technology, the work organization, and the supervision of work is altered. As a complement to these local activities the project also sought to examine obstacles and limits confronting this democratization process.

The overall research goal was to make a contribution to efforts aimed at establishing a more democratic working life. The more detailed objectives of the DEMOS project were stated as making contributions to:[1]

- the theoretical development of an alternative totality of theories, methods and procedures for planning, control and computer use;
- the development of methods and procedures for inter-disciplinary research with trade unions;
- the production of knowledge related to planning and computer use as demanded by workers and their unions;
- the development of procedures for planning and the investigation and analysis of activities which can be used within trade unions.

This was clearly a highly ambitious research program, and in practice the local studies at the different work-places dominated the first three years of the project. The production of study materials, a textbook and articles presenting the findings dominated the last part. More fundamental theoretical and methodological reflections started in this period, but were to a great extent carried out after the conclusion of project.

## Research Methods

The trade union connection and the objective of supporting democracy at work had consequences for the research methods chosen. To us the commission-oriented work research then dominant in Scandinavia seemed to produce results as the basis for decisions by management, rather than being useful to those ultimately affected by the research findings. Therefore we saw a need for a research approach where content and procedures were compatible

[1] Ehn, P. et al.: *Demokratisk styrning och planering i arbets-livet – utgångspunkter för ett forskningsprojekt om datateknik, fackförening och företagsdemokrati*, Demos report no 1, TRITA-IBADB-1023, Department of Information Processing, Stockholm 1975.

with the workers' interests and opportunities for action. Action research was an obvious choice.

In the DEMOS project action research meant that local unions themselves through the use of *investigation groups* made inquiries into the conditions of their own enterprises. The idea was that we as researchers should take part in these investigation groups as 'resource persons'. That is, our academic competence and time should be at the groups' disposal. The starting point of the research should, however, be the workers' own experience and competence.

Inspired by Paulo Freire's *Pedagogy of the Oppressed*[2] and the approach taken by the NJMF project in Norway the idea was to start the work in the investigation groups not with detailed analysis of the specific computer artifacts being designed and used in the work place, but with everyday problems such as time pressure, lack of contact between fellow workers, alienation, and work environment problems. Such a discussion could point at connections with broader but more abstract problems such as the pay system, principles for work organization, long range planning and technology investment policy. From inquiries into such conditions some problems would be ameliorated via demands presented at local negotiations, while other conditions would appear to require collective actions on a higher level e.g. as central investigations, new laws and negotiations on agreements. The perspective would be broadened to include important questions of power and technology in working life. This way it was thought that the workers and the research group could learn from each other while together building up a new understanding essential for democratization of working life. The understanding acquired in the investigation groups should elucidate and widen the possibilities for action. Through education and central unions this knowledge would then be disseminated to other workers, in other workplaces.

[2] Freire, P.: *Pedagogy of the Oppressed*, Herder & Herder, New York 1971.

Besides being 'resource persons' in the investigation groups we as researchers should also conduct more traditional theoretical studies which could both be informed by our practical experiences in the investigation groups and at the same time be brought back for reflections in these groups. The theoretical tradition we leaned towards was a Marxist approach, in the beginning especially inspired by theories on democratic planning,[3] and labor process theory.[4]

The interplay between practical action oriented investigations and theoretical reflective elucidations was what we referred to as *practice research*. This was the base of our research approach.

## The Investigation Groups

The four different workplaces in connection with which the main part of the project work was carried out were chosen after visits to about 25, and discussions with local union representatives there. We tried to find workplaces meeting the following vaguely formulated criteria:

- There should be an acute problem that the local union wanted to work on, and the problem should be of general scientific interest within our research field.
- The local union itself should be committed to developing both independent union knowledge and broad activation of its members.

---

[3] Especially the work by Åke Sandberg, later published in English as Sandberg, Å.: *The Limits to Democratic Planning – knowledge, power and methods in the struggle for the future*, Liber, Stockholm 1976 (dissertation).

[4] In the beginning especially inspired by Braverman, H.: *Labor and Monopoly Capital – The Degradation of Work in the Twentieth Century*, Monthly Review Press, New York 1974, and his theses on the dequalification of work as capitalistic rationalization. Later by Friedman, A.: *Industry and Labour*, Macmillan Press, London 1977, and his theses on direct control and responsible autonomy.

• The concrete problem should be such that it could be developed into an analysis of strategic questions concerning limits and possibilities for democratization.

At the four selected sites *investigation groups* were established. These investigation groups were, in cooperation with the local union, organized to include both workers with a long trade union tradition, and 'ordinary workers' with limited trade union experience. According to the research plan, the investigation groups studied their own workplaces, using the researchers as resource persons, and developed action plans to support local and central negotiations on design and use of computer artifacts. Interesting and activating many union members into dealing with these issues concerning the future of their workplace was also part of the intentions for the investigation groups.

Investigation groups were, as mentioned, ultimately established at a metal factory, a department store, a newspaper and a repair shop.

At the metal factory, the rolling mill at a big steel plant in Oxelösund, the group was responding to management's attempt to develop advanced computer-based systems for production planning and control. The local union was afraid that the new system would dequalify their jobs and also make the workers more isolated from each other.[5]

In the big department-store PUB in Stockholm the initial problem was a planned computer-based system for registration of working hours, sales, and personal data. The union saw a danger of increased control of the workers.[6]

At the newspaper, the Svenska Dagbladet in Stockholm, the typographers were facing the transition from lead and

[5] The work at the metal factory is reported in Perby, M.L. and Carlsson, J.: *Att arbeta i valsverket*, Swedish Center for Working Life, Stockholm 1979.

[6] The work at the department store is reported in Erlander, B.: *Så här var det på PUB*, Swedish Center for Working Life, Stockholm 1980.

Linotype production to computer-based text processing systems. The union wanted to investigate staffing problems, changes in work organization and how this new technology was to be introduced, before it was introduced.[7]

In the repair shop, the State Railroad locomotive repair shop in Örebro, management planned to introduce a computer-based work measurement system. The union had no experience with computer technology and wanted initially to use the 'resource persons' basically as computer experts to check whether the information from management was correct.[8]

Clearly, not all our methodological expectations were met. In the metal factory the investigation group really meant an activation among the members concerning problems with planning and introduction of new technology, but the work in the investigation group was not really taken seriously by the local union committee. At the department store it turned out to be difficult to go from the initial problem investigations to the more action oriented activities. At the newspaper there was a built-in conflict between trade union activists who wished the work to develop fast into concrete actions, and other members that saw the group more as a study group to learn more. Finally, at the repair shop the group was, after the initial investigations, split up into a smaller investigation group (basically with members from the trade union committee) and a more general study group. At all workplaces there was a conflict between using personnel resources for the investigation work and for other trade union work. This gives rise to questions of principle concerning e.g.:

[7] The work at the newspaper is reported in Ehn, P., Perby, M.L., Sandberg, Å.: *Brytningstid*, Swedish Center for Working Life, Stockholm 1984.

[8] The work at the repair shop is reported in Ehn, P. and Erlander, B.: *Vi vägrar låta detaljstyra oss*, Swedish Center for Working Life, Stockholm 1978.

- the combination of broad activity among the member-ship with trade union action oriented investigation work;
- the interplay between knowledge needed for here-and-now negotiations and development of long term per-spectives and action plans; and
- the formulation of 'problems' in cooperation between local unions and researchers/designers.

This will not be further developed here, but after the DE-MOS project such questions were addressed in a special project.[9] Instead I will turn to examples and theoretical reflections illustrated by these examples. Since I was working as 'resource person' in the investigation groups at the newspaper and at the repair shop I will use them as examples. But first a sketch of the theoretical perspective.

## Theoretical Perspective

Marxist labor process theory was theoretically funda-mental to the DEMOS project. On the one hand, we were more users of such theory than really developing it. On the other hand, the work in the investigation groups con-stituted interesting cases for application and reflection, and hence a concretization, especially for understanding design of computer artifacts. The theoretical perspective outlined below reflects this 'dialogue'; i.e. it reflects our reading of theory 'digested' via the work conducted in the investigation groups.

In accordance with Marxist theory we saw the design process as part of a larger organizational development

[9] After the DEMOS project one of the members, Åke Sandberg, ini-tiated the METHOD project to investigate methods problem with our approach. This was done both as a comparative study of different action oriented trade union research projects, and as reflections of the theoretical foundations for action research. This study is documented in Sandberg, Å. (ed.): *Forskning för föränd-ring – Om metoder och förutsättningar för handlingsinriktad forskning i arbetslivet*, Swedish Center for Working Life, Stockholm 1981.

process. Furthermore, this process of organizational development and change was seen in a broader context than traditional organizational development, including and emphasizing trade union activities as well as societal constraints and opportunities.

A central concept was that of *labor processes*. In short, a labor process, in the Marxist tradition, is a process to produce use values; specific products or services of some kind. These use values are produced by people using artifacts (specific machines, tools, techniques etc.) to refine objects of work (specific 'raw materials'; goods, services, ideas, etc.). Planning as well as execution are fundamental parts of human work in this process. The division of labor between different groups of people, their qualifications for accomplishing different tasks, and the quality of the use values being produced are key aspects of the labor process in the context of democratization of work.

The design process reflects, at least conceptually and so far in most cases also practically, a fundamental division of labor, the division between planning and execution. In the *design process*, technology and use values, as well as skill requirements and organizational options for another labor process, the *use process*, are 'frozen'. In the *use process* work is executed given the constraints and opportunities set by the design process. Looked at the other way around, the characteristics of a given use process also set constraints and opportunities for the design process.

The design process as well as the use process are separate labor processes, and at the same time parts of a 'total' labor process. In this perspective an understanding of changes of labor processes must be related to the totality as well as to the separate parts, to the division of labor between different groups of workers within the labor process of design, to the division of labor between the design labor process and the use labor process, and to division of labor within the use labor process.

Given this basic understanding, it is no wonder that the debate and research in the mid-1970s emanating from

Braverman's work[10] came as a great relief and to a large extent formed our general understanding of work and technology. Braverman utilized Marx's analysis of labor processes under the capitalist mode of production, and was able to formulate useful theses on principle driving forces for change of technology and work today.

In summary, the main theses were that the Tayloristic way of organizing work was the most adequate form for division of labor and use of technology in capitalist enterprises. Hence, there was an overall tendency by management to divide the labor process into planning and execution activities. By taking away the planning activities from the shop floor and concentrating them in the hands of management, workers would be easier to control and replace and cheaper to buy. Computer artifacts seemed to be the appropriate technology for the ultimate realization of these basic capitalist interests. Braverman himself provided striking illustrations for the theses from shop floor as well as from office labor processes that had been automated, and the theses certainly affected our view on planning and control systems. Others, elaborating on the same theses, provided illustrations and important contributions to the understanding of the labor process of designing computer artifacts.[11]

However, there were also practical and empirical anomalies that could not be explained by these theses. Work was not deskilled in all cases. More collective forms of work organization than the Tayloristic were sometimes proposed by management. And it happened that workers gained from the introduction of new technology.[12] How-

[10] Braverman, op. cit.

[11] Important contributions were given by Greenbaum, J.: 'Division of Labor in the Computer Field' in Monthly Review, vol 28 no 3, 1976 and by Kraft, P.: *Programmers and Managers – the routinization of computer programming in the United States*, Springer Verlag, New York 1977.

[12] In chapter 18, *Skills and the Tool Pespective* I will return to the contemporary theoretical Marxist discussion on qualifications and technological change.

ever, the Marxist approach was most useful for understanding:

- the relation between capital accumulation and managerial control,
- the role of class struggle at work and workers' resistance,
- the importance of the specific economic, social and historical situation in which a change takes place,
- the role of the existing technology and labor processes.

This holds for the design process as well as the use process and their relations. Here I will not go into a detailed presentation of the labor process tradition and its result,[13] but only present some theses that have been important for our understanding of opportunities and constraints for designing for democracy.

In a Marxist approach capital accumulation or generation of profits is understood as the basic driving force in changes of labor processes. This means that changes that are, at least in the long run, contradictory to this interest are most unlikely to occur. Trade union demands that go further also have to take into account changes of the economic system.

From a Marxist perspective *intensification of work* and *use of new technology* may be understood as two basic strategies for capital accumulation. This means that when a labor process changes, trade unions must be aware of the risk that e.g. new planning and control systems may intensify work beyond acceptable limits. The main reason for introducing new technology is in many cases its ability to intensify work. Especially when technology has been stable in an industry for some time there is a tendency to lower skill requirements and intensify work. However, when really new technology is introduced this may imply increased requirements for skill, especially in the first period, where experience with the equipment is

[13] For references see chapters 3, *Emancipatory Practice – A Marxist approach* and chapter 18, *Skills and the Tool Perspective*.

sparse. In any case, trade unions will hardly be able to resist, at least in the long run, new available more productive technology, especially if other companies introduce it. This reveals the importance of conscious trade union strategies for design of new technology.

*Direct control* and *responsible autonomy* can, in a Marxist approach, be understood as complementary strategies for capital accumulation. This means that even if direct control, the Tayloristic detailed division of labor (intensified, unskilled, cheap labor) in the short run is the most obvious strategy for capital accumulation it is not the only alternative. Opposition from workers and their trade unions to detailed control (strikes, high labor turnover, absenteeism etc.) may imply such high production costs that alternatives are more profitable. Besides, possible economic advantages of using a skilled work force are lost. This produces an opening for complementary strategies, by Friedman labeled responsible autonomy.[14] They are based on some local responsibility, some development of skills and some cooperation among workers. This may for instance explain some of the employer interest in sociotechnical experiments.

To trade unions these strategies are an opportunity for better working conditions, and at the same time a threat. It may well end up in competition between small groups of workers where common interests and solidarity are lost sight of, and where the overall control of the labor process remains firmly in the hands of management. This is even more obvious when considering the fact that the different strategies may be applied to different groups of workers within the same company. Friedman suggests that one of the determining factors in management's choice of strategy towards a group of workers is whether that group is

---

[14] The concepts used here are based on Friedman, op. cit. They have later been developed with special reference to the computer field in Friedman, A. and Cornford, D.: 'Strategies for Meeting User Demands – An International Perspective' in Bjerknes, G. et. al (eds.): *Computers and Democracy – A Scandinavian Challenge*, Avebury, 1987.

central or peripheral to management's interests in capital accumulation and control. Skilled workers or workers in areas with labor shortage may for instance be approached differently than migrant workers, women and other weak-resource groups.

However, the actual outcome of these tendencies toward rationalization of labor processes is not deterministic. It depends on a number of factors such as available technology, the economic situation, the power and strategy of workers and their trade unions, etc. Hence, fundamental to a Marxist approach is not only the attempt to understand the objective side of societal tendencies, but also the subjective side of interests of different groups or classes in society. In a Marxist approach towards understanding technology and work, *class struggle* is an important aspect of actual changes in labor processes. Here, this concerns not only the use process designed, but also the design process and possible integrations in the future.

# Example 1:
# The Locomotive Engine Repair shop

In 1974, the State Employees' Union was informed by the State Railway's central administration that a computer-based planning system, ISA-KLAR, would be introduced in its work shops – among other places in Örebro. It represented the management's alternative to piecework wages, which the union had gotten rid of after a long struggle.

ISA-KLAR involved interviewing workers at the workplace to determine in detail how they carried out their jobs. The employees' knowledge of their jobs was collected, then used by the company management. Work tasks were broken down into small steps, stored in a computer and coupled with an MTM database which was compiled from several big companies.

The following illustrates the work tasks from the loco-motive repair shop produced by ISA-KLAR:

1. Get tools X and Y
2. Go to the carriage
3. Crawl into position
4. Remove the cotter pin
5. Remove the washer and bolt
6. Repeat moments 3-5 for the other bolts
7. Remove

In addition to the specification of detailed work steps and the time and sequence for them, information was also stored concerning the tools that should be used. Company management wanted to use data of this type as a basis for designing the workplace. In this way, possibilities were created for the future control and direction of employees with automatic work orders and instructions.

At the repair shop in Örebro, built in 1901, the main task is engine maintenance. At this repair shop the general system was to be adapted to local and practical circumstances and thus tested.

Management project groups were formed with at least one trade union representative in each group.

Contacts were established with the DEMOS group, when the union had participated in the work with ISA-KLAR for almost two years without really having had any influence or information.[15]

## The Union Investigation Work

In March 1976, the union established an investigative group with 14 participants. With the support of researchers from the DEMOS project, it was to investigate ISA-KLAR and work planning in the locomotive shop. It was

---

[15] Barbro Erlander and myself were the two 'resource persons' from the research group in the repair shop in Örebro. Our work there, from which this summary is extracted, was reported in Ehn and Erlander, op. cit.

also supposed to provide information and support for the union representatives sitting in the project groups.

In the initial discussion between the local union and researchers from DEMOS, the researchers were asked to serve as 'data experts' checking the timings of the various tasks that were to be incorporated into the computer-based system for work measurement. However, we did not consider such an activity consistent with our research perspective.

In subsequent discussions between the researchers and the union it was generally acknowledged that the key implication of the system – that the work being done on the shop floor could be dequalified – was a far more significant issue for the investigation than merely an attempt to adjust particular timings.

The problem under investigation was then reformulated so as to focus on the full range of production planning.

It was further agreed that the union should conduct its own investigation, using the researchers as a medley of resources. Some of the ways in which the researchers could contribute 'expertise' would be, for example, to analyze the computer-based system and to provide a structure for the investigation work.

The investigation group from the trade union was formed after a number of discussions had been held between the local union committee and the research group.

The basic investigation work went on until June 1977, and during this period the group met about twice a month. This work was then followed up for another year by the local union committee and the researchers. Experiences were summarized and 'transformed' by the union into demands for local agreements of codetermination and rationalization.

As a first step, the investigation group issued a report describing the current work situation, pointing out what was good and what was bad. This description was then to be used as a base for the union's strategy for future work regarding planning, control, and computer use as well as a base for collective agreements within the Joint Regulation Act (MBL). It should be stressed that the investigation was initiated before the introduction of MBL.

## The Workers' View Of the Work Place

In the accounting of the current situation, issues such as the work environment and the planning were described. The report stressed that the changeover from piecework to a system of fixed monthly wages was extremely important, not only in terms of group solidarity among the workers and of job satisfaction, but also in relation to the quality of production.

The lack of planning and uneven rate of work on the engines had created major problems, and the fact that neither the tools nor the spare parts were handled effectively had been a great source of irritation at all workshops. Too much time was taken up searching for tools and spare parts. The poorly maintained work facilities had caused a number of problems in the work environment. Some examples were outside draughts and also working positions that were damaging workers' health. The uncertainty as to the consequences of ISA-KLAR did not make the working conditions any better, and there was great dissatisfaction about the lack of information.

## Further Investigation Work

At the same time as the current work situation was described, a more thorough analysis was performed of the ISA-KLAR system.

The purpose of this system (its technical construction, etc.) was described in various documents, and it was mainly the researchers who conducted this investigation. The results of this study were discussed continuously in the investigation group.

Some activities in the investigation group were carried out based on the systems approach of West Churchman.[16] For instance, in planning the work in the group the *purpose* (e.g. an alternative proposal to ISA-KLAR or an action program for the union) was related to *resources* like economy and time, available information, the researchers, etc. This was, in turn, related to the *environment* in the case, e.g. managerial prerogatives. *Measurement of performance* was discussed in terms of working conditions and democratic participation in design work. The *decision-maker* was discussed in terms of the local union committee or the investigation group. Finally, the *client* was discussed in terms of the workers in the repair shop in Örebro, all repair workers of the State Railroad's different repair shops, or the central union in its work with laws and agreements. These discussions created a lot of tension in the group, but were also very important for its progress.

The investigation was completed by studies of various topical questions which were also important for the trade union. For this reason, a study group was formed on planning, control and computer use. Among the topics discussed in the group were the principles of Taylorism, and these were compared to the current work situation at the SJ work shops. It also included basic facts on computers, design, planning methods, etc. One purpose of these meetings was to broaden the discussions and to elicit views from as many members as possible.

One demand of the union – presented in various management project groups – was that the problem with the planning, the material administration and the work organization be solved before the discussion about computer-based time measurement be carried on. As time went by, it became obvious that the union's chances of influencing the design of production planning by participation in the project groups were more or less illusory. Camouflaged by

[16] Churchman, C. W.: *The Systems Approach*, Delta, New York 1968.

technical discussions, the management of SJ and its consultants continued to develop ISA-KLAR. The basic question – how the planning in the shops was to be conducted in the future – never appeared on the agenda. Through this fact, and the analysis of ISA-KLAR, the union's investigation group came to the conclusion that the system had to be stopped until an agreement on codetermination could be reached that would regulate the design and use of this kind of systems. The local union demanded, and got, central union support for this position. Management officially accepted the position of the union.

Instead management appointed so-called planning groups, which were to 'construct and test a planning model' for two different items in the production process (components on bogies and work on certain types of engines). Each of the planning groups consisted of two repair workers, a supervisor, and a production technician.

The investigation group of the union collaborated with the two planning groups. The union participants in the planning group were appointed from the investigation work around ISA-KLAR and the investigation group supported its members in the planning groups. In practice the repair workers themselves did the design work. A technician was asked to look over the proposals, and minor adjustments were made.

## The Propositions of the Bogie Workers

Although the planning groups had very little time at their disposal they still managed to present concrete propositions on changes in work organization as well as other conditions.

The basic idea in the proposition was that repair workers should be flexible between the rates of work. These are pre-demolition, demolition, test of cracks, welding, installation, mounting of wheel axles, and final installation. Flexibility meant that all repair workers were to participate in the entire work cycle, from demolition to final installation, and they should all be able to handle all the existing tasks. The main principles were thus skill, training, and job rotation. In the proposition special stress was placed on the teams' right to plan their own work. This was considered necessary not only as a move toward democratic work organization, but also as a measure facilitating production.

In connection with the proposition on a new bogie workshop, demands were put forward, and possible improvements of methods was discussed.

The repair workers claimed that their proposition had demonstrated that they could have a well-functioning work place without ISA-KLAR, and the local union contended that their way of working with rationalization can serve as a model for other workplaces as well.

## Demands of Rationalization

The local union's experiences in investigation work and its awareness of SJ's role in the ISA-KLAR project were in May 1978 assimilated in a number of demands that served as a basis for local agreements on rationalization and codetermination on design and use of computer artifacts. The demands were adjusted to MBL and to a central collective agreement on codetermination. Among the demands were:

- that long term planning be conducted by SJ for (among other things) technical development, training, and staff policy;
- that the repair and revision work be carried out within SJ;
- that rationalization not lower the requirements for skilled repair personnel;
- that rationalization not result in work measurement of individuals or groups or in incentive payments of any kind.

With special regards to the *design process*, it was demanded:

- that directives for a project be negotiable before it starts;
- that design methods are approved by the union;

- that investigations in the design work not only include technical and economic considerations, but also changes in employment, work environment, work organization, and possibilities for cooperation, codetermination, and development in the daily work;
- that the union get the necessary resources for conducting a parallel independent investigation;
- that the cost for these resources be calculated as part of the investment in the rationalization;
- that participation by trade union representatives and users be a natural aspect of the design work, and that it be planned to allow this; and
- that participants receive what the union regards as the necessary training to participate in the design work.

*Just after DEMOS*

What did the local union win or lose by participating in the DEMOS project? For one thing, it gained experience in planning and in conducting its own investigations, independent of management; it also learned to cooperate with researchers/designers in resolving union problems.

In addition, the union came to understand a great deal about production planning generally, and about computer-based work measurement specifically. The experiences in investigation work, as well as in production planning, entered into the discussion at other repair work shops in SJ.

Our report on the work, *Vi vägrar låta detaljstyra oss* (We are Opposed to Detailed Control),[17] was distributed to all members in Örebro. A new study group on work shop planning, based on the report was set up by the local union.

But the struggle over planning at the work place was far from finished. As a result of the union opposition, ISA-KLAR was not implemented. This was an important victory for the union. But on the other hand, no immediate changes took place in response to the propositions of the bogie workers, and no agreement was reached on code-

[17] Ehn and Erlander, op. cit.

termination with regard to rationalization and use of computers. The ultimate power to plan was not shifted from management to union. No real codetermination was achieved.

## Ten Years After

What was the impact of the DEMOS investigation work at the repair shop in Örebro in a longer perspective? We ourselves did not conduct such evaluations, but a report from a now ongoing democratization project at the State Railroad give some rather positive indications. In the report its is stated that:[18]

> 1976 was a remarkable year. The repair shop in Örebro began to participate in the DEMOS project. (...) The importance of the DEMOS project for developments in Örebro reminds one of the story of the hen and the egg. Obviously the researchers had great influence. Together with the local union they created a frame of reference that still is alive. It is also obvious that the local union already, at this time, had a well developed strategy, and this was perhaps a condition for starting the DEMOS project in Örebro. (...) The core of the debates from the 1970s is still alive and useful. Developments have, however, not been according to the prognoses from the 1970s. An important reason is of course that the debates took place. However, from a trade union point of view, the strategy must be developed to deal with the new reality. The strategy from the 1970s concerned a defense against the threat of that time. Today the threats look different. The new strategy must identify these new threats, and perhaps the union must change part of the frame of reference that was established in the DEMOS period.

---

[18] The report is based on interviews. The quotations are from a draft by Brulin, G. and Ulstad, C.: *DESAM vid halvlek* (forthcoming) (my translations).

And on the investigation work with the work measurement system the report says:

> The struggle forced the union to develop an offensive strategy. The union could not just say no to the proposals from management. DEMOS meant an opportunity to develop the union's competence in relation to control systems, computers, work organization and skills.

As a reflection on interviews concerning the changes in the production process today, the investigators find it

> interesting to note that the rather unstructured alternative presented a long time ago has more and more been developed into a coherent view on production planning. Today this union view also gets some support from management. (...) The message from the managing director concerns many things that we can recognize from the trade union work with DEMOS and collective agreements on design and use of computer artifacts. It is not an exaggeration to say that the management philosophy on efficient organization now has caught up with the one the union developed in the mid-1970s.

As a comment on the draft for a collective agreement on design and use of computer artifacts that the investigation group developed the report says:

> It was written 10 years ago, but is still largely valid.

And the report sums up:

> The trade union work in Örebro from DEMOS onward has given a trade union perspective that perhaps is best formulated in the title of the DEMOS report: *We are Opposed to Detailed Control*. The collective agreement on design and use of computer artifacts created conditions for a dialogue with management. The repair shop in Örebro got a new managing director with a view on efficient organization that, to a great extent, overlaps the trade union perspective. In summary, as we understand it, what happened and is happening in Örebro

can be explained by the abovementioned three moti-
vating forces: a trade union perspective, use of the the
collective agreement on design and use of computer
artifacts, and a real dialogue with management.

If this report is right, the DEMOS project at the repair shop
in Örebro did not just produce yet another research report
on computers and democracy at work.

# Example 2:
# The Newspaper

In January 1976, a project for the introduction of computer-based text processing was initiated at the major
daily newspaper Svenska Dagbladet in Stockholm. At that
time photosetting had already been in operation for many
years parallel to lead composing. However, the major
change, the scrapping of lead, still lay ahead of the graphic
workers' union at Svenska Dagbladet.

Graphic production and the manufacture of newspapers had been carried out in approximately the same
manner for several hundred years. Work in the composing room of a newspaper has, for example, to a great extent been a craft.

In the mid-1970s, however, graphic workers found
themselves in the center of a technological revolution.
Within a short decade, they went from a traditional craft
to a situation in which computers are central to the entire
production process. Text entry, proof-reading, image processing and subsequently page make-up, all were now
done via computer display terminals from which the finished text was produced on a photosetter linked to the
computer-based system.

The labor process no longer consisted of a series of work
stages in which the material gradually was refined by
hand with the assistance of machinery. Instead the 'raw
text' fed into a computer-based system was now automatically transferred – hyphenated and justified – to a
photosetter.

As a result of this new technology, the graphic workers' control over their work was threatened. An increasing number of decisions were programmed into the machines, e.g. the standardization of advertisement formats. To a great extent production speed was determined by the machinery.

In short, the new computer-based technology threatened graphic workers in three areas: control over the labor process, dequalification of work, and employment.

## The Union Investigation Work

In the beginning of 1976 contacts were also established between the graphic workers' local union at Svenska Dagbladet and the DEMOS research group.[19]

An investigation group was formed at a union meeting. The subject of the group was determined as 'new technology', but it was an open question as to how the group should organize its work and which questions to focus on.

The group was set up to include graphic workers with different skills. It also included members of the local union committee as well as members with little union experience. Around twenty workers were active in the group.

An agreement was negotiated with management on the conditions for the investigation. The agreement included the right for the group to meet during working hours, the researchers' access to the workplace, and the group's access to information, such as the right to interview management and technical experts in the company.

The investigation work was planned in two steps – an investigation of what was good and bad in the current situation at Svenska Dagbladet, and a future oriented study.

In the study of the current situation the idea was to utilize the different experiences that the participants had to formulate demands for change. The group should not

[19] Maja-Lisa Perby, Åke Sandberg and myself were the 'resource persons' from the research group working with this case. The presentation of this case is based on our report: Ehn, Perby, Sandberg, op. cit.

narrowly look at the current technological change at the newspaper, but create a general understanding and formulate general demands that were supported by many members.

In three months, and with the researchers as 'resource persons', the group had produced a report which highlighted problems as well as positive qualities in the current work environment, work organization, training, etc. The report concluded that:

- In the composing room, and at the lithographic department, work was still to a high degree, carried out as a craft. Work environment problems had to do with heat and gas from the lead, heavy lifts, and dangerous chemical products used in film processing and plate making.
- At the other technical departments (stereotyping, printing, distribution) the workers were more like machine operators. Work was often monotonous, and heavy lifts were a dangerous aspect of the work environment in all these departments.
- Time pressure was seen as a problem at all the technical departments.
- At all departments work was organized in teams. However, it was only in the composing room that this meant planning by the team and systematic job rotation (among skilled workers, i.e. the female teletypists were excluded).
- Composers and lithographers performed work that required craft skills and long practical training; they also were the only group that had a strong professional pride. Especially in the composing room this represented a problem, since there was a division of labor between on the one hand, craft-trained male composers, and on the other hand, female teletypists with only typewriting and on-the-job training.
- In spite of time pressure and work environment problems most graphic workers got on well with their work at Svenska Dagbladet. Especially the fellowship with

their closest work mates was seen as very positive. The composers, however, did also really like their work (i.e. the composing work).

In the next step technical and organizational alternatives were to be outlined. Here the investigation group was to look into what plans management had, and reformulate the problems and potentials highlighted in the first study into concrete design proposals that could be negotiated by the union committee. This step turned out to be much harder to take, and after another four month the group stopped without really having been able to fulfill the task of formulating concrete design demands.

There were at least three reasons for this 'failure'. One had to do with our *design methods*. Discussions were not enough to envision future possibilities and constraints. We had no method to transform the ideas from the initial investigation into concrete visions of the future. As a result several participants found the investigation work boring, and the trade union committee found it too abstract.

Another problem with the investigation group had to do with *the union's scarce resources*. In practice the investigation work not only created new resources, it also sapped resources from other trade union activities. Many active members participated in the group, and this took most of their time for trade union work.

Finally, the union had a lot of *'burning' here-and-now problems* with the introduction of new technology which they wanted to use their most qualified members to work with.

As a consequence of this, the investigation work was reorganized, and was continued in other organizational forms during the next two years that the union participated in the DEMOS project.

Several smaller groups were established that investigated various issues as a basis for negotiation with management. Some of these groups were 'pure' union design groups, others were joint management and union groups where the union members worked full time with the investigation. In parallel to this some, not very active, general union study groups were established. The researchers from DEMOS worked as 'resource persons' for some of these groups and for the union committee.

## Management's Design Proposal and the Union Response

Management's design project for scrapping lead in favor of full computer-based text processing started in January 1976. For this project management had hired external consultants. The union was well represented in the project group formed to carry out the study. However, this group only met three times and the actual design was carried out entirely by experts from the consulting firm. The consultant's study provided an overall proposal for the introduction of new technology to the composing department.

The proposal, delivered after four months, included the computer-based system to be implemented, and a plan for its implementation. Though formulated in technical terms the proposal meant drastic changes in work organization, including the controversial issues of division of labor between journalists and graphic workers.

At its best, union participation in the project group resulted in only marginal adjustments. For example, in the final proposal management had eliminated statements such as 'the editorial text is entered by journalists'. The technological solution, however, was not altered. The largest number of display terminals were in the editorial departments, as had been suggested in the the original systems proposal.

In this situation, and with the support from the DEMOS researchers, the union formulated a strategy to deal with the design situation. The strategy was discussed at a membership meeting, and then in June 1976 formulated as a letter to the managing director of the company. The union wanted time to prepare themselves for negotiations on directives for a new investigation of consequences of the new technology for work organization, skill requirements, etc. This study was to complement the consultants' report.

In the letter the union stated that 'in SDK (the local union) we are not against the new technology. However, to take a stand we must get *resources to understand* the consequences of the changes and what this means to the graphic workers. Such consequences are not mentioned in the consultants' report.'[20]

What the union wanted time to prepare negotiations on included:

- new forms for decision-making in the design process so that their demands could be taken into consideration, including the right to negotiations whenever found necessary by the union during the design process, and
- a new investigation that gave a detailed picture of what happens to the graphic workers in the whole company, not only in the composing room.

Among the more detailed demands for participation in the design process were mentioned e.g. education of members in design work and computer-based text processing so that they actively could participate in the design process, and resources for seminars and conferences to support the work in the DEMOS investigation group.

Questions to be negotiated about the actual design included e.g. work environment, work organization, opportunities for contacts between workers, education, and demarcations between different groups of workers.

Upon receipt of the letter, the management retreated from their initial proposal. They no longer made reference to a total solution but instead applied an approach of presenting one machine at the time.

Initially, the union attempted to stand fast on the demands put forward in the letter, but gradually they returned to dealing with various issues after they had arisen. Half a year after sending the letter, the union altered its demand for an overall solution to only demanding negotiations prior to the introduction of any new machinery.

[20] Ibid., pp. 105–107.

In 1979, and after many rounds of negotiations, the transition from lead composing to computer-based text processing was completed. By then the local union had done its own investigations in working hours, e.g. concerning education and manning of the new equipment. Union representatives had also participated full-time, and with as many representatives as management, in a project suggesting the new work organization and the layout of the composing room.

No one was fired, and an agreement securing employment was reached in negotiations. An education program to maintain and develop the composers' and the teletypists' skill was also agreed upon after negotiations, but proved, in practice, hard to fulfill. Directions for the future work organization were still an open question.

The union was, however, not really able to influence the choice of technology and therein one of the fundamental preconditions for work content and work organization. The development at Svenska Dagbladet must be viewed against the technical developments in the entire graphic branch. This limit to democratization at the workplace was one of the experiences that led to the UTOPIA project and our attempt to really design computer-based alternatives for skilled work in the printing industry.[21] However, before leaving the experiences from the DEMOS work at Svenska Dagbladet our reflections about the content of a union strategy will be discussed – the need for a comprehensive union view.

### A Comprehensive Local Union View

Basic problems with a union strategy for dealing with technological change came to light in the study at Svenska Dagbladet. These problems concerned differences of interests between different groups of members, technical-economic bindings, and existing technology.

---

[21] See chapter 13, *Case II: The UTOPIA project* and chapter 15, *The 'Tool Perspective' – An Example*.

New technology changes *the division of labor between different groups of workers*. In newspapers this is not only a question of graphic workers versus journalists, or workers at the newspaper versus technical staff from computer companies, it is also an internal demarcation problem for the graphic unions.

The technology in the composing room was emphasized in the suggested design at Svenska Dagbladet. However, the changes meant that the stereotype department would be drastically reduced and several lithographic tasks would also disappear. The union wanted, as mentioned earlier, to negotiate a comprehensive solution for all technical departments. When management refused to negotiate about such a solution, the union came to settle for a solution for the composing room alone. The negative side of this strategy was that the stereotypers and the lithographers to a great extent were left to solve their own work organization and demarcation problems *after* the new technology had been introduced in the composing room. The positive side was the training program for teletypists that was negotiated. It gave the teletypists the opportunity during working hours and at full pay to improve their graphic skills to a level of qualified graphic work.

The *'technical-economic' bindings* posed a hard problem for the union at Svenska Dagbladet. For example how should the union act when management wanted to replace the old photosetters? The union shared the opinion that the old ones had to be replaced, but they also knew that the new 'generation' of photosetters at the same time was an investment in the new computer-based system on which no agreement had been reached in negotiations. More generally it was known that the management board had approved an investment plan for complete transition to computer-based text processing, and yet the union was 'forced' to negotiate on the introduction of single machines at different departments without a comprehensive view of the consequences for the members at different departments.

Finally the union faced the *existing technology* as a problem for a comprehensive view. Did alternatives that fulfilled the union demands on the technology exist? Could the local union at Svenska Dagbladet influence the technological change in the newspaper industry? Negative answers to such questions pointed in the direction of support from central union levels – a union technology policy for the graphic industry – a complementary central union strategy for changing social conditions and for research and development of technological alternatives. This problem with existing technology was also, as mentioned, an important factor in our own shift of research strategy, from support of a defensive local union approach, as in the DEMOS project, towards support for a proactive approach by designing organizational and technological alternatives for skill and democracy at work, as in the UTOPIA project.

## Towards a More Democratic Rationality

Below I will summarize our reflections from the DEMOS project concerning possibilities and constraints for more democratic design processes in Scandinavian working life. The reflections are *formed by the practice research approach taken.* Hence, they reflect our interpretation of the 'interplay' between Marxist labor process theory, and our practical experiences with designing for democracy at work. First, I discuss the limits to democratization in terms of *managerial strategies for rationalization* – the potential changes of the labor process understood as a valorization process for accumulation of capital.[22] Then I discuss local *trade union efforts to counteract this rationality* – a rationality of the oppressed.[23]

---

[22] See chapter 3, *Emancipatory Practice – A Marxist Approach.*

[23] These reflections on strategies were first summarized in Ehn, P. and Sandberg, Å.: 'Local Union Influence on Technology and Work Organization – some results from the Demos Project' in Briefs, U. et al. (eds.): *Systems Design for, with, and by the Users*, North-Holland, Amsterdam 1983. See also Sandberg, Å.: *Techno-*

# Rationalization Strategies for Capital Accumulation

One important reason why the union was successful in preventing the introduction of the computer-based work measurement system into the locomotive work shop was that it was in no way going to effect or alter the actual artifacts of production. Within the graphic branch, however, computer-based systems are themselves production tools. Within the locomotive repair shop, the intention was not to alter the production process; instead, the supervision and control of the work and material was to be altered. In all probability it was this factor that made it easier for the union to successfully reject its introduction. Other alternatives existed which were as profitable. In the graphic branch example, however, there were no equally profitable alternatives available on the market. The maximum *intensity of the use of labor power* (the locomotive repair shop) and the constant *introduction of new technology* which increases the productivity of the work force (in the newspaper) are two central components in management rationalization efforts.

Rationalization and new technology change and shape the labor process. As will be illustrated, rationalization can be directed toward *the worker as human labor*, toward *the artifacts that the worker works with*, or toward *the work objects that the worker refines*. What is of importance is that *regardless of the focus of rationalization, it has consequences for both the organization and the content of work.*

Several of the most basic rationalization strategies are summarized in the illustration below.[24] In the DEMOS

*logical Change and Co-determination in Sweden – Background and analysis of trade union and managerial strategies*, Temple Press (forthcoming).

[24] This Marxist interpretation of 'the frontiers of capital accumulation' was inspired by Björkman, T. and Lundqvist, K.: *Från Max till Pia*, Arkiv, Malmö 1981 (dissertation).

project we found it useful to distinguish between management rationalization strategies for the *use* of production technology, and for the *design* of such technology. One reason for this distinction is that the unions' possibilities and strategies for dealing with technological and organizational changes completely differ in these two areas.

## Rationalization Strategies Directed at Human Labor

The classic strategy employed by management for increasing profits has been to *lengthen the work day* without a corresponding increase in wages. In the Scandinavian countries, as in other industrialized nations, this strategy is primarily of historical interest. As early as 1900, for example, typesetters succeeded in pushing through the eight hour work day even though other groups still worked 9–10 hours per day.

Nevertheless, rationalization measures aimed at *lowering the price of labor* and *increasing its intensity* to the greatest extent continue to be widely employed. They are used in both cases to break down the labor process into simple tasks. In some situations, it has been possible to separate out certain of these tasks which can be performed by those with less training and education – thereby employing cheaper labor. With the assistance of the computer-based planning system in the locomotive repair shop in Örebro, the work cycles would have been divided up so that more skilled labor could have been replaced by unskilled and minutely directed labor. In such situations, skills would not be sought, and nor would training be provided. Another example of this process is the division of labor between composers and teletypists. The degree to which company management succeeds with this strategy of paying lower wage rates to unskilled labor depends of course on the union's response. The union prevented the introduction of the computer-based planning system in the repair shop. As a result of the union's demands, teletypist wages are at the same level as for the average male graphic worker.

Even though company management may not succeed directly in lowering the price of labor by means of the minute division of work tasks, such an approach often offers the possibility of increasing work intensity. It is easier for a company to supervise and control workers who carry out a few simplified tasks. In the case of the computer-based work measurement system in the repair shop, it would have been possible for the company to give repairmen detailed instructions. An example from the composition department is performance measurement and piecework wages for the teletypists.

## Rationalization of Artifacts and Objects of Labor

Within the framework of the existing technology it is possible for a company to reduce its machinery, raw materials and general plant costs. One rationalization strategy in this respect is to *economize on the use of plant space*. This often occurs in connection with changes in technology. For example, with the introduction of new technology in the newspaper the company drastically reduced the space allocated for the composing department. Thus, one of the pre-conditions for a good work environment and organization was affected.

The *increased utilization of machinery* is another rationalization strategy. An example of this is the fact that newspaper composing departments often take on outside work to fill in the idle periods that occur in the production of a newspaper. This affects work organization and control, and perhaps, work intensity as well.

The *reduction of material costs* is yet another possible area for rationalization. One example is the introduction of block setting in order to make better use of expensive photosetting paper. This alters the work organization of paste-up work.

## Rationalization as Design of New Artifacts and Objects of Labor

Competition between companies results in continual developments of work artifacts and objects. The result of this steady technological development is that fewer workers are required to produce the same product quantity. *Labor productivity* can be increased by means of the introduction of various forms of mechanization and automation. Constraints on the organization and content of work are also built into the artifacts.

A historical example of increasing the productivity of labor in this way was the replacement of the composing stick with the composing machine. A current example is the introduction of computer-based text and image processing. To a greater extent the work is performed by unskilled graphic workers. Entire departments (e.g. stereotype and plate preparation departments) disappear when plates are engraved by laser beams directed by a composing department computer.

### Rationalization Strategies in Practice

The rationalization strategies outlined above are theoretical 'ideal types'. In practice, a union will typically be confronted with a mixture of these strategies.

Furthermore, the specific rationalization strategy chosen by the company management in a given situation is also dependent on the technological limitations (for example, paper paste-up presupposes advanced photosetting). Further, the company's economic resources available for investment must also be considered. Finally, it is also dependent upon union strength and strategy.

How can the union deal with management's rationalization strategies for design and use of technology and work organization? How can the union confine rationalization to socially acceptable and union supported forms? I now turn to the overview of our reflections on such counter-rationality design strategies for democratization by the oppressed.

## Rationality of the Oppressed

The technology and work organization in a company often changes gradually – generally at the same pace as new machinery replaces old through normal wear. However, more rapid and thorough changes frequently occur with the design of new production technology.

Whichever of these situations prevail, the union needs to have a good overall grasp of developments to be able to see the connection between various changes which may be occurring simultaneously. It is essential that studies carried out in the light of such changes illuminate issues of importance to the union (such as employment, work organization, work environment) so that the consequences for the entire personnel and all departments are brought to light and possible conflicts can be resolved. The union must acquire a grasp of the ongoing technological-economic developments and the available 'negotiating room' for union influence and the alternatives that exist.

What can the union do at the local level? How can one best work within the union in the face of technological and organizational changes?

On the basis of experiences from the DEMOS project three design strategies which the union can apply will be discussed: Union *participation* in the companies' project groups; a model for independent union design work in connection with the companies' studies – *the negotiation model*; and as a third alternative, perhaps the union should not become engaged in the company management's design work, but instead focus its efforts primarily on the *mobilization and ideological education* of its members.

## Project Participation

Today, design work in companies is often carried out by a project group with the assistance of experts. The group is established by the company's management. It is increasingly common to include representatives from the departments concerned. Not infrequently, the union is offered a position in the project groups. This participation *can* provide the opportunity of becoming involved even at the idea stage of the project. However, the union's chances of exerting significant influence through such traditional project work are very limited. We found participation in project groups appointed by management to be a trade union problem because:

- the appointed project group participants are often not trade union representatives, and if they are
- the union representatives have no real means of exerting power coupled to their project group participation, and hence there is
- the risk that the union will become integrated into a generally unaltered employer decision-making process, especially since
- the union representatives will often have to comment on alternatives and approve decisions without really having a chance to explore the questions from a trade union perspective; besides,
- the return for giving management access to 'shop floor information' is unclear, and
- trade union participation can, in fact, be part of a managerial strategy to make it easier to implement the changes planned by referring to the fact that the union has been involved; and finally,
- language, attitudes and values of management's technical and organizational design experts have a tendency to spread, and in fact by the end of the project it often happens that
- the trade union representative is offered some kind of expert position, and in this way the union loses access to information which its representative inspite of it all acquired while participating in the project work.

There is the risk that the union will become integrated in a generally unaltered employer's design process.

*'The Negotiation Model'*

Against such a background, is there any reason why the union should at all participate in the company's project groups? Yes, given certain pre-conditions. To remain completely outside such groups would close the door to a vital source of information. In our view (i.e. that of the

DEMOS project) the most important pre-condition for such participation was that parallel to the company's project group, an independent union effort takes place to enhance understanding, or for mobilization around union demands.

This involves a clear distinction of the relationship between the parties in the design work, but it does not conflict with demands for democratization of decision-making in the day-to day work in the organization. On the contrary, we found that a demarcation of the relationship between the parties in the design work is a precondition for the democratization of cooperation and planning in the work organization.[25]

A model for the development of union resources and negotiations was created in the DEMOS project. As its basis we stated that:[26]

> the main purpose of this negotiation model is to serve as a form within which the union may develop knowledge and realize its demands in a democratic, efficient manner; a second objective is to facilitate what in planning theory is seen as preconditions for 'quality in investigations' – for example, critical analysis, alternatives, openness. Also, from this point of view it is desirable for the union to make its own investigations and prepare its own alternatives.

More specifically, the purpose of the model and the style of organizing union work is:

- to allow the local union to obtain its own knowledge in new areas, by making its own investigations;

---

[25] This aspect of the relation between democracy and bureaucracy is further discussed in Ehn, P. and Sandberg, Å.: 'Att påverka det påverkbara' in *Tre år med MBL*, Liber, Helsingborg 1980.

[26] Ehn, P. and Sandberg, Å.: 'Systems Development – On strategy and ideology' in *DATA* no 4, 1979, p. 52.

- to decrease the risk of the union being overpowered by management when participating in management project groups;

- to develop a basis for negotiations which is well supported by union members;

- to ensure that the working procedure itself contributes to activating and increasing the participation of union members.

According to the model, *independent union design or investigation groups* work in parallel with the company *management project groups* and provide a basis:

- for discussions at membership meetings and union study groups;
- for union representatives in the company project groups; and
- for the union's position in negotiation with management.

Hence, participation in management's project groups is a process of *gathering information and discussing alternatives*, whereas *major decisions are taken in formal negotiations* between the local union and management. The union's position in these negotiations is based on proposals from the union design group and broad discussions with the membership. In addition to the union design group, other potential resources for the local union in this design process are support from *central levels of the union, workers' consultants*, or researchers. *Study groups* concerned with the actual problem area, for instance with work organization, may serve as reference groups for the design groups and for the external experts.

In practice, including many more local unions than those participating in the DEMOS project, the strategy proved workable and most useful. However, there is a risk that what has been described can become an investigation based on the employer's terms with union representatives as hostages. One reason the union representatives easily can acquire (or appear to acquire) 'co-responsibility' is that they often have a rather unclear mandate (as opposed to the situation, for example, with wage negotiations). They must operate on the basis of the general trust of the members, a trust which assumes that they will come to grips with a complicated problem area while, at the same time, maintaining an appreciation of the interests and wishes of the members. They are forced to independently evaluate and adopt positions on various issues. Participation and co-responsibility means that it is more difficult for them to stand on the outside, to show a 'lack of solidarity' with the design decisions which they themselves participated in.

Another most important obstacle is the limited resources at the local union's disposal. This strategy is extremely resource-consuming from the trade union's point of view, and even if it does its best the local union cannot really compete with management, even if the union design work has the advantage of being based on many members' experience.

Another aspect of the limited resources has to do with priorities. Design of new technology and work organization is a new and certainly very important issue for local unions, but there are other issues which are just as important and even more crucial to their ultimate democratic objectives, such as daily contact with the members and broad studies. A central question for a local union is thus how important the change in technology and work organization is for the members, and whether it should participate and make its own investigation or not.

Given its limited resources, the trade union design groups in most cases have to desist from full participation in the design process. A realistic approach might be a 'shadow investigation' covering aspects of specific interest to the union such as changes in qualifications, work organization, work environment and employment. A complementary action might be to require supplementary investigations from the management design group specifically addressing these issues.

Our practical experience also indicates that some of the problems connected with a strategy based on participation only, affect this approach as well. This is true, for example, as regards the risk of the trade union representatives acquiring a technical expert language and a management view on the problems. In some cases these representatives even make a career for themselves and leave their work mates behind. Of course, this makes those aspects of the strategy that aim at securing internal union democracy key elements of the strategy – aspects such as broad discussions at meetings of members and study groups to activate a well informed membership. It has also been observed that some employers attempt to counter this strategy because they find it too militant, too time and resource consuming, or simply too threatening to have a really well informed union.

Practical experience also indicates that local unions need external resources and support in their design activities. Such basic resources are workers' consultants and central union officials who have access to the workplace and information on the planned changes in order to support the local union and its design groups.

But because of the limited resources at the unions' disposal, and the associated problems involving internal union democracy, still other strategies for designing technology and work may be recommended. One such strategy that some unions have been practicing is a modification of the traditional strategy of wage negotiations.

## Mobilization Around Union Demands

Rather than making its own investigations concerning a specific project, the union can emphasize the development of fundamental union principles, such as the right of the already employed workers to operate the new technology, and their right to qualified training and education. Once such basic principles have been established through negotiations, perhaps the actual design can be carried out by participation in management's project groups. An essential prerequisite for these negotiations is a long-term union activity formulating these fundamental principles, e.g. the development of local union action programs. Furthermore these long-term activities should be carried out in such a way that the members can be mobilized around the fundamental principles in times of concrete negotiations. Another prerequisite for the strategy is that management really has the resources, competence, and will to carry out the investigatory work spelled out in negotiations, e.g. concerning the consequences for qualifications and required complementary education.

Besides the fact that these prerequisites are not always present, there are other risks in this strategy. While the union is involved in working out fundamental principles and negotiating them, the company may take concrete steps which make it either difficult or impossible to realize these fundamental principles. The strategy also implies the risk that the union will fail to accumulate the technological and design competence which would enable it to determine whether or not management's proposals for new technology and organization are in accordance with the union's basic principles.

Nevertheless, this modified traditional mobilization and negotiation approach is a good alternative candidate for local trade union strategy concerning the design and use of new technology.[27]

## Choosing a Strategy

The three strategies outlined above (participation only, investigation and negotiation, and mobilization and negotiation) all have their problems. They may be seen as empirically based 'ideal types', and in practice there will be combinations. However, in the context of democratization it is important that the problems associated with each strategy are kept in mind, either as restrictions or as li-

---

[27] Examples of this strategy, based on experiences from *Dagens Nyheter*, another major newspaper in Stockholm, are given in Ehn, Perby, Sandberg, op. cit.

mits to be overcome. Some of the conditions which may have an influence on the choice of strategy include:

- actual resources available for the local union in a specific situation;
- management's resources and strategy;
- relations to other unions in the company;
- degree of harmony or conflict between management and the local union in the specific area of change;
- type of change and the union's experiences with it;
- type of change and how important it is to the work force; and
- degree of harmony or conflict between different groups of workers and different trade unions in the specific area of change.

The last point has, in practice, turned out to be crucial to the success of trade union efforts to influence new technology and work organization. This is because new technology tends to imply changes in the labor process which make traditional division of labor between different groups of workers obsolete. For instance, changes often affect the distinction between planning and execution of a specific task. Since jurisdictions between different unions are often based on the division of labor within the traditional labor process, especially between blue and white collar workers, the changes in the labor process are a potential source for demarcation disputes. When not overcome, these disputes have in practice been severe obstacles to the development and use of collective resources to support the shaping of more democratic work organizations. This problem is also true for different groups within the same union. There is a tendency that stronger groups within the union support solutions at the expense of weaker groups of workers. The stronger groups are often skilled and male dominated groups, or groups which in the short run benefit from a specific change in the labor process, whereas the weaker are often unskilled or female groups, or groups which are specifically threatened by the specific change.[28] Hence, to be successful a local trade union strategy has to be based on solidarity between the different groups of workers involved, a solidarity which goes beyond the traditional division of labor in the labor process and the traditional jurisdictions between the unions involved.

Such a solidarity could for instance be based on principles like: no one group of workers should be the victim of the new technology. Furthermore, appropriate educational programmes offered to all groups which are involved over a longer period of time.

## And a Fourth Strategy

Local union efforts are important and a basis for democratization in working life. But there are limits to local influence.

There is a need for a coordination of local efforts, a long term, comprehensive and offensive struggle through central organizations – not simply a reaction to local issues. If this is not done there is a risk that interest will be lost at the local workplaces. The local union can be overwhelmed and the offensive for democratization of working life can appear to be little more than interesting rhetoric.

There is a need for collective solutions to local problems. For instance, existing technology may hinder realization of local union demands. This brings me to the UTOPIA project, and a fourth strategy for really designing technological alternatives for, by, and with the ultimate users, as will be discussed in the next chapter.

---

[28] See e.g. Dilschmann, A. and Ehn, P.: *Gränslandet* , Swedish Center for Working Life, Stockholm 1985, Ehn, Perby, Sandberg, op. cit., and Ekdahl, L.: *Att bli maskinens herrar,* Swedish Center for Working Life, Stockholm 1984.

# Dissemination of the Results
# and Further Directions

Our experiences from the DEMOS project were, as part of the project idea, shared with workers and trade unionists in several ways.

On the basic level, the researchers together with the investigation groups at the four participating work sites wrote *reports* on the local work that were distributed to the membership of the local union.[29] These reports were discussed at union meetings and seminars (They were also distributed to management).

A *textbook* for trade unions on computers, trade union activities and design work was written to make our reflections useful to other workers than those from the participating work sites.[30] (The fact that the textbook also became used at many universities all over Scandinavia was not a planned result, but certainly an encouraging one.)

Based on our material the first Swedish *trade union course* on computers and planning from a trade union perspective was designed in cooperation with the Swedish Confederation of Trade Unions (LO). In addition we traveled to union meetings all over Sweden to discuss our experiences.

On a central union level the experiences from the DEMOS project were disseminated in two basic areas – *laws and agreements on democracy at work* and *trade union research policy*. Our experiences were used in discussions with LO on formulating demands for central collective agreements on design and use of computer artifacts, adjusted to the then newly enacted Joint Regulation Act (MBL), and to highlight the limits of MBL with regard to democratic participation in design and use of computer

---

[29] Ehn and Erlander, op. cit., Ehn, Perby, Sandberg, op. cit., Erlander, op. cit., and Perby and Carlsson, op. cit.

[30] Ehn, P. and Sandberg, Å.: *Företagsstyrning och löntagarmakt – planering, datorer, organisation och fackligt utredningsarbete*, Prisma, Stockholm 1979.

artifacts. The experiences from DEMOS were also used in discussions about problems with research conducted in cooperation between researchers and workers and their local trade unions, including discussions of problems with researcher access to the workplaces, the local unions' and the researchers' access to information, and the workers' and local union's resources for participation in research work.

The contact with *the research community* was carried out as an intensive dialogue with other Scandinavian research projects that in different research fields tried to develop a research strategy for democratization of the workplace in cooperation with trade unions.[31] This included researchers with backgrounds in computer science, sociology, architecture, engineering, and industrial administration. In the field of design and use of computer artifacts the DEMOS project was one of the main projects giving form to what we have labeled *the collective resource approach*. This approach and the experiences from the DEMOS project are now part of a wider ongoing dialogue with the research community, and, of course, subject to further reflections.[32]

---

[31] Several of these projects were mentioned in chapter 11, *From Socio-Technical Satisfaction to Collective Resources*.

[32] Besides ongoing 'reporting' on the results at research seminars and as papers at conferences, and besides being a basis for new projects considering e.g. action research methods, conditions for democratization of working life, and design of computer artifacts, two 'documents' showing a change in the dialogue between DEMOS and other projects of the collective resource approach and other research approaches in the field may be of historical interest. In 1978 an IFIP conference focusing on Scandinavian experiences with participation and computers was held in Copenhagen. No researchers from the collective resource projects in Scandinavia were invited. As a response to this we produced a 'white book' on our research experiences and sent it to the conference organizers as a contribution to the lacking 'dialogue'. Later our contribution was published as Sandberg, Å. (ed): *Computers Dividing Man and Work – Recent Scandinavian Research on Planning and Computers from a Trade Union Perspective*, Swedish Center for Working Life, Malmö 1979. In 1985 the academic cli-

One such fundamental reflection concerns creativity and practical skill in design. In the light of the first two parts of this book the Marxist emancipatory approach taken in the DEMOS project was in a way far too rational. There was a strong emphasis on participation and development of collective resources in design of computer artifacts, but the design methods and the design artifacts applied were rather formalist. Focus was on the forms for democratic participation in design, and less on how to make it possible for the ultimate users of the design to express their competence in the design process, and have fun while doing this.

The Wittgensteinian approach of organizing design as a language-game with family resemblance with other language-games that the users participate in at work gives a philosophical ground for such rethinking. And so does the Heideggerian approach towards understanding human ready-to-hand use of artifacts.

Other ways of seeing and doing discussed in Part II, like the *idealized* design suggested by Ackoff, *prototyping*, the ideas of *future workshops*, and *'postmodern' approaches taken in architectural design* are challenges to develop democratic design processes that are both more creative and more fun to participate in. We took a minor step in this direction when we began the UTOPIA project and the design of new technology together with graphic workers.

mate had changed. That year we organized an international conference on the 'development and use of computer-based systems and tools in the context of democratization of work'. The conference gathered participants representing many different research traditions on the issue, not least the collective resource approach. This more open dialogue was published as Bjerknes, G., Ehn, P., Kyng, M. (eds.): *Computers and Democracy – A Scandinavian Challenge*, Avebury, 1987.

## Chapter 13

# Case II: The UTOPIA Project

UTOPIA was a Scandinavian research project on trade union based design of, and training in, computer techno-logy and work organization, especially text and image processing in the graphic industries. (In the Scandinavian languages UTOPIA is an acronym for Training, Techno-logy, and Products from a Quality of Work Perspective).

Graphic workers and computer and social scientists worked together in the UTOPIA project. Besides working directly in the project group, the Scandinavian graphic workers' unions followed and supported the project through a reference group consisting of representatives from Sweden, Denmark, Finland and Norway, appointed by the Nordic Graphic Workers' Union (NGU).

The project was carried out at the Swedish Center for Working Life, at The Royal Institute of Technology, Stockholm, and at Aarhus University in Denmark. At various stages the project cooperated with the computer supplier Liber/TIPS and the newspaper Aftonbladet in Stockholm.

The project began in 1981, and lasted for four years. An average of fifteen people participated in the work, though most did so on a part-time basis. The total input amounted to 15 man-years. The project was financially supported by the Swedish Center for Working Life. Other financial sources were the Swedish Board for Technological Deve-lopment, the Royal Institute of Technology, and Aarhus University.[1]

---

[1] This overview of the UTOPIA project is partly based on our sum-mary report. UTOPIA project group: *An Alternative in Text and*

# The Strategy

The strategic background of the UTOPIA project can be found in our research program from 1980:

> The experience gained by organized labor and the research conducted by trade unions during the 1970s into the ability to influence new technology and the organization of work at local level highlighted a number of problems. One fundamental experience gained is that the 'degrees of freedom' available to design the content and organization of work which utilizes existing technology is often considerably less than that required to meet trade unions demands. Or expressed another way: existing production technology more and more often constitutes an insurmountable barrier preventing the realization of trade union demands for the quality of work and a meaningful job.[2]

Furthermore, the difficulties the unions experienced in influencing technology at its introduction were among the concerns of the project, especially because 'turn-key' systems were purchased by management in more and more cases where management would otherwise have designed systems locally. With these 'turn-key' systems came standard organization of work. Furthermore, the standard training offered by the suppliers was often insufficient. Due to the distance between the designers and the users these issues were hard for local unions to influ-

---

*Images,* Graffiti no 7, Swedish Center for Working Life, 1985. In parts this is also based on our overview in Bødker, S. et al.: 'A Utopian Experience' in Bjerknes, G. et al. (eds.) *Computers and Democracy – A Scandinavian Challenge*, Avebury, 1987.

[2] See Ehn, P., Kyng, M., and Sundblad, Y.: *Training, Technology, and Product from the Quality of Work Perspective, A Scandinavian research project on union based development of and training in computer technology and work organization, especially text and image processing in the graphic industry.* (Research programme of UTOPIA), Swedish Center for Working Life, Stockholm 1981, p. 7.

ence. Trade unions were facing a design process for which the strategy outlined in, for example, the DEMOS project had to be complemented. As we saw it,

> the question of what the trade unions can do to influence technology can be partially answered by looking at what is already being done. Attempts are made to reduce the negative effects of technology on employees by demanding reforms in legislation and concluding agreements. Efforts are made to mobilize forces at local level through the implementation of broad-based programs. Training is demanded in order to obtain and retain control over new technology and to counteract degradation of work. Demands are being made on the actual utilization of technology and the work organization associated with it. Demands have also been initiated on suppliers of production technology primarily in respect of the physical working environment. However, this strategy could best be described as a defensive action. This project is working on a supplementary and as yet untried offensive strategy: The trade union movement itself draws up the technological and training alternatives and takes sole responsibility for their implementation and development at local level.[3]

To support the local unions in their struggle for influence on technology, training and organization of work, we saw the need for an offensive, long-term strategy conducted by the central unions. The trade unions at the central level had to assume responsibility for working towards collective solutions to the local demands in the areas of training, technology and organization of work, in addition to giving central support for actions taken at the local level.

However, enormous resources have been invested in the new technology utilized by companies. When, on the other hand, a trade union presents demands for possible technological alternatives, the question of whether such

[3] Ibid., p. 8.

technology exists and is feasible comes up, together with the question of whether designing an alternative is realistic, economically, for one single company.

To conduct a trade union technological design project was seen as one contribution to resolving these two problems. The UTOPIA project could hopefully contribute to changing the trade union's range of possible actions at the local level. Instead of defending the status quo, an offensive strategy was to be developed for another type of technology and improved products. We would seek for a type of technology that improves the quality of work and the products, a type of technology that is not inflexible but dynamically changeable at individual workplaces as the employees develop their skills. The project would enable this by the design of technology and training programs combined with sociological and historical analyses of the prerequisites for the alternatives, and an understanding of the forces acting on technological development nationally and internationally.

The aim of the project was to produce a 'demonstration example' showing that trade union design of technology is a feasible strategy under certain favorable conditions. We did not, however, intend to produce a strategic design model that is generally applicable regardless of the application domain. Nonetheless, the idea was that the project could constitute an important source of inspiration for the development of strategies on technology policy in different application domains where e.g. the economic, technical or trade union conditions are different.

The more specific aim of the UTOPIA project was to design computer support and professional education for integrated text and image processing. This design was to be based on the principles of

- quality of work and products,
- democracy at work, and
- education for local development.

## Research Approach
## and Theoretical Perspective

Our theoretical perspective in the UTOPIA project was a continuation of the Marxist approach taken in the DEMOS project. Labor process theory was still important for understanding technological change, and so was the interest in emancipatory practice for democratization of work. There was, however, a shift in focus. Now the emphasis was on trying to design computer artifacts for skilled work, to really design 'utopian' alternatives and reflect about a strategy for this 'utopian' design process, as well as a strategy for implementation of the 'utopian' alternatives in reality. *By a proactive approach we were investigating social, political, technological and methodological limits to a more democratic design process and the design of skill enhancing computer artifacts in the interest of the ultimate users.*

Close cooperation with the users was still very important, but the political conditions for doing this 'utopian' design locally at one or several work sites in Scandinavia did not exist. The work had to be carried out in a research environment, but with skilled graphic workers and trade unionists participating directly in the research group.

Close cooperation with the Nordic Graphic Workers' Union (NGU) was also important. A pre-condition for 'implementing' the 'utopian' alternative technology, work organization, and training was that the union found the alternatives interesting enough, and that they could give concrete examples in negotiations with the employer federations, and in mobilization of the membership around these alternatives. Negotiated agreements and a better understanding of technological alternatives at the workplaces were seen as a necessity for practical implementation. NGU played a key role with respect to both aspects.

In addition we saw an ongoing dialogue with graphic workers throughout Scandinavian workplaces during the project as essential to the strategy. To this end a magazine called *Graffiti* was created.[4]

## The Research and Design Process

*Building Scenarios and a 'Knowledge Platform'*

In the first phase of the UTOPIA project we investigated existing technology, working practices, and training in the graphic industries, as well as the prerequisites for designing alternatives.

A major aspect in this first phase of the project was the mutual learning process in which the participants – graphic workers, and computer and social scientists – established a common 'knowledge platform' for their future work.

In cooperation with NGU, the UTOPIA project organized a three day workshop where graphic workers from all the Nordic countries participated. The aim was to give more substance to the research goal stated in the research program.

Joint visits to newspapers, technical exhibitions, suppliers, and research laboratories in Scandinavia and abroad to collect information were a major activity. Especially a study of the development of technology and working practices in American newspapers came to play an important role as the antithesis of a desired development.[5]

Another activity in this phase consisted of so-called 'quality workshops'. In these workshops graphic workers, graphic designers, and journalists participated in discussions of good use quality of graphic products.[6]

Based on the investigations various scenarios were outlined as possible alternatives for the future work in the

---

[4] During the project seven issues of *Graffiti* were produced and widely distributed.

[5] See Dilschmann, A. and Ehn, P.: *Gränslandet*, Swedish Center for Working Life, Stockholm 1985.

[6] See *Graffiti* no 2, Swedish Center for Working Life, Stockholm 1982.

project, e.g. 'pre-press production', 'the graphic work-shop', 'the newspaper production plant', 'image process-ing in 1990', and 'the automated paradise'. The work re-sulted in suggestions for the design of either of the follow-ing: *pre-press production of newspapers*, or *the graphic workshop*.

Ironically, the scenario of the graphic workshop which we as researchers favored was thought of as less impor-tant by the graphic workers. This scenario came close to what today is known as desktop publishing, one of the most expanding domains in graphic production. Instead it was decided to concentrate on pre-press newspaper pro-duction, since this was seen as the technological front line, and a domain concerning many graphic workers.

In the research group many difficulties had to be over-come. The graphic workers, who were used to rapid con-crete results in their daily work, found that work pro-gressed too slowly and was too abstract. It also became ap-parent that we had underestimated the costs of developing technical alternatives on our own, especially if we were to work with integrated newspaper production.[7]

## Vendor Cooperation

After about 18 months the UTOPIA project was approa-ched by the Swedish state-owned printing concern and computer supplier Liber through the Graphic Workers' Union in Sweden. This provided an incentive to delimit the project and make it more concrete. Liber wished to examine the possibilities for cooperation around the com-pany's design project TIPS (Text and Image Processing System), a $10 million project for designing an integrated computer-based system for text, image, and full page make-up for newspaper production.

As we saw it, Liber was interested in cooperating be-cause it had to acquire a substantial share of the domestic

---

[7] In Ehn, P.: *UTOPIA-projektet* (Status rapport (fas I) och arbets-plan (fas II)), Swedish Center for Working Life, Stockholm 1983, the early phases of the project are described in detail.

market in order to be successful in marketing, and this would require attentiveness to the demands for technology and training posed by the Scandinavian trade unions for graphic workers. In the UTOPIA project, the aim of which was to formulate such requirements and try to technically realize them, Liber/TIPS found a natural discussion partner.

After final discussions with the board of the NGU, a cooperation agreement was signed in late 1982. The basic idea of the agreement was that the TIPS project should exploit the competence of the UTOPIA project (work organization, quality of work, training, human-computer interaction, graphic skills, etc.) in its design work. In this way the UTOPIA project obtained the opportunity to try out many of its ideas. The cooperation would also offer valuable experience in exercising influence over a large technical development project. However, the agreement did not force Liber in the TIPS project to follow the requirement specifications of the UTOPIA project. Correspondingly, the agreement gave the UTOPIA project complete freedom to cultivate and inform others about its viewpoints, and about requirements which the TIPS system might not fulfil.

The cooperation with TIPS had many consequences for UTOPIA. The project came to focus on page make-up and image processing for newspapers; and not only the Swedish Center for Working Life, but also the Swedish Board for Technical Development was now willing to support the UTOPIA project's development of requirement specifications.

### 'The Design Workshop'

During the next year the UTOPIA project concentrated on requirement specifications. This, however, called for the development of working practices so that the researchers and graphic workers together could formulate the requirements. To this end we established a *design workshop* with design tools to simulate different kinds of page make-up, image processing, and the surrounding organization, thus making it possible for the graphic workers in the project to develop requirements and wishes on a concrete level by actually carrying out the page make-up and image processing on simulation equipment. As researchers we could contribute by pointing out possibilities and limitations of equivalent real equipment, and by structuring the experience in requirement specifications.

This *design-by-doing* approach was not applied from the beginning. We started out by using traditional, more or less formalized description methods ranging from scenarios to data flows. However, these were too abstract and did not function very well as a vehicle for communication with the graphic workers. The situation was drastically improved when we built a *mock-up* to simulate computer-based page make-up.

## Workstation Mock-Ups

The principle behind the mock-up was simple. Using sheets of paper, matchboxes, some plywood, etc., one 'builds' a workstation with a 'high-resolution display', a 'mouse', etc.

The process in which this equipment was used is one in which the work with the computer-based tools, such as page make-up, is done simultaneously with the creation of the needed display images drawn on paper. The graphic worker and the designer work together. The graphic worker does the page make-up step by step. For each step the corresponding display image is drawn on paper. The product is a series of snapshots simulating the work done while using the workstation.

The designer takes part in the process by pointing out possibilities and limitations of the corresponding 'real' equipment, and by collecting and structuring the demands and wishes formulated by the graphic worker while doing the make-up work.

In addition to experimenting with the display images, experiments with the interaction devices can be conducted by means of the mock-ups.

This kind of design-by-doing simulations turned out to be a very good way to get started. First of all it enabled skilled workers to take an active part in the design process. The method is quite cheap, as expensive equipment or time-consuming programming is unnecessary. New features of the workstation can be designed and added as they are needed.

Another advantage of this approach is that experiments are not limited to available equipment. Both equipment that just does not happen to be at hand, for example, for economic reasons, and future computer equipment can be simulated. We could, for example, play with super high-resolution display screens big enough to show a real size newspaper page.

The mock-ups were later given a more realistic exterior. The interaction devices were still made out of paper and plywood, but color slides projected on a screen were used to simulate the graphic display screen. Applying the color slides made it look more realistic, and it was much easier to redo the simulation sequences, meaning that it was easier to have the graphic workers sit down and try out the design.

A real computer workstation with a high-resolution screen and a tablet with a 'puck' was also employed to experiment with and illustrate aspects which were difficult to simulate with the mock-ups, such as co-ordination between puck movements and display changes, and the readability of text in different sizes and resolutions. This workstation did not provide any real prototyping environment. But the fact that the graphic workers tried to use real computer artifacts, helped them relate the mock-ups to the 'real' applications that were to come out of the process.

Compared to our earlier attempts this approach allowed the graphic workers to articulate their demands and wishes in a concrete way by actually doing make-up work on the simulated equipment. Even the first extremely simple 'paper and wood' mock-up allowed the graphic workers to play a very active role in the design work.

## Organizational Simulation

The design artifacts in our design workshop were not only used for simulation of how work could be conducted at the workstations. Another important aspect was to simulate *relations between the designed technology and work organization.*

How we used an empty box with the sign 'laser printer' on it can illustrate this. In newspaper production the co-operation between the layout person (journalist) and the make-up person (graphic worker) is of crucial importance. In the 'old' technology the journalist always got a hard copy of the page before it was delivered for print. With computer-based text processing this had become a problem, and there were repeated conflicts between graphic workers and journalists concerning how the work should be organized. The box simulating a cheap laser printer envisioned a new possibility where the make-up person can produce alternative solutions to the page, based on the instructions from the layout person. The layout person would then get alternative hard-copy prints of the page as a basis for determining the final layout.

## The Work Organizational Tool Kit

As a supplement to the simulations, we needed design artifacts for analysis and design of current work organization as well as of organizations supporting quality and democracy.

Traditional methods for system description turned out to be too abstract for this design work to be carried out in cooperation with the graphic workers. Instead we developed a *work organizational tool kit* to be used for analysis and design in group discussions.

The basic ideas behind the organizational tool kit were that:

- it should be fast and easy for a group of people to work with,
- it should be cheap and flexible to use, allowing several alternatives to be tested during discussions,
- it should be based on concepts relevant to newspaper production and support involved reflections about existing and future work functions.

To this end we started by analyzing the functions which have to be undertaken at a newspaper production plant to produce a ready-for-press original.[8] All these functions were symbolized with icons on cardboard bricks. Work material and work artifacts were symbolized in the same way.[9] The bricks were waxed on the back, which made them easy to place and move again. The idea behind the organizational tool kit resembles what is known as wall graphs. However, the idea here was that each icon as such must reflect an insight into the specific labor process, e.g. newspaper production.

A reminder of the work organization at a newspaper can quickly be made with the icons of the organizational tool kit. However, similar to other graphical descriptions, this kind of descriptions easily becomes very complicated,[10] and thus, hard to change and inaccessible to others than the creators. For this reason it is important to stress that the creation process is very important as a process of mutual learning. It was not our goal to make descriptions to be used for other people than those taking part in the design process. Our emphasis was on the *use* of the tool kit, not on correctness in the descriptions.

The organizational tool kit was used for discussions about conflicts like 'demarcation disputes', that is, which functions should be carried out by editorial staff, and

[8] These functions are described in Dilschmann and Ehn, op. cit.

[9] The organizational tool kit is described by Dan Sjögren in Dilschmann and Ehn, op. cit.

[10] Bødker, S. and Madsen, K.H:: 'More or Less Systems Descriptions' in Lassen, M. and Mathiassen, L.: *Report of the Eight Scandinavian Conference on Systemeering*, part I, Aarhus 1985.

which should be carried out by make-up staff. It was also used to discuss, for example, conflicts concerning the right to operate graphic page make-up workstations and organizational solutions to this. Games with the organizational tool kit were not only played by the graphic workers and the researchers participating in the UTOPIA project. Sessions were also held together with journalists, and in negotiation sessions with management representatives.

## *The Requirement Specification*

Based on the work in the design workshop the first version of UTOPIA's requirement specifications for computer-based page-make up and image processing was published in late 1983.[11] They were made in constant discussions with TIPS, but the requirements were meant to be generally applicable when introducing new systems for newspaper production. Thus, they were meant for all suppliers and newspapers, not only for Liber/TIPS.

In many respects the requirement specifications looked like traditional ones. It was a forty-eight page technical document filled with *musts* and *ought-to's*, and *questions* to be answered by the suppliers. There was a description of requirements for work procedures, display screens, human-computer interaction, and operations for page make-up and image processing equipment.

What was new was that these technical requirements were derived from the principle that the equipment should serve as *tools for skilled work* and for production of *good use quality products*. The requirement specifications were also different in the sense that they also specified requirements for work organization, work environment and training. Technology bringing about poorer working conditions than those already existing was not accepted. A minimum requirement was that graphic workers must be able to carry out the same work operations in page

---

[11] Ehn, P. and Sundblad, Y. (eds.): *Kravspecifikation för datorstödd bildbehandling och ombrytning*, Swedish Center for Working Life, Stockholm 1983.

make-up and image processing as they could do with traditional technology. Product quality inferior to what could be obtained with traditional technology was also rejected.

## Professional Training

Our next step in the UTOPIA project was, while still working in the design workshop, to aim the resources of the project at professional training. Many of the reports produced in the project were written to be applied in professional training of graphic workers. The list includes textbooks on computer-based page make-up,[12] on computer-based image processing,[13] on work organization when integrated computer-based technology is introduced,[14] and on work environment in this new environment.[15] A large part of the educational material was tested in training of graphic workers in 1984 in the Graphic Industries Department of the Royal Institute of Technology (Stockholm). Valuable experience was also gained by using the design artifacts from the design workshop in teaching situations.

## Investigations of History and Future

Parallel to these design and professional training activities, a historical study of the printing industry and a study of democratic technology policy were conducted within the UTOPIA project.

The historical study compared the introduction of new technology in the printing industry around the beginning of this century with the situation in the 1980s. The report suggests, against the historical background, the need for

---

[12] Ehn, P. et al: *Datorstödd Ombrytning*, Swedish Center for Working Life, Stockholm 1985.

[13] Frenckner, K. and Romberger, S.: *Datorstödd Bildbehandling*, Swedish Center for Working Life, Stockholm 1985.

[14] Dilschmann and Ehn, op. cit.

[15] Gunnarson, E.: *Arbetsmiljökrav*, Swedish Center for Working Life, Stockholm 1985.

broad cooperation between the different unions involved in the technological changes in the graphic industry today. The conclusion is that a counterpart to labor's united front at the turn of the century with its rather successful strategy concerning the introduction of new technology, today only can be established through closer cooperation, or even amalgamation of the unions within the graphic industry.[16]

The technology policy study discussed the UTOPIA project in the light of a 'new Scandinavian model' for technological research and development activities supporting more democratic solutions, and new, more democratic demand patterns based on voices from the workplaces.[17]

*Back to Reality*

The cooperation between the UTOPIA project and Liber/TIPS also included an evaluation phase. This evaluation was to include the TIPS system and active development of work organization in connection with the first pilot installation at the Swedish newspaper Aftonbladet. Based on these experiences updated requirement specifications were to be written. Here the original intentions proved difficult to realize. The management at Aftonbladet was not particularly interested in a well-defined experiment on work organization in connection with the pilot installation. The journalists' union was also opposed to an organized experiment. All this meant that the ideas of the UTOPIA project for active participation in an organizational experiment where graphic workers and journalists together in practice seek new ways, had to be abandoned.[18]

[16] Ekdahl, L.: *Att bli maskinens herrar,* Swedish Center for Working Life, Stockholm 1984.

[17] Sandberg, Å.: *Mellan alternativ produktion och industriell FOU,* Swedish Center for Working Life, Stockholm 1984.

[18] However, after the project ended an evaluation of the use of the equipment has been carried out. See Bartholdy, M et al.: *Studie av datorstödd bildbehandling på Aftonbladet,* Swedish Center for Working Life, Stockholm 1987. An updated version of the requirement specifications based on this evaluation and post-UTOPIA

## Scandinavian Models?

Before ending this chapter on UTOPIA with some general reflections on the impact of the project for a more democratic design and use of computer artifacts, I will illustrate our reflections on designing for democracy at work with two 'Scandinavian' paradigm cases from the project – *a work organization model* for 'peaceful coexistence' of graphic workers and journalists in newspaper production, and *a model for participative and democratic technological research and design*.[19]

# Example 1:
# Work Organization in the Borderland

Questions concerning work organization in connection with integrated text and image processing in newspaper production were important study areas in the UTOPIA project, especially prerequisites for designing future ways of organizing work 'from manuscript to plate'.

This is a question full of conflicts causing confrontations between professional groups and their trade unions. This is not only true where newspaper employees are concerned; metal workers and engineers confront each other, chemist's assistants and chemists, and many others. Management introduces new technology to save manpower. Journalists, graphic workers, and administrative staff confront each other in the struggle over a decreasing number of jobs.

Is there a basis for solving these demarcation disputes across professional and union-based frontiers? Can a new way of organizing work create peaceful coexistence in the borderland?

changed technological possibilities is now being produced. This work is also being carried out by Merete Bartholdy in cooperation with the former members of the UTOPIA project.

[19] The skill aspects of the UTOPIA project will be further developed in the part on *Designing for Skill*.

I will exemplify this by considering the 'borderland' between editing and making-up, one of the many borderlands in newspaper production.[20]

## Editing and Making-Up

Journalists are afraid of losing their control over the layout if the graphic workstations are placed in the composing room and are operated by the graphic workers. Alternatively, they naturally see a possibility for creating new jobs for themselves if the sub-editors obtain the right to operate the workstations. The graphic workers not only risk losing jobs, but they also risk losing page make-up, a corner-stone in graphic work, if the journalists obtain the right to operate the graphic workstations.

The connections between editing/layout/make-up can be seen as follows: The result of the sub-editor's work (planning content, planning pages, and text editing) may be called a journalistic model of the newspaper page. The journalistic competence involved lies in improving the readability of the product. The make-up person refines the product by giving the journalistic model a graphic design. The graphic competence involved lies in improving the legibility of the product.

## The 'Traditional Way' of Organizing Work

With the introduction of graphic workstations it may seem apt to try to maintain the traditional way of organizing work. The make-up staff in the composing room gets powerful computer-based tools. The sub-editors may get expensive electronic sketch pads. Both professional groups and their respective competences are intact, and may even be developed. But the technical possibilities for a more flexible production with a later deadline for manuscripts, and hence a higher product quality, are not exploited.

---

[20] This example is further elaborated in Dilschmann and Ehn, op. cit.

The strict division of labor between journalists and graphic workers is maintained. The instructions from the editorial staff to the composing room are written instructions, primarily rough layout sketches even in situations where oral instructions would have been sufficient. If the sub-editors have electronic sketch pads, the instructions are communicated electronically in the form of boxes on a display. Sub-editors and make-up staff do not cooperate closely, even though they work with the same pages. The division between the news-room and the composing room obstructs the necessary dialogue in connection with questions, suggestions, changes, follow-up, and exchange of ideas.

## An 'American Way' of Organizing Work

In fact, when integrated computer-based systems for make-up and image processing first were implemented, the traditional model was rejected by management, though the unions often wanted to stick to it. The newspaper *Star News*, published in the Los Angeles suburb of Pasadena, was in the early 1980s the technically most advanced newspaper in the world. The management of this paper has consciously introduced new technology in order to get rid of graphic workers. The graphic workstations were placed in the news-room, where they were operated by editorial staff as well as by new groups of employees. The organization did not allow any room for make-up staff, but the journalistic model was still transformed into a graphically designed page.

The problem is that the people who performed the work did not have the necessary graphic competence, which results in a deteriorating product quality. Furthermore, the new staff was not organized in trade unions, received lower wages, and usually had not received a journalistic education.

## The 'Scandinavian Way' of Organizing Work?

In the UTOPIA project we found neither the 'traditional' nor the 'American' model to be the work organization of the future. The 'traditional' model was rejected because it meant a misuse of the technological potential for higher quality in newspaper production. The 'American' model was rejected on ground of its anti-democratic and de-skilling approach. Instead, we found inspiration for an alternative work organization at the newspaper *Østlændingen*, which is published in Elverum, Norway. It represented a Norwegian answer to the American challenge. The first steps on the path towards what hopefully may be called the 'Scandinavian way' of organizing integrated production had been taken.

Below I will expand this example to a more general model for discussions of future work organization.[21] This model grew out of a number of discussions in many sessions where the organizational tool kit was used, often starting with the work organization at Østlændingen. In the model we assumed that technology according to the UTOPIA requirement specifications was used.

In this model the reporters have access to display terminals. Here they write and process their articles, if they wish to. The reporters do not do any actual typographical coding. Furthermore, the display terminals will give them access to text files, administrative databases with public information and maybe even foreign databases. When the reporters choose to use typewriters, the manuscript is entered by the teletypist.

A central journalist and technical production unit called the *central production* is established. This unit is the central part of the production process. Here journalists and graphic workers cooperate closely and smoothly. However there is a clear division of responsibility between the professional groups.

In the central production and in its immediate vicinity, a number of other work functions have been integrated. Besides page editing and make-up there are functions

---

[21] Here I shall restrict myself to summarizing aspects of the 'borderland' between journalists and graphic workers. The model, however, covers the entire pre-press production process.

such as typing of paper manuscripts, proof-reading, major corrections, editing of strictly standardized material such as lists of television programs, and coding and make-up of individual articles.

Sub-editors take on more responsibility in relation to the editors. The latter still have both editorial and administrative tasks, but delegate more responsibility for the final selection. The editorial tasks of the editors in relation to the sub-editors are first of all to maintain a general view of things and to act as support and discussion partners for the sub-editors and the reporters. The sub-editors usually work on paper print-outs. The reason for this is partly the diminished eye-strain involved, and partly to keep a general view of the texts, as they often read both long continuous texts, and several texts simultaneously. Some of the text is corrected directly on the display screen by the sub-editors, while other corrections are made by the tele-typist.

Sub-editors work closely together with page make-up staff. Apart from the rough planning of pages, and the enhanced text editing and image thinking, the sub-editors, among other things, have access to display terminals to do administrative work on the material. The ease of trying out alternatives, and of making late evaluations of and changes on the page is improved through the electronic page make-up process, and good and easy proof print possibilities are available via small laser printers.

For the make-up staff the most important change is that the work is performed at graphic workstations. It is no longer necessary to wait for film from photosetters when changes are made in the typography. The possibilities for enhancing the typography with graphics are considerably increased. Images can be changed in size directly in the make-up process. Quality is improved because several alternatives can be tried out. Cooperation with the sub-editors plays a very important part.

Because the electronic page make-up tools make it possible to do rapid changes on the page late in the process, the make-up person can start the make-up process before all parts are ready. The journalistic planning is thus made easier. Feature articles, and entertainment pages, etc., can be produced and made up beforehand.

The teletypists in the central production, or in its close vicinity, have enriched their work content. They cooperate with the sub-editors and the make-up staff. The teletypists type the text from paper manuscripts, code and make-up articles and type the more extensive corrections. They may also perform certain administrative tasks in the central production.

Image processing staff handles the editorial images. Work of high quality is made with black and white reproduction. The processed images are transferred electronically to page make-up, where the sub-editor can get a copy if needed. The image processing staff also has access to conventional reproduction equipment, for example, for color work. Photosetting is performed the same way as before. However, requirements for quality control are stricter now. Now it is not only a question of columns, but of whole pages with images which are going to be produced directly on plate.

## Possibilities in the Borderland

It was our conviction in the UTOPIA project that this work organization model could serve as a paradigm case for discussions on technology and organization for quality and efficiency in production. These would be solutions where skills, professional identity, and the professional pride of graphic workers and journalists could live on. We intended to show that they provide a basis for graphic workers and journalists to jointly influence and improve the product, working practices, and working conditions. By now the model has also inspired many negotiations and agreements on work organization at different newspapers in Scandinavia.

# Example 2:
# Research and Development for
# a More Democratic Technology

A national technology policy for democratization is another area where experiences from the UTOPIA project can be utilized as an inspiring paradigm case. This applies to the process as well as to the results.

So far it is just an idea or a perspective with only a few practical examples. This aspect of the project was highlighted in a study by Sandberg.[22] He related the UTOPIA experiences to other similar approaches, both international examples like the LUCAS workers' approach and the strategy developed by Greater London Council, and Swedish trade union approaches like the ones developed by the Metal Workers' Union, the Food Workers' union, and the State Employees' Union. The idea may be outlined as follows:[23]

- technology which supports good working conditions and good use quality products should be designed;
- the trade unions should play an active role in formulating requirements for this technology, since they are best fitted to capture and draw upon the employees' knowledge and experience of work and work environment;
- this helps to design technology which satisfies the demands of the employees, and that is useful, since it is based on their practical understanding of the labor process;
- this is a unique opportunity and resource which our Scandinavian high tech industry should utilize;

---

[22] Sandberg, op. cit.

[23] For more details see Sandberg, Å.: *Technological Change and Co-determination in Sweden – Background and analysis of trade union and managerial strategies*, Temple Press (forthcoming).

- our governments should foster and support such activities with national and Scandinavian research and development programs;
- furthermore, its traditionally calm labor markets make many sectors of Scandinavian industry good 'test sites' for these technological and organizational alternatives;
- and give opportunities for domestic markets of realistic size for at least initial production of this kind of technology, especially if the demands for it are supported by the trade unions and by government requirements;
- in the long run this kind of technology (which supports quality of work and products) could give Scandinavian industry opportunities in foreign markets.

As pointed out, there are only a few activities going on along these lines today, and it would not be correct to describe them as a trend. Furthermore, other future scenarios would probably be more realistic. However, there is a growing interest in this 'new Scandinavian model', not only within trade unions, and the experiences from the UTOPIA project suggests that it is a promising approach to support more democratic design and use of new technology.

Needless to say, this approach must be accompanied by changes in the public educational system. One important aspect is to enhance the designers' interest in and qualifications for dealing with this kind of objectives for democratic technological and organizational development. Another (just as important) aspect is to provide good opportunities for qualification and requalification of workers in different branches of industry. This is not a question of short retraining courses, but of real professional education fostering technological skills as well as genuine understanding and practical mastering of tools and materials in specific labor processes. Again, this may turn out to be just pious hopes. But it is hard to see how any truly democratic design and use of new technology can be achieved without these prerequisites being fulfilled.

## Dissemination of the Results

As with the DEMOS project it was a deliberate aim of the
UTOPIA project to disseminate the results from our research and design outside the walls of our design workshop.

Our major concern was with the graphic workers in
Scandinavia. The many textbooks for professional training of graphic workers in computer-based technology and
work organization have already been mentioned, as has
our newsletter *Graffiti*. Our summary report, *Graffiti
no 7*, addressed graphic workers at the workplaces. It was
translated into the different Nordic languages, and 50,000
copies were distributed by the graphic workers' unions.
For international use we also produced an English
version, and an Italian graphic workers' union made its
own translation.

Our dissemination of the results, however, did not only
address graphic workers alone. At a three day conference
and workshop in May 1984, we presented the results of
our efforts to graphic workers, journalists, and administrative staff and their unions jointly.

The project was also presented at several technical and
management conferences on new technology in newspaper production.

The requirement specifications especially received a
great deal of attention in graphic trade journals, at seminars and at conferences on newspaper production technology. Many representatives from journalists' unions
reacted critically to the fact that the requirement specifications did not include editorial systems, and that they
(the journalists) only played a minor role when the requirement specifications were worked out. Reactions
from employers were mixed. 'Technically competent, but
too political', was a common assessment. The Scandinavian journal on newspaper technology, *Tidningsteknik*, let
various opinions be heard in a special report. The
managing editor of the Danish newspaper *Berlingske
Tidende* wrote in his contribution that 'the UTOPIA report

concludes with a range of good questions meant as inspiration for trade unionists, but these are just as thought-provoking for newspaper management.'[24] Graphic trade unions have made extensive use of the requirement specifications in connection with collective bargaining and local negotiations. The Greater London Council (GLC) translated the requirement specifications and meant to use it for a new graphic industry project along the lines sketched by UTOPIA. (This project, like most of the other projects that GLC initiated, was later stopped by the conservative British government.)

Public debate of technological alternatives for skill and democracy was another arena for dissemination of UTO-PIA as a paradigm case. Participation in meetings and seminars, also far outside Scandinavia, writing of articles and discussions with different trade unions were aspects of this work. To the public debate the UTOPIA project also contributed to two films. One was an educational program on new technology for Danish television. The other was an American view of 'the new Scandinavian model' for design of computer artifacts.

The Marxist approach for understanding possibilities and limits for democratization at work from the earlier collective resource projects (e.g. NJMF, DEMOS, and DUE) also formed part of the basis for the UTOPIA project. Hence, just as in the earlier projects, this project's contacts with the research community studying labor process theory and emancipatory practice were important. Again, we did not really develop theory, but at research seminars and conferences we have contributed to the scholary dialogue by discussing the UTOPIA project as a practical application of a Marxist approach.[25]

However, the UTOPIA project also meant a new theoretical orientation. Our attempts to really design computer artifacts for skilled work also brought us in contact

---

[24] *Tidningsteknik,* no 2, 1984, p. 18 (my translation).

[25] The relations to the theoretical Marxist qualification debate are discussed in chapter 18, *Skills and the Tool Perspective.*

with research fields like human-computer interaction, software engineering, and philosophy of design, as has been discussed in the first two parts of this book. An incitement for this wider theoretical orientation was our practical experience with the rather successful use of mock-ups, our 'design-by-doing' approach, and our 'tool perspective'. We lacked a theoretical frame of reference for understanding why it worked so well, and for getting ideas on how to further develop our design approach. Again we started out as users of theory, rather than as developers of new theory, but our combination of a a theoretical approach focusing on the social issue of designing for democracy at work and at the same time on the technical issue of designing skill-enhancing computer artifacts has met with a great deal of appreciation in these more technical research fields.[26] We are now contributing to this 'new dialogue' by developing our practical experience into a theoretical perspective. Besides papers at conferences, a more comprehensive theoretical account of our UTOPIA experiences has been presented in a Ph.D. thesis on human-computer interaction.[27] One main purpose for writing this book on work-oriented design of computer artifacts is to contribute to this new dialogue in the research community.

## The UTOPIA Project: Success or Failure?

Looking at the UTOPIA project in retrospect: was it a success or a failure?

First some positive opinions. When the UTOPIA project was finished the *decision-makers* from the Nordic Graphic Workers' Union and the graphic workers that

[26] See e.g. the comments by one of the leading researchers in human-computer interaction and cognitive science, Don Norman in Norman, D. and Draper, S. (eds.): *User Centered System Design – New Perspectives on Human-Computer Interaction*, Lawrence Erlbaum, London 1986.

[27] Bødker, S.: *Through the Interface – A Human Activity Approach to User Interface Design*, DAIMI PB-224, Department of Computer Science, University of Aarhus, 1987(dissertation).

had participated in the project were interviewed about their view on the results.[28]

Gunnar Kokaas, chairman of the reference group from the Nordic Graphic Workers' Union, stated that:

> The UTOPIA project has been a good model for Scandinavian cooperation, a model which ought to be studied by other Scandinavian trade unions. The work has shown that conditions in various countries are similar, and that it would be a waste of resources to carry out parallel work in various countries. The contact with graphic workers from other countries and with researchers has been valuable for the participants from the workplaces. Finding the financial resources has been a big problem. Before similar projects are initiated it is important to ensure financial support from sources all over Scandinavia. The Scandinavian trade unions and certain public authorities should jointly demand government support for objective research, i.e. including research on the premises of the workers.
>
> I see two important results. First the reports themselves. For the first time the trade unions are a step ahead in the assessment of the new technology, even before the technology actually exists. The workers can read about that in the reports. Then there is the content. Several reports state that there is no incompatibility between making profits and demanding quality of training, work, and product. Skills will always – independent of technology – be very important in the graphic process. Some new skills will be acquired, but knowing what a good product looks like will always be important. Human beings determine the needs of human beings. I would like to say the following to all Scandinavian trade unions: Make good use of the experiences generated by the UTOPIA project. New projects must soon be initiated, as it is important to stay

[28] UTOPIA project group, op. cit.

up-to-date where technology, work organization, and training are concerned.

Åke Rosenquist, chairman of the Nordic Graphic Workers Union and of the Swedish Graphic Workers Union, concluded that:

> We will continue to disseminate our findings in the form of material from the UTOPIA project to our sections and local unions. (...) The material will also be used in courses and at conferences. (...) The UTOPIA project has given us several contacts concerning technological questions. Active discussions of new ways for Scandinavian trade unions to cooperate have already started. (...) In this connection I might mention that the interaction between researchers and graphic workers has been problematic. The participating graphic workers sometimes felt that things 'took so long'. Also the researchers didn't always take up the questions which seemed most important to the graphic workers. The most important results are that the trade unions have started to cooperate with researchers, and the reports themselves which can form the basis for the work of the trade union.

Kaj Pedersen, chairman of the Danish Graphic Workers' Trade Union:

> The UTOPIA project has first and foremost taught us some working practices which make it easier to communicate with other professional groups in the business, and with employers. Negotiations concerning work organization in connection with computer-based page make-up had almost come to a stop in Denmark. We have chosen to use the UTOPIA reports and the working practices as a starting point in the current negotiations. (...) The working practices of the UTOPIA project are also important where training is concerned. Up to now we have been forced to arrive at some kind of agreement with the employers to get resources for training. The simulation methods developed by the

UTOPIA project give us possibilities to start on our own, because they require far less resources.

Kjell Christoffersen, chairman of the Norwegian Graphic Workers' Union:

> The UTOPIA project has brought us abreast of techno-
> logical development. Now we can define the employees'
> requirements on the new technology. The Union ad-
> ministration has just allocated $4,000 for a number of
> UTOPIA reports which will be distributed to local unions
> and negotiators. We think it important to disseminate
> findings such as the requirements on the design of the
> systems, work environment, and work organization,
> and especially demarcation problems between different
> professional groups. I think that the results will benefit
> us generally at the local level, and especially in connec-
> tion with training and negotiations.

Gunnar Rasmussen, one of the Danish graphic workers participating directly in the project group, emphasized that:

> The project has succeeded in working out a compre-
> hensive report on requirements concerning computer
> based page make-up and image processing. This report
> has been widely praised. The project has succeeded in
> the same way with organization of work. New tech-
> nology requires new ways of thinking in the field too:
> the project has worked out a very applicable and com-
> prehensive method for describing work organization.
> In addition a number of important suggestions for trai-
> ning have been formulated.

And Malte Eriksson, one of the Swedish graphic workers that directly participated in the project work, summarized:

> For the union the UTOPIA project may mean every-
> thing or nothing. Just a pile of reports or something
> which they can turn into practice. We know more
> about new technology. And we know more about the

limitations, for instance in communication both inside
the computer and between man and computer. The
*requirement specification* is easy to use, even on both
sides of the negotiation table. The *organizational model*
is already being applied in at least five newspapers. The
most important result is the cooperation between trade
unions and researchers based on the unions' objectives.
The reports and cooperation with a supplier, TIPS, that
was exceptional, and worked out quite well. I am quite
optimistic where the future is concerned. The organizational model presented by the UTOPIA project allows
room for qualified graphic workers of the future.

Finally, an international research perspective. An appre-
ciative article in *MIT Technology Review* analyzing
*UTOPIA – where workers craft new technology* concluded:[29]

So the impact of UTOPIA is continuing to expand, and
the idea that workers and their unions have an important role in the design of new technology is reaching
a wider and wider audience. Today Scandinavia. Tomorrow, perhaps, the rest of the world.

However, as in all 'success' stories, UTOPIA, too, has its
dark sides on which the light more seldom is shed. Let me
in conclusion drag some of them into the light.
   Clearly one dark side is what happened to the vendor
Liber that the UTOPIA project cooperated with, and the
destiny of the TIPS system. The problems of carrying out
practical technical and organizational experiments with
the TIPS system have already been mentioned. There
were, however, many more problems.
   Liber really did implement most of the requirement
specifications for image processing, and the system
worked well. When it came to page make-up, Liber decided (for market considerations) to make two versions.

[29] Howard, R.: 'UTOPIA – Where Workers Craft New Technology'
in *Technological Review*, vol 88 no 3, Massachusetts Institute of
Technology, 1985.

One was according to the UTOPIA specifications, and intended for the Scandinavian market with strong trade unions. A completely different one was destined for the U.S.A market. This latter version was a less skill-based one, not relying on a democratic work organization. Neither of the versions were really well implemented, at first due to technical problems, then, as a consequence, due to financial problems.

The TIPS system was implemented at several 'test site' newspapers. However, before finalizing it as a market product the vendor was short of capital and the rights to the system were sold to another company primarily focusing on the image processing part. This illustrates a problem with 'the Scandinavian model' for technological development. The small Scandinavian countries may lack both the technological competence and the financial resources for really successful participation in the international technological race.

The UTOPIA project clearly showed that the latest technology may be designed and put into use to improve, not decrease, the skills of the graphic workers. If not a dark side, it is perhaps a dark horse, as to whether this really will happen. Will the Scandinavian newspaper owners exploit the possibilities for a constructive discussion on technology, organization, and training? This to a great extent depends upon whether the graphic workers and journalists succeed in overcoming their professional clash of interests, and together develop a common strategy. The historical study conducted by the project provides some insight into this. The new technology creates 'demarcation disputes' between professional groups, as well as between trade unions. This presents a large and very real problem. This is true for graphic workers and journalists, as well as for other professional groups. However, the UTOPIA project demonstrated that solutions can be found. For newspapers there are technical and organizational alternatives where no professional group is unilaterally lost, and where product quality and reasonable efficiency can be ensured. Nevertheless, the lack of trade union cooperation, not the technology, not the newspaper owners, nor the suppliers, may ironically become the decisive factor frustrating the dream of Utopia.

Given this background it seems reasonable to ask why only the graphic workers' unions directly participated in the UTOPIA project, and not also the journalists' and the administrative staff's unions. I find this question very important. Such participation would, at least in theory, have contributed to a better design. It was a deliberate choice by the research group to cooperate with the graphic workers, since we considered them as the weakest party in the current technological change in graphic industry. However, we also consciously were seeking close cooperation with the other unions concerned. The fact that we first had contacts with the graphic workers made the other unions, on good grounds or not, critical towards UTOPIA, and thus frustrated the dream of a joint design.

Finally a note on the design process in the UTOPIA project. It was really utopian. The preconditions for such a design process are not present in corporate business as we know it today. Resources for skilled workers, trade union people, computer and social scientists to work together over a long period of time designing tools in the interest of the end users do not generally exist as yet, not even in Scandinavia. UTOPIA was not only a challenge to design, but also to a more democratic working life.

Chapter 14

# Reminders on Designing for Democracy at Work

In this part I have discussed *the democracy aspect of work-oriented design of computer artifacts*. I have outlined *the collective resource approach* developed in the Scandinavian setting, especially focusing on our *practice research* experiences from the DEMOS and UTOPIA projects.

Together with Morten Kyng a few years ago I made a summary of 'some theses on the collective resource approach', based on our shared experiences.[1] In the light of the philosophical discussion in the first part of this book I will below restate the results from DEMOS, UTOPIA and other collective resource projects as a number of 'reminders', in the Wittgensteinian sense, on designing for democracy at work. These reminders, argued throughout the chapters of this part of the book, are not scientifically proved 'theses' in a strict sense.

The *practice research* approach applied certainly can contribute to practical change and theoretical development, and my claim is that in both respects it has done so, but this case and practical change based approach does not really produce scientific theses in the form that e.g. controlled experiments do. (The theoretical status of scientific theses produced that way is another matter that

---

[1] Ehn, P. and Kyng K.: 'The Collective Resource Approach to Systems Design' in Bjerknes, G. et al (eds.) *Computers and Democracy – A Scandinavian Challenge*, Avebury, 1987.

will not be examined here. Every research approach has
its own practical and methodological problems.[2])

The methodological problems with the practice research approach we applied derive from the close interaction between existing theory used for understanding
and intervening in practice, and this changing practice as
the inspiration for further theoretical reflections – a hen-
and-egg problem. Furthermore, results can not only be
measured in terms of 'new theory', but must also be seen
in the light of practical change – a related action and reflection problem. Another problem, one specific to design
research, is related to the aim of not only contributing to
substantial theory concerning the research field, but also
of creating new design artifacts and working practices
related to this theory – a design research problem.

With this in mind, the following reminders from the
chapters on designing for democracy at work are summarized for further reflection and action:

# Reminders

*Reminders on the General Theoretical Framework for
Understanding Design and Use of Computer Artifacts in
the Context of Democratization of Work*

- The design process is part of a larger organizational
  development process. Furthermore, this process of organizational development and change should in the
  context of democratization be understood as including
  trade union activities as well as societal constraints and
  opportunities.

- A central concept for understanding design and use of
  computer artifacts is that of labor processes. A labor

---

[2] The methodological problems with our *practice research* approach in cooperation with trade unions has, as mentioned before, been reflected in a separate research project. See Sandberg,
Å. (ed.): *Forskning för förändring – Om metoder och förutsättningar för handlingsinriktad forskning i arbetslivet*, Swedish
Center for Working Life, Stockholm 1981.

process is a process to produce use values: specific products or services of some kind. These use values are produced by people using artifacts (specific machines, tools, techniques etc.) to refine objects of work (specific 'raw materials'; goods, services, ideas, etc.). Planning as well as execution are fundamental parts of human work in this process. The division of labor between different groups of people, their qualifications for accomplishing different tasks, and the quality of the use values being produced are key aspects of the labor process in the context of democratization of work.

- The design process reflects, at least conceptually and so far in most cases also practically, a fundamental division of labor, the division between planning and execution. In the design process, computer artifacts and use values, as well as skill requirements and organizational options for another labor process, the use process, are anticipated and 'frozen'. In the use process work is executed given the constraints and opportunities set by the design process. Turning matters the other way around, the characteristics of a given use process also set constraints and opportunities for the design process.

- The design process as well as the use process are separate labor processes, and at the same time parts of a 'total' labor process. In this perspective an understanding of changes in labor processes must be related to the totality as well as to the separate parts, to the division of labor between different groups of participants within the labor process of design, to the division of labor between the design and the use labor process, and to the division of labor within the use labor process.

- Capital accumulation or generation of profits is the basic driving force in changes of labor processes.

- Intensification of work and use of new technology are two basic strategies for capital accumulation.

- The relations between on the one hand workers and their trade unions, and on the other hand management and capital owners has its origin in the labor contract.

This is an exchange relation between two kinds of commodity possessors – capital (which owns the means of production and the workplace) and labor (which owns its labor power). To produce profit the capital owner needs to buy labor power; to earn a living the worker needs to sell his or her labor power and work at the workplace.

- Class struggle at work is an important aspect of actual changes in labor processes, not only of the use process designed, but also of the design process and of possible integrations in the future.

- A participative approach to the design process is not sufficient in the context of democratization at work.

- In democratization of design and use of computer artifacts in Scandinavia, trade unions – especially on a local level – must play an active role.

*Reminders on Democratization by Local Trade Union Participation in the Design of Computer Artifacts*

- A clear distinction based on negotiations between union and management roles in the design process is not in opposition to, but a prerequisite for the democratization of cooperation and decision-making in the work organization.

- Design and use of computer artifacts requires new trade union activities.

- The most important prerequisite for trade union participation in the traditional design process is a parallel and independent process of accumulation of knowledge on the part of the union.

- The union investigation and negotiation strategy, 'the negotiation model', is a democratic and workable complement to traditional design strategies. But it is very resource consuming for the local unions. Hence, in many situations less participative strategies like mobilization around general union principles for use of computer artifacts, and negotiations based on these principles, may be a more realistic alternative.

- Local unions need external resources and support in their design activities.
- A local trade union strategy has to be based on solidarity between the different groups of workers involved, a solidarity which goes beyond the traditional division of labor in the labor process and the traditional jurisdictions between the unions involved.

## *Reminders on Central Trade Union Support for Democratization of Design and Use of Computer Artifacts*

- The existing computer-based technology in many cases restricts the possibilities to locally reach trade union objectives, especially with respect to skill, but also with respect to work organization.
- However, it is possible to design computer-based technology based on criteria such as skill and democracy at work.
- Central trade unions must influence the process of research and development of new technology to change the supply of technological and organizational solutions.
- Equally important is a trade union strategy to influence the demand for these technological and organizational alternatives.
- Central trade unions must provide training with a trade union perspective on design and use of computer artifacts, and influence the supply of professional training for skilled work.
- A strategy like the 'new Scandinavian model' for research and technological development – focusing on a new form for cooperation between governments, trade unions and high tech industry in production of new technology which supports good working conditions and good use quality products and services – is a promising approach to support more democratic design and use of computer artifacts.

*Reminders on Design Artifacts for User Participation in*
*Design in the Context of Democratization of Work*

- 'Design-by-Doing' design methods like the use of mock-
  ups and other prototyping design artifacts make it
  possible for ordinary users to use their practical skill
  when participating in the design process.
- 'Systems description' design artifacts should not primarily be seen as means for creating true 'pictures of
  reality', but as means to help the users (and the designers) discuss current situations and envision and discuss
  future ones. To this end, as the 'organizational tool kit',
  they must support a 'family resemblance' with the
  users' ordinary work practice, and be easy to use in
  group work.

## Beyond DEMOS and UTOPIA

What are the relations between these 'reminders' and the
reflections on *Design Philosophy* and *The Art and Science
of Designing Computer Artifacts* discussed in the previous
parts?

A first comment must be that my reason for writing the
previous parts to a great extent is rooted in a desire to
further reflect upon our experiences from the DEMOS and
the UTOPIA projects. These parts are *post hoc* theoretical
reflections to illuminate our 'achievements' as well as our
'shortcomings'. They relate our research to a more general philosophical and academic research context. They
constitute a frame of reference which permits others to
understand and criticize the basis for our research, as well
as for allowing us to rethink some of our research
'findings'.

In relation to the part on *Design Philosophy*, the collective resource approach is best captured as a *Marxist approach*. However, in the case of the DEMOS project there
were also elements of a rationalistic Cartesian approach,
with regard to its emphasis on formal procedures for democratization. In the UTOPIA project elements of a *Hei-*

*deggerian approach* and a *Wittgensteinian approach* entered with the 'tool perspective' and the 'design-by-doing' methods, but by no means as an *a priori* philosophically conscious choice. Rather, our practical experiences led us in these philosophical directions.

In relation to the part on an *Art and Science of Designing Computer Artifacts* and the 'definition' of design of computer artifacts, the *social, historical,* and *planning* aspects of design of computer artifacts were, both in the DEMOS and the UTOPIA project, extensively treated in the context of democratization of work.

However, the *creative* aspect was not really taken into account in the DEMOS project, whereas the UTOPIA project came to focus on skill both in design and use of computer artifacts.

With respect to *the contradiction between tradition and transcendence* in design, both projects highlighted crucial aspects in the context of democratization. To mention a few examples: There was the contradiction between adherence to traditional local trade union working practices of negotiations on behalf of the members, and at the same time the development of new ways of preparing negotiations on new technology. There was adherence to traditional project participation, and at the same time the development of new complementary participative structures.

In retrospect, a 'family resemblance' between the approach taken in the DEMOS and the UTOPIA projects and the 'social systems design methods' (Churchman, Ackoff, and Checkland) discussed in the previous part is obvious, though it was far from clear as the projects were carried out. In the case of the UTOPIA project, the relations to new prototyping design approaches suggested by Floyd, and to the new theoretical foundation of design suggested by Winograd and Dreyfus are rather obvious too. Compared to the above approaches I find that the strength of the collective resource approach is our ability to integrate social theory on democratization with design, and as the ability to practically participate in the democratization process. Just as obvious is our methodological weakness as compared to more 'mature' design approaches. In relation to design approaches in other fields discussed, a 'family resemblance' between the Bauhaus movement and the collective resource approach can be noticed concerning the focus on democracy and skill. In relation to 'postmodern' architectural design the collective resource approach lacks the playfulness suggested.

The list of reminders on designing for democracy at work grow out of the experience that socio-technical participation in design is far from sufficient. In the light of our own practical shortcomings (and some progress in the UTOPIA project), and the more 'creative' approaches discussed in the previous part I will end the list by suggesting that

• formal democratic and participative procedures for designing computer artifacts for democracy at work are not sufficient. The design process must also be organized in a way that make it possible for ordinary users to utilize their practical skill in the design work, and having fun doing this.

In the next part of this book I will elaborate on the skill aspect of creativity in design and use of computer artifacts.

# Part IV

# Designing for Skill

*'If we could rid ourselves of all pride,*
*if, to define our species,*
*we kept strictly*
*to what the historic and the prehistoric periods*
*show us to be*
*the constant characteristic of man and of intelligence,*
*we should say not Homo sapiens, but Homo Faber.*
*In short, intelligence,*
*considered in what seems to be its original feature,*
*is the faculty of manufacturing artificial objects,*
*especially tools to make tools,*
*and of indefinitely varying the manufacture.'*

Henri Bergson in *Creative Evolution*

# Introduction

Craft work unions, like those of typographers, have historically played a major role in the struggle for democracy at work and in society in general. The skilled worker and his union have often been in the front line, fighting for democratic rights. As was discussed in the previous part on *Designing for Democracy at Work*, democratic rights at work to a great extent concern the worker's ability to counteract tendencies towards deskilling of the work force. Not surprisingly, craft work has been an ideal for the trade union movement. There are historical and political connections between the ideal of democracy at work and the ideal of skilled workers producing good use quality products – my normative point of departure for work-oriented design of computer artifacts. Though the connection between democracy at work and craft work is obvious, it is also a problematic one. Craft work may end up in the kind of undemocratic elitism that many professional groups exercise. There is also a contradiction between craft workers' interests, and the interests of unskilled or unemployed workers. Furthermore, the ideal of high quality products may lead to the production of luxury products for the happy few who can afford them, rather than to good use quality products for the many. Finally, there is more to life than work. There is a contradiction between acquisition of high skills at work and time for realization of perhaps more important aspects of our lives. These kind of contradictions between democracy and a craft ideal are important to consider. Nevertheless, I maintain the position that designing for skill should be a fundamental aspect of work-oriented design of computer artifacts. This position will be elaborated in this part.

# Craftsmanship as Design Ideal

It is easy to become romantic about craft work. It is everything industrial work is not. John Seymour is one of its bards. In the introduction of his guide to traditional skill *The Forgotten Arts* he writes:[1]

> Radically every artifact a person uses today can easily be made from oil-derived plastic, in a large factory, by machine-minders whose chief quality is their ability to survive lives of intense boredom. Even the machine-minders are rapidly being replaced by robots who, we are told, don't get bored at all. Artifacts so produced often do their jobs perfectly well. They are ugly, for beauty in an artifact depends on the texture of some natural material combined with the skill and loving care of an artisan; they are short-lived, so consequently our world is becoming choked with partly degraded, broken-down plastic objects, and their production is causing the pollution of our planet on a scale never before experienced. But, by and large, they work. If everything we use is to be ugly and boring to make, what is the purpose of living at all? Was there once really something people called quality of life? A good and satisfying quality, that is. Could there be again? Or are we, as a species, doomed to live out the rest of our destiny doing boring jobs and surrounded by mediocrity and ugliness?

No matter how convincing the above argument may be, its critics could easily demonstrate that in many respects an assembly-line worker who in 1988 works in a Scandinavian workplace and is a member of a union has more freedom and autonomy in general than his fellow worker who was a member of a guild several hundred years ago. In addition he earns more money.

---

[1] Seymour, J.: *The Forgotten Arts – A practical guide to traditional skills*, Dorling Kindersley, London 1984, p. 6.

The social and political conditions under which crafts-manship was acquired in the guild system are far from being worth romanticizing about.

However, since early industrialism attempts have now and then been made to counteract the negative sides of industrial work as machine-minding, and to reintroduce craft work traditions – focusing on skilled work for pro-duction of good use quality products.

William Morris was one of these great utopians from the nineteenth century. His interests in quality ranged from good typography to ideal factories. His craft work visions are still worth reading.[2]

Today craft ideals are mostly associated with the alter-native production movement, which deals with funda-mental issues of our environment. Typically there is a fo-cus on low technology small scale crafts production.

The UTOPIA project was a rare example of trying to apply craftsmanship principles to the design and use of advanced computer artifacts, but not the only one.[3] These examples suggest designs which on the one hand norma-tively support the craft ideal of quality of work and prod-uct, and on the other try to utilize the flexibility of com-puters as material to design really skill-enhancing tools.

However, if we want to design and use computer arti-facts based on the practical skill of craftsmen, rather than just the calculus of engineers, then we need new means of designing. The design approach we applied in the UTOPIA project demonstrated some ways of moving in that direc-tion. These ways are also theoretically supported by the role given to practical understanding in the Wittgen-

[2] See e.g. Morton, A.L.: *Political Writings of William Morris*, Lawrence & Wishart, Berlin 1973, and Morton, A.L.: *Three Works by William Morris, News from Nowhere, The Pilgrims of Hope, A Dream of John Ball*, Lawrence & Wishart, Berlin 1968.

[3] The design efforts by the workers at Lucas Aerospace, and the work by research teams around Mike Cooley and Harold Rosen-brock in Britain, the work by IG Metal and researchers around Peter Brödner in Germany, as mentioned in the *Prologue*, demonstrate similar attempts.

steinian and Heideggerian approaches discussed in Part I on *Design Philosophy*. In addition, it will be argued in this part that modern workstation technology and user interface design styles constitute new opportunities for practically designing computer artifacts as tools – for and with skilled workers.

Obviously, the design approach advocated here is heavily influenced by traditional craft work. This goes for the *product ideal* – a tool under complete control of the user, as well as for the *design ideal* – the role of tradition, and the master-apprentice relation. There are, however, several points where one may criticize these ideals.

One concerns *the possibility of designing computer artifacts in such a way that using them resembles craftsmanship*. This is, for example, questioned by many craftsmen as well as by researchers.

Craftsmen fear that their kind of skill will have to vanish when computer artifacts replace traditional tools and materials. Researchers support them in this view by stressing that abstract technical qualifications are replacing craft skills. It is the engineer, not the craftsman, that will be the ideal future user. In this part I will try to argue that though both may be right in their critique of our UTOPIAn ideal, they do not have to be.

Another critique is of the desirability of *the ideal of craftsmanship in design and use of computer artifacts*. Why craft work and autonomy as an ideal? What is it more than a historically specific pre-industrial and pre-capitalistic form of work? Moreover it is a form of work that carries an inherent individualistic and male centered ideal. Yes, let us try to extend it to something that is cooperative and human centered. And let us at the same time reflect upon whether the ideal of craftsmanship is too high an ideal, as has also been argued: The point is that if craft skill and autonomy are set as the ideal then we will in working life only find deskilled workers.

I am not arguing that this critique is wrong. On the contrary it should be taken as a challenge to change and develop the craftsmanship ideal. But no matter how much we change and develop it, there are two aspects of crafts-manship that I think should remain as cornerstones in our design ideal.

The first one is *the priority of practical understanding in design and use of computer artifacts,* as opposed to just relying on theoretical detached reflection. No matter how technically complex a computer artifact is, it is possible and desirable to anchor design and use in practical understanding. That is a a position I theoretically and empirically try to demonstrate in this book.

The second cornerstone I want to maintain is the design ideal of *computer artifacts as tools augmenting skills* rather than replacing them. Again the claim is that theoretically as well as empirically this can be shown to be a possible way of designing.

## Structure of Part IV

In the UTOPIA project we developed some design princip-les we have referred to as *the tool perspective*. Traditional craft work was used as an ideal both for the design process and for the tools and materials to be designed. Hence, there was a strong emphasis on practical understanding both in design and in use. The design ideal for computer artifacts was seen as a set of tools under the skilled wor-ker's control. The ideal for the design process was as an activity of 'design-by-doing', as a practical learning pro-cess. In chapter 13, *Case II: The UTOPIA Project* I gave a general background. In chapter 15, *The 'Tool Per-spective' – An Example*, I will in more detail describe the tool kit for computer-based page make-up designed ac-cording to these principles.

In the following three chapters of this part I will elabo-rate on the ideal of computer-based tools for skilled work. An important aspect of computer artifacts that I will in-vestigate in these chapters concerns how tool-like we may design them to be. I will refer to this aspect as the *toolness* of computer artifacts.

In chapter 16, *Tools*, the concept of a tool is investigated. The chapter has the form of an inventory of tool aspects of computer artifacts. Pros and cons of understanding computer artifacts as tools, as well as alternative views, are discussed. The conclusions are far from unambiguous. I find strong support for a tool perspective, as well as fundamental criticism.

In chapter 17, *The 'Toolness' of Computer Artifacts* is discussed in terms of 'state of the art' hardware and software supporting this toolness. As paradigm examples I refer to a number of 'classical' computer artifacts displaying such features. I also discuss the tool perspective in the light of some general principles for user interface design. The chapter is introductory, intended as a background for readers unfamiliar with the field of human-computer interaction design, rather than as a contribution to the field.

Finally, in chapter 18, *Skills and the Tool Perspective*, skill aspects of design and use of computer artifacts are further elaborated. The problematic concept of tacit knowledge is defended. At the same time the blindness a tool perspective may create towards social, collective and cooperative skills is acknowledged. The chapter ends with a section in which the tool perspective and the craft work ideal are confronted with a number of empirical sociological studies of changes of qualifications in relation to use of computer artifacts in working life.

*Chapter 15*

# The 'Tool Perspective' – An Example

In the UTOPIA project we developed a design approach which we called the tool perspective.[1] The tool perspective takes the labor process as its origin rather than data or information flow. This means: not detailed analysis, description and formalization of qualifications, but development of professional education based on the skills of professionals; not information flow analysis and systems description, but specification of tools and materials. The ideal for designing a computer artifact is a tool kit containing craft tools which under complete and continuous control of the user can be applied to fashion materials into more refined products or services. The user is seen as a person who possesses skills relevant for the task to be accomplished. Computer-based tools are developed to be used by skilled users to create good use quality products and services.

In the tool perspective, essential parts of the user's skills relevant when using a tool are tacit, and as such they neither can nor should be made explicit and formalized. Hence, the intention is not to automate parts of the skills,

---

[1] The tool perspective was first outlined in Ehn, P. and Kyng, M.: 'A Tool Perspective on Design of Interactive Computer Support for Skilled Workers' in *Proceedings of the Seventh Scandinavian Research Seminar on Systemeering*, Helsinki 1984. See also Bødker: 'Utopia and the Design of User Interfaces' and Kammersgaard, J.: 'On Models and their Role in the use of Computers' in *Preceedings of the Aarhus Conference on Development and Use of Computer Based Systems and Tools*, Aarhus, 1985.

but to build computer-based tools by which craftsmen can still apply and develop their original skills.

In this chapter I will exemplify the tool perspective with our efforts to design computer artifacts for full page make-up in newspaper production. I will make a few comments on the design process, but my primary emphasis will be on the product designed.

The main purpose of the chapter is to give a concrete example of an application of the tool perspective. This example will then be utilized in the coming chapters, where both the tool aspect and the skill aspect of a tool perspective are scrutinized.

## The Design Process – 'Design-by-Doing'

The tool perspective was deeply influenced by the way the design of tools takes place within traditional crafts. The idea is that new tools should be designed as an extension of the traditional practical understanding of tools and materials used within a given craft or profession. As a consequence of this, design must be carried out by common efforts of skilled, experienced users and design professionals. Users possess the practical understanding necessary as the basis for the design, but to support their technical imagination they must gain insight into new technical possibilities as well. The designer has to spend a great deal of time trying to gain some insight into the specific labor process. The goal is not to become, for example, a make-up person, but to be able to contribute constructively in the design process. But the designer must also be a design professional. Computer-based tools which for the skilled worker are simple, powerful and accurate to use, are often technically highly complex.

In the UTOPIA project we tried out such a process of mutual learning: here, graphic workers learned about the technical possibilities and constraints of computer technology, and we as designers learned about the work of the craft or profession in question. Initially the group worked with building up a mutual understanding of the specific labor processes of the profession, of the design situation, and of the technical possibilities and limitations. Apart from discussions, visits to workplaces with different 'generations' of technology as well as visits to research laboratories and vendors proved to be important early activities in the mutual learning process.

However, as mentioned in chapter 13, *Case II: The UTOPIA Project*, we, as designers, ran into severe difficulties – with regard to communication with the graphic workers and with regard to really designing artifacts for skilled work – when at the beginning of the project we used traditional design artifacts like data or information flows in designing computer artifacts for page make-up. It was also described how the situation drastically improved when we shifted towards a *design-by-doing* approach. With the use of mock-ups and other prototyping design artifacts the skilled workers could actively participate in the design process, *expressing their craft skills, in the design process, by actually doing page make-up.*

In a philosophical frame one can say that we came to reject the rationalistic and dualistic Cartesian design approach of descriptions based on a picture theory of reality. The basic design strategy was no longer one of correct descriptions of the user's skill and practice as a basis for formal descriptions of the correct design by a rational observing designer, but one of shared doing both design and page make-up. The main emphasis was instead on a mutual learning process resembling the traditional master-apprentice relation in a double sense. As designers we had to learn practically from the skilled graphic workers doing page make-up. As users participating in the design process, the graphic workers had to learn from us as more experienced in design of computer artifacts. The fundamental problem was to establish a context in which this shared practice could be cultivated. The use of mock-ups and other prototyping design artifacts helped in shaping this context.

The philosophical foundation for such a design strategy has been discussed at length, in Part I on *Design Philoso-*

*phy*, both as a Heideggerian approach and as a Wittgensteinian approach.[2]

In summary, the Heideggerian approach provided a
basis for understanding *human use of artifacts as a pre-
reflective involved everyday activity*, and design-by-doing
as a process of anticipation of future use situations based
on the dialectics between support for the users' gaining
*ready-to-hand* practical experience of using their 'future'
artifacts, and support for creative *breakdowns* as a means
for *present-at-hand* reflections of the desirability of different alternatives. The Wittgensteinian approach provided
a basis for understanding design-by-doing as *a language-
game*. The users can participate in this language-game
because it has *family resemblance* with the language-
games played in their ordinary use situations. And by actually doing, for example, page make-up they can make
use of their practical understanding in the design process.
Design-by-doing becomes a language-game in which the
users learn about possibilities and constraints of new
computer artifacts that may become part of their future
ordinary language-games. Users learn from designers
how to participate in the language-game of design. However, to create a language-game of design-by-doing designers have to learn a great deal from the users.

In design-by-doing the traditional division of the design
process into an application-oriented phase (carried out by
application-oriented designers) followed by a computer-
oriented phase (carried out by computer-oriented designers) also becomes problematic. The designer must be able
to organize the design process, to master design artifacts
for dealing with work organization, to contribute to education and training, etc. But this cannot be done in a first,
isolated phase. Hardware considerations play an important role even in the initial stages of design. The communication with the graphic workers about existing

---

[2] See chapter 2, *Existential Phenomenology – A Heideggerian
Approach* and chapter 3, *Language-Games – A Wittgensteinian
Approach.*

technology, for example display resolution, response times and interaction devices, in the beginning of the design process, was of major importance in our design of the tools for page make-up. Hardware considerations have to be dealt with in parallel with the software design considerations in all stages of a design project, thus supporting the generation of new ideas. We found the use of simple mock-ups highly useful in this process, but obviously in terms of performance such mock-ups have many limitations. By being non-computer-based, however, they can be very useful in highlighting limitations of current, and future, computer technology.

## A Tool Perspective Use Model for Page Make-Up

As pointed out, the opportunity for the users to relate these computer-based tools to their experience and knowledge is an important prerequisite for making computer artifacts applicable as tools in a labor process. To facilitate this we did in the UTOPIA project design what we (with a badly chosen label) called *use models*.[3] We developed use models for tools for page make-up and image processing.[4] The use models relate the use of the computer-based tools to the use of the users' traditional tools. The use models were intended to encourage the graphic workers to apply expe-

[3] The concept use model was inspired by Newman, W. and Sproull, R.: *Principles of Interactive Computer Graphics*, Mc-Graw-Hill, Tokyo 1979. For a detailed discussion about use models, see Kammersgaard, op. cit. For a parallel discussion of user models, mental models, and design models in the context of cognitive science see Norman, D.: 'Cognitive Engineering' in Norman, D. and Draper, S. (eds.): *User Centered System Design*, Lawrence Erlbaum, London 1986.

[4] See Ehn, P. et al.: *Datorstödd Ombrytning*, Swedish Center for Working Life, Stockholm 1985, Frenckner, K. and Romberger, S.: *Datorstödd Bildbehandling*, Swedish Center for Working Life, Stockholm 1985, and Ehn, P. and Sundblad, Y. (eds.): *Kravspecifikation för datorstödd bildbehandling och ombrytning*, Swedish Center for Working Life, Stockholm 1983.

rience, knowledge and skills from working with the old technology when designing and using computer-based tools for newspaper production.

The idea can be interpreted in our Wittgensteinian language of language-games and family resemblance. The practices of users and designers are different. A use model is a means to bridge this gap, in design, as well as in use, of the artifact being designed. The user is experienced in his or her work, and knows how to play the language-games in the work or use situation. Similarly, professional designers are experienced in the language-games of design. Both aspects are important. The way we learn the practice of new language-games is by participating in them, and by their family resemblance with other language-games we are familiar with.

A use model may be seen as a 'dramatic context' based on the professional language related to the labor processes in question, enhanced with new concepts developed from possibilities and restrictions of the new technology being used and of external metaphors. It is proposed that this model be instrumental in supporting family resemblance between the language-games of design, education and use.

In *design* a use model should support communication between users and designers, and the design of functionality and user interface of the computer computer artifact. In the UTOPIA project the use models for page make-up and image processing evolved in our use of mock-ups.

In *education* a use model should support activities aiming at enhanced competence as practical understanding. The textbooks on computer-based page make-up and image processing that we wrote in the UTOPIA project were, for example, based on our use models.[5]

In *use* a use model should support the user's ready-to-hand focus on the work, making the artifact 'transparent' (preventing breakdowns like technical distortions).

A way of expressing the relations between the design of tools and a use model is to say that the use model consti-

[5] Ehn, et al., op. cit., and Frenckner and Romberger, op. cit.

tutes a useful *context* for understanding computer-based tools as reminders of traditional ones. In design of computer-based tools *we not only design the new tools, we also design the material for the skilled worker to work with.*

Below I will give a summary of the tool perspective use model for page make-up that we designed in the UTOPIA project. However as a necessary background I will first make a few comments on traditional tools and computer-based systems for this labor process.[6]

## Tools for Page Make-Up

Page make-up is the process by which full newspaper pages are made up of material such as articles, pictures, advertisements, frames, and lines.

Seen in a historical perspective three different page make-up technologies can be distinguished according to the material with which the make-up person works.

In the first generation technology the make-up person works with tangible material in the form of types, clichées, and printing blocks originally made of wood, later of metal. This technology has its roots in sixth century China and mid-fifteenth century Europe (Gutenberg). The material is put together in a form which is later used in the printing process. The tools employed, such as the composing stick and the bodkin, were, like the material itself, tangible.

In the second generation the material is paper-based, and the form is replaced by a paper page ground onto which the material is pasted. Text, headlines, and galleys are produced on photographic paper by means of a photosetter. Images are half-tone paper photographs, and the graphic materials are tape rules, dry transfer symbols, half-tone boxes, etc. The original make-up is photographically transferred to printing plates. This technology, which became common in the 1960s, is based on the application of computer-based text processing and offset

---

[6] The presentation of our tool perspective use model for page make-up is based on Ehn, et al., op. cit.

printing technology. The most important tools are the knife and wax.

In the early 1980s, a third generation technology was on its way. The material and form are no longer tangible, but are presented as reminders on the display of a computer workstation. The tools are more abstract: with a pointing device the worker can move a cursor on the display, choose part of or the entire material, and by means of buttons indicate what is to be done with the chosen material.

Thus the production process for page make-up has changed from working with concrete, tangible material to working with reminders on a display. The stability which characterized the first generation technology in the form of a limited choice of type sizes and exactly horizontal and vertical texts, columns, and lines, has not always been considered in the more flexible second generation technology, where it is far easier to make errors in matching type sizes and mounting horizontally and vertically.

Our ideal in the UTOPIA project was a computer-based tool kit that combined the strengths of the earlier technologies and avoided their weaknesses, and at the same time utilized new technological possibilities for improving product quality.

We envisioned a design which was based on the following: When making up a page on a graphic display, the page displayed on the screen should remind the user as much as possible of the final printed page, and the work should consist of using tools for placing and adjusting the material until a satisfactory result is obtained. The make-up person should, in principle, work in the same way as in paper paste-up. Another important consideration was to exploit the possibilities for supporting the advantages of both lead composing (firmness of typography) and paper paste-up (flexibility). Designed for skilled graphic workers, these computer-based tools should facilitate and encourage the graphic workers to fully use their creative abilities.

However, even the best current technology had its limitations where for example graphic displays are concerned:

- they emitted light rather than reflected it as paper pages do;
- they were too small to reproduce a whole page in natural size;
- their resolution was too poor to make the body text legible in its natural size.

To take an example: Imagine the resolution necessary to show a full page of a newspaper in A2-format (560x410 mm) in photosetter quality (typically 1500 points per inch) on the display. A 27" display with 34,000x25,000 pixels would be necessary. Imagine further that the display has a refresh rate of 100 Hz to eliminate flicker. To control the display a memory of 1 Gbit would be needed and each pixel should be processed in approximately 10 picoseconds. Available processors were at least 100 times too slow, and the best available 'high resolution' raster displays had a resolution of approximately 1400x2000 pixels on a 19' display. As the comparison shows the use of modern computer-based technology could mean a drastic reduction of quality as compared with the traditional paper paste-up technology for page make-up.

The question was whether these drawbacks could be counterbalanced by new possibilities, such as:

- changes in typography and graphic material may be executed more easily later in the process, and carried out faster;
- the relative ease of changing the typography and the graphic design makes it possible to try several alternatives in a short time;
- the ease of changing the material makes it feasible to start making up the pages at a much earlier stage in the production, before all material is available, and then to successively complete and correct them;

- the positioning can be made more precise – all text may be set exactly horizontally; it is possible to get exactly the same leading between all sections in the article; the material in the surrounding columns can be exactly aligned, etc.

The tool perspective use model should not only be a reminder of the users' ordinary work practice, it should also be both a way to overcome technical constraints imposed by the computer technology, and a way to envision how new technical possibilities could be used. The use model we envisioned should technically be realized on a graphic workstation where the material is displayed and processed on a high-resolution bit-mapped display, and the work is carried out by the make-up person using tools designed as a combination of graphic operations and physical interaction devices.

## The Use Model

In the use model we imagined that *page ground*, *menus*, *list of material*, and *status information* are placed on a *desk*. The desk also contains a *work area*. On the desk the make-up person works with materials like *articles*, *pictures*, *logotypes*, *advertisements*, *frames*, *lines*, etc.

As it was not possible to show the whole desk on the display (unless the page was considerably reduced), the make-up person will have to look at selected parts, which are appropriately enlarged (or reduced). We therefore imagined that a number of *lenses* are at the make-up person's disposal and through which different parts of the desk can be viewed. The make-up person can choose which lenses to put on the display.

Each lens enlarges or reduces according to the scale employed. A limited number of scales should be available. These scales should be chosen so that each of the following criteria is met by at least one scale:

- the body text is easy to read: for precise allocation and changes in the text;

- the material is shown in natural size: for assessment of optical and aesthetical balance;
- the whole page can be seen on the display screen: for rough allocation;
- a miniature picture of the page: for guidance.

Using fixed scales instead of a more or less continuous degree of enlargement helps the make-up person estimate what the real page will look like.

The interaction is supported by the following two capabilities: The lenses can be directed at different parts of the page ground, work area, and material; and the material visible through the lens can be moved in all directions.

The make-up person may wish to work on several pages at the same time, for example to get a comprehensive view of a spread, or an advertisement which fills several pages. Hence, several pages can be placed on the desk so that the pages can be seen together through one or more lenses on the display.

Naturally the *lenses* and the *desk* are reminders based on metaphors which we used to conceptually overcome the technical constraints of today's computer and display technology which prevent the make-up person from working directly on the full page in natural size and in full resolution. These aspects of the use model were necessary in order to ensure that certain possibilities for qualitative assessment are not lost in the computer-based page make-up process.

However, the imaginary tools called lenses are not just an impediment in the page make-up process. They help the make-up person keep in mind that what is seen on the display is not the final page, but only a reminder. The make-up person looks at the page through a lens which carries with it intentional and unintentional distortions. The make-up person must always have the final page in mind. This is one of the reasons why the use model also includes facilities for getting proof-prints of the page as a basis for complementary assessment (for example via a laser-printer).

So far the desk and the lenses have been outlined. What about the tools for refining the material, for moving it, for measuring it, etc.? In the use model we imagined that tools for computer-based page make-up are realized through a combination of general interaction devices and graphical operations as reminders of traditional make-up tools.

As an example imagine that the make-up person is to pick up some material from the work area and place it on the page ground. He or she will point at the material with the pointing device, or rather, with the cursor which he or she controls with the pointing device. The make-up person will also indicate that he or she wishes to use a *move* tool. Using the move tool, by moving one's hand, the make-up person controls the positioning of the material with the pointing device.

The move tool is an example of a tool for positioning material. The material can be placed anywhere on the page ground or in the work area.

Imagine, however, that the make-up person wants to position a piece of text so that it exactly aligns with a column rule. Then he or she would, for example, with the other hand use the *support tool for gravity pointing*. Applying this tool the make-up person has only to move the material close to the column rule. It will be 'sucked' into the exact position. This is one of the advantages of lead composing (firmness of typography) as opposed to paper paste-up.

Using the other way around, we can imagine that the make-up person wants to position a piece of text to slightly overlap a logotype. He or she would than use a *magnifying glass tool*. When using the move tool to position the text on the logotype he or she looks at the text and the logotype 'through' the magnifying glass to see exactly where to place it (thus having the flexibility available in paper paste-up).

The examples illustrate how both 'lead' and 'paper paste-up' aspects of page make-up are envisioned in the use model. Another aspect of the use model for page make-up that the examples illustrate is the importance of the capability that allows the make-up person to use several tools from the tool kit at the same time.

We envisioned and tried to implement the following types of computer-based tools for page make-up:

- tools for *selecting and positioning the material*. For example tools for selecting, moving, column setting, contour setting, centering, indenting, and leading.
- tools for *support for page make-up*. For example tools for gravity pointing, aligning, magnifying, and various construction lines and construction points.
- tools for *text operations*. For example for changing column width, font and size; for kerning and letter spacing; and, of course, for adding and deleting text.
- tools for *picture operations*. For example for changes of size of pictures and for cropping them.
- tools for *make-up of advertisements*. In addition to the 'normal' make-up tools, tools for more imaginative typography like curve setting.
- tools for *administrative operations*. For example for allocating material from one page to another, for status information about pages and articles, and for requesting different types of proof prints.
- tools for *controlling 'desk' and 'lenses'*. For example for directing, and changing size, of the lenses.
- tools for *general support*. For example for getting 'help' information, for 'undoing' mistakes, and for saving and later resuming a job as it was left. Furthermore for 'furnishing' the desk with regard to display layout, type faces, scales, units of measurement, amount of help and status information, etc.

The computer-based make-up tools can be designed to be extremely powerful in the hands of a skilled user. Well-designed, they are founded upon a more than 500 year old tradition. Nevertheless, they are new and untested and need further elaboration. In our use model for page make-up we have assumed that a large part of this can be done by the make-up person directly on the shop floor. At the least it must be possible to *combine* existing graphic tools

with *personalized tools* which can be added to the operation menus or implemented as function keys. In the long
run the make-up person must have more advanced *programming tools* at his or her disposal to be able to *modify*
existing graphic tools, or *create completely new ones*.
These are necessary tools for our use model of the computer-based page make-up desk to be fully realized,
though we ourselves in cooperation with a vendor were
unable to implement all of them.

## Summary

Today the design of a tool-kit for computer-based page
make-up like the one outlined seems far from utopian.
Several professional page make-up systems, as well as
desktop publishing systems for relatively small computers, have many of the tools described, and support a work
practice like the one suggested. This positive development
was far from obvious for us when at the beginning of the
1980s we did our design in cooperation between graphic
workers and professional designers. In fact, the main
trend in the newspaper industry at that time was to design computer-based systems that deprived graphic
workers of their skills, which meant an acceptance of a
impoverished product quality.

I can see several reasons for this change. One obvious
reason is economic. There have been drastic reductions in
the cost for the computer technology required, and with
desktop publishing reaching far outside the newspaper
industry a mass market for standard software has
emerged, thus reducing the programming costs. Sticking
to the economic arguments, it also seems, as was discussed
in Part III on *Designing for Democracy*, that there for the
time being is a changing managerial rationalization attitude suggesting that the skilled worker might be the most
profitable one.

Other reasons have more to do with changes in design
practice. Of course, the UTOPIA project was far from the
only design group that had learned from paradigm ex-

amples in the history of designing computer artifacts as tools.[7] Finally, the best systems for computer-based page make-up on the market today, have, as the case was with the UTOPIA project, been designed in close cooperation with skilled graphic workers.

In summary the observations on design of computer-based tools for page make-up in the UTOPIA project may be formulated as the following reminders:

- Designing advanced computer artifacts for skilled work based on skilled work is a possibility.
- Important aspects of labor processes, in relation to design of computer artifact, neither can nor have to be formally described.
- Design should be done with users, not just for them.
- Mutual learning should be an important part of the work in a design group.
- Design-by-doing and the design of use models are ways of making it possible for users to utilize their practical skills in design and use.
- Hardware should be considered early in the design, in parallel with software, not after.
- The tool perspective is not such a bad idea.

In the three coming chapters of this part some light will be shed on several of these reminders.

---

[7] Such examples will be discussed in chapter 17, *The 'Toolness' of Computer Artifacts*.

*Chapter 16*

# Tools

The craft ideal is often upheld as the antithesis of using computers. A representative craftsman's view was given by Tomas Temte at a research symposium, some years ago, addressing the question: Is the computer a tool?. Tempte stated:[1]

> I am a master cabinet-maker in Stockholm, and have worked in the trade for 19 years. (...) For a craftsman, a tool is an object which is used to fashion raw material into a more refined product. By its weight, its hardness or its sharpness, the tool creates a more refined or practical product. The tool is a necessary condition for material production. For thousands of years, the tool has been wielded by the worker's hand, but often in combination with a machine. The lathe is one of the oldest machines in history. With it, the tool could both be incorporated into a machine and be guided by the worker's hand (...) Today, I believe that the lathe is undergoing its ultimate development. Numerical control, which is programmed in the computer, is the most that can be done with this mechanical device. In practice, the craft of lathe work will disappear with this generation of craftsmen. As a craftsman, I cannot see the computer as a tool based on what I have demonstrated and presented with my assistants. Not in any sense at all.

[1] Tempte, T.: 'Is the Computer a Tool? – A Craftsman's View' in Sundin, B. (ed.) *Is the Computer a Tool?*, Almqvist & Wiksell, Stockholm 1980, pp. 64, 69.

Let me state our position, in the UTOPIA project, regarding a tool perspective clearly. We did not, without qualifying the statement, claim that a computer artifact *is* a tool. What we considered was *whether the craft design process and craft use of tools could be used as prototypical examples for good design*. In the UTOPIA project we found strong support for such an ideal in practice. Below I will elaborate this position as a 'conversation' with different views I have found in the literature.

First I will 'define' computer artifacts as tools proper, distinguishable from our other privileged human instruments. Then I will discuss some criteria for good tools. Next, relations between computer artifacts, machines and traditional tools are considered. This includes a discussion of 'autonomous machines' from the clock to the computer, and some reflections on 'intelligent tools'. An ideological and technical critique of computer artifacts understood as tools is then considered. Finally, I also discuss alternatives to a tool perspective, like the design ideal of computer artifacts as playful 'postmodern' media.

## The Computer is a Tool

### Body, Language, Institutions, and Tools Proper

To 'define' tools I will start at a most general level, distinguishing *tools proper* from other *human instruments*. In *Teknokosmos* philosopher Ole Thyssen suggests such a distinction, which is well in line with the philosophical foundation of this book. He distinguishes four interrelated privileged human instruments – our bodies, our language, our social institutions, and our tools proper.[2] We use them all in the social construction of reality.

The first privileged instrument is our *body*. It is not an artifact in the sense that it is man made, nor is it a physical machine. But we change through practice, and we

[2] Thyssen, O.: *Teknokosmos – om teknik og menneskerettigheder*, Gyldendal, Viborg 1985, pp. 17–29.

certainly use our cultivated bodies. Merely think of everything we do with our hands.

Our second privileged instrument is our *language*. It is used to recreate the world, for communication and to carry our consciousness. But like our bodies it did not emerge as an artifact. We dwell in our language just as we are in our bodies. Our use of language is only possible within a certain form of life that sets conditions for our actions. But we certainly use language as an instrument.

Our third privileged instrument is our social *institutions*. As with language we are born into them. But we can also recreate them and use them to achieve certain ends.

The forth privileged instrument is the *tool proper*. It is physically objectified work and knowledge, dead labor in Marxist terminology. In contrast to the other three privileged instruments *all tools are designed*, constructed, maintained, and redesigned. Obviously computer artifacts are tools in this fourth sense. The question is: What kind of tools can they be designed to be?

When asking that question it should be kept in mind that design and use of tools in this sense is interrelated to the other instruments: our bodies, our languages, and the social institutions that we live in. In the context of Part I on *Design Philosophy*, the Heideggerian approach concerns use of tools as our existential condition, and how we practically understand the world. In design we are concerned with intentional and unintentional breakdowns of understanding and use of these tools. In the Marxist approach we are concerned with design and use of tools in labor processes, as purposeful work activity transforming objects of work by the use of tools. We are interested in the design labor process and how it is related to the use labor process. Finally, in the Wittgensteinian approach we are interested in the same relation. Here we are interested in the language-games of design and use, not of the labor processes. But practical understanding of the use of tools is just as fundamental. I think it can be justified to suggest that all three approaches are concerned with the use of tools as fundamental to human practice, but with different weight and emphasis on the tools, our bodies, our language and our social institutions.

However, in asking the question of what kind of tools computer artifacts can and should be designed to be, the tool perspective focuses on a specific kind of tools – the tools of craftsmen. To investigate this ideal I will look into the relation between tradition based technically simple hand tools, and complex natural science and engineering-based machines. However, first I will make a comment on what a good tool might be.

## Transparent Tools

> When we use a hammer to drive a nail, we attend to both nail and hammer, but in a different way. (...) The difference may be stated by saying that the latter [i.e. hammers] are not, like the nail, objects of our attention, but instruments of it. They are not watched in themselves; we watch something else while keeping intensely aware of them. I have a *subsidiary awareness* of the feeling in the palm of my hand which is merged into my *focal awareness* of my driving the nail.[3]

This comment by Michael Polanyi, the philosopher of tacit knowledge, is fundamental to my understanding of what is characteristic of a good tool. It is something that, when we have the skill to handle it, *is transparent to us; something that lets us have focal awareness on the task or on the material* we are working with. A good tool becomes an extension of our bodies. Or even, as Polanyi puts it, 'we pour ourselves out into them and assimilate them as parts of our own existence. We accept them existentially by dwelling in them.'[4]

---

[3] Polanyi, M.: *Personal Knowledge*, Routledge and Kegan Paul, London 1973, p. 55.

[4] Ibid., p. 59. According to Polanyi this is also the case with 'intellectual tools', and an argument is that 'when we accept a certain set of pre-suppositions and use them as our interpretative framework, we may be said to dwell in them as we do in our own body. Their uncritical acceptance for the time being consists in a

But there is also a fundamental risk inherent in good tools and skillful use of them. They not only strengthen our instrumental abilities, they also make us *extremely dependent on them, and weakened without them*. What can a blind man do without his stick, or a carpenter without his hammer? This risk of being weakened is more severe using computer artifacts instead of traditional machine-tools, no matter how tool-like the computer artifacts may be designed to be.

Tools for graphic work is a good illustration. The traditional typographical tools were not changed for long periods. The tools you learned to use as an apprentice were something you could be quite certain of using also as a journeyman or master for the rest of your working life, and you knew how to make, repair and maintain them. Even with the best tool-like designed computer artifacts for graphic work you can have no such expectations. A computer-based system remaining without changes for ten years, is more than you can expect. *To survive as a skillful tool-user of computer artifacts you have to adapt to changes, not just get more experienced with the tools you already know.*

## Tools for Conviviality

Ivan Illich, the well known critic of our contemporary technological society, argues that most industrial tools today deny the users the opportunity to invest the world with his or her own meaning, allowing designers – not users – to determine the meaning and expectations of others. He argues that we need *tools for conviviality*.[5]

> Tools foster conviviality to the extent to which they can be easily used, by anybody, as often or as seldom as desired, for the accomplishment of a purpose chosen by the user. The use of such tools by one person does not restrain another from using them equally. They do not

process of assimilation by which we identify ourselves with them.' (Ibid., p. 60.)

[5] Illich, I.: *Tools for Conviviality*, Calder & Boyars, London 1973.

require previous certification of the user. Their existence does not impose any obligation to use them. They allow the user to express his meaning in action.

According to Illich most hand tools, like primitive ham mers, good modern pocket knives or pedal-driven sewing machines, lend themselves to convivial use. However, it is not in principle a question of level of technology. The telephone is an example from the other end of the scale.

Tool for conviviality could be a strong candidate as an ideal for work-oriented design of computer artifacts. Hence, it is important to notice the difference between this ideal, and the ideal of powerful skill-enhancing tools for skilled workers advocated by a tool perspective. The latter tools are not convivial in the sense that they are designed to be easily used by anybody as often or seldom as desired. They are not 'user-friendly' in general, but requires specific skills to be used, like extensive *typographic* skill to operate a computer artifact for page make-up. In this sense they lack in conviviality by becoming the monopoly of one profession, no matter how well designed they are to let the user have focal awareness on making up the page.

However, what Illich seeks is not total abandonment of these kind of tools, 'but the balance between those tools which create the specific demands they are specialized to satisfy and those complementary, enabling tools which foster self-realization.'[6]

I find, taking design of computer artifacts for graphic production as my example, that there is a need for tools both for typographically highly skilled workers to produce high quality products, and for more casual use that does not require previous certification of the user, like some tools for elementary desktop publishing. In both cases I find the ideal of self-realization just as important.

*Tools, Machines and Computer Artifacts*

Let me recapitulate the characteristics of design and computer artifacts discussed in an earlier chapter. I outlined design as a concerned social and historical activity in which artifacts and their use are anticipated, an activity and form of knowledge that is both planned and creative, and that deals with the contradiction between tradition and transcendence. It was also suggested that in designing artifacts we should consider them as mediating instrumental and/or communicative activities; as supporting individual and/or cooperative activities; as augmenting and/or replacing human activities; as function and form that are irrevocably interconnected. Furthermore, computer artifacts are based on a material or medium – computers having a specific capacity for symbol manipulation – that can be shaped quite flexibly with regard to the different activities and aspects summarized above. Thus, a special characteristic of computer artifacts seems to be the kind of reminders they can be designed to be. These reminders may be in the tradition of the use of artifacts in a specific use activity, or they may transcend it.

In short: computer artifacts are what they are used for, but they can also be designed as the reminders we want them to be. Below I will argue that no matter how complex computers are, these characteristics make it possible for us to design computer artifacts as reminders of craft tools, and I will try to show which implicit and explicit values, both intended and unintended, such a tool ideal carries.

*From Craft Tools to Computer Artifacts*

The craftsman and his tools are to a great extent the epitome of the traditional pre-industrial society. These tools like hammers, planes, wrenches, saws and braces were designed based on traditional knowledge, and on practical understanding. They were often specialized, like the blacksmith's sledge hammer, shoeing hammer, and ball peen hammer, or the cooper's heading knife, hollowing knife and jigger, but they kept basically the same shape, form and function for centuries. From the Middle Ages until the era of industrialization the tools of a carpenter or a smith did not undergo any radical changes. New tools were basically designed because of the appearance of better materials or the development of new crafts for which tools different from the ones already existing were needed.

Practical experience and socialization into traditional values are how use of craft tools is learned. The craftsman controlled his individual labor process. His skill in using the tools and in understanding the material he shaped was of ultimate importance. The *skill* of the user was what made the tool, both in use and in design.

This skill and the quality of the products were guaranteed by the function of the craft guild. It controlled, if, and when, a man could become an apprentice. It used examinations to ensure that the apprentice by education and training had acquired journeyman skills. Then the journeyman had to travel far and wide for perhaps five years to work with masters of the trade in different places and even foreign countries, before he could produce a masterpiece to get his mastership diploma and be his own master. This work was carefully examined by the guild-master.

Via the travels of the journeymen new tools and the practical understanding of how to work with them were learned and spread far around, and there was an accumulation of new knowledge about tools and their use.

But the guild had on the other hand a very conservative influence on changes in tools, in ways of designing and using them. When a journeyman in his work to achieve his mastership diploma designed his tools, they had to be just as the guild-master prescribed.[7] With craftsmanship followed high skill in design and use of tools, and high standards for quality of products, but there was from the guilds a strong resistance to changes, that only to some

[7] A description of the development from hand tools to industrial robots can be found in Strandh, S.: *Maskinen genom tiderna*, Nordbok, Gothenburg 1979, especially chapter 3.

extent was balanced by the diffusion of new tools and their
use caused by the travels of the journeymen.

When I argue for a tool perspective for design and use
of computer artifacts I do that with an emphasis on the
role of skill, practical understanding, and quality of products, the mastery of the tools, the transparency of these
tools, and the sensitiveness for tradition in design and use
of these tools, not the conservative resistance to change. It
is the contradiction between tradition and transcendence
which I find fundamental to design.

With the industrial revolution of the nineteenth century traditional craft tools started to be replaced by machines, though machines like the lathe or the drill had existed long before. Machines as opposed to traditional tools
were to a greater and greater extent based on detached
theoretical understanding, and were much more complex.

A craft tool is 'transparent' to a user that knows what it
is intended for. This is far from obvious in the case with a
complex machine. However, as Lewis Mumford has
pointed out in his classical study of *Technics and Civilization*:[8]

> the essential distinction between a machine and a tool
> lies in the degree of independence in the operation from
> the skill and motive power of the operator: the tool lends
> itself to manipulation, the machine to automatic action.

Given these 'definitions' of tools and machines, computer
artifacts take a peculiar position. On the one hand they
are obviously machines: once started they can perform
automatic actions. They are the automatic machine *par
excellence*. On the other hand, we can design computer
artifacts for the most skillful tool use. Or at least as reminders of such.

The prototypical example for such an understanding of
computer artifacts as tools is in a way neither the hand

[8] Mumford, L.: *Technics and Civilization*, Harcourt Brace Jovanovich, New York 1934, p. 10.

tool nor the automatic machine. It is the *machine-tool*, like the lathe or the drill.

We can design computer artifacts that remind us of traditional machine-tools. The question is whether it is a good design ideal, and how far we can develop this familiarity in specific language-games of use. To shed some light on these questions I will further investigate a few more aspects of tools, and what it means to use them.

## Prosthetic Tools and Autonomous Machines

In 1976 Joseph Weizenbaum published *Computer Power and Human Reason*,[9] a milestone in the humanistic critique of contemporary use of computer artifacts. According to Weizenbaum there are two basic kinds of tools or machines. He calls them prosthetic tools and autonomous machines.[10] This is a most important distinction for design of computer artifacts.

*Prosthetic tools* add functional capacity to the human body. Some of them are virtually prostheses of *physical power*, like a lever or a steam shovel. Others extend our *physical reach*, like a spear or a radio. Still others are extensions of our *sensory apparatus*, like a microscope, a telescope and various measuring instruments.

*Autonomous machines* are intellectual tools. Once started they run by themselves on the basis of an internalized model of some phenomena in the world. They are reminders and paradigm cases in the Wittgensteinian sense: they make us think of something we already are familiar with.

## The Clock and the Computer

To date, the most important autonomous machine in our culture is the clock. It neither extends our physical power or reach, nor our senses. It is a reminder or a 'use model'

---

[9] Weizenbaum, J.: *Computer Power and Human Reason – from judgment to calculation*, W.H. Freeman and Company, San Fransisco 1976.

[10] Ibid., pp. 20-25.

of the planetary system. Its products are hours, minutes, seconds, or even pico-seconds, as a basis for predictions. Lewis Mumford calls the clock, not the steam engine 'the key machine of modern industrial age.'[11] The first 'modern' clocks were designed and used in monasteries. In the fourteenth century the clock spread out of the monastery, and in the words of Mumford,[12]

> the regular striking of the bells brought a new regularity into the life of the workman and the merchant. The bells of the clock tower almost defined urban existence. Time-keeping passed into time-serving and time-accounting and time-rationing.

In the same way the rationalization of the labor process in early industrial capitalism was characterized by 'scientific management', the Taylor system. It combined accurate time measurement of detailed operations of the worker, with deskilling division of labor, concentrating control in the hands of management.[13]

But there is another aspect of the clock that is just as important. This autonomous machine changed our reality from reasoning based on practical and direct experience to reasoning from an abstract model. Weizenbaum writes:[14]

> It is important to realize that this newly created reality was and remains an impoverished version of the older one, for it rests on a rejection of those direct experiences that formed the basis for, and indeed constituted, the old reality. The feeling of hunger was rejected as a stimulus for eating; instead, one ate when an abstract model had achieved a certain state, i.e., when the hands of a clock pointed to certain marks on the clock's face (the anthropomorphism here is highly significant too), and similarly for signals for sleep and rising, and so on. This

---

[11] Mumford, L., op. cit p. 14.

[12] Ibid., p. 14.

[13] See the previous part on *Designing for Democracy at Work*.

[14] Weizenbaum, op. cit., p. 25.

rejection of direct experience was to become one of the principal characteristics of modern science.

Computer artifacts, like clocks, are autonomous machines, only much more general. Not only can they be used to change our understanding of the planetary system, they can literally be designed to simulate and remind us of any situation, existing or fictitious. As general autonomous machines they can be designed as reminders of craft tools, or any kind of prosthetic tool, just as well as artificial intelligence. The question is to what extent practical understanding of this new reality can substitute the former experience. That is a context in which design of computer artifacts as tools for skilled work must be put. If we take the example with the computer-based tool kit for page make-up of newspaper pages, it is obvious that the direct experience of using these tools is different from working with hot metal or in paper paste-up. However, we cannot be sure that practical experience from this new situation is less useful for development of typographical skills and products of good quality. It may be true that signs on the display are all there is to work on, but these signs do not have to be numbers and formulas. They can be most various and interesting pictures or graphics that we manipulate with most of our senses via interaction devices. Certainly computer artifacts can be designed to be used as reminders of traditional tools. But there are also reasons to be skeptical to this 'toolness'. However, before exploring this skepticism, let me first consider the vision of computer artifacts as 'intelligent tools'.

### *'Intelligent Tools'?*

I have earlier argued that good tools let the user retain focal awareness on the task he or she is working with, leaving only a subsidiary awareness of the tools. This requires *control* over the tools. But what about 'intelligence' in the tools?

Neither the problem of 'tool intelligence' nor the use of 'intelligent tools' are new phenomena, slavery being the most inhuman historic example of human use of other humans as 'intelligent tools'. Slaves seen and used as 'intelligent tools' by their oppressors could to some extent be controlled by violence and ideology. However, this widely practiced non-human use of human beings as 'intelligent tools' later continued in the emerging capitalistic society. Here it took the (by then socially accepted) form of divided wage labor. However, this human use of human beings represents a fundamental control problem for the oppressing 'owner' of the 'intelligent tools': He might get the commanded job done, better than he ever could have done himself, but he lacks control or understanding of *how* it is done. The human 'intelligent tools' are by no means transparent. Taylorism and 'scientific management' were an attempt to regain this control and transparency – on behalf of management.

The history of human use of animals as tools further demonstrates the conflict between control and 'intelligence'. Horses, camels and llamas were for example preferred to gorillas as means of transportation, despite the fact that gorillas are both stronger and more 'intelligent'. The obvious advantage of the horse over the gorilla is its 'toolness' – the locomotive power of a horse can be pretty well controlled by human beings manually and continuously.

But certainly horses are more 'intelligent' than artifacts like cars. Still cars are preferred over horses. This is not only because of more horse-power, but also because of their superior 'toolness'. They are designed to allow the driver full control. But could not some artificial intelligence, compensating for driver inadequacies, be desirable for make driving a bit safer?[15]

This is not the place to discuss the high hopes of artificial intelligence, but to address a practical question of the

[15] These examples of historical 'intelligent tools' are inspired by Ghandchi, H. and Ghandchi. J.: 'Intelligent Tools – The Cornerstone of a New Civilization' in *The AI Magazine*, fall 1985. However, the authors' future prospects of artificial intelligence as a cornerstone of a new civilization is as far away as one can get from my basic ideas of work-oriented design of computer artifacts.

toolness of computer artifacts: to what degree are we interested in tools that do more than 'what they are told' to follow our intentions, or as it often is expressed as an interface design ideal: tools that do what we mean, not what we say.[16]

An illustration from the UTOPIA project's tool kit for page make-up is the use of gravity pointing when, for example an article is placed on the page ground.[17] The user just has to place the article near the column line. Automatically it aligns with the column line when the 'lead make-up' effect of gravity pointing is chosen. This is not magic to the user, because he or she can understand this feature from the use model, and can control whether to use this effect or not.

A fancier example is an office information systems use model that Dionysious Tschritzis has called *Objectworld*.[18] Users are seen as controlling independent 'knowledge bases'. In this world of knowledge bases there live animal-like knowledge objects known as *Knos*. They travel around in Objectworld collecting and disseminating information. Some of them are specialized as *carriers* that move information around while leaving it intact, others as *parasites* that follow other knos to collect information from them, still others as *hunters* that move around and assemble other knos that have gone astray. Knos are understandable for the user from the use model, Objectworld, but most of them are not under the user's control.

There is a conflict between 'toolness' and 'intelligence', between control and automation. However, since the toolness of computer artifacts is a designed reminder, there is

[16] Classical examples are such as having the computer executing the right command, though it may be wrongly spelled. See e.g. Teitelman, W and Masinter, L.: 'The Interlisp Programming Environment' in *Computer*, April 1981.

[17] See the chapter on *The 'Tool Perspective'*.

[18] Tsichritzis, D.: 'Objectworld' in Tsichritzis, D. (ed.): *Office Automation*, Springer, Berlin 1985.

the opportunity to design more or less 'intelligent tools', trying to meet both the tool requirement for control and the 'intelligence' requirement for getting done what actually was intended. In this sense 'intelligent tools' may be designed to strengthen rather than weaken the user's control.[19]

In summary: the usefulness of 'intelligence' designed into a tool is a question of how well this 'illusion' supports the user's ultimate control, which in turn depends on how the 'intelligent tool' can be understood from the use model shaping the metaphorical understanding.

# The Computer is not a Tool

## Critique of Tool Ideology

Now to the criticism of the toolness of computer artifacts. There is a point in Weizenbaum's earlier discussed argumentation on tools that I have not mentioned so far.

> Once man could kill another animal only by crushing or tearing it with his hands; then he acquired the axe, the spear, the arrow, the ball fired from a gun, the explosive shell. Now charges mounted on missiles can destroy mankind itself. That is one measure of how far man has extended and remade himself since he began to make tools.[20]

This illustrates an obvious risk of understanding computer artifacts as tools. The computer as a tool metaphor may suggest that we are in control, whereas in reality we

[19] For similar views on tools and intelligence see Norman, D.: 'Cognitive Engineering' in Norman, D. and Draper, S. (eds.): *User Centered System Design*, Lawrence Erlbaum, London 1986, and Kay, A.: 'Computer Software' in *Scientific American*, vol 251, no 3, September 1984.

[20] Weizenbaum, op. cit., p. 20. I can only add that since direct experience is rejected, we can skillfully fire these deadly weapons, imagining that we are only fighting horrible creatures from outer space in a computer game.

may be completely alienated and out of control. This illusion of control has ideological significance.

Art Historian Linda Gardiner Janik participated in the abovementioned conference which addressed the question: Is the computer a tool?. In reflections over the contributions she especially was struck by this ideological use of the tool metaphor. If the computer is not just a machine, but also a tool, then an emotive tone is added:[21]

> the concept of a 'tool' implies what I might call *mereness*, a sense of the subordinate, the manipulable, the non-threatening or non-determining part of our world which *we* have made for *our* ends and can therefore control. (...) What this usage suggests to me is that in asking whether computers are tools we are not talking specifically about computers at all, but more generally about all our machines, especially the more 'autonomous' ones in Weizenbaum's sense; the oddness, in an everyday context, of calling an oil-tanker, a guided missile or a computer a tool, derives not from the particular characteristics of those artifacts but simply from the tension between their extreme mechanical complexity and the contrasting notions of technical simplicity and availability attaching to the ordinary concept of a tool. By calling such machines 'tools', we are in effect assuring each other that in spite of their complexity, autonomy, and unforeseeable social consequences, they are after all nothing but fancier kinds of canoe, spear or abacus. And this metaphorical extension of the concept of a tool is perhaps most attractive when in reality the machines in question are slipping out of our control to an ever greater extent.

I find Janik's critique striking, indeed, and I basically agree with it. The 'computer is only a tool' metaphor has the ideological function of reassuring us that our fears of

---

[21] Janik, L. G.: 'Some Reflections on the Topic of the Sigtuna Symposium' in Sundin, B. (ed.): *Is the Computer a Tool?*, Almquist & Wiksell, Stockholm 1980.

being controlled and replaced by computers are without grounds. This is one of the ways in which the 'computer is only a tool' metaphor has become an ideological tool of modern capitalism (for example turning our attention away from alienated assembly-line work controlled via computer-based planning systems, or unemployment tragedies caused by the introduction of labor saving computer artifacts.) Another obvious use is as a sales argument for vendors of computer artifacts (regardless of whether they in practice are tool-like or not).

More generally Weizenbaum has argued the ideological aspect of tools, that we not only use them to transform our environment, but that they also strongly determine our understanding of the world and ourselves. In the era of the computer, cognitive psychology has transformed our brains into computers, and our minds into information processing systems. This is a later version of the original Cartesian mind-body dualism, in which the mind became a ghost in the machine. Before that God was a craftsman.

On what happens when we lose our tools Weizenbaum writes:[22]

> The six-shooter of the nineteenth-century American West was known as the 'great equalizer', a name that eloquently testifies to what that piece of hardware did to the self-image of gun-toters who, when denuded of their weapons, felt themselves disadvantaged with respect to their fellow citizens.

This example could easily be extrapolated to modern hardware such as the desktop computer of middle managers today. And certainly, if we go back in time, deprived of his tools, a craftsman was no one.

### Critique of Tool Rationality

A critique similar to Janik's of metaphorically understanding computer artifacts as tools has been presented by

[22] Weizenbaum, op. cit., p. 19.

the philosopher of science, Bo Dahlbom. However, he also argues that the tool metaphor is the fundamental metaphor of the modern purposive rational society (a term he uses in Max Weber's sense of 'Zweckrationalität'). When computer artifacts are seen as tools, questions of values and norms are reduced to second order. First value neutral tools are designed. Then it is instrumentally decided which values they should be used to control.[23]

The understanding of computers as tools that I have argued for is the *opposite*. The tool perspective as a design ideal emphasizes designing computer artifacts to support the user's development of skills and the quality of the product. If anything, the design ideal of a tool perspective is that of the traditional craft skills. More generally I argue that the role skill has in a tool perspective, and skill and democracy in work-oriented design design, is as consciously articulated values on which design should be based. This is what Dahlbom, with reference to Weber, calls value rational action ('Wertrationalitet'). I agree with Dahlbom that a simple return to traditional values is no solution to the problems of the modern purposive rational society, and that only approaches that explicitly deal with their own values, and use them as a basis for change of technology and organizations, can be a challenge to the modern society. My point is that the tool perspective is such a humanistic value rational design principle.

When, despite different kinds of valid ideological critiques of understanding computers as tools, I keep insisting on the usefulness of a tool metaphor as a design perspective the argument is not that computer artifacts are craft tools proper. The argument is that we should be challenged to try to design computer artifacts as skill-enhancing tools for production of good use quality products and services, and to the extent that we find this impossible we should reflect over the obstacles and try to make them

[23] Dahlbom, B.: *Humanisterna och Framtiden – fyra varianter över ett tema av Max Weber*, Department of Science, University of Umeå, Draft 1986, p. 56.

clear. At the same time, as part of a strategy for work-oriented design we should fight back against any ideological or commercial attempt to label computers as tools, where they in practice alienate our lives.

## Critique of Technical Lack of 'Toolness'

I now turn to a more technical critique in arguing why computer artifacts not are tools. Such a critique has been articulated by Bernd Wingert and Ulrich Riehm.[24] In addition to the kind of general use of the tool metaphor criticized above, they find a weak and a strong thesis proposing that computer artifacts are tools.

The strong thesis, which argues that computer artifacts are the new tools, they reject with reference to the sensuous control of the object being refined which is lost when a tool is replaced by a computer artifact. What you work with is a software program which has a complex structure that is strictly different from physical objects. This difference is evident.

The weaker thesis, which argues that computer artifacts can be metaphorically designed so that working with them resembles work with tools, is of special interest here, since it is fundamental to the tool perspective. Wingert and Riehm reject this thesis on the following three grounds.

Firstly, when using computer artifacts the user to a great extent gives values to global parameters rather than performing the detailed operations – the operational activity is replaced by the computer artifact. My comment: This is not that different from *preparing* materials, in work with traditional tools. Furthermore, 'direct manipulation' user interfaces provide a means to overcome this obstacle.[25]

[24] Wingert, B. and Riehm, U.: 'Computer als Werkzeug – Anmerkungen zu einem verbreiteten Missverständnis', in Rammert, W. et al. (eds): *Technik und Gesellschaft*, Jahrbuch 3, Campus Verlag, Frankfurt 1985.

[25] See the next chapter on *The 'Toolness' of Computer Artifacts*.

Secondly, what the user acts on is a piece of software, not the 'real' object, which instead is controlled by the software and produced via some peripherals. It is the computer artifact, not the user, that refines the object. This means that you to a large extent have to rely on trial and error procedures, hoping that the result will be good. My comment: Trial and error is also common in work with traditional tools. It takes a long time before the user can see the result of many operations he or she performs with traditional tools on physical materials. But the more experienced the user becomes in using specific tools and materials the better he or she becomes in knowing how the result will be. Just as when using computer artifacts, including their peripherals.

Thirdly, no matter how well designed a computer artifact is, what the user interacts with and gets feed-back from is a simulation, not the real object. Hence, the user can never be sure that the 'representation' on the display really has taken place. My comment: This is doubtless a fundamental difference for the user as compared to actually performing work on the ultimate object. However, in practice this situation may not be too different from the one above. It is important to get feed-back not only of what happens on the display but also continuously from the ultimate results of the interaction. As the users get experienced they will be quite good at predicting the results, even when the simulation suggests something slightly different. Of course, there can be major technical breakdowns where the user keeps on working in good faith, while nothing happens but as reminding signs on the display. This is a difference from traditional tools.

The differences between traditional tools and even the most tool-like designed computer artifacts that Wingert and Riehm highlight are fundamental differences. The computer is not a tool in the same sense as a craft tool, and I agree that it is important to be aware of what is specific to computer artifacts. However, I see no fundamental argument why it should not be a good and in principle realizable design ideal to metaphorically design computer artifacts as tools for skilled work. These new 'tools' will be different from the traditional ones, and it will be different to work with them. This difference may be in two directions, as with the tool kit for page make up that we designed in the UTOPIA project: not only were the simulations of some traditional tools pale copies, there were also some totally new, extremely useful and previously inconceivable tools.

## Computers and Computer Artifacts as Media

Finally, I will comment upon the view that computer artifacts not are tools, but *media*. I will suggest that rather than arguing the one view over the other we should concentrate on the productive relation between the two.

Firstly, on the most general tool level, where I have called the computer the material out of which we design specific computer artifacts, *the computer is a medium*.[26] Computers are vehicles for signs just like books, gramophone records, and other media are. But they are a different kind of medium or material, that, due to the capacity for signal manipulation, can be designed to change operations according to our interaction with them. Alan Kay has put it this way:[27]

> The protean nature of the computer is such that it can act like a machine or like a language to be shaped and exploited. It is a medium that can dynamically simulate the details of any other medium, including media that cannot exist physically. It is not a tool, although it can act like many tools. It is the first metamedium, and as

---

[26] Peter Bøgh Andersen has made interesting attempts on this level to replace the dominant information processing view with theory from traditional linguistics and semiotics focusing on both form and content of messages, and on the implied communication not only between users, but also between users and designers and programmers. See e.g. Andersen, P.B.: *Edb-teknologi set i medieperspektiv*, University of Aarhus 1984.

[27] Kay, op. cit., p. 47.

such it has degrees of freedom for representation never before encountered and as yet barely investigated.

Secondly, since *computers* are media or materials we can deliberately design *computer artifacts* as media (just as we can design them as craft tools). They can be designed as media, like advanced books, as hypertexts, as mail handlers, as shared materials for planning, control and coordination of activities, etc.

The problem with the tool perspective is that it may create a blindness towards the media aspects of use of computer artifacts. But I see no real contradiction. However, as an ideal for work-oriented design we then have to consider *a media design ideal*. Whereas the tool perspective has the skill of the user, the control of the tools, and the quality of the product as its design ideal, it seems with my frame of reference reasonable to suggest that the corresponding media design ideal should be emancipatory dialogues free from coercion. Research on computer support for cooperation in small groups along such an ideal has recently been emphasized. For example in our own efforts in Århus in a recently established research program for computer support for cooperative design and communication we try to unite the skill ideal and the free dialogue ideal, seeing computer artifacts both as tools and as media.[28] A reason for this is that even when we focus on design of computer artifacts as media, these media might best be operated with tools designed according to a craft tool ideal.

However, computer artifacts are not only designed as tools and media. The computer as a medium can also, for example, be designed into computer artifacts that appear as 'intelligent dialogue partners' using natural-like language. Clearly we can design many aspects of this popular 'illusion', but what can it accomplish but disillusion, if, or

[28] Andersen, P.B. et al.: *Research Programme on Computer Support for Cooperative Design and Communication*, Department of Information Science and Department of Computer Science, University of Aarhus 1987.

when, the user finds out that the partner is a puppet on a string, and that someone unknown and invisible holds and control the string? Is this not in a way the ultimate alienation of human beings, and a serious distortion of human communication?[29]

There is, however, another approach to the design of computer artifacts that utilizes the computer as a medium to design computer artifacts as completely new media, an approach that I find most interesting. I am thinking of the design of computer artifacts as games or plays where the user is the main actor in a fictitious 'world' or context. As the dialogue partner design ideal it supports the idea of fictitious characters. The big difference is that here the user knows that he or she is playing a game. This 'postmodern' media design approach supports *an ideal of fantasy, playfulness and sheer fun*, rather than emphasizing skill and free communication. Below I will exemplify this playful challenge to the more serious design of computer artifacts as traditional tools and media for hard work.

## Computer Artifacts as Interactive Plays

In *Interfaces as Mimesis* [30] Brenda Laurel, who has been involved with companies developing computer games, gives an introduction to this 'postmodern' media design ideal.

Since all we can experience from interaction with a computer artifact is simulations, why then not make the most out of the special characteristics of the computer as a medium? Why not try to design *fictions that we really can experience*? That is the question this design ideal focuses on.

---

[29] For a detailed critique of the dialogue partner model see Bødker, S.: *Through the Interface*, Department of Computer Science, University of Aarhus, 1987, chapter 4.

[30] Laurel, B.K.: 'Interfaces as Mimesis' in Norman, D. and Draper, S. (eds.): *User Centered System Design*, Lawrence Erlbaum, London 1986.

Laurel describe her own motives for such a design as springing out of her 'impatience with 'dumb' computer games, a fascination with the idea of 'interactive movies', and a perverse desire to become Captain James T. Kirk.'[31]

If we see computer artifacts as plays then we focus on designing a 'world' that the user can virtually live in and commit him/herself to. As a user I know that when I enter this dramatic context or 'world' it is fictitious, just as when I watch a play. As Laurel stresses:[32]

> I know that the people on the stage are actors and that the castle parapets are cardboard, but I choose, in order to have the pleasure of unencumbering emotional and rational participation, to suspend that knowledge for the duration of the play.

Computer artifacts as media can as an ideal be designed for such pleasurable engagement, by giving them a dramatic form like plays, with the intention to be acted out, rather than read as descriptions. Designing computer artifacts this way becomes a form of artistic imitation, a *mimesis*, an art that has been studied and practiced from Aristotele's *Poetics* and onwards.

But there are differences between a play and a computer artifact if we compare a user with a member of an audience. The latter can only marginally interact in the play (except in some avant garde plays), whereas computers as media lend themselves very well to design of such interaction. Computer artifacts can be designed as *interactive mimesis*. This makes possible a user-artifact/ 'world' relation that Laurel calls *first-personness*.

First-personness is a grammatical metaphor. It is the designed simulation of *thrown* activity of, for example attending a meeting, wielding a hammer, or eating a meal. This is different from say how most movies or novels are told. The viewer or reader is often a third-person entity outside the action. It is also different from say computer

[31] Ibid., p. 85.
[32] Ibid., p. 76.

artifacts to which the user makes imperative statements and asks questions, and where the computer artifact as feed-back 'tells' the user what to do, and what it has done. This is second-personness. First-personness supports 'direct awareness' of being in the fictitious 'world'.[33]

This first-person direct awareness not only requires a good plot, it also has to be supported by interaction devices that allow interaction in all relevant sensory modalities, for example physically pointing or speaking as opposed to typing, spatial and graphic reminders as opposed to textual ones.

Laurel's suggestion is that in design of computer artifacts we use the principles of mimesis and first-personness to 'indicate how the material and structure of a mimetic world can be orchestrated to create the experience we desire.'[34]

Say we want to design a computer artifact to be an encyclopedia, and use the principles of interactive mimesis. When looking up the word Hamlet, the user would *not read* about a prince of Denmark, *but experience* a drama in Kronborg Castle. In the entry on ancient Egypt he or she would not look for information about pyramids, but 'be climbing them, looking around their musty innards, reading hieroglyphs, or reincarnating pharaohs.'[35]

What if the user looks up the word for a tool, for example a hammer? Will he or she be able to *use* it? I think that it depends not only on if there is a dramatic context to use it in, but also on the *user's skill*. Laurel is very critical to the computer as a tool metaphor, arguing that the tool comes in between the user and the 'world', preventing him or her from acting in it. I find computer artifacts as interactive plays supporting direct awareness for pleasurable engagement a most challenging design ideal. However, with Polanyi's tool concept in mind, it becomes

---

[33] Principles for design of 'direct awareness' will be discussed in the next chapter on *The 'Toolness' of Computer Artifacts*.

[34] Laurel, op. cit., p. 77.

[35] Ibid., p. 85.

clear that there always is a price for direct awareness: we must by practical experience acquire the skills necessary to have focal awareness on what we are doing, leaving only subsidiary awareness for the tool. This is the case when we use a hammer as well as when we use computer artifacts designed as interactive mimesis. On the other hand, in design of computer artifacts as tools for skilled work we may benefit a great deal from design principles of computer artifacts as interactive plays. In a way a tool perspective is just a special case of designing computer artifacts as interactive plays – a case where the first-per-sonness is carried out by a skilled tool user acting in a context of useful materials from which he or she can create good use quality products. It is a challenge to design, to create such tools for pleasurable engagement, tools that when used help the user transcend the boredom of machine work.

## Summary

In this chapter I have discussed the consequences of understanding computer artifacts as tools. I started by distinguishing tools proper from other human instruments – our body, our language, and our social institutions. 'Transparency' and 'conviviality' were then discussed as ideals for the design of tools. Differences between tools, machines and computer artifacts were then outlined. The critique of the ideology suggesting that 'the computer is only a tool', and the more technical critique denying the 'toolness' of computer artifacts, were also discussed. Finally, the complementary understanding of computer artifacts as media, especially in a 'postmodern' version, was highlighted.

To sum up: I have tried to show how computer artifacts

- *are tools proper* in the general sense of being designed as means to an end,
- tools proper that on a more concrete level *are machines*, in the sense that once started they perform au-

tomatic action, and hence differ from simple hand tools, but that

- these machines *metaphorically can be designed as reminders of traditional craft tools* for a specific craft or profession, just as well as they *metaphorically can be designed as new media*, utilizing interactive hardware devices and the capacity of signal manipulation to create these reminders, but that
- there also exists an *ideological use of a tool metaphor* suggesting that we are in control of the development of the social, political and technical use of this technology, when in practice we may be more alienated than ever, and that this ideological use of the 'the computer is only a tool' metaphor may, as discussed in Part III on *Designing for Democracy*, have to do with the fact
- that *in industry today computer artifacts are more often designed as machines, in the sense that they take control away from the user and automate skill.*

In this chapter I have pointed at many problems with a tool perspective. A tool perspective for design of skill-enhancing computer-based tools may unintentionally create a blindness, both for other design ideals such as interactive media, and for the ideological use of a tool metaphor as a smoke screen for what really goes on, not only in our working lives. However, when this is said, I still find the craft tool ideal of the tool perspective a most useful paradigm case for design of computer artifacts.

In the next chapter I will refer to developments in user interface hardware and software design that support the 'toolness' of computer artifacts.

*Chapter 17*

# The 'Toolness'
# of Computer Artifacts

The Apple Corporation set the standard for small computer workstations in the marketplace when they introduced the Macintosh in 1984. Tool-like software/hardware, based on the 'mouse', the 'desktop metaphor', icons and 'windows' on a graphic display, suddenly spread from universities and research laboratories to literally millions of users.

This machine was by no means the first tool-like computer artifact, nor was it the most powerful one. But it was unique in that it created a commercial breakthrough after more than twenty years of ideas and efforts by visionary designers.

Apple recognized the importance of developments in hardware and software concerning the 'user interface' of computer artifacts in creating the 'toolness' of the Macintosh. This represented a shift in design. As Alan Kay, one of the visionary designers of computer artifacts as tools has put it:[1]

> The user interface was once the last part of the system to be designed. Now it is the first. It is recognized as being primary because, to novices and professionals alike, what is presented to one's senses *is* one's computer.

To design tool-like user interfaces we have to understand both software and hardware. The user interface is a com-

---

[1] Kay, A.: 'Computer Software' in *Scientific American*, vol. 251, no. 3, September 1984, p. 42.

bination of hardware and software that the user experiences in use. In an earlier chapter it was suggested that in designing user interfaces we should be aware of the *physical aspects* that set conditions for the physical handling of the artifact, the *handling aspects* that involve conditions for operating and controlling the artifact, and the *subject / object directed aspects* that constitute the conditions for activities on 'objects' or with 'others' via the artifact. The subject/object directed aspects relate to both the physical and the handling aspects, as well as to the desired functionality.[2] The basic interest in user interface design is in which way the artifact *augments*, and is *transparent*, in human activities directed towards the subject/object. Additionally we are also interested in the *aesthetic and ergonomic aspects* of the user interface.

All these aspects are relevant to the toolness of computer artifacts. Does the artifact really allow the user to be fully engaged in the task he or she is performing, requiring only subsidiary awareness of the artifact? Does the handling or control of the artifact break down this involvement – this thrownness? Does the physical design of the input/output devices support functionality, ergonomics, and aesthetics in a way that prevents a shift in awareness from involvement in the task towards the artifact itself?

The main hardware and software developments that in these respects have changed the toolness of computer artifacts are related to the technology of *graphic workstations, including new interaction devices.*

In this chapter I will take a brief look at the main features of concepts and styles for designing the user interface of computer artifacts as tools, or at least as reminders or simulations of tools.

The first main section is an overview of the 'state of the art' of computer-based tools. First the workstation concept is introduced and briefly discussed. Then I turn to the his-

---

[2] See Bødker, S.: *Through the Interface – A Human Activity Approach to User Interface Design,* DAIMI PB-224, Department of Computer Science, University of Aarhus, 1987 (dissertation).

tory of design visions that have contributed to the *toolness* of computer artifacts. The section ends with a list of state of the art prototypical examples.

In the second main section, drawing on the field of human-computer interaction state of the art *principles for designing toolness of computer artifacts,* are introduced and discussed. Based on the workstation technology, software for *directness* and the use of *metaphors, use models,* and *systematic domains* are discussed as ideals for designing computer artifacts as tools.

The chapter is of a background character, where my claims of a tool perspective as a design ideal are seen in the light of current technical developments, and research in the field of human-computer interaction.

## Computer-Based Tools – State of the Art

### The Workstation

From a user point of view the main hardware characteristics of the contemporary computer workstation are the visual display unit and the input devices. The traditional computer terminal has been given a considerable face-lifting.[3]

[3] Concerning displays there has been a shift from traditional alphanumeric screens with typically 24 lines of 80 fixed font characters, to graphic displays with up to 20 inch bit-mapped displays and a typical resolution of 1000x1000 pixels. Simple alpha-numeric text as output and feedback has largely been replaced by graphics, pictures, icons, etc. As main input device the traditional QWERTY keyboard has been complemented and sometimes almost replaced by combined pointing and selecting devices related to the graphic display. The pointing and selection devices typically control a cursor on the graphic display. They are not only used for making graphics on the display, but perhaps more typically for a variety of tasks like selecting or positioning an object on the graphic display for further operations on it. Input from the pointing devices is closely related to changes of output on the graphic display. Typical examples are the *mouse* (control of a cursor by hand movements of the mouse on the table, and buttons for 'clicking'/ selecting objects on the display), *joystick* (a handle e.g. to indicate cursor movements like direction (by pushing it in the correspon-

Interaction with a computer workstation is no longer constrained to reading fixed characters on the display and writing text via a keyboard. Bit-mapped displays with high-resolution graphics in combination with new interaction devices, like the mouse, have opened up the opportunities for completely new design styles, often referred to as *direct manipulation*. The means used to support this are *windows* (frames that the user can size and move around on the display, and in which, or 'through' which, the user can manipulate or 'view' objects and actions), *menus* (to select objects and actions from), and *icons* (that 'picture' the object or action they are intended to remind one of).

ding direction) and speed (by the power or magnitude of the push), *trackball* (that moves the cursor through rotating movements of the ball in a box), *graphic tablet* (a touch-sensitive surface separate from the screen that 'maps' the display, and where the cursor is moved by corresponding movements of a pointing device on the tablet), *light pen* (direct pointing with the pen at spots on the display), *touchscreen* (pointing with fingers on a pressure sensitive membrane covering the display), etc. Scanners and laser printers are also important computer workstation devices to input and output text and graphics that more or less directly correspond to what is displayed on the screen. Developments of workstation technology include refinements of the pointing devices and a better understanding of how they can be combined and specially designed for specific applications. Also the displays will be improved. Not only can they be made larger, have better resolution, color, and increased facilities for manipulating images, but they may also be flat, lightweight and non-light emitting as opposed to today's CRT-displays. Other examples are built-in modems and network capabilities that drastically increase the data available for manipulation with computer workstation based tools, and new technologies for speech input and output that widen the interaction possibilities. For an introduction to workstation interaction devices see e.g Schneiderman, B.: *Designing the User Interface*, Addison-Wesley, USA 1987, chapter 6, and for a critical view of how little has been done in the area, Buxton, W.: 'There's More to Interaction Than Meets the Eye: Some Issues in Manual Input', in Norman, D. & Draper, S. (eds.): *User Centered System Design*, Lawrence Erlbaum, London 1986.

These technical achievements may contribute to the toolness of computer artifacts, making the artifact more transparent and letting the user focus his/her awareness on the task, to the aesthetics of using computer artifacts, and also to the ergonomics of use. But there are also contradictions, such as between increased functionality with a larger display versus less eye-strain and perhaps lower radiation with a smaller one. And there is of course no guarantee that a nice user interface corresponds to aesthetically better designed products. The many disgraceful graphic products resulting from desktop publishing are evidence enough of that. Discussions of these kinds of pros and cons of workstation technology were important in our design of computer-based tools for page make-up and image processing in the UTOPIA project.[4]

However, even though there lately has been a dramatic development of the interaction devices of computer artifacts, many possibilities still seem untried. In *There's More to Interaction Than Meets the Eye*, William Buxton lets us imagine a time far into the future where an anthropologist dig into a fully stocked computer store from our days with all of the hardware and software in working order. Buxton guesses that the anthropologist's conclusions would be that we had:[5]

> a well-developed eye, a long right arm, a small left arm, uniform-length fingers and a 'low-fi' ear. But the dominating characteristics would be the prevalence of our visual system over our poorly developed manual dexterity.

What Buxton draws our attention to is, except for seeing how little use is made of our senses in design of user interfaces of computer artifacts. In sewing, driving a car or playing the organ we find it natural to use our feet. Why

---

[4] See chapter 15, *The 'Tool Perspective' – An Example*, and Gunnarson, E.: *Arbetsmiljökrav*, Swedish Center for Working Life, Stockholm 1985.

[5] Buxton, op. cit., p. 319.

not so in the design of computer-based tools? And why not interaction devices for both hands? Imagine having to turn off your shower in order to adjust the water temperature! That is the one-handedness most computer artifacts are designed for.

Buxton gives examples of improvements using already existing interaction devices, but his main point is that:[6]

> managing input is so complex that it is unlikely that we will ever totally understand it. No matter how good our theories are, we will probably always have to test designs through actual implementation and prototyping. The consequence of this for the designer is that prototyping tools (software and hardware) must be developed and considered as part of the basic environment.

This recommendation is well in line with our UTOPIAn experiences of designing computer-based tools, and with the skill-based design strategy being argued in this book.

## From Design Visions to Technical Reality

Now to some design visions which have contributed to the toolness of computer artifacts. Examples from this history are worth mentioning for several reasons. One is the time it may take to technically realize good design ideas. Another is the creative way of thinking that guided some of these 'prophetic' designs.

The perhaps oldest reference is to Vannevar Bush's 'memex' from 1945.[7] His imagined 'memex' device transformed one's desktop into tools for easy access, annotation, and elaboration of all recorded information in the world. The concept included ideas of personal workstations, associative indexing, windows, database trails, etc. Not only were ideas concerning personal tools envisioned, but also cooperation using hypertexts, for example

[6] Ibid., p. 321.

[7] Bush, V.: 'As We May Think' in *Atlantic Monthly*, July 1945, pp. 101–108.

sharing recorded paths through textual and image archives.

In the early 1960s Douglas Engelbart developed such ideas in a detailed scenario on how computer artifacts could be designed for *augmenting human intellect*.[8] His augmentation tools basically concerned the organization of ideas and the production of text (including the hypertext notion). Engelbart got support for trying to realize these ideas, and the Augmentation Research Center at Stanford Research Institute was established. New interaction devices like the joystick and lightpen were tested in practice, and the first 'mouse' was born. The experimental oN-Line System (NLS) was designed to provide a complete 'knowledge workshop' for a user writing and editing documents, running programs, etc. The user was equipped with tools for navigating in an 'information space', and there were tools for personal as well as for cooperative work. At the Fall Joint Computer Conference in 1968 the system and the basic concepts were presented.[9] Still more impressively, Engelbart demonstrated the system at the conference using a computer workstation and utilizing a three-button mouse, and a five-piece key set as complement to the traditional keyboard, all with remote connections to the Augmentation Research Center at Stanford Research Center. A point of special interest in our context of tools is Engelbart's commitment to tools for skilled work, i.e. that augmentation is what is fundamental, not the easy-to-use criterion.[10]

[8] Engelbart, D. C.: *Augmenting Human Intellect: A Conceptual Framework*, AFOSR-3223, Stanford Research Institute, Menlo Park 1962.

[9] Engelbart, D. C. and English, W. K.: 'A Research Center for Augmenting Human Intellect' in *AFIPS Proceedings – Fall Joint Computer Conference*, 1968.

[10] For more details on the work of Douglas Engelbart see the appendix in Bannon, L. J.: *Extending the Design Boundaries of Human-Computer Interaction*, Institute for Cognitive Science, University of California, San Diego, May 1985.

Another early and influential contribution to the toolness of computer artifacts is Ivan Sutherland's *Sketchpad*,
ideas for a graphic design program from 1962.[11] The user
should interact by using a light pen for adding, moving,
and deleting parts of drawings directly on the display. The
display was metaphorically seen as 'sheets of paper'. Pictures were composed from primitive picture types like
points, line segments, and circle arcs, as well as from user
defined pictures. The user could *copy* these picture definitions, and modify the copy to create a new picture. A picture definition could also be used as a *master* for arbitrar-
ily many *instances*. If the master was edited, each instance would change correspondingly. Sutherland's work
has helped create many graphic interface ideas supporting the toolness of computer artifacts, ideas that only
now are being fully explored.

A list of historical contributions to the toolness of the interface of computer artifacts would be most incomplete
without reference to the researchers and designers at
Xerox Palo Alto Research Center. At the beginning of the
1970s Alan Kay initiated the Learning Research Group to
realize design ideas from his Ph.D. dissertation on *The
Reactive Engine*.[12] The design ideal for the Learning Research Group was the *Dynabook* – a personal medium
the size of a notebook by which everyone could have the
power to handle virtually all of his or her information-re-
lated needs. This is how the vision was described:[13]

Imagine having your own self-contained knowledge
manipulator in a portable package the shape of an ordinary notebook. Suppose it had enough power to out-
range your senses of sight and hearing, enough capac-

[11] Sutherland, I.E.: *Sketchpad – A Man-Machine Graphical
Communication System*, MIT, Cambridge 1963 (dissertation).

[12] Kay, A.: *The Reactive Engine*, University of Utah, 1969 (dissertation).

[13] Kay, A. and Learning Research Group: *Personal Dynamic Media*, Xerox Palo Alto Research Center, Technical Report no SSL
76–1, March 1976.

ity to store for later retrieval thousands of page-equivalents of reference materials, poems, letters, recipes, records, drawings, animations, musical scores, waveforms, dynamic simulations, and anything else you would like to remember and change. We envision a device as small and portable as possible which could both take in and give out information in quantities approaching that of human sensory systems. Visual output should be, at least, of higher quality than what can be obtained from newsprint. Audio output should adhere to similar high-fidelity standards. There should be no discernible pause between cause and effect. One of the metaphors we used when designing such a system was that of a musical instrument, such as a flute, which is owned by its user and responds instantly and consistently to its owner's wishes. Imagine the absurdity of a one-second delay between blowing a note and hearing it.

The influence from these ideas on the research and design at Xerox PARC as well as on the development of the workstation concept and actual design in general has been immense.

The user interface of the 'interim Dynabooks' the Learning Research Group designed was from the user's point of view very similar to today's workstations – a high resolution bit-map display, mouse, windows, pop-up menus, local disk memory etc. It had programming and problem solving tools, a text editor, tools for drawing, painting and animating pictures, for generating music, etc.

The first prototype of this 'interim Dynabook' was the programing environment *Smalltalk*. The user interface of this object-oriented programming language was later developed at Xerox PARC into one of the most powerful set of tools for programmers developed to date.[14]

---

[14] See e.g. Goldberg, A.: *Smalltalk-80: The Interactive Programming Environment*, Addison-Wesley, Reading 1984.

Other important design efforts at Xerox PARC were the development of the experimental *Alto* workstation and (based on these prototyping experiences) the implementation of the *Star* office system – a system of workstations and peripherals like laser printers connected in a local area network. The use of icons, windows, and the desktop metaphor in a consistent use model, as well as of the 'what you see is what you get' principle in the user interface design makes it one of the most tool-like office systems so far. And the design principles behind the system are far from outdated.[15]

The ideas of toolness of computer artifacts have been around for quite some time, but their implementation and further exploration have just began. This is especially true, when it comes to the visions of tools for cooperative work. However, the technical opportunities should be great, not least since the capacity of the multi-million dollar machines required in the late 1960s now can be achieved for a few thousand dollars.

# Prototypical Examples of Computer-Based Tools

Now to some prototypical examples of computer-based tools, a 'snapshot' of some of the 'state of the art' computer-based tools around today. I have a double reason for mentioning them. Firstly, they illustrate what I mean by computer-based tools. Secondly, investigations of practical designs are, in our field just as in other design fields, an important source for further theoretical development.

## Tools for Typography and Graphic Design

Given my background in graphic industry technology in the DEMOS and UTOPIA projects, tools for typography and graphic design come first to mind.

---

[15] See e.g. Smith, D. C. et. al.: 'Designing the Star User Interface' in *Byte Magazine*, vol 7, no 4, April 1982.

Word processors are fundamental tools in this category. Word processors let the user constantly view the document he or she is working on. The user has first of all tools for manipulating the text in the writing process. In addition several word processors (like *Word* 3.01 from Microsoft) have integrated other tools. Hence, when working on a document with the tools the user can view the document from different perspectives. There are tools for typography, layout and graphics, as well as for structuring the ideas in the document. Furthermore, there are tools for checking spelling and for hyphenation.[16]

Other programs for graphic design support the user with a set of tools for drawing and painting (like *MacPaint* from Apple and later *Fullpaint*). These programs give the user a feeling of full control over pencils, brushes, paint etc. Whereas these programs remind the user of traditional painting (what the user manipulate is the bitmap of the display), other programs let the user in addition move, combine and in other ways manipulates graphical 'objects' like circles and free form shapes (like *MacDraw* from Apple, and *Illustrator* from Adobe).

A third type of computer-based graphic design tools are those for page make-up. (The first really powerful set of make-up tools for small computer workstations was *Pagemaker* from Aldus.) These tools remind the user of traditional make-up tools. The user interactively places text and pictures, changes fonts, edits text, crops pictures, etc. The operations the user performs on the page are those he or she could do in hot metal and in paste-up technology. In addition there are new operations like 'pouring' text into the galleys. (In fact the best of the desktop publishing page make-up systems today fulfill most of the

---

[16] Word processors may rather be tools for creative writing than for graphic design. However, in producing this desktop published book I have experienced word processing tools in all the above mentioned respects.

requirements we in the UTOPIA project specified for professional newspaper systems in 1983.)[17]

The toolness in all these graphic design programs is based on the metaphor that what the user sees on the display is the 'paper' he or she is working on. The tools and materials used are typically picked from menus and then handled with a mouse (and in addition a keyboard). In addition, via windows the user can (again metaphorically) see the material from different perspectives and in different magnifications. Clearly, the toolness of the page make-up 'use model' and of the image processing 'use model' in the UTOPIA project were designed with similar ideas.

## 'Desktop' Tools

Another popular set of computer-based tools are those associated with the *desktop metaphor*. The display is graphically designed as a 'desktop' with icons for a mailbox, documents, a filing cabinet, a wastepaper basket, different tools the user needs for specific tasks like writing documents, sending mail, searching for data in files and documents, writing programs, etc. The user has a mouse to handle the tools and documents he or she works on (e.g. by double-clicking on them). Objects on the desktop are moved around by 'dragging' them with the mouse. For example, the user drags a document to the wastepaper basket if he or she want to throw it away (delete).

The first well known example of the desktop metaphor was the previously mentioned *Xerox Star* office system, where toolness was created this way. *Finder*, the operating system for the Apple Macintosh, utilizes a similar metaphor in the view the user is given. Another example worth mentioning is the *Switcher* by Andy Hertfield, one of the most creative Macintosh programmers. It goes be-

---

[17] See chapter 15, *The 'Tool Perspective' – An Example*, and Ehn, P. and Sundblad, Y. (eds.): *Kravspecifikation för datorstödd bildbehandling och ombrytning*, Swedish Center for Working Life, Stockholm 1983.

yond the desktop metaphor, by also supporting the user with a metaphor of tools, not for manipulating the programs on the desktop, but for looking into the memory of the machine and then moving around between and within programs.

## Explorative Programming Environments

Explorative programming environments like *Smalltalk* and *Interlisp* from Xerox, and the operating system *Unix*, may also be seen as examples of sets of tools (though the concept here is used in a more abstract sense) for acting in, and manipulating, a 'world' of programs and data. Windows and menus on the display are related to pointing devices, and function in a similar way as in the examples above to create the toolness.

*HyperCard* by Bill Atkinson represents a new dimension of programming environments. Admittedly, it lacks much of the power of the above mentioned programming environments, but the toolness has been given new features. All programing objects have a visual graphic shape that is displayed on the screen. Furthermore, depending on the user's experience, he or she can manipulate the objects with tools on different levels, at first simply with tools for copying and modifying existing prototypical examples, later by really programming new objects. In contrast to traditional 'off-the-shelf' programs HyperCard applications are 'open' – as in programming environments, the user can at any time modify the application and build new tools.

## Dynamic Spreadsheets

Dynamic spreadsheets are computer-based tools for a wide range of applications. (The best know examples are *VisiCalc*, the first dynamic spreadsheet, designed by Daniel Bricklin and Robert Frankston and the contemporary *Excel* from Microsoft.) The visual metaphor is here that of the old ruled-paper spreadsheet. But in addition each cell is given a value rule specifying how its value is to be determined. These rules can easily be copied and modified to other cells. When the user enters or changes a value anywhere in the spreadsheet, all values that are dependent on it change too. Interaction takes place as in the earlier examples, and the user literally sees how the whole spreadsheet changes as he or she manipulates a single cell. The spreadsheet metaphor is most helpful for simulating different strategies: 'What happens to the spreadsheet if I change the value or the rule of this cell?' 'Instantly' the user sees the changes on the spreadsheet. Other tools in the tool kit let the user design and edit business graphics like pie charts, by just selecting a set of cells from the spreadsheet, and then applying a graphic tool. A spreadsheet application is an example of a computer-based tool that transcends properties of traditional tools and materials. (The tools for 'pouring' text into galleys that some page make-up programs have display the same 'magic'.)

*Computer Games*

I will end this list of examples of computer-based tools, which certainly could have been made much longer, with the toolness that some computer games represent. These games resemble programming environments. The player operates in a dramatic context, which he or she has tools to operate in and on. *Lode Runner* from Bröderbund is a good example. It is a game where the player moves around in labyrinths of bricks and ladders, collecting treasures while being chased by evil men. The action is continuously displayed on the graphic display and the player controls his or her 'man' with the mouse – all the time the player sees and hears what he or she does. (As in most computer games the narrative lacks literary quality, but has a most dramatic theatrical context.)

However, the interesting toolness is that the player has an editor for 'building' new, and changing old labyrinths and games – tools to make tools. Much as in the graphic design programs discussed above the player picks a tool for placing objects like bricks, ladders, treasures etc. By exiting the editor the player moves into the just recreated brave new world to find out if it works as intended (and to have some fun).

I am not suggesting that all the examples above demonstrate tools in the sense of traditional tools. In particular, the role of professional skill and aspects of the quality of the product have to some extent been left out. Nevertheless, to me the examples demonstrate important features and inspiring ideas for design of 'transparent', and 'convivial', computer-based tools. In the next sections principles for designing this toolness of computer artifacts will be discussed.

## 'Directness'

'Direct manipulation' is a basic principle for designing toolness of computer artifacts. The principle was coined by Ben Schneiderman in 1974, and he and others have later developed it into one of the main principles for user interface design.[18] He has described driving a car as his favorite example of direct manipulation.[19]

> The scene is directly visible through the front window, and actions such as braking or steering have become common knowledge in our culture. To turn left, the driver simply rotates the steering wheel to the left. The response is immediate and the scene changes, providing feedback to refine the turn. Imagine trying to turn by issuing a command LEFT 30 DEGREES and then having to issue another command to see the new scene.

In user interface design this is typically simulated by pointing at visual reminders of objects and actions on a display. Tasks can rapidly be carried out, and the results are immediately observable. Keyboard entry of commands is replaced by pointing devices for selecting objects and actions.

[18] Schneiderman, op. cit.
[19] Ibid., p. 180.

In a recent article Edwin Hutchins et al. have further developed the principles for *directness*. They suggest that this directness is achieved by a change of central metaphor for the user interface.[20] Traditionally a *conversational metaphor* has been used. The user is in contact with linguistic structures, structures that can be interpreted as referring to the objects of interest. The interface becomes an *intermediary* to a hidden 'world'. Focal awareness is on 'conversations' with the intermediary about the task, not on performing it. The interface stays in the way for the user, as a badly designed tool.

Alan Kay has argued that:[21]

> a person exerts the greatest leverage when his illusion can be manipulated without appeal to abstract intermediaries such as the hidden programs needed to put into action even a simple word processor. What I call direct leverage is provided when the illusion acts as a 'kit' or tool, with which to solve a problem.

This can be accomplished by the design of a *dramatic context* for the user to act in. This dramatic context is often referred to a *model world metaphor*. The user does not describe actions, but rather performs them in the dramatic context. This world of action, rather than language of description, is typical of the examples above, not only of the computer games, but also of all the others, like graphic design environments, spreadsheets, and exploratory programming environments.

The tool perspective from the UTOPIA project can be seen as a special case of creating a dramatic context by the use of a model world metaphor. The user is the skilled actor, and the 'world' is designed by 'tools' that the actor can

[20] Hutchins, E.L. et al. 'Direct Manipulation Interfaces' in Norman, D. and Draper, S. (eds.) *User Centered System Design*, Lawrence Erlbaum, London 1986. I have chosen to use this article as my main point of reference to the field of human-computer interaction since, in my view, it is one of the best accounts of state of the art design principles in the field.

[21] Kay, 1984, op. cit., p. 42.

use to refine 'materials'. This is a 'meta'-metaphor that can be applied to many practical situations, but of course completely different meta-metaphors can be created as well. Such an alternative meta-metaphor of viewing computer artifacts as interactive plays was discussed in the previous chapter.

However to establish directness in use of tools in these dramatic contexts, certain requirements of the user interface have to be fulfilled. Hutchins et al. suggest that (translated to the language used in this book):

- It must be possible for the user to practically treat *reminders of objects or actions as the objects or actions themselves*. This is not equivalent to saying that the reminders cannot be verbal, and have to be graphical, using pictures and icons. The point is rather that menus, icons and pictures on a display have proved to function much as onomatopoetic words do.
- There must be *an inter-referential relation between input and output 'language'. Input expressions must be allowed to incorporate or make use of previous output expressions*. Directness is typically designed by use of the same 'object' as both input and output. With interaction devices the user 'controls' the changes of the display.
- There must not be *delays between a user input issued to change an object and the corresponding change of the output* (unless such delays are 'natural' in the dramatic context).
- It must be possible for the user to 'view' *the objects from different perspectives*, and in this sense obtain different reminders of the same object.

In the examples of tool-like computer artifacts given earlier, as well as in the design of tools for page make-up and image processing in the UTOPIA project, these means to achieve toolness have typically been utilized.

More analytically, Hutchins et. al. suggest that *semantic directness, articulatory directness,* and *direct engage-*

*ment* are central concepts for designing the directness of computer artifacts.

## Semantic Directness

In a language more in line with this book *semantic directness* involves how close the dramatic context is to the user's conceptual competence, i.e. how well the user interface relates to the practice and language the user is familiar with. Frequent users can in this respect break through most poorly designed interfaces and overcome semantic breakdowns, but that is no excuse for not trying to design consistent dramatic contexts in the language of the users. However, a user interface that supports semantic directness for a skilled user does not necessarily do it for a novice, and vice versa, which is a well known design dilemma.

Another dilemma of semantic directness is the level of tools in the user interface. The primitive command of a Turing machine gives the user the tools to perform any task that can be done with a computer artifact, but there are not many users that would be helped by this in their ordinary work practice. Hutchins et. al. refer to this as *the Turing tar-pit* in which everything is possible but nothing of interest is easy.[22] But they also warn for the converse, where over-specialized tools make operations easy, but little of interest is possible.

However, as Don Norman argues in another article in the same book:[23]

> We want higher-level tools that are crafted to the task. We need low-level tools in order to create and modify higher-level ones. The level of tool has to match the level of intention. Again, easier to say than to do.

---

[22] Hutchins, et al., op. cit., p. 101.

[23] Norman, D.: 'Cognitive Engineering' in Norman, D. and Draper, S. (eds.) *User Centered System Design*, Lawrence Erlbaum, London 1986, p.54.

Fundamentally there seem to be two ways out of this dilemma of semantic directness. The first is to design the tools in close cooperation with the future users, close to their practical experience and professional language. This is how the tool metaphor was used in the UTOPIA project and in the graphic design examples given above. The complementary way is to give the user access to tools on different levels for manipulating and incrementally expanding a whole and consistent dramatic context, reaching from basic programming tools to the most aggregated application tools. This is, for example, how a user interacts with a *Smalltalk* machine as opposed to traditional environments of separated operating systems, programming languages and application programs. *HyperCard* demonstrates the same principle.

## Articulatory Directness

*Articulatory directness* has to do with the relation between concepts used in the interface and their physical form. As mentioned earlier onomatopoeia is a technique used in spoken language. Hutchins et al. argue that:[24]

> in many ways, the interface languages should have an easier time of exploiting articulatory similarity than do natural languages because of the rich technological base available to them. Thus, if the intent is to draw a diagram, the interface might accept as input the drawing motions. In turn, it could present as output diagrams, graphs, and images. If one is talking about sound patterns to the interface language, the output could be the sounds themselves. The computer has the potential to exploit articulatory similarities through technological innovation in the varieties of dimensions upon which we can operate.

Most significantly high resolution bit-mapped displays facilitate the creation of direct articulation. Expressions like pictures and icons on a display and their immediate

[24] Hutchins, et al., op.cit., p. 110.

changes according to input issued by the user, or sounds
from a tone generator, are means that extend the articulatory directness of verbal language. On the input side we
can achieve articulatory directness by mimicking actions
like cursor movements by moving a mouse, a trackball, a
lightpen, etc. Certainly it is the articulatory directness, not
the semantic one, that has made computer games so at-
tractive to many people.

Output devices like bit-mapped displays and input devices like the mouse are in these games, and in several of
the examples above, used to support a *spatial metaphor*.
The spatial metaphor can be used to create completely
new concrete tools for tasks that earlier have been purely
formal or abstract. Furthermore, even in computer-based
systems with poor support for a spatial metaphor users
tend to use it for 'moving around in the system' or for
'going from one place to another'.[25] It has also been observed how young people in our contemporary media societies develop unique competence in dealing with spatial
and graphical representations. It started with film and
television, but computer games and personal computers
have accelerated this tendency.[26]

### 'Direct Engagement'

Finally, *direct engagement* is, according to Hutchins et al.,
a feeling of involvement directly with a world of objects.
These objects must be of interest to the user, and it must be
possible to perform actions on them and watch how they
react. To provide the user with the opportunity of this engagement, designers have to utilize means for creating
semantic and articulatory directness of computer artifacts. However, in addition the use of these artifacts has to

[25] Andersen, P.B. and Madsen K.H.: 'Design and Professional
Languages' in Larsen, S.F. and Plunkett, K. (eds.) *Computers,
Mind and Metaphors* (forthcoming).
[26] Greenfield, P.: 'Video Games as Tools of Cognitive Socializa-
tion' in Larsen, S.F. and Plunkett, K. (eds.) *Computers, Mind and
Metaphors* (forthcoming).

be interesting enough for the user to engage in. After all, the user interface is, as Kay has put it, 'essentially a theatrical context'.[27] It is the design of an engaging *dramatic context in which the user can have focal awareness on action in this 'world'*, leaving only subsidiary awareness of the tools used, which is the hardest challenge to designers of user interfaces. This is a challenge for design of tools and contexts for professional use just as much as for design of computer games. This *narrative aspect*, especially the creation of first-personness interaction with computer artifacts as interactive mimesis, was exemplified in the previous chapter. Here I will elaborate on the use of 'metaphors', 'use models' and 'systematic domains' in creating toolness or directness of computer artifacts.

## Metaphors, Use Models, and Systematic Domains

### Metaphors

The use of metaphors in design of computer artifacts has frequently been mentioned in this chapter: a tool metaphor, a desktop metaphor, a spatial metaphor, a model world metaphor, a page make-up metaphor, etc. Metaphors typically mean understanding one situation in terms of another.[28]

When using computer artifacts, metaphors may remind the user of a set of useful tools, for example for page make-up or for organizing documents on a desktop, rather than using a computer. The metaphors are sug-

---

[27] Kay, A., op. cit., p. 42.

[28] For a detailed discussion of computers and metaphors see e.g. Andersen, P.B.: 'Semiotics and Informatics – Computer as a Media' in Ingwersen et. al.: *Information Technology and Information Use*, Taylor Graham, London 1986, see also Madsen, K.H. 'Breakthrough by Breakdown – Metaphors and Structured Domains' in Klein, H. and Kumar, K. (eds.) *Information Systems Development for Human Progress in Organizations*, North-Holland (forthcoming).

gestions to the user that working with the computer artifact is similar to the work the user is familiar with in ordinary work situations. Other metaphors relate more to
the user's general experiences than specifically to their
professional practice. Thus, the suggestion is made that
the computer artifact is an almost physical 'information
space' which the user can move around in, or a model
world that the user can play in, like the office information
system *Objectworld* mentioned in the previous chapter.

Furthermore the reminders are typically created with
layers of metaphors. For example the metaphor of a tool
kit for page make-up is based on the more general tool
metaphor, which in turn utilizes both the spatial metaphor and the model world metaphor.

However, if the user interface of a computer artifact is
understood as essentially a dramatic context, it is not just
metaphors proper, but any narrative means that can be
used to create useful reminders in the dramatic context of
a user interface that we should be concerned with in design. What is important is what the user interface re-
minds the user of. This may be in the tradition of the
user's familiar tools and professional language, or it may
transcend them reminding the user of other experiences,
providing the user with opportunities to see and do familiar things in new ways.

In our Wittgensteinian language we could say that the
user interface is a sign that plays the role of reminding the
user about what he or she can do with a specific computer
artifact in specific situations in specific language-games.
All the metaphors listed above are intended for design of
such signs, as such useful reminders. These signs are just
as important in design for professional work as for more
amusing games.

## Use Models

In designing for skill there is a clear relation between the
user interface of a computer artifact, the user's professional language and competence, and the design situation.
To facilitate this, in the UTOPIA project we designed what

we called *use models* (outlined in an earlier chapter). Use models for tools for page make-up and image processing were developed.[29]

Here I shall return to the role of use models in *use*. Fundamental aspects of the use models created were (on a meta-level) a tool metaphor, a physical space metaphor, and a model world metaphor.

These meta-metaphors in the use models supported family resemblance with the users' ordinary professional language and practice of page make-up and picture processing work. In these language-games work was performed with tools like a knife, in a physical space like the page ground, in a given world of typographical tools and materials.

The choice of these or other metaphors in a use model is by no means 'natural'. They are hopefully creative design choices that fit well with the ordinary language-games in the users' normal practice. They are developed in interaction between designers and the prospective users. The same applies to the reminders created of the specific tools and materials.

However, the use models did not merely have a family resemblance with the users' traditional tools. They also included new tools that were introduced because of limitations in use of computers; and new tools with which the users could do things that were not possible with traditional tools. An example of the first is cropping a picture, an example of the second is the 'magnifying glass' needed because of too low display resolution and limited display size and resolution, while an example of the third is a tool for 'pouring' articles into a given column space on a page ground.

In the use model for page make-up, the resemblance of the properties of the working material was straightforward. As in the user's practice with traditional materials articles could be composed of text, pictures, and graphics. Texts could be ingress, headline, subtitle, picture text, etc.

---

[29] See chapter 15 on *The 'Tool Perspective' – An Example*.

These materials could be composed of paragraphs, sentences, words, word spaces, characters, character spaces, lines, leadings, columns, groups, etc.

However, in the use model we designed for picture processing we in contrast decided to give the material some fundamentally new properties as compared to traditional graphic material.

Traditional graphical material for picture processing are either opaque (reflecting light) like paper photographs, or transparent like dia frames (letting some light from behind pass through the picture). However, on the display we can simulate both these properties in the same picture material, which gives some new opportunities for image manipulations (imagine a partly transparent and partly reflecting picture). Hence, graphic materials were seen as having both a transparent layer and an intensity (or light reflecting) layer that the user has tools to control independently.

As designers we were quite pleased with this extension of the properties of graphic material and the new graphic operations it made possible, and so were the participating graphic workers, but it should also be admitted that this aspect of the use model for picture processing was the hardest one for new users to get used to. The 'innovation' in picture processing that the use model suggested had no obvious immediate family resemblance with graphic worker's ordinary use language and practice. It did not support new ways of doing picture processing for *all* graphic workers. To what extent this aspect of the use model should be redesigned, and to what extent the learning process based on the use model could be developed is a design challenge – the fundamental dialectics of tradition and transcendence in design. We tried both ways.

The above outlined use models were designed in close cooperation between professional graphic workers and designers. They were developed based on the use of simple mock-ups and prototyping tools on which different versions of the use models were 'implemented'. Changes and new design ideas were based on the typographers' experience from actually doing (simulated) graphic work with the mock-ups and prototypes, and designers' and users' joint reflections on the usefulness of the simulated tools for graphic work.

When the users were satisfied with their simulated use of the use models 'implemented' on the mock-ups, we as designers used these models (understood as reminders and paradigm cases) to make traditional requirement specifications for construction.[30]

## Systematic Domains

What about formalization of skills when designing use models? In the terminology of Winograd and Flores a *systematic domain* must be generated.[31] This systematic domain must then be formally represented in a way that can be put into a computer. The objects in this systematic domain possess no other properties than those we have designed them to and have been able to formalize.

Thus far there is no difference, as compared to the problem of 'knowledge engineering' in the design of artificial intelligence expert systems.

However, the difference becomes clear when we ask what is represented as the systematic domain. In an expert system the knowledge of an expert is what one tries to capture in the model. Hence, the expert's knowledge is reduced to what can be stated explicitly as facts or rules. The model is an attempt to include the expert's knowledge. As has been discussed earlier there seems to be much more to professional competence than what can be formally described.[32]

---

[30] See chapters 15 on *The 'Tool Perspective' – An Example,* and 13, *Case II: The UTOPIA Projects.*

[31] The concept of systematic domains, and the problem of formal representations in e.g. expert systems are discussed at length by Winograd, T. and Flores, F.: *Understanding Computers and Cognition – a new foundation for design,* Ablex, Norwood 1986.

[32] In the next chapter I will return to the role of 'tacit knowledge'.

If we take a tool perspective as our design approach, the systematic domain created is designed to be under the user's skillful control. His or her understanding is not modelled. *What are modelled are the tools and materials the skilled user works with.*

To take the graphic example, what are modelled are typographical materials and tools, not the far more complex knowledge about typographical design that expert system 'knowledge engineers' try to capture.

However, a fundamental problem is what we can know about existing or desirable properties of tools and materials in a given craft or profession. In some cases these objects and their properties already exist *present-at-hand,* to use our Heideggerian language – as already objectified designed tools and materials within the professional domain. Typographic material became a systematic domain a long time ago. Mathematics and bookkeeping are other examples. This has paved the way towards success for computer-based tools in these professions.

The design of new systematic domains requires that a world that is *ready-to-hand* for the user *breaks down*, that it partly becomes *present-at-hand*, objectified as for example new tools or materials to work with and on. However, if these tools are good, they will, as all good tools, become ready-to-hand in the hands of an experienced user, extending his or her control of the task to perform. Hence, in this sense formalization may help develop rather than decrease competence in a domain, may create glasses for new views rather than just a new blindness.

In which existing professions and crafts can we design such new systematic domains? If so, how do we do it? What may be achieved? And what blindness do these new systematic domains create, which is the knowledge and competence that might get lost in this process? These are fundamental questions to which the *answers may be given in actual design based on a creative dialogue between professional users and designers, rather than in theoretical reflection.*

I find design of computer artifacts as tools for skilled workers to be a challenging, highly exciting, and technically quite possible direction for our design efforts. In design of computer-based tools the limits set by formalization are wider than for expert systems, since there is no attempt to replace human competence by formalization, but instead to augment human competence by skill-enhancing artifacts. The creation of metaphors, use models, and new systematic domains provides challenging aspects of designing the toolness of computer artifacts. But we should not be so blinded by this fact (i.e. that we can design systematic domains with tools for skilled work) as to believe that all professions and crafts lend themselves to such tool manipulation.

## From Concrete Experience to Abstract Formalisms to Concrete Experience?

To sum up on the toolness of computer artifacts, I will return to some concluding remarks (by Hutchins et al.) on the new opportunities for practical understanding:[33]

> On the surface, the fundamental idea of Direct Manipulation interface to a task flies in the face of two thousand years of development of abstract formalisms as means of understanding and controlling the world. Until very recently, the use of computers has been an activity squarely in that tradition. So the exterior of Direct Manipulation, providing as it does for the direct control of a specific task world, seems somewhat atavistic, a return to concrete thinking. On the inside, of course, the implementation of direct manipulation systems is yet another step in a long formal tradition. The illusion of the absolutely manipulable concrete world is made possible by the technology of abstraction.

[33] Hutchins et al., op. cit., pp. 119–120.

There is no ultimate farewell to abstract formalisms in the design of computer artifacts, but there are promises of a revival for practical skills in design and use.

In another context Bo Göranzon has made the following reflection on the consequence of Cartesian abstract algebraic formulation of concrete geometric points, lines, surfaces and volumes. The new mathematic-algebraic language made concrete geometric thinking redundant. Göranzon gives the example of the equation $x^2 + y^2 = 25$ – a representation of a circle's properties. The properties of the circle are all there in the formula. Has algebra replaced geometry, and the brain the 'eye', he asks?[34] However, it is somewhat a paradox that the Cartesian mathematical-logical replacement of, for example, concrete geometric thinking, now can be used to recreate conditions for concrete thinking. The circle is there on the display, round as ever, ready for the user to manipulate it in a spatial, geometric and concrete way. In fact we are only in the beginning of exploring user interfaces as tools supporting such concrete actions. Computer workstation technology, design principles of directness, and the use of metaphors and use models are steps in the direction of designing computer artifacts as highly useful tools to be practically manipulated and concretely experienced. The possibilities are there. As was discussed in the part on *Designing for Democracy at Work*, however, the question of who will benefit from them is a rather different one, indeed.

[34] Göranzon, B.: 'Vad är en dator?' in Göranzon, B. (ed.): *Datautvecklingens Filosofi – tyst kunskap och ny teknik*, Carlsson & Jönsson, Malmö 1984, pp. 41–42.

*Chapter 18*

# Skills and the Tool Perspective

In this chapter skill aspects of the tool perspective will be discussed. The basis for the discussion was already formulated in Part I on *Design Philosophy*.

With the Heideggerian and Wittgensteinian approaches the importance of practical understanding in design and use of computer artifacts was stressed. Here I will further elaborate on the highly controversial concept commonly referred to as *tacit knowledge*. I will also make some reflections on the blindness that the tool perspective may create with regard to skill as social competence in intersubjective communication.

With the Marxist approach (first generally discussed in Part I on *Design Philosophy*, and then further elaborated in Part III on *Designing for Democracy at Work* with reference to the practice research carried out in the DEMOS and UTOPIA projects) a frame of reference for understanding societal aspects of design and use of computer artifacts was outlined. In this chapter I will go one step further by explicitly relating the skill aspect of the tool perspective to the ongoing 'Marxist debate' on qualifications and new technology.

## Tacit Knowledge

An essential aspect of the tool perspective was the assumption that tacit knowledge neither can nor should be formalized into algorithmic procedures.

Tacit knowledge exists, and it is by no means mysterious – this is what we can learn both from a Wittgensteinian and a Heideggerian approach.

In a Wittgensteinian approach tacit knowledge is referred to as the kind of knowledge that involves practical understanding by familiarity and by 'rule following behavior' in practice. We acquire tacit knowledge by practical sensuous experience from earlier cases and by learning to follow rules in practice, rules that are neither explicit nor distinguishable from the actual perfomance of them. Understanding practice as participation in intertwined *language-games* is fundamental to the Wittgensteinian notion of tacit knowledge.

In a Heideggerian approach tacit knowledge is related to the involved, rapid, fluid and intuitive performance typical of proficient and expert behavior. This proficient and expert behavior we all acquire in some situations in our lives. It is performance in a world that has become *ready-to-hand* and where detached reflections are secondary to our performance.

However, in a discussion of the 'tacitness' of practical understanding I find it reasonable to start with explicit reference to Michael Polanyi, who coined the term *tacit knowledge*.[1] He uses well-known human activities like swimming or riding a bicycle to establish[2]

> the well known fact that the aim of a skillful performance is achieved by the observance of a set of rules which are not known as such to the person performing them.

And he argues that:[3]

---

[1] Tacit knowledge is discussed in Polanyi, M.: *The Tacit Dimension*, Anchor Books, Doubleday & Company, New York 1967, and Polanyi, M.: *Personal Knowledge*, Routledge and Kegan Paul, London 1973.

[2] Polanyi, 1973, op. cit., p. 49.

[3] Ibid., p. 53.

an art which cannot be specified in detail cannot be transmitted by prescription, since no prescription exists. It can be passed on only by example from master to apprentice.

The role of *tradition* is, according to Polanyi, crucial to learning tacit knowledge:[4]

> To learn by example is to submit to authority. You follow your master because you trust his manner of doing things even if you cannot analyze and account in detail for its effectiveness. By watching the master and emulating his efforts in the presence of his example, the apprentice unconsciously picks up the rules of the art, including those which are not explicitly known by the master himself.

These are basic assumptions of the tool perspective, and the design principles and recommendations based on it. However, as we participate in many language-games, and are skillful in different situations in our lives, there is also a possibility of transcendence from traditions in the meeting between different groups, with different practices and knowledge. And as will be discussed, transcendence is in fact also the hallmark of skillful and creative rule following behavior.

## Tacit Knowledge and Non-Explicit Knowledge

However, not all non-explicit knowledge is genuinely tacit knowledge. According to the philosopher and Wittgenstein expert Allan Janik there are at least three different kinds of tacit knowledge that in principle *can* be made explicit and formally described.[5]

His first example is knowledge that is *kept tacit for political or economic reasons*. Trade secrets of craftsmen and their guilds provide a historical example which at

---

[4] Ibid., p. 53.

[5] Janik, A.: *Tacit Knowledge, Working Life and Scientific Method*, Brenner Archive, Innsbruck University, 1986.

least had this as an ingredient. The craftsmen's status, power and standard of living often depended on keeping others away from their knowledge. This was also part of the tacit knowledge that typographers had in the era of lead composing. The same could probably be said about many professionals today, including designers of computer artifacts. When we, with a tool perspective, argue that tacit knowledge neither can nor should be made explicit, tacit knowledge based on this kind of professional trade secrets is not what we have in mind.

The second example concerns the kind of knowledge that *in principle could have been articulated but that never was*, because no one had an interest in doing it. As Janik put it : 'nobody pays much attention to the practice of blacksmiths until those practices are in danger of going out of existence.'[6] However, it is not until we try to make explicit the tacit skill of a craft that we find out to what extent it also was tacit in a more fundamental way.[7] The history of Taylorism from the beginning of our century demonstrates that tacit knowledge does get lost if we assume that all skilled work can be reduced to algorithmic procedures. The use of computers in working life in the 1960s and 1970s was perhaps the peak of this mistake, that is unless artificial intelligence and expert systems in the 1980s take us yet another step down the deskilling ladder.

The third example of tacit knowledge that in principle can be explicitly articulated is, according to Janik, *the absolute presuppositions of everyday practice*. A trivial example may be that when I write a text with my word processor and move the mouse I assume without reflec-

[6] Ibid., p. 4.

[7] In Göranzon, B. (ed.): *Datautvecklingens Filosofi – tyst kunskap och ny teknik*, Carlsson & Jönsson, Malmö 1984, pp. 12-13, Göranzon calls the kind of consequences that we do not observe until after perhaps 4–5 years, 'third order consequences', as distinguished from immediately observable consequences, and consequences like eye strain that we can observe within a year or so.

tion that the cursor will move accordingly. Only in breakdown situations, to use our Heideggerian language, does this presupposition appear to me, for example if there is a technical problem with the mouse. A more general and serious example may be the presuppositions that the work mates I have today also will be around tomorrow. Certainly we can also purposely bring these assumptions to our attention, and in that sense make the tacit knowledge explicit – *make the-ready-to-hand present-at-hand*. But we live our everyday life embedded in a background of such assumptions. To make them explicit is at times an important endeavor, in social science typically performed as critique of ideology, and in professional activities, like design, as reflection-in-action.[8] However, to make absolute presuppositions explicit again only partly makes tacit knowledge explicit. We could not perform skillfully if we had to be aware of them all the time – that would literally mean a breakdown of professional competence, regardless of whether we talk about riding a bike, using a computer artifact or attending a meeting in a design team.

The examples above demonstrate tacit knowledge that can be made explicit and to some degree formalized. Hence when we talk about tacit knowledge it is often something else we have in mind. We think of knowledge that defies precise description by its very nature.

## Tacit Knowledge as Sensuous Experience

Following Wittgenstein, Janik suggests that knowledge by familiarity is a kind of tacit knowledge that results from sensuous experience. This is sensuous experiences that are not limited to seeing. Most of us know how coffee smells and a clarinet sounds. But how do we describe it to someone that does not? Once you know by experience,

---

[8] This was, with reference to Schön D. A: *The Reflective Practitioner – How Professionals Think in Action*, Basic Books, New York 1983, discussed in chapter 9, *Other Ways of Seeing and Doing – External Alternatives*.

then you know, and there is no mystery about it. You will perfectly well understand when someone else talks about the sound of a clarinet. But to 'describe' this sound to someone that does not know it, the best thing you can do is to use paradigm cases, for example metaphors, analogies, and hints that remind him or her of something familiar. The skill involved in this kind of tacit knowledge is associated with the ability to make subtle discriminations – like between the sound of a clarinet and an oboe. We are all capable of such judgments, but we are not equally good at it.

However, in some respects these kinds of sensuous knowledge also can be formalized and automated. It is an easily accomplished task to design a computer artifact to distinguish between a clarinet and an oboe. It is quite different with the social competence of making judgments such as whether a clarinet sounds nice, a cup of coffee smells awful, or a page layout has a nice balance. The skill to make sensuous, typically aesthetic and moral judgments is communicated by examples under the guidance of someone more skillful, and learned by experience. This kind of knowledge for making judgments based on sensuous experience defies rational formalization in the sense discussed in the tool perspective.

Tacit knowledge based on sensuous experience also concerns another aspect of the tool perspective. How does a computer artifact differ from traditional tools with respect to sensuous experience, especially when there is more to it than meets the eye? Not many years ago, it would have been perfectly correct to say that all we can sense using a computer artifact is the text from the display that meets the eye, and the feeling of the keys when touching the keyboard. Hence, traditional knowledge by familiarity was by necessity constrained when computer artifacts replaced traditional tools. Current developments of computer workstation technology and in user interface design are widening the scope considerably. The tool perspective suggests that we think of traditional tools as a design ideal in the following respects: What kind of sensuous experiences are possible with them? How can we design computer artifacts in these respects? But certainly there are not only limitations: computer artifacts based on modern workstation technology also open up possibilities for new sensuous experiences. We may not be used to thinking of the knowledge of a young expert computer game player as tacit knowledge. But is this not exactly what it is? Hence, it seems that in designing computer artifacts as tools we must investigate both constraints and new possibilities for acquisition of tacit knowledge based on sensuous experience. Maybe we will find that the possibilities are only pale copies of the originals, like a simple computer-based tone generator is of a clarinet. But we will also find new challenging tools for composing and playing electronic music that defies some of the limits of traditional instruments.

## Tacit Knowledge – Tradition and Transcendence

Now to the paradox of rule following behavior. As mentioned, many rules that we follow in practice are scarcely to be distinguished from the behavior in which we perform them. Tacit knowledge that involves following specific rules in practice is the practical understanding that Wittgenstein as well as Polanyi emphasize. It is the kind of knowledge, as a rule following activity, that only can be acquired as practical experience. This is typically how craftsmanship is acquired. The tacit knowledge is passed on by example from master to apprentice. The rules are only rarely made explicit as prescriptions. In most cases we simply do not know how to do that. They are tacit knowledge. We do not know that we have followed a rule until we have done it. *The most important rules we follow in skillful performance defy explicit formalization, but we still understand them.* As Polanyi put it:[9]

It is pathetic to watch the endless efforts – equipped with microscopy and chemistry, with mathematics and

[9] Polanyi, op. cit., p. 53.

electronics – to reproduce a single violin of the kind the half-literate Stradevarius turned out as a matter of routine more than 200 years ago.

*This is the traditional aspect of human rule following behavior.* Polanyi points out that our perhaps most explicit rule based system – the practice of Common Law – also uses earlier examples as paradigm cases:[10]

This procedure recognizes the principle of all traditionalism that practical wisdom is more truly embodied in action than expressed in the rules of action.

According to Polanyi this is also true for science, no matter how rationalistic and explicit it claims to be, the point being that:[11]

while *the articulate contents of science* are successfully taught all over the world in hundreds of new universities, *the unspecifiable art of scientific research* has not yet penetrated to many of these.

The art of scientific research defies complete formalization; it must partly be learned by examples from a master whose behavior one trusts. The suggestion in the tool perspective to actively include skilled users in the design of new computer artifacts, when their old tools and working practices are redesigned, can hardly be given better illustrations. After all, few social activities have been under such pressure of rational formalization as Law and Science, and still they are heavily dependent on practical experience and paradigm cases. Why should we expect other work practices that have been under less pressure of formalization to be less based on practical experience, paradigm cases and tacit knowledge? To take the extreme example, Tayloristic reduction of work to algorithmic procedures is not only a democratic failure, but has also

[10] Ibid., p. 54.
[11] Ibid., p. 53.

failed in terms of utilizing the workers' tacit knowledge as practical understanding of the labor process.

In rule following behavior there is also the aspect of *creative transcendence of traditional behavior*. Again, this is what is typical of skillful human behavior, and exactly what defies precise formalization. By mastery of the rules comes the freedom to extend them. This *creativity* depends on what Janik calls 'the open-textured character of rule-following behavior.'[12] To begin with, we learn to follow a rule as a kind of dressage, but in the end we do it as creative activity. To be able to follow a rule is to have learned how to in practice continue an example we have been given. Mastery of the rules puts us in a position to invent new ways of carrying on. This skill is tacit knowledge. In Janik's words:[13]

> Another way of putting the matter would be to say that there is always and ineliminably the possibility that we can follow the rule in a wholly unforeseen way. This could not happen if we had to have an explicit rule to go on from the start. (...) The possibility of radical innovation is, however, the logical limit of description. This is what tacit knowledge is all about.

This is why rule based expert systems cannot completely replace the creativity of a human competence, and why in the tool perspective there is such strong epistemological focus on skill both in design and in use of computer artifacts. *The tool perspective focuses on traditional skill, not at the cost of creative transcendence, but as a necessary condition for it.*

## Not Just Instrumental Skill

Now to some critical points concerning skill and a tool perspective.

---

[12] Janik, op. cit., p. 8.
[13] Ibid., pp. 11-12.

The competence involved in using tools in a labor process can, with reference to Jürgen Habermas, be understood according the kind of interest that is supported.[14]

An important aspect in use of tools is *instrumental action*, as when a carpenter uses a hammer to drive a nail. He realizes more or less defined goals under given conditions. The purpose is effective technical control and correct evaluation of the environment. By learning rules of instrumental action we acquire *skills*. They put us in a position to solve problems. *Incompetent* behavior reveals itself in instrumental failure.

However, there is more to competence than instrumental skills, as there is more to labor than instrumental work. In use of tools in a labor process we do not only perform instrumental actions, we also participate in language-games, or in Habermas' words, an institutional framework of symbolic interaction. We perform ordinary-language *intersubjective communication* actions. As internalization of the social conventions of the labor process the carpenter learns 'correct' behavior, the competence *to follow (and sometimes skillfully break) consensual norms or rules. Deviant* behavior reveals itself as violation of social conventions, and provokes social sanctions.

To use computer artifacts in a specific labor process is both instrumental action and communicative action; it requires both instrumental work skills and social interaction competence. We can distinguish between what it means to follow a rule to perform instrumental actions like operating a computer artifact, and what it means to follow a rule in the sense of knowing how to act according to the norms for social interaction in which the instrumental use of the artifact is embedded. It is in practice by repetition and experience that we learn both kind of rules.

---

[14] These *knowledge interests* were referred to in the introduction to both Part I on *Design Philosophy* and Part II on *The Art and Science of Designing Computer Artifacts*. See e.g. Habermas, J.: *Toward a Rational Society*, Heinemann, London 1971.

Professional skill as expertness or proficiency is to know the rules so well that you know when to creatively transcend them and eventually create new rules. Both instrumental and communicative aspects of the tacit knowledge of skillful following of rules in practice are important to understand in design of computer artifacts.

However, no matter how much we, given the tool perspective, acknowledge the tacit professional competence of the users there is inherently an unfortunate bias towards the instrumental use of computer artifacts. The tool perspective may create *a blindness for tacit knowledge that stems from the maintenance of the institutional framework* in which computer artifacts are embedded.[15]

This critique could also be extended to a *gender critique* of the tool perspective, since women traditionally are more socialized to perform actions to follow and maintain social norms of institutional frameworks than to perform instrumental actions. The traditional tacit knowledge of women remains invisible in the background.[16]

Another similar critique of the tool perspective involves the focus on *individual skill*, whereas less attention is paid to *collective competence* of a group of workers. Typically work and interaction in labor processes are performed as cooperation. The individual's work is dependent on that of others. Communicative actions are important aspects of this cooperation, but there are also cooperative instrumental actions, mediated via the artifacts and the materials being used. The labor process is highly integrated,

---

[15] In the UTOPIA project we tried to focus on such aspects, but more as a complement to the tool perspective than as rethinking of it.

[16] The importance of the social competence of office workers has using a theoretical approach close to the one outlined in this book been analyzed by Wynn, E.: *Office Conversation as an Information Medium*, University of California, Berkeley 1979 (dissertation). With special reference to the work of women see e.g. Lie, M. and Rasmussen, B.: *Kan 'kontordamene' automatiseres?*, IFIM, Trondheim 1984, or Ressner, U.: *Den dolda hierarkin*, Tema Nova, Stockholm 1985.

requiring both coordination and planning of the individual activities, and of joint activities. There is no reason why cooperation and collective control as design ideals in work-oriented design should be subordinated to the ideal of individual skill.

Hence, the tool perspective as design ideal needs to be supplemented with ideals that help focus on cooperative aspects in general and especially on the tacit knowledge performed as social interaction competence in a labor process.

## Qualifications and New Technology

In this last section I will return to the Marxist approach focusing on changes in skill when new technology is introduced.[17] I will relate the tool perspective to influential 'Marxist' empirical studies of qualifications in working life. What do these studies conclude about constraints and possibilities for skilled work when computer artifacts are being used in working life? Which are the constraints on a craft design ideal?

### Is Craft Work Just of Historical Interest?

The craftsman worked with hand tools and machine-tools, and had a great autonomy in using these tools. Planning of the job was integrated with the manual execution of *craft work*. He was a highly skilled worker.

*Mechanization* came with the use of machinery. Machines replaced hand tools. The craftsman was transformed into an operator of these machines. At the same time planning of the work was done by engineers and administrators as 'intellectual' planning and design work distinguishable from the 'manual' work of operating the

---

[17] Hence, the theoretical context is the same as in the discussions of the *democracy* aspect of the DEMOS and UTOPIA projects in Part III on *Designing for Democracy at Work*, although the emphasis is a different one.

machines. There was a division between practical and theoretical work.

*Automatization* comes into its own especially with the use of computers. It changes the work of not only operators, but also engineers and administrators. A new relation between 'manual' and 'intellectual', or practical and theoretical work is taking form. Is it more like craft work than mechanized industrial work? Is it neither, but something completely new?

Craft work is the point of reference in many studies of qualifications and automation. In *Labor and Monopoly Capital*,[18] the influential work by Harry Braverman from 1974, it is both point of reference and ideal. This is also true of Robert Blauner's classical study from 1964, *Alienation and Freedom*.[19] However, as will be discussed below, this point of reference is questioned by several later studies, especially German ones. Moreover the results of the various studies differ drastically.

The results from the different studies can be categorized according to their main conclusions. They are: *qualification (upgrading), dequalification (degrading), polarization, requalification and segmentation*.[20]

*Qualification (Upgrading)*

Work for craft printers is a source of involvement and commitment. It is not chiefly a means to life, but an ex-

---

[18] Braverman, H.: *Labor and Monopoly Capital – The Degradation of Work in the Twentieth Century,* Monthly Review Press, New York 1974.

[19] Blauner, R.: *Alienation and Freedom – The Factory Worker and His Industry*, The University of Chicago Press, London 1964.

[20] For a more detailed overview of these 'theses' see Björkman, T.: 'Reparatörsyrkets utveckling' and 'Från polarisering till omkvalificering' in Nyberg, P. et al.: *Yrkesarbete i förändring,* Carlssons, Stockholm 1984, Broady, D. and Helgeson, B.: 'Farväl till arbetsdelningen?' in Broady, D. (ed.): *Professionaliseringsfällan,* Carlssons, Täby 1985, Björkman, T. and Lundquist, K.: *Yrkeskunnande och datorisering,* Statskontoret, Stockholm 1986, and Aronzon, G. (ed.): *Arbetets krav och mänsklig utveckling*, Prisma, Stockholm 1983.

pression of their selfhood and identity. For craftsmen, work is almost the expression of an inner need, rather than the grudging payment of a debt imposed by external sources. Since the printer is almost the prototype of the non-alienated worker in modern industry, he can provide a useful reference point with which to compare the situation of workers in a number of different industrial settings. Yet, it is not certain how long printers can maintain this position, for technological innovations and economic developments threaten to eliminate not only the typesetter's control but the job itself. The newspaper industry has developed a process by which printed type can be set automatically by a columnist or reporter as he writes out his copy on the typewriter. The craft unions may remain strong enough to resist this and other similar technological developments, but if they do not, printing may change rapidly from a craft to an automated industry, and this chapter will remain only of historical interest.[21]

This is how Robert Blauner ends his chapter on 'The printer: a free worker in a craft industry' in the classical study on *Alienation and Freedom*. It is for several reasons of interest to our discussion of skill and technological change.

Blauner found that graphic workers were highly skilled, and had considerable freedom and control in the labor process. Work was not very divided, and it was meaningfully related to the total organization of work. Graphic workers even controlled conditions of employment. Their unions were strong. All the graphic workers really lacked were ownership of the shop they worked in and the rights to the finished product of their work. This was in the U.S.A. in 1964. There is no doubt, that to Blauner the craft work of the printer was an ideal, the ideal of the independent craftsman of pre-industrial times.

[21] Blauner, op. cit., pp. 56–57.

It is this ideal he compared with developments in the textile, auto and chemical industries. What he generally found when production got more mechanized was, as compared with the ideal of craft work, deskilling, less control, and alienation of workers, combined with a decline in number of jobs. But there was hope for the future, the future of automation. The automation workers, working with the remaining non-automatable work in control rooms or with repair and maintenance, were the new 'non-manual' craft workers replacing the unskilled alienated factory jobs of machine and assembly-line technologies. (Programmers and designers definitely fit into this category as well.) Not that the new craft workers shared the traditional manual skill with older crafts, but the responsibility required in exercising judgment gave similar opportunities for discretion and initiative. Compared with mechanization work, there was an *upgrading*.

This was of course good news for the trade unions. Problems and critiques of the consequences arising from the introduction of new technology reported from many work places were important, but could be seen as temporary, and due to vanish when mechanization was replaced by automatization. This was the dominant trade union view when computer artifacts started to be introduced on a large scale in Swedish industry.[22]

More than twenty years have now passed since Blauner conducted his study. We should be able to give some of the answers to what happened to the printer as craft worker.

In short: The printers' newspaper unions in the U.S.A could not resist the introduction of new technology. Many typographers have not only lost control over their work, but also their jobs. Newspapers have since the mid 1960s gone through several drastic changes of technology and organization. Management has actively 'busted' their

[22] This was the main analysis in *Fackföreningsrörelsen och den tekniska utvecklingen*, an approved report to the LO, (The Swedish Federation of Trade Unions) 1966 congress.

unions. In Europe the peak of this trend was perhaps reached in 1986 when newspaper capitalist Robert Murdock fired the typographers from the venerable *Times*, and set up a new computer-based printing factory in Wapping outside London. Typographers and their unions were not allowed inside the fences of the heavily protected factory. The machines are now operated by electrical workers with a minimum of typographic training and skill. In this sense his chapter on the craft printer remains only of historical interest.

On the other hand the same threat from new technology has (as has been discussed earlier) been met in Scandinavia by other strategies from the graphic workers and their unions. The UTOPIA project with the tool perspective has been part of a strategy of demanding that new technology must maintain and develop rather than decrease quality of work and products. And this strategy has been quite successful. Trade unions have remained relatively strong. Many graphic workers still have challenging skilled jobs working with computer-based page make-up and picture processing. These are results of their acceptance of new technology on certain conditions. The unions have accepted that the number of jobs might decrease when new technology is introduced, but the condition for this acceptance has been that no one is fired. That has been part of the agreement with management. Skilled graphic workers are still demanded in many areas of the printing industry.

However, what we witness today may only be a temporary prolongation of craft work in the printing industry, to eventually be replaced by work in other media and desktop publishing in the offices. In another twenty years we will know. Today printing has and has not changed 'from a craft to an automated industry'.

## Dequalification (Degrading)

However, what happened in the early 1970s when computer artifacts became commonplace in industry was not the automation Blauner had been describing. Computers were used in planning and control systems supporting a separation of planning from the practical execution of work. Jobs got even more divided and controlled than before. If anything, we were witnessing a giant deskilling of the work force with the aid of computers. As was discussed in Part III on *Designing for Democracy*, Harry Braverman's *Labor and Monopoly Capital* had a subtitle giving the clear message: *the degradation of work in the twentieth century*, which seemed much better to capture and explain what was happening.

As for Blauner, traditional craft work, the worker who plans, controls and executes complete tasks, was an ideal for Braverman. In modern computer-based versions of Taylor's 'scientific management' Braverman saw the ultimate means of deskilling workers in the interest of control and profit. Not only was the deskilled worker easier to control with the new technology, he was also cheaper to buy. Though Braverman shared with Blauner the craft ideal, his reading of Marx was certainly different from Blauner's, and so were the illustrative cases he presented.

As has been mentioned I was deeply involved in action research to support industrial democracy both in the printing industry[23] and in repair- and maintenance work.[24] And in both cases Braverman, rather than Blauner, seemed to be right. Computer-based systems were deliberately used in attempts to deskill workers, make them easier to control and cheaper to buy. Historical studies by David Noble on the emergence of numerical controlled machines also demonstrated the deliberate aims of designing the new technology so that it required less skill to operate and took control away from the work-

[23] Ehn, P. et al.: *Brytningstid*, Swedish Center for Working Life, Stockholm 1984.

[24] Ehn, P. et al.: *Vi vägrar låta detaljstyra oss*, Swedish Center for Working Life, Stockholm 1978.

ers.[25] Several studies argued that the new computer workers, like computer operators and programmers, also seemed to be under the same deskilling attack. Signs of standardization of these jobs were already seen.[26]

Braverman's dequalification thesis had a similar positive reception in Swedish trade unions as had Blauner's upgrading thesis ten years earlier.[27]

However, as was discussed in Part III on *Designing for Democracy at Work*, there were many cases the dequalification thesis failed to explain. Some managerial strategies advocated the use of skilled workers, computer artifacts were sometimes used in a way that increased rather than decreased qualifications, patterns were different in different branches of industry, etc.

It was in this period that the UTOPIA project and the tool perspective were born with the idea of counteracting the main dequalification trend by actually, as a part of a trade union strategy, attempting to design skill based computer artifacts for newspaper production. This was *a design approach*, an attempt to use action research to investigate the possibilities for design and use of skill-enhancing computer artifacts. For more *elaborated qualification research* the interest in Scandinavia now turned to German theoretical and empirical investigations.

---

[25] Noble, D.: 'Social Choice in Machine Design – The Case of Automatically Controlled Machine Tools, and a Challenge for Labor' in *Politics & Society*, nos 3–4, 1978.

[26] See e.g. Greenbaum, J.: 'Division of Labor in the Computer Field' in Monthly Review, vol 28 no 3, 1976 and by Kraft, P.: *Programmers and Managers – the routinization of computer programming in the United States*, Springer Verlag, New York 1977.

[27] In the report *Solidariskt Medbestämmande* which was approved by the LO congress 1976 (LO: *Codetermination on the Foundation of Solidarity*, Prisma, Stockholm 1977), the control and dequalification thesis was the main message in the analysis of the use of computers in working life. The 'data ombudsman' (who was a woman) also actively supported that Braverman's book was rapidly translated to Swedish.

## Polarization

With Horst Kern and Michael Schumann the polarization thesis was introduced in Scandinavian debate.[28] What they found in their extensive empirical study was neither dequalification nor upgrading, but a *polarization* of skills. There was a small group of winners in the automation race, getting relatively qualified and autonomous jobs, whereas most workers got even more repetitive and alienated conditions to work under. The changes also heavily depended on type of industry and production process. However, these empirical results reported in the now classical *Industriarbeit und Arbeiterbewusstsein* from 1970, were already questioned not only by other researchers, but also by Kern and Schumann themselves when the polarization thesis by the end of the 1970s reached the Scandinavian debate and took over as the major explanation.

The craft ideal may also be seen as the point of reference for Kern and Schumann. Autonomy as the possibility of independent and self-governed work activities was a highly ranked property of a job. This included autonomous planning and control of the work involved, methods and tools to be used, when to perform a task, the pace of the work, quality and quantity of products, spatial mobility, etc.

With German accuracy they defined in detail the qualifications to be measured. A main distinction was between process dependent and process independent qualifications.

Among the *process dependent qualifications* they investigated craft qualifications like manual skill, feel for materials and knowledge about them; technical qualifications including knowledge about abstract technical functions and relations; knowledge about construction of the technical equipment used and the layout of the machinery, and knowledge about how to operate the machinery.

[28] Kern, H. and Schumann, M.: *Industriarbeit und Arbeiterbewusstsein I und II*, Europäische Verlagsanstalt, Frankfurt am Main 1970.

As *process independent qualifications* they mention
flexibility, technical 'intelligence', perception, technical
sensibility, responsibility, accuracy, reliability, and independence.

Other measures had to do with opportunities for social
interaction, both as actual cooperation in the labor process,
and as informal contacts. This included aspects like influence and control from others, and on others' work, opportunities for cooperation and helping each other, and opportunities to exchange information about production.

The skill categories Kern and Schumann used in their
investigation were much more refined than the skill concepts applied by Blauner and Braverman, and doubtless
more elaborated than the skill concept we were operating
with in the UTOPIA project applying the tool perspective.
For further refinement of the tool perspective as an approach to skill-based design of computer artifacts their
categories seem extremely useful.

As to the strategic conclusions and the contradiction
between theoretical technical-scientific knowledge and
the workers' practical empirical understanding Kern and
Schumann advocated that the practical base should be
maintained, and that production workers should incorporate theoretical knowledge into their practice, rather than
strive to become engineers. This position, based on a vast
empirical material, comes close to the strategy we in the
UTOPIA project tried out as action research and actual
design.

*Requalification*

Still another influential German research group is *Projektgruppe Automation und Qualification* (PAQ).[29] Their
extensive investigations and their somewhat differing results, and especially recommendations, are perhaps the
most popular thesis in qualification research today. To

[29] See e.g. Projektgruppe Automation und Qualifikation (PAQ):
*Widersprüche der Automationsarbeit,* Argument Verlag, Berlin
1987.

them the deskilled or low-skilled end of the polarization thesis mainly consists of 'rest functions'. These are left from earlier forms of production. It is work that in principle can be, but has not yet been, automated. PAQ's position has been called the *requalification* thesis. They focus on how work tasks are redistributed and reintegrated, such as between typographers and journalists concerning e.g. page make-up, layout, and editing. They also focus on completely new tasks and qualifications, like those of programmers and designers.

PAQ present a much more comprehensive view than Blauner's early study, but it is about as optimistic as his concerning the promises of automation. Theoretically they see automation as a major change of human work. 'The necessary work' in the future is what cannot be automated, like handling fault and errors; supervision and programming of production equipment; and research and development.

The requalification thesis is of special interest in the discussion of skill-based design and the tool perspective. Craft work is by no means an ideal for PAQ. They ask: What reason is there to measure the 'new' with the old as its measure? What are we told if we find that a job is more or less craft-like, i.e. more or less like a historically specific form of work?

The point is that not only do old qualifications vanish, but also completely new ones develop. And new integrations occur. Think of the typographers in a longer perspective than the one we had in the UTOPIA project. What would they have been without the dequalification of the writing monks? Certainly some important product qualities were lost, but still we are quite happy with Gutenberg's invention of the movable type. Without this technological change there would not have been any typographers. With computer artifacts for desktop publishing in the 1980s a similar change may occur. Maybe the unborn typographer is a secretary or a middle manager that will integrate graphic design in their other tasks. Beyond the typographers, who will deplore this change? How will it affect the strength of the trade union movement, not only the graphic workers' union? What are the consequences for the quality of different kinds of typographical products? Arguing for a tool perspective, we will have to consider these kind of wider reflections on changes in qualifications. This is especially the case if we make claims that the tool perspective is a cornerstone in work-oriented design of computer artifacts as a strategy for democratization and skill in the interest of *all* workers.

PAQ's position concerning qualifications for automation runs counter to the tool perspective. PAQ argues the need for extensive technical-scientific knowledge to operate, maintain, and re-program computer artifacts. In this perspective a craft work approach based on the workers' practical understanding must seem to be a dead end.

In my view, PAQ may have committed the mistake of just extrapolating from the computer technology they found in use. But things happen fast in the development of computer artifacts. Today, not many years after their study, it is possible to design computer artifacts , based on workstation technology, where formal training in mathematics and logic is far from the most essential qualifications to operate and re-program this technology. Think of what a skilled graphic artist can do with most advanced computer artifacts for picture processing. Or think of all Macintosh users. It is not technical-scientific knowledge that marks the master in these achievements.

A reply could be that these are not 'real systems', that this kind of programming is not 'real programming', etc. But what reason is there to think that the way computer artifacts were designed, and programmed, in the 1970s is more real than the new tool-like computer artifacts, discussed in the previous chapter, that now are becoming more and more commonplace?

However, the gap between the PAQ perspective and the tool perspective may not be as wide as it seems. PAQ has observed that experimentation is a main way in which workers learn to operate computer artifacts, and recommends this kind of experimental practice. This is how many professional programmers work, supported by modern exploratory programming environments designed according to craft-like principles, and it is a basic idea in the tool perspective.

PAQ argues that the practical experimentation must be based on scientific theory, as opposed to the tacit knowledge of craft-like practice. I am not arguing that theoretical knowledge is irrelevant when operating and programming computer artifacts. Some of the tools for this may be highly abstract and theoretical models, but others may rather be designed as practical tools reminding one of traditional work practice. As discussed in the previous chapter: They already exist, and they are most useful. If the user wants to change the size of a circle, why not do it right away, by hand, on the screen as direct manipulation, instead of bothering with its theoretical formula and the appropriate parameters?

## Segmentation

*Das Ende der Arbeitsteilung?*[30] was published in 1984 by Kern and Schumann. It was a kind of replication of their earlier study, but this time with a new result. The low-skilled end in the polarization had melted away. In the most automated plants there were no need for unskilled labor. What was left were the skilled workers. This resembles the requalification thesis, but there is less technology optimism. What automation really may lead to, according to Kern and Schumann, is even more problematic than the polarization between high and low skilled workers. It is a *segmentation* of the work force, between those who have a qualified job, and those who never will get a job at all.

But the whole situation is most complex. Kern and Schumann see new production concepts and coming political changes as determining factors. Trends today can-

[30] Kern, H. and Schumann, M.: *Das Ende der Arbeitsteilung? Rationalisierung in der industriellen Production: Bestandsaufnahme, Trendbestimmung*, Verlag S.H. Beck, München 1984.

not just be extrapolated. The coming development cannot be reduced to extrapolations from past rationalizations. It has become more important for management to utilize skills and trade unions as productive forces to optimize profits. To use the concepts from an earlier chapter: responsible autonomy rather than direct control may in the era of the computer be the dominant managerial strategy. To call this new situation capitalism with a human face might definitely be to go too far. But the situation certainly opens up some new and challenging opportunities for skill-based design of computer artifacts. The risk is that the democracy aspect of work-oriented design may be lost. This risk does not merely concern the subordination of skill-based design to managerial interests and the loss of a clear view of desirable changes in the interest of labor, but just as much the risk of skill-based design to be diminished to a strategy for the already privileged, those who were lucky enough to get a job. Designing for skill *and* democracy, not the one without the other – that is the challenge to work-oriented design.

# Epilogue

*'In all important matters, style,
not sincerity, is the essential.'*

Oscar Wilde in *Chameleon*

*Epilogue*

# Postmodern Reflections on Work-Oriented Design of Computer Artifacts

What is the future of work-oriented design of computer artifacts?

The times are postmodern, we are told. Everything has become style. We live our lives in subcultures, all with their own styles. Life is style, as are science, philosophy, art, literature, architecture, etc. In all important matters, style, not sincerity, is the essential. Our conditions are postmodern, because the 'modern project' of Enlightenment has failed. The 'master narratives' of emancipation have collapsed. The rationality of modern science, technology and industry has taken us beyond the pre-capitalistic tradition-based society, but brought us to the eve of destruction. The Utopia of freedom through liberalism has failed. So has, however, the alternative Utopia of communism. We are left with fragmentation and chaos. We live in an era of lost innocence – in a postmodern condition.

If this is the case; where does it leave us with our project of work-oriented design of computer artifacts? In this epilogue I will, as a summary, make a few comments on this. I will characterize the outlined project in terms of the traditional, the modern, and the postmodern, and I will reflect about the future of work-oriented design in the postmodern condition.

First it should, however, be noticed that the postmodern condition refers to two quite different, but interrelated conditions. One is a postmodern mode of thinking, expressed as trends or styles in philosophy, science, art, literature, etc. The other is a characteristic of our contemporary high technology societies in the West, typically referred to with names like the media society, the information society, post-industrialism, etc.

In other words: The postmodern condition both refers to contemporary language-games played in art and science, language-games of resistance to modern rationality, and to a fragmented society of subcultures and local language-games, life-styles rather than social classes.

The postmodern suggestion in the postmodern condition is that we have to abandon all our master narratives – scientific and political – and the very idea of representations of 'truth'. What is suggested is a strategy of resistance by 'deconstruction' and 'suspecting', not a construction of an oppositional alternative–a better and greater 'truth'. In art, literature, and architecture this takes the form of irony and meta-linguistic play.

This is, of course, a gross simplification of major theoretical and artistic discourses today. But it is a challenge to 'revisit' our own story with some suspicion and irony.

## A True Story?

What do we find if we 'revisit' work-oriented design of computer artifacts in the light of the postmodern condition?

- A romantic and neo-conservative return to tradition-based values such as tools, craft, competence, care, and relationship? The emphasis on practical understanding and tacit knowledge, the ideal of the skilled craftsman making high quality products, and the frequent references to a Heideggerian approach could be signs of this. A return to the good old days before industrial capitalism in the era of the computer.
- A modern rationalistic project? A late (too late?) example of 'the modern project' of Enlightenment from the

French Revolution and onwards? The emancipatory ideal of freedom, change and progress, the emphasis on knowledge, work, and technology, the Marxist labor process approach, and the purpose of humanizing the rationalization process, could be signs of this – a persistence in the 'master narrative' of a Utopia of democratic socialism, when it, in practice, has collapsed in most so-called socialistic countries, and when only a minority in the societies of contemporary Western capitalism seek this ideal.

• A postmodern resistance to machine slavery in an era of lost innocence in the simulation culture of the 'information and media society'? The critique of the modern obsession with rationalistic thinking and 'true' representations, the emphasis on local language-games, the acknowledgement of the importance of styles in science and design as well as in art, and the plea for playfulness and pleasurable involvement in the use of those artifacts we call computers could all be signs of this.

All these signs are there. Are we then left with an eclectic postmodern play with words, without a comprehensive or coherent *scientific and political* orientation? The question becomes even more important to address in the light of the philosophical foundations involved. Frequent references are made to a Heideggerian, a Marxist, and a Wittgensteinian approach, in a way corresponding to a traditional, a modern, and a postmodern mode of thinking, although the conflicts between them have not really been resolved. The suggestion of a need to transcend the disciplinary boundaries, not only between human, natural, and social sciences, but also between art and science, and between the language-games of science, design, and of use, and the attempt to integrate the knowledge interests of intersubjective communication, instrumental control, and emancipation, does not make the approach less eclectic. Eclecticism, what could be worse? Maybe that Heidegger really was a Nazi, that Stalin was a Marxist, and that Wittgenstein ...

Still there is a 'truth' which I have tried to legitimate, not innocently, but constructively – an alternative of opposition. In summary it reads as follows:

Work-oriented design of computer artifacts could be a *modern* emancipatory project, a language-game among many in a political process towards the Utopia of not only a democratic, but also a pleasurable and creative working life in the era of the computer. This project may be set in motion by struggles for qualitative changes in the participative structures of design and use of computer artifacts, emphasizing both new local democratic procedures, and the creation of family resemblance between the language-games of design and use, beyond the limits of systems descriptions and formalization of skills.

Furthermore, this modern project suggests that *traditional* values of work, like the craft skill ideal and pleasure in work, can and should be applied when designing perhaps the most significant artifact of all in the *postmodern* simulation culture – the computer.

The project even goes one step further, suggesting that computer artifacts can, and perhaps even should, be designed to transcend the borders between work and play – the use of computer artifacts at work as a playful and enjoyable activity.

Though based on a critical attitude to the contemporary social, cultural, political, technological and scientific conditions it is an optimistic view of opposition – an alternative of opposition argued under the postmodern condition.

## The Postmodern Society

There are family resemblances between postmodern thinking and work-oriented design of computer artifacts, for example with regard to the critique of the major contributions of science and the scientific method, with regard to the emphasis on language-games and styles, the suggested playfulness, and a transcendence of the borders between art and science. In short: *an acceptance of a postmodern mode of thinking or form of knowledge.*

After two hundred years of modern 'enlightenment' we have in society reached a postmodern condition of fragmented language-games and lost Utopias. This political analysis of lost innocence is also shared with postmodernism. However, the postmodern political answer to this chaos seems to be 'anarchy' – resistance but no alternative. In this sense *postmodernism as a political practice is rejected* by an approach of work-oriented design of computer artifacts, especially by keeping to the emancipatory ideal, a belief in progress, in work as a fundamental category in human life, in democratic rationality, and even in an important role for trade unions to play in the future.

In these 'postmodern' times we are certainly witnessing fundamental changes of capitalism, and our conditions for living in an 'information and media society'. However, this postmodern society is more than ever a market economy. The only really existing rationality is success or failure on the market. Not only scientific rationality, but also the rationality of social institutions like local, national and international bureaucracies (which we have all reason to be critical of, but also to defend), and the rationality of democratic institutions (which we have all reason to defend, but also to be critical of) are subordinated to the market rationality. We are all free to play our local language-games in a society of fragmented subcultures only related to each other via the market, a market made more effective than ever by the use of computers and the media industry. However, in this postmodern information and media society we are not only free, we are also all trapped in networks of products and pictures produced by multinational companies. It is a chaotic society where we are forced to market ourselves and gain self-respect by as much individualism as possible. But we have not gone beyond capitalism. The market keeps on producing inequality, and an opposing strategy based on solidarity and democracy has never been more in need than today to create at least some overview and justice – in society as a whole as well as at work.

# Democracy?

To transcend the postmodern condition politically it seems
that, with sincerity (and maybe with some irony) we must
revisit our democratic institutions, including the trade
unions, and discuss new strategic perspectives. What
Marx taught us about capitalism could still be relevant,
even if work and workers look different today, the working class in a broad sense is a most heterogeneous category, and the revolutionary model has failed. The forms of
the labor contract and the workers' collective have
changed but still exist in the postmodern condition. We
could, aware of our lost innocence, try to rebuild a Utopia,
a dream of different, but peacefully coexisting language-
games mediated by a democratic rationality. We could
name our way towards this Utopia – that we have understood we never will finish working on – something
different than class struggle, for example the creation of
family resemblance between the different language-
games, or the establishment of an open dialogue free from
coercion, but we would have to challenge the power of capital.

The question is whether the practices of work-oriented
design of computer artifacts can be a contribution in the
never ending emancipatory process of building this
Utopia, to help pave the way out of the postmodern fragmentation. Is the tool perspective a too traditional answer
to the postmodern challenge? Is the trade union base an
outdated modern approach? Is the suggested postmodern
playfulness in use of computer artifacts just cynical
manipulation?

# Work?

In addition to these questions there is an even more fundamental one for a project of work-oriented design of
computer artifacts: If work gets less and less important in
our lives in the postmodern or post-industrial society,
what, then, is the value of a work-oriented approach?

Unemployment, shorter working-hours, a decline of industrial labor and increased service labor, heterogenization of the working class, maybe even a new postmodern class of 'information workers' or a post-industrial class of 'care' workers, a new or lost work morality, and many other signs are referred to as the death of the industrial work society. The language-games we participate in at work have changed, and their importance in our lives may have diminished. We have been made aware of the blindness that an emphasis on instrumental skills in the labor process creates towards the fundamental communicative competence of social interaction.

Industrial labor may have lost its position as *the* major sociological category, but still most of us live our lives as wage-workers, and the computer is increasingly more present in these activities. Is it really untimely to propose that a language-game of work-oriented design of computer artifacts can and should be played as one of many language-games with family resemblance to other language-games we play at work and in everyday life?

## Back to Bauhaus
## and beyond Postmodernism?

What has been suggested in this book is *a design approach*. It has grown out of the experiences that I have shared with scholars and workers in research for skill and democracy in design and use of computer artifacts in Scandinavia in the 1970s and the 1980s. But it has also borrowed shape and content from many past and ongoing discourses, discourses in computer and information science, in other design arts and sciences, in sociology, in philosophy, in the media, in everyday life, etc.

As a final attempt to position this approach, I will return to two paradigm examples from architectural design.

Bauhaus was a beautiful program for the design of artifacts based on progressive social and cultural values, artifacts designed to engender social change. It was a style of design based on a democratic and participative ideal, a merge of arts, craft skills and industrial production, using 'modern' materials for design of quality products for ordinary people.

This looks like a blueprint for work-oriented design of computer artifacts. The problem is that we know that the program failed. As Bauhaus developed into Modernism and the International Style, it turned into elitism, just instrumental rationality, a sheer expression of the market economy, and ugliness and uselessness for ordinary people. Yet even so: is there a better design approach to learn from in design of computer artifacts?

Postmodernism in architectural design rejects Bauhaus functionality. It suggests a semiotic play with signs. Buildings are understood as sign artifacts. Emphasis is on small or local narratives, often with built-in irony, eclectically gathered from many traditions.

If buildings can be designed as sign artifacts for postmodern playfulness, computer artifacts must be *the* postmodern artifacts, since they are designed based on a material for symbol manipulation. The problem is only that we so far really have not developed our stylistic competence to design this playfulness. And when we have, we have in a way come to copy postmodern elitism and cynicism. I think of the 'double-coding' of postmodern architecture to 'reconcile' the language-games of ordinary users and of experts.

As an example we can take the postmodern attitude to a classical Greek temple.

The expert could delight in the construction of the columns, their shape and order. The slaves would understand nothing of this beauty, although they could appreciate the mythological motive on the frieze.

A parallel in our design field: Real computers for the experts to enjoy the subtlety of the design, a metaphorical user interface for the 'machine-slaves' to appreciate. And still: Is there a better paradigm example of a design of computer artifacts than the Apple Macintosh?

How to create useful and pleasurable, maybe even enjoyable, narratives in the design and use of the most postmodern of all artifacts, the computer – this is a question of style, competence, moral and sincerity that I find of decisive importance in the postmodern era of lost innocence. In doing this we should accept the challenge of designing beyond 'reconciliation' of the language-games of experts and ordinary users – a design based on family resemblance between mediated language-games.

As a program for the future of work-oriented design of computer artifacts, I suggest that we should 'revisit' Bauhaus functionality and Postmodern playfulness, but we should do so in a spirit of lost innocence.

## Moral

The moral of the story: style is important in work-oriented design of computer artifacts, but what really matters is sincerity. In addition: There are two equally dangerous extremes – to shut reason out and to let nothing else in. Blaise Pascal, the 'inventor' of the computer, noted that in his *Pensées* more than three hundred years ago. To criticize reason and style, we have to reason within a certain style. That is the irony of our language-games.

# Bibliography

Abrahams, P.: 'What is Computer Science' in *Communications of the ACM*, vol 30, no 6, June 1987.

Abrahamsson, B.: *Varför finns organisationer*, Nordstedts, Stockholm 1986.

Ackoff, R.L.:, 'A Black Ghetto's Research on a University' in *Operations Research*, September 1970.

Ackoff, R.L.: 'The Social Responsibility of OR' in *Operational Research Quarterly*, 25, 1974.

Ackoff, R.L.: *Redesigning the Future*, John Wiley, 1974.

Ackoff R.L.: 'A Theory of Practice in the Social Systems Sciences' IIASA International roundtable on *The Art and Science of Systems Practice*, IIASA, November 1986.

Aguren, S. and Edgren, J.: *Annorlunda fabriker – Mot en ny produktionsteknisk teori*, The Swedish Employers' Confederation, Stockholm 1979.

Ahlin, J.: *Arbetsmiljösanering – förnyelse genom demokratisering av planeringsprocessen*, Royal Institute of Technology, Stockholm 1974 (dissertation).

Alexander, C.: *Notes on Synthesis of Form*, Havard University Press, Cambridge 1964.

Andersen, C. et al.: *Syskon – en bog om konstruktion av datamaiske systemer*, Gads Forlag, Copenhagen 1972.

Andersen N.E. et al.: *Professionel Systemudvikling*, Teknisk Forlag, Copenhagen 1986.

Andersen, P.B.: *Edb-teknologi set i medieperspektiv*, University of Aarhus 1984.

Andersen, P.B.: 'Semiotics and Informatics: Computers as Media' in Ingwersen et al.: *Information Technology and Information Use*, Taylor Graham, London 1986.

Andersen, P.B. et. al.: *Research Programme on Computer Support for Cooperative Design and Communication*, Department of Information Science and Department of Computer Science, University of Aarhus 1987.

Andersen, P.B. and Madsen K.H.: 'Design and Professional Languages' in Larsen, S.F. and Plunkett, K. (eds.): *Computers, Mind and Metaphors* (forthcoming).

Archer, L.B.: 'What Became of Design Methodology?' in Cross, N. (ed.): *Developments in Design Methodology*, John Wiley & Sons Ltd, Bath 1984.

Argyris, C. and Schön, D.A.: *Organizational Learning: A Theory of Action Perspective*, Addison-Wesley, Reading 1978.

Aronzon, G. (ed.): *Arbetets krav och mänsklig utveckling*, Prisma, Stockholm 1983.

*Artificial Intelligence*, no 31, 1987.

Bahro, R.: *Die Alternative – Zur kritik des real existierenden Sozialismus*, Europäische Verlagsanstalt, Köln 1977.

Bannon, L. J.: *Extending the Design Boundaries of Human-Computer Interaction*, Institute for Cognitive Science, University of California, San Diego, May 1985.

Bannon, L. 'Issues in Design – Some Notes' in Norman, D. A. and Draper, S. W. (eds.): *User Centered System Design – New Perspectives on Human-Computer Interaction*, Lawrence Erlbaum Associates, London 1986.

Bansler, J. and Bødker K.: *Experimentelle teknikker i systemarbejdet*, DIKU report no 83/7, 1983.

Bansler, J.: *Systemudvikling – teori og historie i skandinavisk perspektiv*, Studentlitteratur, Lund 1987 (dissertation).

Bartholdy, M. et al.: *Studie av datorstödd bildbehandling på Aftonbladet*, Swedish Center for Working Life, Stockholm 1987.

Bergson, H.: *Creative Evolution*, Henry Holt, New York 1911.

Bjerknes, G. and Bratteteig, T.: 'Florence in Wonderland – Systems Development with Nurses' in Bjerknes, et al. (eds.): *Computers and Democracy – A Scandinavian Challenge*, Avebury, 1987.

Bjerknes, G., Ehn, P., Kyng, M.(eds.): *Computers and Democracy – A Scandinavian Challenge*, Avebury, Aldershot 1987.

Björkman, T. and Lundqvist, K.: *Från Max till Pia*, Arkiv, Malmö 1981 (dissertation).

Björkman, T.: 'Reparatörsyrkets utveckling' and 'Från polarisering till omkvalificering' in Nyberg, P. et. al.: *Yrkesarbete i förändring*, Carlssons, Stockholm 1984.

Björkman, T. and Lundquist, K.: *Yrkeskunnande och datorisering*, Statskontoret, Stockholm 1986.

Bjørn-Andersen, N. (ed.) *The Human Side of Information Processing North-Holland*, Amsterdam 1980.

Bjørn-Andersen, N. (ed.): *Information Society, for richer, for poorer*, North-Holland, Amsterdam 1982.

Blauner, R.: *Alienation and Freedom – The factory Worker and His Industry*, The University of Chicago Press, London 1964.

Blomberg, J.: 'The Variable Impact of Computer Technologies on the Organization of Work Activities' in *Proceedings of CSCW'86*, Austin 1986.

Boguslaw, R.: *The New Utopians – A Study of System Design and Social Change*, Prentice-Hall, Englewood Cliffs 1965.

Bottomore, T.B.: *Karl Marx – Selected writings in Sociology and Social Philosophy*, Penguin Books, Harmondsworth 1971.

Braverman, H.: *Labor and Monopoly Capital – The Degradation of Work in the Twentieth Century,* Monthly Review Press, New York 1974.

Briefs, U. et al. (eds.): *Systems Design for, with, and by the Users,* North-Holland, Amsterdam 1983.

Broadbent, G.: 'The Development of Design Methods' in Cross, N. (ed.): *Developments in Design Methodology*, John Wiley & Sons Ltd, Bath 1984.

Broady, D. and Helgeson, B.: 'Farväl till arbetsdelningen?' in Broady, D. (ed.): *Professionaliseringsfällan*, Carlssons, Täby 1985.

Brock, S.: 'Wittgenstein mellem fænomenologi og analytik' in Brock, S. et al.: *Sprog, Moral & Livsform*, Philosophia, Århus 1986.

Brown, J. S. 'From Cognitive to Social Ergonomics and Beyond' in Norman, D. and Draper, S. (eds.): *User Centered System Design*, Lawrence Erlbaum, London 1986.

Brulin, G. and Ulstad, C.: DESAM *vid halvlek* (forthcoming).

Brödner, P.: *Fabrik 2000 – Alternative Entwicklungspfade in die Zukunft der Fabrik*, Sigma Rainer Bohn Verlag, Berlin 1985.

Budde R. et al. (eds.) *Approaches to Prototyping*, Springer Verlag, Berlin 1984.

Bunge, M.: *Scientific Research. The Search for System. The Search for Truth*, Springer Verlag 1967.

Bush, V.: 'As We May think' in *Atlantic Monthly*, July 1945.

Buxton, W.: 'There's More to Interaction Than Meets the Eye: Some Issues in Manual Input', in Norman, D. and Draper, S. (eds.): *User Centered System Design*, Lawrence Erlbaum, London 1986.

Bødker, S. and Madsen, K.H.: 'More or Less Systems Descriptions' in Lassen, M. and Mathiassen, L.: *Report of the Eight*

*Scandinavian Conference on Systemeering*, part I, Aarhus 1985.

Bødker, S.: 'Utopia and the Design of User Interfaces' in *Proceedings of the Aarhus Conference on Development and Use of Computer Based Systems and Tools*, Aarhus 1985.

Bødker, S. et al.: 'A Utopian Experience' in Bjerknes, et al. (eds.): *Computers and Democracy – A Scandinavian Challenge*, Avebury, 1987.

Bødker, S.: *Through the Interface – A Human Activity Approach to User Interface Design*, DAIMI PB-224, Department of Computer Science, University of Aarhus, 1987 (dissertation).

Carlson, J., Ehn, P. Erlander, B., Perby, M-L, and Sandberg, Å.: 'Planning and Control from the Perspective of Labour: A Short Presentation of the Demos Project' in *Accounting, Organizations and Society*. vol 3, no 3/4, 1978.

Checkland, P.B.: 'Systems Thinking in Management: the Development of Soft Systems Methodology and its Implications for Social Science' in Ulrich, H. and Probst, G.J.B. (eds.): *Self-organisation and Management of Social Systems*, Springer Verlag, 1984.

Checkland, P. B.: 'The Politics of Practice', IIASA International roundtable on *The Art and Science of Systems Practice*, IIASA, November 1986.

Cherns, A.: 'The principles of socio-technical design' in *Human Relations*, no 29, 1976.

Churchman, C.W.: *The Systems Approach*, Delta, New York 1968.

Churchman, C.W.: *The Design of Inquiring Systems – basic concept of systems and organization*, Basic Books, New York 1971.

Churchman, C.W.: *The Systems Approach and its Enemies*, Basic Books, New York 1979.

Churchman, C.W.: 'Who Should Be the Client of Systems Design', IIASA International roundtable on *The Art and Science of Systems Practice*, IIASA, November 1986.

Cooley, M.: *Architect or Bee? – The Human/technology Relationship*, Langley Technical Service, Slough 1980.

Cross, N. (ed.): *Developments in Design Methodology*, John Wiley & Sons Ltd, Bath 1984.

Dahlkvist, M.: *Att studera kapitalet,* Bo Cavefors, 1978 (dissertation).

Dahlbom, B.: *Humanisterna och Framtiden – fyra varianter över ett tema av Max Weber*, Science of Science, University of Umeå, Draft 1986.

Dahlström, E. et. al.: *LKAB och demokratin*, W & W, Stockholm 1971.

Dahlström, E.: *Bestämmande i arbetet – Några idékritiska funderingar kring arbetslivets demokratisering*, Department of Sociology, University of Gothenburg, Gothenburg 1983.

Daley, J.: 'Design Creativity and the Understanding of Objects' in Cross, N. (ed.): *Developments in Design Methodology*, John Wiley & Sons Ltd, Bath 1984.

Daressa, L and Mayers, J: *Computers in Context*, California Newsreel 1986 (film).

Descartes, R.: *A Discourse on Method and Selected Writings*, J.M. Dent and Sons, London 1912.

DIALOG project group: *Årsrapport för 1984*, Department of Computer Science, Royal Institute of Technology, Stockholm 1985.

Dilschmann, A. and Ehn, P.: *Gränslandet*, Swedish Center for Working Life, Stockholm 1985.

Dreyfus, H. L. and Dreyfus, S. D.: *Mind over Machine – the power of human intuition and expertise in the era of the computer*, Basil Blackwell, Glasgow 1986.

Dreyfus, H. L.: *What Computers Can't Do – A Critique of Artificial Reason*, Harper & Row, New York 1972.

DUE project group: *Demokrati, udvikling og edb — Rapport fra første fase*, DUE report no 2, Computer Science Department, Aarhus University, Århus 1978.

DUE project group: *Klubarbejde og EDB*, Fremad, Copenhagen 1981.

Eco, U.: *Postscript to The Name of the Rose*, Harcourt Brace Jovanovich, USA 1984.

Eco, U.: *The Name of the Rose*, Pan Books Ltd, London 1984.

Edwards, R.: *Contested Terrain*, Heinemann, London 1979.

Ehn P.: *Bidrag till ett kritiskt social perspektiv på datorbaserade informationssystem*, TRITA-IBADB-1020, Stockholm 1973.

Ehn, P. and Göranzon, B.: *Perspektiv på systemutvecklingsprocessen*, Department of Information Processing, University of Stockholm, 1974.

Ehn, P. et al.: *Demokratisk styrning och planering i arbetslivet – utgångspunkter för ett forskningsprojekt om datateknik, fackförening och företagsdemokrati*, TRITA-IBADB-1023, Department of Information Processing, Stockholm 1975.

Ehn, P. and Erlander, B.: *Vi vägrar låta detaljstyra oss*, Swedish Center for Working Life, Stockholm 1978.

Ehn, P. and Sandberg, Å.: *Företagsstyrning och löntagarmakt –
planering, datorer, organisation och fackligt
utredningsarbete*, Prisma, Stockholm 1979.

Ehn, P. and Sandberg, Å.: 'God utredning ' in Sandberg, Å. (ed.):
*Utredning och förändring i förvaltningen*, Liber förlag, Stockholm 1979.

Ehn, P. and Sandberg, Å.: 'Systems Development – On strategy
and ideology', in DATA no 4, 1979.

Ehn, P. and Sandberg, Å.: 'Att påverka det påverkbara' in *Tre år
med MBL*, Liber, Helsingborg 1980.

Ehn, P., Kyng, M. and Sundblad, Y.: *Training, Technology, and
Product from the Quality of Work Perspective, A Scandinavian
research project on union based development of and training
in computer technology and work organization, especially text
and image processing in the graphic industry.* (Research
programme of UTOPIA), Swedish Center for Working Life,
Stockholm 1981.

Ehn, P. and Sandberg, Å.: 'Local Union Influence on Technology
and Work Organization – some results from the Demos
Project' in Briefs, U. et al. (eds.): *Systems Design for, with, and
by the Users, Amsterdam*, North-Holland 1983.

Ehn, P.: *UTOPIA-projektet* (Status rapport (fas I) och arbetsplan
(fas II)), Swedish Center for Working Life, Stockholm 1983.

Ehn, P. and Sundblad, Y. (eds.): *Kravspecifikation för datorstödd
bildbehandling och ombrytning*, Swedish Center for Working
Life, Stockholm 1983.

Ehn, P. and Kyng, M.: 'A Tool Perspective on Design of Interactive Computer Support for Skilled Workers' in M. Sääksjärvi
(ed.): *Proceedings of the Seventh Scandinavian Research
Seminar on Systemeering*, Helsinki 1984.

Ehn, P., Perby, M.L., Sandberg, Å.: *Brytningstid*, Swedish Center
for Working Life, Stockholm 1984.

Ehn, P. et al.: *Datorstödd Ombrytning*, Swedish Center for Working Life, Stockholm 1985.

Ehn, P. and Kyng K.: 'The Collective Resource Approach to Systems Design' in Bjerknes G. et al. (eds.): *Computers and
Democracy – A Scandinavian Challenge*, Avebury, 1987.

Einhorn, E. and Logue, J. (eds.): *Democracy at the Shop Floor –
An American Look at Employee Influence in Scandinavia
Today*, Kent Press, 1982.

Ekdahl, L.: *Arbete mot kapital*, Arkiv, Lund 1983 (dissertation).

Ekdahl, L.: *Att bli maskinens herrar*, Swedish Center for Working Life, Stockholm 1984.

Emery, F. and Thorsrud, E.: *Democracy at Work: The Report of the Norwegian Industrial Democracy Program*, Martinus Nijhoff, Leiden 1976.

Emery, F. (ed.): *The Emergence of a New Paradigm of Work*, Centre for Continuing Education, The Australien National University, 1978.

Engelbart, D. C.: *Augmenting Human Intellect: A Conceptual Framework*, AFOSR-3223, Stanford Research Institute, Menlo Park 1962.

Engelbart, D. C. and English, W. K.: 'A Research Center for Augmenting Human Intellect' in *AFIPS Proceedings – Fall Joint Computer Conference*, 1968.

Engeström, Y.: *Learning by Expanding*, Orienta-Konsultit, Helsinki 1987 (dissertation).

Erlander, B.: *Så här var det på PUB*, Swedish Center for Working Life, Stockholm 1980.

Flensburg, P.: *Personlig databehandling*, Studentlitteratur, Lund 1986 (dissertation).

Floyd C.: 'A Systematic Look at Prototyping' in Budde R. et al. (eds.) *Approaches to Prototyping*, Springer Verlag, Berlin 1984.

Floyd, C.: 'Outline of a Paradigm Change in Software Engineering' in Bjerknes, et al. (eds.): *Computers and Democracy – A Scandinavian Challenge*, Avebury, 1987.

Foged, J. et al.: *Håndbog om klubarbejde, edb-projekter og nye arbejdsformer*, HK kommunal, Århus 1987.

Fox Keller, E.: *Reflections on Gender and Science*, Yale University Press, New Haven 1985.

Freire, P.: *Pedagogy of the Oppressed*, Herder & Herder, New York 1971.

Frenckner, K. and Romberger, S.: *Datorstödd Bildbehandling*, Swedish Center for Working Life, Stockholm 1985.

Friedman, A.: *Industry and Labour*, Macmillan Press, London 1977.

Friedman, A. and Cornford, D.: 'Strategies for Meeting User Demands – An International Perspective' in Bjerknes, et. al (eds.): *Computers and Democracy – A Scandinavian Challenge*, Avebury, 1987.

Fry, J. (ed.): *Towards a Democratic Rationality – Making the Case for Swedish Labour*, Gower, Aldershot 1986.

Ghandchi, H. and Ghandchi. J.: 'Intelligent Tools – The Cornerstone of a New Civilization' in *The AI Magazine*, fall 1985.

Goldberg, A.: *Smalltalk-80: The Interactive Programming Environment*, Addison-Wesley, Reading 1984.

Goldkuhl, G.: *Framställning och användning av informations-modeller*, TRITA-IBADB-4099, University of Stockholm, 1980 (dissertation).

Greenbaum, J.: 'Division of Labor in the Computer Field' in *Monthly Review*, vol 28 no 3, 1976.

Greenbaum, J.: *The Head and the Heart – using gender analysis to study the social construction of computer systems*, Computer Science Department, Aarhus University, Denmark 1987.

Greenfield, P.: 'Video Games as Tools of Cognitive Socialization' in Larsen, S.F. and Plunkett, K. (eds.) *Computers, Mind and Metaphors* (forthcoming).

Groat, L. and Canter, D.: 'Does Post-Modernism Communicate' in *Progressive Architecture*, December 1979.

Gulowsen, J.: 'A measure of work-group autonomy' in Davis, L. and Taylor, J. (eds.): *Design of Jobs*, Penguin, Harmondsworth 1972.

Gunnarson, E.: *Arbetsmiljökrav*, Swedish Center for Working Life, Stockholm 1985.

Gustavsen, B.: 'Workplace Reform and Democratic Dialogue' in *Economic and Industrial Democracy*, vol 6, Sage, London 1985.

Göranzon, B. (ed.): *Datautvecklingens Filosofi – tyst kunskap och ny teknik*, Carlsson & Jönsson, Malmö 1984.

Göranzon, B. et al.: *Datorn som verktyg – krav och ansvar vid systemutveckling*, Studentlitteratur, Lund 1983.

Habermas, J.: *Erkenntnis und Interesse,* Suhrkamp, Frankfurt 1968.

Habermas, J.: *Technik und Wissenschaft als 'Ideologie'*, Suhrkamp, Frankfurt 1968.

Habermas, J.: *Toward a Rational Society*, Heinemann, London 1971.

Habermas, J.: *Theorie des Kommunikativen Handelns*, I, II, Suhrkamp, Frankfurt 1981.

Hedberg, B.: 'Using Computerized Information Systems to Design Better Organizations' in Bjørn-Andersen, N. (ed.): *The Human Side of Information Processing North-Holland*, Amsterdam 1980.

Hedberg, B. and Mehlmann, M.: *Datorer i bank*, Swedish Center for Working Life, Stockholm 1983.

Heidegger, M.: *Being and Time*, Harper & Row, New York 1962.

Helgeson, B.: *Arbete, teknik, ekonomi*, Högskolan i Luleå, 1986 (dissertation)

Holbæk-Hanssen, E., Håndlykken, P. and Nygaard, K.: *System Description and the DELTA Language*, Norsk Regnesentral, Oslo 1975.

Hooper, C.: 'Architectural Design – An Analogy' in Norman, D. and Draper, S. (eds.): *User Centred System Design -New Perspectives on Human-Computer Interaction*, Lawrence Erlbaum, London 1986.

Howard, R.: 'UTOPIA – Where Workers Craft New Technology' in *Technological Review*, vol 88 no 3, Massachusetts Institute of Technology, 1985.

Hutchins, E.L. et al.: 'Direct Manipulation Interfaces' in Norman, D. and Draper, S. (eds.): *User Centered System Design*, Lawrence Erlbaum, London 1986.

Illich, I.: *Tools for Conviviality*, Calder & Boyars, London 1973.

Ingwersen et al.: *Information Technology and Information Use*, Taylor Graham, London 1986.

Israel, J.: *The Language of Dialectics and the Dialectics of Language*, Harvester Press, London 1979.

Ivanov, K.: *Quality Control of Information*, Royal Institute of Technology, NTIS no PB219297, Stockholm 1972 (dissertation).

Ivanov, K.: *Systemutveckling och ADB-ämnets utveckling*, Department of Computer and Information Science, University of Linköping, Linköping 1984.

Jackson, M.: *System Development*, Prentice Hall, 1983.

Jackson, M.C.: 'The nature of 'soft' systems thinking' in *Journal of Applied System Analysis*, vol 9, 1982 and vol 10, 1983.

Janik, A.: *Om Wittgenstein och Wien,* Swedish Center for Working Life, Stockholm 1985.

Janik, A.: *Tacit Knowledge, Working Life and Scientific Method*, Brenner Archive, Innsbruck University, 1986.

Janik, L. G.: 'Some Reflections on the Topic of the Sigtuna Symposium' in Sundin, B. (ed.): *Is the Computer a Tool?*, Almquist & Wiksell, Stockholm 1980.

Jencks, C.: *Current Architecture*, Academy Editions, London 1982.

Jencks, C.: *The Language of Postmodern Architecture*, Rizzoli, New York 1984.

Jones, J. C.: 'A Method of Systematic Design' in Jones, J. C. and Thornley, D. (eds.): *Conference on Design Methods*, Pergamon Press, Oxford 1963.

Jungk R. and Müllert, N. R.: *Zukunftwerkstätten, Wege sur Wiederbelebung der Demokratie*, 1981.

Kaasbøll, J.: *A Theoretical and Empirical Study of the Use of Language and Computers,* Department of Informatics, University of Oslo, forthcoming (dissertation).

Kammersgaard, J.: 'On Models and their Role in the use of Computers' in *Preceedings of the Aarhus Confererence on Development and Use of Computer Based Systems and Tools*, Aarhus, 1985.

Kay, A.: *The Reactive Engine*, University of Utah, 1969 (dissertation).

Kay, A. and Learning Research Group: *Personal Dynamic Media*, Xerox Palo Alto Research Center, Technical Report no SSL 76-1, 1976.

Kay, A.: 'Computer Software' in *Scientific American*, vol 251, no 3, september 1984.

Kensing, F.:'Generation of Visions in Systems Development' in Docherty, P et. al. (eds.) *Systems Design for Human Development and Productivity – Participation and Beyond*, Elsevier Science Publishers, North Holland, IFIP 1987.

Kern, H. and Schumann, M.: *Industriarbeit und Arbeiterbewusstsein I und II*, Europäische Verlagsanstalt, Frankfurt am Main 1970.

Kern, H. and Schumann, M.: *Das Ende der Arbeitsteilung? Rationalisierung in der industriellen Production: Bestandsaufnahme, Trendbestimmung*, Verlag S.H. Beck, München 1984.

Kling, R.: 'Computerization as an Ongoing Social and Political Process' in Bjerknes, et al. (eds.): *Computers and Democracy – A Scandinavian Challenge*, Avebury, 1987.

Kosik, K.: *Die Dialektik des Konkreten*, Suhrkampf, Frankfurt 1967.

Kraft, P.: *Programmers and Managers – the routinization of computer programming in the United States*, Springer Verlag, New York 1977.

Kubicek, H.: 'User Participation in System Design' in Briefs, U. et. al. (eds.): *Systems Design for, with, and by the Users*, North-Holland, Amsterdam 1983.

Kuhn, T.S.: *The Structure of Scientific Revolution*, Chicago 1962.

Kyng, M. and Mathiassen, L.: 'Systems Development and trade union activities', in Bjørn-Andersen, N. (ed.): *Information Society, for richer, for poorer*, North-Holland, Amsterdam 1982.

Langefors, B.: *Theoretical Analysis of Information Systems*, Studentlitteratur, Lund 1966.

Langefors, B.: *Samband mellan modell och verklighet*, IB-ADB 66, no 1, (rewritten 1971-11-02).

Lanzara, G.F. and Mathiassen, L.: 'Mapping Situations Within a System Development Project' in *Information & Management*, no 8, 1985.

Laurel, B.K.: 'Interfaces as Mimesis' in Norman, D. and Draper, S. (eds.): *User Centred System Design -New Perspectives on Human-Computer Interaction*, Lawrence Erlbaum, London 1986.

Leontiev, A.N.: *Problems of the Development of the Mind*, Progress, Moscow 1981.

Lie, M. and Rasmussen, B.: *Kan 'kontordamene' automatiseres?*, IFIM, Trondheim 1984.

Lindqvist, S.: *Gräv där du står – Hur man utforskar ett jobb*, Bonniers, Stockholm 1978.

LO: *Fackföreningsrörelsen och den tekniska utvecklingen*, Report to the congress of LO, 1966.

LO: *Handlingsprogram för företagsdemokrati och data*, Swedish Federation of Trade Unions, Stockholm 1975.

LO: *Solidariskt Medbestämmande*, Report to the congress of LO, 1976.

LO: *Codetermination on the Foundation of Solidarity*, Prisma, Stockholm 1977.

Lundeberg, M.: *Some Propositions Concerning Analysis and Design of Information Systems*, TRITA-IBADB-4080, Royal Institute of Technology, Stockholm 1976 (dissertation).

Lundeberg, M. et al.: *Systemering*, Studentlitteratur, Lund 1978.

Lundeqvist, J.: *Norm och Modell – samt ytterligare några begrepp inom designteorin*, Department of Architecture, Royal Institute of Technology of Stockholm, 1982 (dissertation).

Lundeqvist, J.: 'Ideological och teknologi' in Göranzon, B. (ed): *Datautvecklingens filosofi*, Carlsson & Jönsson, Malmö 1984.

Lyotard, J.F.: *The Postmodern Condition – A Report on Knowledge*, Manchester University Press, 1984.

Lysgaard, S.: *Arbeiderkollektivet*, Universitetsforlaget, Stavanger 1961.

Madsen, K.H.: 'Breakthrough by Breakdown – Metaphors and Structured Domains' in Klein, H. and Kumar, K. (eds.): *Information Systems Development for Human Progress in Organizations*, North-Holland (forthcoming).

March, L.: 'The Logic of Design' in Cross, N. (ed.): *Developments in Design Methodology*, John Wiley & Sons Ltd, Bath 1984.

Marx, K.: *Thesis on Feuerbach*, (first published in 1845), (translated in Bottomore, T.B.: Karl Marx – Selected writings in Sociology and Social Philosophy, Penguin Books, Harmondsworth 1971).

Marx, K. and Engels F.: *The Communist Manifesto*, (first published 1848), Penguin Books, Harmondworth 1980.

Marx, K: *Wage Labour and Capital*, (first published in 1848), (translated in Bottomore, T.B.: *Karl Marx – Selected writings in Sociology and Social Philosophy*, Penguin Books, Harmondsworth 1971).

Marx, K.: *Grundrisse der Kritik der politischen Ökonmie*, Diets Verlag, Berlin 1953.

Marx, K.: *Capital – A Critical Analysis of Capitalist Production*, vol. I-III (first published 1867, 1885, 1895), Progress Publishers, Moscow 1953 -1971.

Mathiassen, L.: *Systemudvikling og Systemudviklingsmetode*, DAIMI PB-136, Department of Computer Science, University of Aarhus 1981 (dissertation).

Mayall, W.H.: *Principles in Design*, Design Council, London 1979.

Mead, G.H.: *Mind, Self and Society*, University of Chicago Press, Chicago 1934.

Morton, A.L.: *Three Works by William Morris, News from Nowhere, The Pilgrims of Hope, A Dream of John Ball*, Lawrence & Wishart, Berlin 1968.

Morton, A.L.: *Political Writings of William Morris*, Lawrence & Wishart, Berlin 1973.

Mumford, E and Ward, T.B.: *Computers: Planning for People*, Batsford, London 1968.

Mumford, E.: *A Comprehensive Method for Handling the Human Problems of Computer Introduction*, Manchester Business School, 1970(?), mimeo.

Mumford, E.: *Designing Human Systems*, Manchester Business School 1983.

Mumford, E.: 'Sociotechnical System Design – Evolving Theory and Practice', in Bjerknes, et al. (eds.): *Computers and Democracy – A Scandinavian Challenge*, Avebury, 1987.

Mumford, L.: *Technics and Civilization*, Harcourt Brace Jovanovich, New York 1934.

Naur, P. and Randell, B.: *Software Engineering*, report from a conference sponsored by the NATO Science Committee, Brussels 1969.

Naur, P.: 'Intuition and Software Development' in *Formal Methods and Software Development*, Lecture Notes in Computer Science no 186, Springer Verlag, 1985.

Newman, W. and Sproull, R.: *Principles of Interactive Computer Graphics*, McGraw-Hill, Tokyo 1979.

Nissen, H.E.: *On Interpreting Services Rendered by Specific Computer Applications*, Gotab, Stockholm 1976 (dissertation).

Noble, D.: 'Social Choice in Machine Design – The Case of Automatically Controlled Machine Tools, and a Challenge for Labor' in *Politics & Society*, nos 3-4, 1978.

Nordenstam, T: 'Två oförenliga traditioner' in Göranzon, B. (ed.): *Datautvecklingens Filosofi*, Carlsson & Jönsson, Malmö 1984.

Nordenstam, T.: *Technocratic and Humanistic Conceptions of Development*, Swedish Center for Working Life, Stockholm 1985.

Norman, D. and Draper, S. (eds.): *User Centred System Design – New Perspectives on Human-Computer Interaction*, Lawrence Erlbaum, London 1986.

Norman, D.: 'Cognitive Engineering' in Norman, D. and Draper, S. (eds.): *User Centred System Design -New Perspectives on Human-Computer Interaction*, Lawrence Erlbaum, London 1986.

Nurminen, M.: *Three Perspectives to Information Systems*, Studentlitteratur (forthcoming).

Nyberg, P. et. al.: *Yrkesarbete i förändring*, Carlssons, Stockholm 1984.

Nygaard, K. and Bergo, O. T.: *Planlegging, Styring og Databehandling*, part 1, Tiden Norsk Forlag, Oslo 1973.

Nygaard, K. and Bergo, O.T.: *En vurdering av styrings- og informasjonssystemet KVPOL*, Tiden Norsk Forlag, Oslo 1975.

Nygaard, K. and Bergo, O.T.: 'The Trade Unions – new users of research' in *Personal Review*, no 2, 1975.

Nygaard, K.: 'The Iron and Metal Project: Trade Union Participation' in Sandberg, Å. (ed.) *Computers Dividing Man and Work*, Swedish Center for Working Life, Malmö 1979.

Oakley, K.: *Man the Toolmaker*, British Museum, London 1965.

Offe, C.: *Disorganized Capitalism*, Polity Press, Oxford 1985.

Perby, M.L. and Carlsson, J.: *Att arbeta i valsverket*, Swedish Center for Working Life, Stockholm 1979.

Perby, M.L.: 'Computerization and the Skill in Local Weather Forecasting' in Bjerknes, G. et. al.: *Computers and Democracy – A Scandinavian Challenge*, Avebury, 1987.

Polanyi, M.: *Personal Knowledge*, Routledge & Kegan Paul, London 1957.

Polanyi, M.: *The Tacit Dimension*, Anchor Books, Doubleday & Company, New York 1967.

*Proceedings from the Conference on Computer-Supported Cooperative Work*, Austin, Texas 1986.

*Produktionslivets förnyelse – teknik, organisation, människa, miljö*, conference in Uppsala, The Swedish Work Environment Found, 1978.

Projektgruppe Automation und Qualification: *Theorien über Automationsarbeit*, Argument-Sonderband AS 31, Berlin 1978.

Projektgruppe Automation und Qualifikation : *Widersprüche der Automationsarbeit*, Argument Verlag, Berlin 1987.

Qvale, T.: 'A Norwegian strategy for democratization of industry' in *Human Relations*, no 5, 1976.

Ressner, U.: *Den dolda hierarkin*, Tema Nova, Stockholm 1985.

Rittel, H.: 'Second-generation Design Methods', in Cross, N. (ed.): *Developments in Design Methodology*, John Wiley & Sons Ltd, Bath 1984.

Rommetveit, R.: 'Meaning, Context, and Control – Convergent Trends and Controversial Issues in Current Social-scientific Research on Human Cognition and Communication', in *Inquiry,* no 30, 1987.

Rosenbrock, H.: *Social and Engineering Design of an FMS*, CAPE 83, Amsterdam 1983.

Ryle, G.: *The Concept of Mind*, Penguin Books 1949.

Rønnow, U.: *Ny Teknologi – UTOPIA*, Danmarks Radio, 1984 (film).

Sandberg, T.: *Work Organization and Autonomous Groups*, Liber Förlag, Uppsala 1982 (dissertation).

Sandberg, Å.: *The Limits to Democratic Planning – knowledge, power and methods in the struggle for the future*, Liber, Stockholm 1976 (dissertation).

Sandberg, Å. (ed.): *Computers Dividing Man and Work – Recent Scandinavian Research on Planning and Computers from a Trade Union Perspective*, Swedish Center for Working Life, Malmö 1979.

Sandberg, Å. (ed.): *Forskning för förändring – Om metoder och förutsättningar för handlingsinriktad forskning i arbetslivet*, Swedish Center for Working Life, Stockholm 1981.

Sandberg, Å.: *From Satisfaction to Democratization – On socio-logy and working life changes in Sweden*, Swedish Center for Working Life, Stockholm 1982.

Sandberg, Å.: 'Trade union-oriented research for democratization of planning in work life – problems and potentials' in *Journal of Occupational Behaviour*, vol 4, 1983.

Sandberg, Å.: *Mellan alternativ produktion och industriell FOU*, Swedish Center for Working Life, Stockholm 1984.

Sandberg, Å.: *Technological Change and Co-determination in Sweden – Background and analysis of trade union and managerial strategies*, Temple Press (forthcoming).

Sartre, J.P.: *Critique de la Raison Dialectique*, Librairie Gallimand, 1960.

Schneidermann, B.: *Designing the User Interface*, Addison-Wesley, USA 1987.

Schädlich, C.: *Bauhaus i Dessau 1925 – 1932*, Catalogue from Randers Art Museum, 1985.

Schön D. A: *The Reflective Practitioner – How Professionals Think in Action*, Basic Books, New York 1983.

Searle, J.: *Speech Acts*, Cambridge University Press, Cambridge 1969.

Seymour, J.: *The Forgotten Arts – A practical guide to traditional skills*, Dorling Kindersley, London 1984.

Shotter, J.: 'Consciousness, Self-consciousness, Inner Games, and Alternative Realities', in Underwood, G. (ed.): *Aspects of Consciousness*, vol 3., Academic Press, London 1983.

Simon, H.: *The Sciences of the Artificial*, The MIT Press, Cambridge 1969.

Sjögren, D. (ed.): *Nyhetsblad från Snickeriprojektet*, Swedish Center for Working Life, 1979-83.

Sjögren, D. (ed.): *Bakom Knuten*, newsletter from the KNUT project, Swedish Center for Working Life, Stockholm, September 1987.

Skjervheim, H.: *Deltagare och åskådare*, Prisma, Halmstad 1971.

Smith, D. C. et al.: 'Designing the Star User Interface' in *Byte Magazine*, vol 7, no 4, April 1982.

Steen, J. and Ullmark, P.: *De anställdas Mejeri*, Royal Institute of Technology, Stockholm 1982.

Steen, J. and Ullmark, P.: *En egen väg – att göra fackliga handlingsprogram*, Royal Institute of Technology, Stockholm 1982 (dissertation).

Strandh, S.: *Maskinen genom tiderna*, Nordbok, Göteborg 1979.

Sundin, B. (ed.): *Is the Computer a Tool?*, Almqvist & Wiksell, Stockholm 1980.

Sutherland, I.E.: *Sketchpad – A Man-Machine Graphical Communication System*, MIT, Cambridge 1963 (dissertation).

Svensson, L.: *Arbetarkollektivet och facket – en lokal kamp för företagsdemokrati*, Studentlitteratur, Lund 1984 (dissertation).

Sveriges Standardiseringskommission: *Riktlinjer för administrativ systemutveckling*, SIS-Handbok 113, Stockholm 1973 (English version: *Systems Development – A Constructive Model*, SIS handbook 125, Stockholm 1975).

Taylor, F.W.: *Principles of Scientific Management*, 1911.

Teitelman, W and Masinter, L.: 'The Interlisp Programming Environment' in *Computer*, April 1981.

Tempte, T.: 'Is the Computer a Tool? – A Craftsman's View' in Sundin, B. (ed.): *Is the Computer a Tool?*, Almquist & Wiksell, Stockholm 1980.

Thorsrud, E. and Emery, F. E.: *Mot en ny bedriftsorganisation*, Tanum, Oslo 1970.

Thyssen, O.: *Teknokosmos – om teknik og menneskerettigheder*, Gyldendal, Viborg 1985.

*Tidningsteknik,* no 2, 1984.

Trist, E. and Bamforth, K.: 'Some social and psychological consequences of the longwall method of coal getting' in *Human Relations*, no 4, 1951.

Tsichritzis, D.: 'Objectworld' in Tsichritzis, D. (ed.): *Office Automation*, Springer Verlag, Berlin 1985.

UTOPIA project group: *An Alternative in Text and Images,* Graffiti no 7, Swedish Center for Working Life, Stockholm 1985.

Vedung, E.: *Det rationella samtalet*, Aldus, Stockholm 1977.

Vygotsky, L.S.: *Thought and Language*, The MIT Press, Cambridge 1962.

*Websters New World Dictionary*, 1982.

Weinberg, G.M.: *The Psychology of Computer Programming*, Van Nostrand Reinholt, New York 1971.

Weizenbaum, J.: *Computer Power and Human Reason – from judgment to calculation*, W.H. Freeman and Company, San Francisco 1976.

Wellmer, A.: 'The Dialectic of the Modern and the Postmodern' in *Praxis International*, no 4, 1984.

Williams, R.: 'Democratising Systems Development – Technological and Organisational Constraints and Opportunities' in

Bjerknes, et al. (eds.): *Computers and Democracy – A Scandinavian Challenge,* Avebury, 1987.

Winch, P.: *The Idea of a Social Science and its Relation to Philosophy,* Routledge & Kegan Paul, London 1958.

Wingert, B. and Riehm, U.: 'Computer als Werkzeug – Anmerkungen zu einen verbreiteten Missverständnis', in Rammert, W. et al. (eds): *Technik und Gesellschaft,* Jahrbuch 3, Campus Verlag, Frankfurt 1985.

Winograd, T. and Flores, F.: *Understanding Computers and Cognition – a new foundation for design,* Ablex, Norwood 1986.

Wittgenstein, L.:*Tractatus Logico-Philosophicus,* Kegan Paul, 1923.

Wittgenstein, L.: *Philosophical Investigations,* Basil Blackwell, Oxford (1953) 1963.

Wynn, E.: *Office Conversation as an Information Medium,* University of California, Berkeley 1979 (dissertation).

Yourdon, E.: *Managing the System Life Cycle,* Yourdon Press, New York 1982.

Zimbalist, A. (ed.): *Case Studies on the Labor Process,* Monthly Review Press, New York 1979.

Österberg, D.: *Metasociologisk essä,* Verdandi, Stockholm 1971.